The Great Catastrophe of My Life

STUDIES IN LEGAL HISTORY

Published by the University of North Carolina Press

in association with the American Society for Legal History

Thomas A. Green & Hendrik Hartog, editors

THOMAS E. BUCKLEY, S.J.

The Great

DIVORCE IN THE OLD DOMINION

Catastrophe

THE UNIVERSITY OF NORTH CAROLINA PRESS

# of My Life

CHAPEL HILL AND LONDON

© 2002 The University of North Carolina Press
All rights reserved
Manufactured in the United States of America
Set in Cycles by Tseng Information Systems, Inc.

The paper in this book meets the guidelines for
permanence and durability of the Committee on
Production Guidelines for Book Longevity of the
Council on Library Resources.

Library of Congress
Cataloging-in-Publication Data
Buckley, Thomas E., 1939–
The great catastrophe of my life : divorce in the Old
Dominion / by Thomas E. Buckley.
    p. cm.
"Published . . . in association with the American Society
for Legal History"—Series t.p.
Includes bibliographical references and index.
ISBN 0-8078-2712-6 (alk. paper) —
ISBN 0-8078-5380-1 (pbk. : alk. paper)
1. Divorce—Virginia—History—19th century.
2. Divorce—Law and legislation—Virginia—History—
19th century.   3. Marital conflict—Virginia—History—
19th century.   4. Virginia—Social conditions—19th
century.   I. Title.
HQ835.V8 B83   2002   2001059840

cloth   06 05 04 03 02   5 4 3 2 1
paper   06 05 04 03 02   5 4 3 2 1

For

Michael and Eleanor Fletcher Buckley

In Thanksgiving for Their Marriage

1926–1999

CONTENTS

ILLUSTRATIONS

ACKNOWLEDGMENTS

Too many years ago, while sifting through the legislative petition collection at the Library of Virginia, I happened upon some divorce petitions. Their poignant accounts of marital tragedy captured my attention. I had been tracking various religious and moral issues for a study of church-state relations, but over many lunches and cups of frozen yogurt, Sandy Treadway, aided and abetted by Brent Tarter and John Kneebone, persuaded me to postpone that project and concentrate on divorce. For better or worse, this volume is the result. I am deeply grateful to Sandy, Brent, and John for their encouragement, suggestions, and friendship over the years. Conversations with other researchers at the Library of Virginia as well as that institution's superb publications staff, particularly Sara Bearss, Julie Campbell, and Gregg Kimball, helped keep me on track and enthused. Meanwhile, during my many summer visits, Conley Edwards and his special collections staff hauled out literally hundreds of boxes of petitions for my perusal. I am especially grateful to Chris Kolbe and Minor Weisiger, who helped me track down elusive legislative and legal records.

My second home in Richmond has been the Virginia Historical Society, where Charles Bryan Jr., Frances Pollard, Lee Sheppard, Howson Cole, Nelson Lankford, and the entire staff provide a wonderfully hospitable environment for research and the exchange of ideas and information among scholars. As my manuscript moved through various redactions, I have benefited enormously from the constructive help of numerous friends and colleagues, especially Cara Anzilotti, Jane Censer, Nicholas Curcione, Melvin Ely, Martha Hodes, Cynthia Kierner, Jan Lewis, Susan Miller, Philip Morgan, Jack Rogers, William Shade, and John Witte Jr., who first proposed a legal focus for this book. Hendrik Hartog and Thomas Green, the legal studies editors for the University of North Carolina Press, provided expert guidance through the final stages of revision, along with liberal doses of encouragement.

Many librarians and archivists provided indispensable assistance during the research phase. I want to thank the staffs at the Earl Gregg Swem Library at the College of William and Mary, the Albert H. Small Special Collections at the University of Virginia, the Union Theological Seminary Library in Richmond, the Tompkins-McCaw Library at the Medical College of Virginia, the Virginia Baptist Historical Society, the Bishop Payne Library at the Virginia Theological Seminary, the Library of Congress, the Maryland Historical Society, the Maryland State Archives, the Pennsylvania Historical Society, the Presbyterian Historical Society in Philadelphia, the Perkins Library at Duke University, the Southern Historical Collection at the University of North Carolina, and the Henry E. Huntington Library in California.

Two Mellon Fellowships from the Virginia Historical Society and grants from Loyola Marymount University and the Graduate Theological Union helped to support summer research. A Bannon Fellowship at Santa Clara University in 1995–96 provided a congenial environment in which to put together the first draft. The final revisions were completed during a sabbatical while I enjoyed a Mellon Faculty Fellowship from the Association of Theological Schools. Portions of Chapter 4 were first presented at a meeting of the Pacific Coast Branch of the American Historical Association. I am grateful to Edith Gelles of the Institute for Research on Women and Gender at Stanford University for the opportunity to deliver a paper that developed into Chapter 5. The *Virginia Magazine of History and Biography* has graciously allowed me to draw upon two articles: "'Placed in the Power of Violence': The Divorce Petition of Evelina Gregory Roane, 1824," 100 (1992): 29–78, and "Unfixing Race: Class, Power, and Identity in an Interracial Family," 102 (1994): 349–80, which was republished in *Sex, Love, Race: Crossing Boundaries in North American History,* edited by Martha Hodes (1999).

Throughout the years of research and writing, my family, friends, and students have provided large reservoirs of support. Virtually every summer the priests and people of St. Bridget's Parish have hosted me in Richmond, and I particularly want to thank Bill Sullivan and Tom Miller for their hospitality and friendship. In northern Virginia Peg and Steve O'Brien have regularly welcomed me into their home. At Loyola Marymount University, where I began this study; then at Santa Clara University during a Bannon Fellowship; and now at the Jesuit School of Theology in Berkeley, my Jesuit brothers and faculty colleagues have listened to my tales of divorce, sometimes with a dash of incredulity, but always with patience and good humor. I am enormously grateful for the multiple ways in which they bless my life.

Spending the past decade with divorce has deepened my awareness of how precious a good marriage is. My parents lived a sacramental marriage for seventy-three years. In thanksgiving for them and the legacy of love and fidelity they have given to their children, grandchildren, and great-grandchildren, this book is dedicated.

The Great Catastrophe of My Life

Petitions

Writing in a careful hand on a single sheet of paper, in 1786 Susanah Wersley begged Virginia's General Assembly for a divorce. She described herself as a victim of the American Revolution. Five years earlier, while the fighting raged close to her home in Hanover County, her family had sheltered a sick colonial soldier, John Wersley, who claimed to be an officer from North Carolina. During a prolonged convalescence he courted the impressionable young woman. Susanah fell in love and, against the advice of her parents and other relatives, married him the following spring. The newlyweds had lived together for just a month when her husband announced that he needed to visit his mother briefly in New Bern. Susanah eventually discovered that he was in Boston. Obviously John had deceived her into marriage and never intended to live with her again. She petitioned the legislature to pass a private bill dissolving their marriage.[1] No other venue existed where she might seek relief. The state had no divorce code, and the courts lacked jurisdiction.

The approach Susanah Wersley took to remedy her situation was not unusual. Throughout the colonial period and at least until the Civil War, women and men, singly or in groups, sought relief of varied kinds and expressed their views on a host of subjects by petitioning their elected representatives. At each session the lawmakers approved dozens of private bills to assist individuals and communities.[2] But they rejected Susanah's petition, as they would hundreds of others from unhappy spouses for the next sixty-five years. During that time the assembly approved divorces for only one-third of the applicants. Meanwhile, decades passed before the courts gained even the most limited authority. The way Virginians terminated marriages dramatically illustrates how far removed we are from their world. In our no-fault era the very idea of asking legislators to provide a divorce by private bill boggles the mind. But well into the nineteenth century, Virginia law afforded no other option for desperately unhappy women and men trapped in loveless relationships.

The Honble Genl. Assembly of Virginia

The petition of Susanah Wersley of Hanover County humbly sheweth, that in the beginning of the year 1781 a Mr. John Wersley who professed himself an officer of the North Carolina Line came to the house of your Petitioner's Father, in a weakly, unhealthy situation where he was admitted to continue while he might recover of his indisposition — the said Wersley after a few weeks paid his addresses to, and in March following, much against the approbation of your Petitioner's Parents and connections did marry your said Petitioner about one month after which, he observed that his mother lived in the Town of Newborn North Carolina, and that he must go to see her, but should certainly return in the course of a few weeks — the said Wersley set out accordingly, and instead of going to North Carolina your Petitioner has very reason to believe that he went to Boston having heard of him at that place about three years ago — but never obtaining any further accounts of him either before or since the time aforesaid — which gives reason to your Petitioner to believe that he never intends returning again, and a that he was actuated by a principal of convenience and deception alone in marrying your Petitioner — Your Petitioner therefore most earnestly prays your Honble House may pass an Act causing effectually, the matrimonial engagements between her and the

Susanah Wersley's petition for divorce, Hanover County, 1786
(Courtesy of The Library of Virginia)

The stories of their troubled marriages and the multiple obstacles to ending them form the core of this book. The experiences of the petitioners reveal the harsh legal culture that surrounded divorce in the Old South. Although each case must be taken on its own terms, the structure of the legal system ensured that all petitions shared certain features. Each attempted divorce played itself out in a series of minidramas with multiple legal actors and institutions. In virtually every scene various parties debated, explicitly or implicitly, core values such as personal happiness, family stability, and the welfare of society. Husband and wife possessed the principal roles even though, as in the case of John Wersley, one party might have been absent during some or all of the legal exchanges. Domestic settings vary dramatically, yet some tragedies are strikingly familiar. One spouse might simply have abandoned the other. More often a third party emerges as the source of alienated affections. If that person is African American, race heightens the tension. Sometimes extreme verbal abuse and physical brutality arrest one's attention and arouse sympathy for the aggrieved individual, usually a wife. Fraud at the time of marriage presents another familiar scenario, and economic issues invariably surface at some point in the contest.

In every divorce the presence of family members, neighbors, and friends during domestic altercations brings a communal aspect to the conflict. Later, when a justice of the peace takes depositions, they become sworn witnesses to the conduct of one or both spouses. Churchyards, courthouse greens, and neighborhood taverns provide settings for the local community to exchange news and gossip about the marital conflict, to argue over the merits of a particular case or divorce in general, and to offer support for one or both spouses. Some people may also assume a legal role in vouching for the good character of the husband or wife, or when seated as a jury in the courtroom, they determine the truth or falsity of the alleged facts in a particular case. County magistrates, lawyers, and sheriffs all play important parts. Finally, the central act opens on the legislators in the capitol as they receive the plea for a divorce, sift the evidence, and render judgment. At times the discussion becomes heated and spills over into the press. Afterward, whether the application for divorce is granted or denied, the spouses, family, and community must cope with the results.

This study, therefore, contextualizes tales of marital failure and the search for divorce within the boundaries of politics, law, religion, family, and community as these elements clashed, shifted, and changed between the Revolution and the Civil War. Over these years the competition among conflicting values dominated the statewide debate. The struggle to escape the bonds of matrimony pitted individuals, couples, and sometimes families and whole communities against an ethic inherited from colonial Anglicanism and rigidly maintained within a legal system promoted at the political center. Only ever so slowly did the legislators formulate general divorce laws and allow courts to dissolve marriages.

The huge collection of petitions in the archives of the Library of Virginia provided the principal research materials. In expressing the concerns and anxieties of ordinary Americans, these texts expose a multitude of social, political, and economic issues. An important subset of the collection pertains to divorce. Over the decades from 1786 to 1851, 242 women, 218 men, and 5 couples submitted 583 divorce petitions to the Virginia assembly, some of them repeating their request as much as two or three times. Of the total number of divorce petitions, 471 (80 percent) have been located. They came from 204 women, 171 men, and 4 couples.[3] What makes their petitions fascinating is the absorbing firsthand accounts they present, often with extraordinary detail, as they interpret their troubled marital situations to other southerners and to themselves. Cutting across boundaries of gender, race, and class, these manuscripts provide intimate perspectives on the lives of mostly white men and women from every type of background and socioeconomic condition as they confronted the multiple problems of troubled marriages and broken families. All the emotions of marriage gone sour—anger, shame, betrayal, hurt, jealousy, and rage—bleed from those pages.

In addition, every petition file includes whatever supporting materials the suppliant collected to bolster a case for divorce. The affidavits relate harrowing incidents of domestic turmoil. Accounts of adultery, cruelty, battery, fornication, and desertion specify the grounds for positive legislative action. Warmly supportive letters, often from prominent local figures, might accompany a petition. Sympathetic community members might endorse a statement of the petitioner's good reputation and the veracity of the charges to forward to Richmond. Besides these often hefty files amounting to dozens of pages, other resources abound to complete the picture. Census, tax, and property records yield evidence of wealth, age, and relationships. Legal documents such as deeds and wills explain family ties. Records of county courts and municipal jurisdictions detail brushes with the law and abusive situations. Private correspondence and even the contemporary press may further flesh out the circumstances of a particularly messy divorce. Frequently these sources expose the relative strengths and weaknesses of husband and wife in their marriage and fix their social, economic, and political status in the community. Taken together, this mass of documentation makes it possible to reconstruct the tragic married lives of these couples.

Some historians have delved into this rich source material. Nancy Cott and Lyle Koehler, for example, successfully mined the colonial Massachusetts divorce petitions. Bertram Wyatt-Brown utilized a variety of petition collections in *Southern Honor: Ethics and Behavior in the Old South.* For her discussion of divorce, Brenda Stevenson studied eight petitions submitted from Loudoun County, Virginia, during the pre–Civil War era. Suzanne Lebsock found the petition collection helpful for *The Free Women of Petersburg.* Cynthia Kierner included a sample of divorce petitions in *Southern Women in Revolution.*[4] Yet discussions of divorce in the South by these scholars as well as in books by Peter Bardaglio, Victoria Bynum, Catherine Clinton, and Stephanie McCurry reinforce the need for more systematic studies.[5] The single book-length treatment for a southern state, Richard Chused's quantitative study of legislative divorce in Maryland, focuses on lawmakers and legislation. The best analysis of divorce in the antebellum South remains an article that Jane Turner Censer wrote two decades ago.[6]

In the past some researchers have shied away from exploiting the petition collection out of the belief that such autobiographical documents are too subjective to be reliable. More than thirty years ago James Hugo Johnston published his 1937 doctoral dissertation, which included extensive excerpts from some of these memorials. Reviewing Johnston's book, Robert McColley warned against taking the divorce petitions "literally" and urged a "cautious skepticism."[7] The same caution, however, applies to virtually every historical document, particularly those of a completely private nature such as letters and diaries. Newspapers are notoriously inaccurate. In the divorce files, some individuals undoubtedly lied, and every petitioner pleads a cause. Affidavits and depositions wear the bias of the witness. Unlike private papers or the press, however, the veracity of each petition is checked by the public nature of the process; the presence, quality, and number of notarized affidavits from witnesses; conflicting testimony; the real possibility of counterpetitions; the watchdogs in legislative committees; and after 1827, the jurors who passed judgment on the facts of a case. Moreover, a petition's usefulness rests as much in the attitudes, values, and beliefs it expresses as in a recital of events. Male and female petitioners drafted texts they hoped would persuade. Thus their rhetoric exposes the cultural outlook of the legislators they sought to impress.

The petition collection provides not only firsthand accounts from people's lives but an unusual opportunity to move outside the elite circles of the literate upper classes and examine the attitudes, values, and situations of middle and lower classes and even poor folk. Research is always easier when the subjects could read and write. But drawing on the assistance of friends and sympathetic neighbors to draft their requests and provide supporting affidavits, the poor submitted petitions, too, an abundance of them, and scratched their mark next to their names. Working from Superior Court records on divorce, Jane Turner Censer discovered a class bias in a southern judicial system that was more available and responsive to "ladies" than to women further down the socioeconomic ladder.[8] Legislative divorce, when and where it was available, offered a cheaper and more egalitarian venue to the bottom 90 percent of the population.

Yet for good reason, as we will see, historians have not treated this procedure kindly. A century ago, in his magisterial three-volume study, *A History of Matrimonial Institutions,* George Elliott Howard decried legislative divorce as a terrible evil, a stumbling block on the road to progressive reform. In the southern states, he wrote, "it bore its most evil fruit." Later historians echo his lament and applaud the turn toward the courts and the easing of legal strictures against divorce as yet another beneficial effect of advancing modernization.[9] The petitions reveal the legislative divorce system as people experienced it in all its harshness and inconsistency. The assembly's *Journals,* reports from the press, and frank criticism in private letters evidence the desire for change on the part of some members of the governing elites. But the discursive process that marked the transition to judicial divorce extended over six decades. Agents included the estranged spouses, members of their immediate families and kinship groups, friends and neighbors, local officeholders, judges, legislators, journalists, clergymen, educators, and a broadly interested public that by turns observed or joined the discussion.[10]

Participants structured their discourses in terms of multiple concerns, but repeatedly they returned to the central point at issue: the conflict between the commitment most of Virginia's leaders felt to the indissolubility of marriage as an essential component of a Christian society and the concrete evidence of human misery and gross injustice in particular marriages. For multiple reasons divorce touched a raw nerve in southern consciousness. Breaking the marital bond between husband and wife not only assaulted a religious tradition that rejected divorce; it undermined the foundations of a close-knit, slaveholding society based on the hierarchy and solidarity of the household unit. Individuals, couples, families, kinship networks, churches, local communities, and state assemblies agonized over the subject. Indeed, the texts that prompted or reacted to the discussion of general and private divorce bills elucidate southern attitudes on a spectrum of issues. Thus divorce provides a fascinating prism through which we can examine the cultural values of Virginians and, by extension, the rest of the South before the Civil War.[11]

Though my research is based on a single state, Virginia mirrors much of the diversity of the entire South. In population the Old Dominion ranked first in the Union in 1790 and remained first in the South throughout the antebellum era. As the largest state east of the Mississippi River before its division during the Civil War, it stretched from the Eastern Shore of Chesapeake Bay to the Ohio River. The vast landscape presented enormous regional variations as one moved through the Tidewater below the fall line of the rivers across the rolling Piedmont to the mountains and valleys beyond. The counties along and south of the James River contained wealthy plantations with fertile tobacco lands and large numbers of slaves, while west of the rich loam and prosperous farms of the Shenandoah Valley the hollows of the Appalachian Mountains held mainly subsistence white farmers and their families, generally hostile to slavery and resentful of the political power it gave the easterners. Across the commonwealth the majority of the population engaged in agriculture and lived on the land, but the number of urban dwellers increased steadily. During the antebellum era, older towns such as Richmond, Norfolk, and Alexandria became cities, and new commercial and mercantile centers sprang up. Thus pre–Civil War Virginia provides a geographical and socioeconomic diversity and a rural-urban mix sufficient to reflect the southern population as a whole.[12]

This book argues that most southern men and women regarded divorce as a personal, familial, and social disaster. It dissolved the bond that both husband and wife, albeit from different perspectives and for diverse

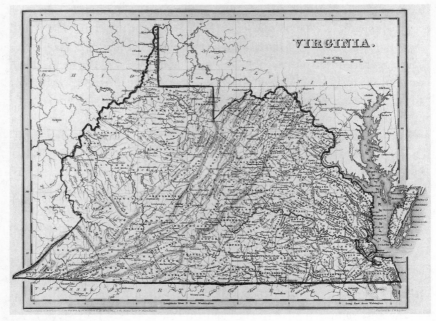

Map of Virginia, 1838
(Courtesy of Virginia Historical Society)

reasons, viewed as essential to personal happiness and fulfillment, and
for many of the people whose lives it touched, divorce left deep psychic
scars. Moreover, divorce in this time and place held serious implications
for kinship and community. While it obviously destroyed the immediate
family, it also strained the extended ties of blood and marriage so integral to southern life. Because marriage fixed a person's place in the social structure and established the households on which the whole South
rested, divorce represented a fundamental assault on society. Nevertheless, using the law to end a disastrous marriage sometimes proved necessary, the only reasonable way to cope with an impossible situation.
During the first half of the nineteenth century most southerners gradually adjusted to that reality. As acceptance grew, a further question arose.
Who should decide the fate of individual marriages? With great reluctance the assembly gradually gave that responsibility to judges and juries.
But the removal of divorce cases from the legislative hall to the courtroom was not an expression of a collective desire for liberal reform or
an effort to make divorce easier. Virginians permitted judicial divorce
on precise, narrow grounds and hedged it about by rules of procedure

and jurisdiction in order to strengthen a fundamental commitment to marriage as foundational to their society.[13]

Three sections comprise this narrative. The first, containing three chapters, contextualizes legislative divorce in its political, legal, religious, familial, and communal aspects, using various divorce cases as points of entry. Chapter 1 focuses on the politics of divorce, the attitudes and policies of legislators, and the widespread resistance to divorce, particularly at the political center. Concerned primarily for the common good of society as rooted in marriage and the family, a conservative legislative temper found support in a perspective on marriage derived from Anglicanism and reinforced by nineteenth-century evangelical Protestantism. This religious culture, the subject of Chapter 2, undergirded the politics of the antebellum South and helps to explicate the nature of the settlement Virginia worked out in 1851. Religious references and language interlaced discussion of divorce, and English church law guided the assembly's adjudication of individual cases and eventually the passage of general divorce laws. Within this religiously oriented culture, women and men commonly derived their attitudes and values from family and local community. Chapter 3 locates the critical roles of relatives and neighbors in marital disputes and explores in particular the problems of marriages between kin. In this familial arena, local mores frequently conflicted with the larger society's established values and even the state's legal code. The treatment of divorced persons in the community reinforces the view that localism dominated life in the Old South.

The next three chapters form the second section of this study. Utilizing cases drawn from the collection of petitions, they explore the principal reasons that drove women and men to seek legislative divorces and the legal boundaries within which they operated. Chapter 4 examines instances of interracial sex as grounds for marital dissolutions. White males proved to be the chief beneficiaries of the "double standard" in morality. The earliest divorces women received in any number involved physical battery as the crucial complaint. Chapter 5 studies these abusive situations, drawing on modern psychological and sociological research to analyze the patterns they followed. Not all women were victims, however, nor were they necessarily repressed. Chapter 6 explores the challenge that female adultery and desertion presented to husbands, families, and society. Southern women as well as men could give free rein to their sexual urges.

The third section presents in a final chapter an extended case study of one woman's inner experience of marital disaster, the social stigma she bore as a divorced woman in the 1840s and 1850s, and her ultimately successful struggle to overcome social prejudice and her own fears to enter a new marriage. By way of conclusion, it summarizes the legislative process of divorce while examining the profound conflict southerners faced in coping with broken marriages within a resolutely conservative society.

I Contexts

CHAPTER 1

A *Vexata Questio*

THE POLITICAL ARENA

Robert Turnbull's obvious misery alarmed and puzzled his friends in the autumn of 1790. The wealthy merchant and planter in Prince George County near Petersburg should have been content and even cheerful. He had remarried just the previous spring, a year after the death of his first wife, Mary Cole Turnbull. By all accounts their nineteen years together had been idyllic. Mary's brother, William Cole, who had lived in their home, later described them as "an exceeding happy couple" and Robert as "a most affectionate and tender Husband." He had depended upon his wife. Her death left the widower emotionally bereft as well as solely responsible for a large family of at least seven children ranging in age from three to sixteen.[1] Thus Robert's remarriage to Sarah Lee Buchanan, a Baltimore widow, should have alleviated his sorrow and marital loneliness while it lifted the burden of raising his children by himself.

In terms of Sarah's personal background, social position, and wealth, it seemed an excellent match. Born Sarah Brooke Lee, she was closely related to the prominent Virginia family of that name. Her only brother, Thomas Sim Lee, served as governor of Maryland in the last years of the Revolutionary War. Sarah's first husband had been Archibald Buchanan, a well-to-do Baltimore merchant. Their marriage had apparently been a happy one. After Archibald's death in 1785, Sarah inherited a huge estate in money, land, and slaves.[2] Before the wedding Robert spoke enthusiastically about his new bride, telling his friends that Sarah possessed "great mental endowments" and promised to be a great help with his young children. Although not yet fifty years old, Turnbull wanted no increase in the size of his family, and since Sarah had been childless in her previous marriage and was now in her mid-forties, further offspring appeared unlikely. From every point of view, she seemed the ideal wife and companion. The wedding took place on 15 March 1790 near Baltimore at the plantation home of Sarah's half-sister, Eleanor Hollyday, with a circle of friends that included Thomas Jefferson in attendance.[3]

Soon afterward, however, Robert returned to Virginia without his bride and did not bring her to White Hill, his plantation on the Appomattox River, until October. He spent most of the six-month interval in Virginia, seldom mentioned Sarah, and never wrote to her. That fall, when Robert finally introduced his new wife to his friends and relations, he seemed troubled, and over the next several weeks his melancholic behavior began to worry them. Finally William Cole appealed to his former brother-in-law to unburden himself, but the latter refused, stating that the problem was too personal to discuss. Then one night in December Sarah sent urgently for William, claiming that Robert was suffering from a "fit of Appoplixy." A quick examination, however, showed the problem to be profound depression rather than a seizure. After Sarah left the room, Robert's male reserve cracked; he admitted his distress and promised an explanation. A week later while riding with William to Petersburg, Robert confided that the source of his unhappiness was his recent marriage because Sarah "was not a compleat Woman . . . in her feminine construction and disqualified for the Nuptial enjoyments."[4]

Shortly after the wedding, Robert told William, he had confronted Sarah with her "defective formation" and implored her to confer with her sister and other women friends in order to find some way "for their mutual relief." But she adamantly refused and insisted that he conceal her disability; in return she promised to take excellent care of his children. That did not satisfy Robert. He wanted a full marital relationship of sexual reciprocity and mutuality, not just a well-ordered household presided over by a wife in name only. His expectations, rooted in the experience of his first marriage, bear out the importance of romantic love and affectivity for men as well as women of the late-eighteenth-century Chesapeake planter class.[5] For a time he had tried to make the best of the situation, but eventually Robert decided that the marriage endangered "his health and life." Either Sarah's "frame" was corrected, or Turnbull wanted "legal redress."

Virginia, however, like the rest of the southern states in 1790, had no statutory machinery to address the desperate planter's situation. The civil code did not mention divorce. No courts possessed jurisdiction to dissolve marriages. The solution lay in legislative action, but at that time and for decades to come the General Assembly refused to establish systematic judicial procedures or to specify grounds for divorce. Instead the legislators themselves handled individual divorce petitions, and they rejected most of them. Not until 1851 did the third state constitution finally end legislative divorce. While generations of unhappy women and men waited in the capitol vestibule, Virginia's elected representatives debated the place of divorce in their society. This chapter explores their long argument within the shifting political framework of legislative divorce and the legal procedures through which individuals sought marital dissolutions. In these contexts, which changed over time, it seeks to answer three critical questions. First, why did the assembly for so many years refuse most petitions for divorce and deny or severely limit judicial authority? Second, in the face of almost certain rejection, why did unhappy spouses continue to request legislative divorces? Third, why did Virginia's leaders finally allow the courts a role in the process?

A STRANGE AND INDELICATE CASE

Robert Turnbull's case offers a useful point of entry. Wherever he turned for help, the merchant-planter faced resistance. A friend, David Robertson, enumerated the almost insurmountable difficulties in dissolving a marriage in Virginia. Pointing out that Sarah had come all the way from Maryland, David urged Robert to live with her. Robert replied that he would rather kill himself. Over the next months the relationship between husband and wife grew increasingly strained. Robert wrote to Sarah's brother and to John Hollyday, her brother-in-law, describing the problem in general terms and imploring them to come to Virginia and help the couple discover "some means for their mutual relief." Pleading the press of business affairs, both men declined. Robert then asked Sarah to return to Maryland with him, but she adamantly refused. Finally he proposed a legal separation, in either Maryland or Virginia.

As the conflict escalated into open warfare, Robert's frustration increased and Sarah felt besieged. If her husband had previously sought a companionate marriage with a loving partner, he now reverted to the role of domestic patriarch by taking full command of the family and household and marginalizing Sarah. Robert operated within his legal rights. As a married woman Sarah lived under coverture—that is, her husband controlled her person and whatever property she possessed at the time of the wedding. The common law made a married couple one person and subordinated the wife.[6] After several stormy scenes, Sarah retreated into a remote corner of the plantation house and gave up any attempt to manage domestic affairs. Robert removed his younger children from White Hill to keep them from witnessing the turmoil. Husband and wife now communicated only by unsigned notes.

Throughout these months, while steadfastly denying her husband's charges, Sarah refused to submit to a physical examination. Robert and others pointed out that if the accusation was false, "she could easily demonstrate the fallacy of it, by occular proof, to some female friend; and that such a disclosure before a lady, could not much wound her delicacy." Sarah disagreed, stating flatly that she would "never . . . submit to an investigation." Nor at first would she consent to return to Maryland. If there must be a separation, she told William Cole, that would be "the last place" she wanted to go. Rather than endure the humiliation of facing her family and friends as a discarded wife, she preferred to remove to the Virginia frontier or the West Indies. But her real wish was to remain at White Hill, resume the care of Robert's home and children, and once more be treated with kindness and consideration by her husband.

Sarah had dug in her heels, but so had Robert. He now bluntly accused her of deliberately tricking him into marriage. By this time he was contemplating a drastic step. When she changed her mind and offered to return to Maryland, provided he accompanied her, Robert refused, declaring "that he could not possibly appear in public as her husband." His lawyer had advised against permitting Sarah to leave Virginia before he had formally informed her of his intention to petition the legislature. When the notice arrived that her husband was applying for a divorce, Sarah considered it "a most violent outrage."[7]

The legal context severely reduced Robert's options. In both Maryland and Virginia, divorce procedures depended on English precedent. In Britain, courts of the established Church of England possessed jurisdiction over marriages and could annul them by granting absolute divorces *a vinculo matrimonii* (from the chain of matrimony) for impediments or disabilities existing at the time of marriage, such as bigamy, an inability to consummate marriage, consanguinity (blood relationship), affinity (relationship created by marriage), insanity, and lack of proper age or consent. All of these considerations rendered a marriage invalid. Annulment ordinarily left both parties free to marry again, provided the same impediments did not carry over to a new marriage. For serious causes, such as adultery or extreme physical cruelty, church tribunals might provide a divorce *a mensa et thoro* (from board and bed), that is, a legal separation. But this mode of divorce did not permit remarriage.

Someone who was legally separated from a spouse and desired to re-marry needed an act of Parliament.[8]

During the colonial period absolute divorce was unknown in Virginia or in the other colonies where the Church of England was established by law. America lacked the church courts as well as the bishops who would have supervised them, though county courts occasionally granted separations for causes such as desertion, cruelty, and bigamy. On the eve of the Revolution, Jefferson became involved as a lawyer in a celebrated Williamsburg divorce case that never achieved resolution because one of the parties died.[9] The revision of the laws that he helped to draft during the war included an act that would have annulled "marriages prohibited by the levitical law"—an effort to adapt English ecclesiastical law to statutory law in the new republic—but the General Assembly failed to pass this bill. Eventually in 1792 it approved a statute defining the norms for legal weddings and forbidding incest, bigamy, and interracial marriages.[10]

Thus when Robert Turnbull sought a dissolution of his marriage in the autumn of 1791, Virginia, like all the other states south of the Mason-Dixon line, possessed no legal procedures by which he could obtain a divorce. He needed a private bill passed by the assembly. The state courts lacked jurisdiction over matrimony except when a statute explicitly granted it. In the few cases received since the Revolution, the legislators had operated on an ad hoc basis. Initially they seemed willing to permit divorce on grounds such as adultery and desertion. Only two years earlier they had turned the case of Anne Dantignac over to the courts. As Anne recounted events, her first husband had died soon after their marriage and left her his entire estate. She was then persuaded to marry John Dantignac, who had falsely presented himself as a wealthy merchant from France. He had treated her cruelly, squandered her property, and finally absconded with her slaves to South Carolina, where he reportedly lived with another woman who had borne his child. Though he had been gone for many years, Anne was still legally bound as his wife; whatever property she possessed belonged to him, if he ever returned to claim it. She asked the assembly for a "full divorce" that would terminate his authority over her or at least "Enable her to acquire, enjoy, and dispose of property in the same manner, as if she had never been Married."[11]

A bill dissolving her marriage passed two readings before the legislators flinched. They had, after all, heard only Anne's point of view. The final act provided that she could obtain a writ from the General Court and publish it in the press for eight weeks, to give her husband an opportunity to respond. The court would take depositions, subpoena witnesses, and conduct a jury trial. If the jury found that her allegations of abuse, desertion, and adultery were proven, then the marriage would be "totally dissolved," and Anne Dantignac would be "declared . . . a *feme sole*," that is, a single woman.[12] The next year the assembly followed a similar procedure in the case of Lewis Robarts of Kentucky district, who appealed for a divorce from his wife, Rachel Donelson, on the grounds of desertion and adultery with Andrew Jackson, the future president. In this case the district's supreme court would issue a writ for a trial, and if the jury found for Robarts, the marriage was to be "totally dissolved."[13]

Such precedents encouraged Robert Turnbull to apply for a divorce. In a petition to the legislature carefully crafted to appeal to male solidarity, he explained that he had discovered "the imposition and injury which had been practic'd upon him" only after the wedding, when he found his wife "unable, incompetent and incapable to consummate Marriage." Direct disclosure ended there, so far as Sarah was concerned. In an age of reticence about sexual matters, "a due regard to decorum," he explained, kept him from detailing her "injury" more precisely. Instead Robert invited his male peers to enter vicariously his experience by describing his emotional reaction to his wife's condition: it had revolted him, destroyed his "tranquility," and rendered existence a "burthen"; "human nature" could not "conquer the disgust" he felt.

Yet Robert did not couch his argument simply in terms of personal distress. He embedded that subjective appeal within the framework of paternal duty toward his "rising offspring." Writing for men of his own class who knew similar obligations, Turnbull contextualized his situation in familial terms and linked "his own happiness and that of his family." Because his mercantile business required extensive travel, the responsibility of raising "a large family of young Children" had dictated his remarriage; now, because he could not live with Sarah and his children needed a mother, it necessitated a divorce. Thus he shifted the center of his case from his personal dissatisfaction as a husband to his objective duty as a parent. While reassuring the legislators that he valued as "sacred . . . the rights of Marriage" and properly regarded the "other sex" with "tenderness and delicacy," he asked the assembly to authorize an inquiry into the "facts" by a court empowered to annul his marriage. In closing he circled back obliquely to Sarah's alleged impotence by declaring that the marriage violated "all Laws," including God's.[14]

State capitol in Richmond, 1802, designed by Thomas Jefferson.
The legislature ordinarily met here from November until March.
(Courtesy of The Library of Virginia)

The significance of the proceedings may be aptly gauged by each party's counsel. Patrick Henry and John Marshall represented Robert Turnbull and Sarah Turnbull, respectively. With those two luminaries guiding the debate, the House of Delegates consumed an entire day on what one observer styled "the strange and indelicate case of Mrs. Turnbull." Perhaps the oratorically skilled Henry beat around the linguistic bush concerning Sarah's "Incompetency," but he managed to embarrass the male legislators. Delegate Francis Corbin found the whole business "shocking even to think of" and informed James Madison that a case so "full of Indecency" would be "better related in person than by Letter."[15]

What was Sarah Turnbull's problem? From Robert's claims about her "defective formation" and the need to correct her "frame," we might conclude that Sarah had a physical abnormality or deformity. Yet Robert never proposed that she consult a physician or surgeon. Moreover, her difficulty in achieving "the Nuptial enjoyments" involved her husband also. He repeatedly held out the hope that the advice of friends might bring them "mutual relief."[16] Sarah may have suffered from vaginismus, a psychosexual disorder that causes painful, involuntary spasms of the vagina in response to physical contact or pressure. The existence of this condition, which would prevent sexual intercourse, also explains Robert's growing frustration in the marital relationship. Not generally known or written about before the middle of the nineteenth century, vaginismus was not covered in the medical literature available to women or the doctors who treated them when Sarah and Robert needed assistance.[17] Nor would Corbin or Virginia's other male legislators, more than a century and a half before the work of Masters and Johnson, have been familiar with this problem or had the medical resources on which to draw.

Extensive discussion and amendments in both the House and the Senate eventually resulted in a lengthy bill that authorized the High Court of Chancery to hear the case and subpoena Sarah to answer the charges. The act specified that if the facts alleged by her husband were true, then "by the common law" the marriage was annulled. Technically English canon law rather than common law had cognizance of marriage, annulment, and divorce cases. At Independence in 1776 the Virginia legislature had declared English common law to continue in force, but it said nothing about canon law. Yet for the sake of trying this case, the assembly in effect instructed the court to treat as common law that portion of the ecclesiastical law of the Church of England that specified grounds for annulments. This procedure was not unusual in England. As William Blackstone pointed out, "Common lawyers . . . have borrowed (especially in ancient times) almost all their notions of the legitimacy of marriage from the canon and civil laws." Future Virginia assemblies would depend on English church law and procedures in formulating divorce statutes.[18]

The legislators also recognized the delicate nature of the allegations Robert made. Chancellor George Wythe was to "adopt such mode of trial and proof . . . , as he in his discretion shall think best adapted to come at the truth of the facts." If Sarah failed to appear or to cooperate, the court could declare the marriage "null and void." Unfortunately the chancery court records were burned at the end of the Civil War, so the proceedings in Wythe's court can only be surmised. Marshall continued to represent Sarah Turnbull, and in the spring of 1792 Judge Wythe named a commission that included the well-known physician Benjamin Rush of Philadelphia. Then Robert apparently receded from his demands. Sarah had evidently accepted a court order for a medical inquiry, at her husband's expense, only to have Robert withdraw from the field. That August

John Marshall informed Rush that Turnbull "declines calling you on this business."[19]

By December Sarah was back in Baltimore with a settlement from her husband, when her cousin Arthur Lee of Virginia applauded her "triumph over one of the blackest conspiracies of which human life has any example. The Ladies ought to erect a statute to you," Lee wrote, "for the unexampled firmness with which you resisted an attempt to which, if you had [yield]ed, as most Women would have done, no wife could have been safe from the dark and wicked machinations of a bad husband." Lee surmised that Robert had been "brought by degrees to the extreme of perjury and wickedness" thinking Sarah would give way. "Having, like Macbeth, stepped in so far, he thought that retracting his charges would cover him with as much shame as an ultimate detection; and hoping that some accident might intervene to save him, he was drawn on to the most dreadful ultimatum of wickedness."[20]

Perhaps. But another interpretation of Robert's action is plausible. With Sarah's return to Maryland, her consent to a settlement, and the public airing of his matrimonial tribulations, Robert had achieved his objective. Liberated from a marriage that had never in fact been one, Robert was not obliged to force the physical inspection that he knew Sarah dreaded. He moved, after all, within the upper echelons of an eighteenth-century patriarchal society that made the rules. His Virginia friends and associates could recognize one of their own. They understood the need at times to function outside the letter of the law. Legal divorce had never been part of their world. Thus Robert's good-faith public effort to gain a marital dissolution served as a discursive process that ultimately justified his repudiation of Sarah as his wife while enabling him to maintain his honor uncontested. No other male challenged his conduct outside the formal courtroom structure. Sarah's brother and brother-in-law had refused to become involved. As the unquestioned dominant party, Robert generously waived for Sarah the examination that she would have found degrading. He had never sought deliberately to injure or embarrass her. Male honor also played its part in forbidding the ill treatment of a woman. Although the chancery court never annulled the marriage, his peers in the Virginia gentry undoubtedly reached the conclusion that counted for just as much in their society and regarded him as free to marry again. He soon did so, to Hannah Jones Minor, a widow whose children guaranteed her capacity for complete sexual relations.[21]

Sarah Turnbull, however, still had a score to settle and, again with

Arthur Lee's encouragement and Marshall's assistance, she brought suit in chancery court for a separate maintenance. Because this court's records were burned, we do not know the terms of her settlement, if she ever received one. Based on Marshall's accounts, it may have ended out of court. As her husband, Robert was obliged to support Sarah financially and to pay whatever debts she incurred. He could well afford the cost. Whatever money, land, slaves, household furniture, clothes, jewelry, and other assets she brought to the marriage belonged to him, unless Sarah had arranged for a separate estate before their wedding. She does not appear to have done so. But because she died an extremely wealthy woman in 1811, Robert may have simply returned to her the property she owned before their marriage.[22]

THE PROCESS OF LEGISLATIVE DIVORCE

The role that the General Assembly prescribed for the courts in the cases of Anne Dantignac, Lewis Robarts, and Robert Turnbull showed Virginians the possibilities for judicial divorce on grounds such as abuse, adultery, and desertion as well as the impediments specified in English canon law. By the 1790s those northern states that had not already done so were passing general divorce laws defining such grounds and establishing court procedures. Advocates for judicial divorce in Virginia wanted to follow suit, but they failed to sway the assembly. Instead the legislators reasserted southern colonial practice. Before discussing Turnbull's petition in its session of 1791, the House of Delegates, which initiated all legislation, quashed a motion to establish "a court for granting divorces," by a vote of 51 to 84. Confronted five years later with nine petitions—two from women, six from men, and one from a couple—the delegates considered a bill authorizing the High Court of Chancery to grant legal separations or divorces *a mensa* in cases of adultery. But they tabled even this extremely limited measure that followed the practice in English church courts.[23] Clearly, in the minds of most legislators a prejudgment against divorce existed from the outset.

Not until the beginning of the nineteenth century did the Virginia assembly divorce a couple. As in Maryland a decade earlier, the case involved interracial sex between a white woman and a black man. In 1801 Dabney Pettus asked for a divorce from his wife, Elizabeth, who had borne a mulatto child several months after their wedding. The lawmakers routinely rejected it; but when Dabney resubmitted his petition in 1802, the assembly granted him an absolute divorce. In addition to Elizabeth's adultery across the color line, he also charged fraud at the time of marriage. In subsequent decades petitioners who could prove impotence or fraud at the time of marriage were most successful in obtaining divorces. In the first half of the nineteenth century, the assembly passed bills for 17 (10 men and 7 women) of the 27 people (19 men and 8 women) who alleged those grounds. They represented, however, only a small portion of the petitions. Between 1786, when the assembly received its first divorce petition, and 1827, when it finally assigned a limited jurisdiction to the courts, 115 women, 101 men, and 3 couples submitted 268 petitions. Some of these people repetitioned as many as three and four times. In response the assembly approved only 42 divorce bills, 25 of them *a vinculo.* Thus during a forty-year period when the legislature exercised sole jurisdiction over divorce, it granted absolute divorces or legally separated the parties in just one-fifth of the cases submitted for judgment. Only 23 women and 19 men received divorces.

Although the assembly repeatedly rejected them, divorce petitions continued to arrive in Richmond in growing numbers from every level of society and every section of the state. They ordinarily followed an elaborate procedure. The person requesting the divorce first notified his or her spouse that a petition would be submitted at the next assembly session. A notarized messenger delivered this missive, and often it also appeared in the press. A signed divorce petition drafted either by the petitioner or by legal counsel formed the centerpiece of the case. It usually narrated the background of both parties, the problems of their marriage, and the grounds for a divorce. As legal documents the petitions were deliberately crafted to appeal to the legislators and at times possess an almost formulaic quality. The petitioner also submitted affidavits from supporting witnesses, who were sworn before a local justice of the peace. Often these manuscripts, as in the Turnbull case, were lengthy eyewitness accounts. At times the almost identical language demonstrates that someone, perhaps a lawyer, had coached the witnesses in advance, but other files present extremely diverse, even conflicting testimony. In some cases relatives, friends, and neighbors lined up and signed a statement to verify the good character of the petitioner and the truth of the allegations. The spouse had to be informed of the date, time, and place for taking affidavits in order to have the opportunity to hear the testimony in favor of the divorce. Of course, the spouse was also free to present a counterpetition and opposing affidavits to the assembly.

In divorce cases the General Assembly functioned as a court, sifting and evaluating the testimony and debating the evidence. The petition would first be presented to the House of Delegates, usually by a member from the county where it originated. Ordinarily the House would then refer it to a standing committee for evaluation. In the 1790s the committee on religion handled divorce cases, but in the nineteenth century the legislature eliminated this body and turned divorce petitions over to the committee on the courts of justice. After studying the evidence, the committee recommended that the House either accept or reject the petition. If the delegates voted to accept it, the committee drew up and presented a bill. During the mandatory three readings that followed, the House might reject or amend it. After a third successful reading, the bill went to the Senate. If the senators passed the House bill, it became law. But they could also veto or amend it. In the latter case it then returned to the House for concurrence or negotiation.

Given the assembly's general unwillingness to pass private divorce bills, why did so many people continue to submit them? Perhaps because, as the example of Robert Turnbull suggests, the public ritual involved in seeking a divorce served within the local community as a discursive process designed to maintain or restore the petitioner's social standing and justify a remarriage regardless of what the legislature decided. This might be particularly true for men, who formed the bulk of petitioners before 1809. For a southern male the divorce procedure necessitated a sequence of interchanges with an estranged or discarded wife, family members, neighbors, and local leaders. Rather than asserting the autonomy of the individual, the result emphasized the importance of the community's judgment and solidarity. Whatever the legislature decided, the process formally terminated the marriage, so far as the local community was concerned. At the same time it ritualized the assertion or restoration of masculine honor. Perhaps the most important exchanges occurred on court days at the local county seat. That could prove an ideal time to gather affidavits with a magistrate present to notarize them. Then, outside the courthouse, the man divorcing his wife might circulate a statement for the signatures of other males in the community. By testifying to the truth of the allegations, the veracity of the witnesses, and the good reputation of the petitioner, they confirmed his standing as one of them. His honor remained intact.[24]

The cases of Samuel Ritchie and John Bonnell exemplify this process. From Scott County in the west, Ritchie wrote the assembly in 1792 that he had joined Ann Parker "in the Holy rites of Matrimony" expecting "to pass his life in all the sweet enjoyments" of the married state. But her "wicked disposition" soon surfaced, and she abandoned "the Solemn *ties* and *Obligations* of the married state" to live in adultery with various men. When the assembly rejected his petition, Ritchie took a common-law wife, Frances Kindrick. Over the years they had six children. His neighbors obviously thought no less of Samuel despite his irregular marriage situation, because they later chose him repeatedly for important positions in local government. Relations with his legal wife also remained amiable. After Samuel's death in 1818, Ann, technically his widow, deeded her dower portion of his estate to the children of Samuel and Frances.[25]

John Bonnell was another frontier Virginian who faced a situation similar to Ritchie's. After discovering love letters to his wife, Hannah, from John Asa, "a married man," Bonnell confronted her. A brazen Hannah admitted the adultery with her paramour. Despite pressure from her family and friends and even her husband's attempt to reclaim her, Hannah left him and their two small children to set up housekeeping with Asa, who presumably deserted his spouse also. In the autumn of 1796 the county court fined Hannah Bonnell and John Asa $20 apiece for their adultery, and a short time later John Bonnell filed his petition for divorce. While agreeing with the "tenderness" of the legislature in divorce cases, his best efforts to save his marriage had failed. Therefore, he announced to the assembly and the world, "I Consider myself Devorced from her by the Devine Law." At least a segment of the local community evidently agreed, because twenty-four people signed a petition affirming his recital of events and stating their support for his position.[26] For Ritchie and Bonnell the judgment of neighbors counted far more than the views of the distant legislature and enabled them to reconstruct their lives within the community.

This process, however, did not work for women. If the legislature refused a wife's divorce petition, she remained under coverture and legally bound to her husband. In exceptional circumstances, as we will see, relatives and neighbors might intervene, particularly in cases of extreme abuse. But unless a wife possessed a separate estate, she held no property in her own right. Rather than seeking an unlikely divorce, the preferred alternative for the majority of unhappy wives lay in flight. Abandoned husbands regularly published notices in the press indicating that their spouses had absconded from "bed and board."[27] Only a small fraction of these men ever petitioned for a divorce. But because married men bore financial responsibility for their wives, deserted husbands advertised the fact in order to escape liability for their debts. Wives who managed business affairs for fleeing husbands also gave public notice.[28]

Because divorces were so difficult to obtain, spouses sometimes arranged separation agreements before county courts. The local government in mostly rural Virginia, these courts were self-perpetuating bodies of gentry who exercised a variety of executive, legislative, and judicial functions. On one or more court days each month the justices of the peace heard presentments from the grand jury, tried criminal and civil cases with petit juries, and sat as a chancery court to determine equity (fairness) cases. Among their myriad duties they witnessed documents that divided property between spouses who desired to separate. John Netherland, for example, had visited Kentucky to purchase property and prepare a home there, but when he returned to Powhatan County to collect his wife, Mary, and their children, he discovered that she had formed a liaison with a younger man named David Owen. The husband and wife separated, and John formally gave Mary some "slaves and other personal property" worth "about five hundred pounds" over which she received complete ownership and control in place of her dower rights. Several months later Mary and David departed for parts west, and only then did John Netherland petition for a divorce to assuage the "disgrace" she had brought upon him. But the lawmakers rejected John's request, despite his prominent family connections. Perhaps they thought his arrangements with Mary through the county court sufficient to cover legal concerns.[29]

In such settlements, which Suzanne Lebsock styled "do-it-yourself" divorces, separating couples commonly signed a formal statement before a justice of the peace. Sometimes they also published the text in the press. One such separation agreement succinctly expressed its purpose: "that the matrimonial tie may be broken, and that they may be hereafter, two people." In a similar situation a petitioner informed the assembly that he and his wife had agreed "by Solemn Contract in writing agreed to Separate and be *Divorced*."[30] These documents, by their detailed, precise terms, expose the extensive legal controls a husband held over a wife, as well as his obligations to her and their children. In 1808, after the assembly had denied his petition for a divorce on the grounds of adultery, George Whitfield and his wife, Elizabeth, signed a formal indenture that stated that henceforth she would be free to go wherever she wished and engage in "such trade and business as She . . . shall think proper." George promised that he would not take her to court "for living separate and apart from him, or compel her to reside or cohabit with him, or sue any person or persons whatsoever for receiving or entertaining her." In effect, Elizabeth would live "as if She was a feme sole and unmarried" and have full capability to acquire, hold, and dispose of her own property and manage her finances. George further agreed to pay her $500 and "keep support and maintain at his own proper costs his four Children" and allow them "at proper and convenient times to visit their Mother . . . and their Grandmother." For her part, Elizabeth accepted the money as fully satisfying her dower rights and for the full "support, and in maintenance during her natural life" of herself and her bastard child, whom she agreed to raise. She gave up "all other claims whatsoever to any part or proportion of [George's] . . . estate." The document named a trustee, who would ensure that Elizabeth "will and truly fulfil and abide by the Covenants and agreements on her part to be done and performed."[31]

Despite the legal language and the presence of a notary, judges and lawyers questioned the validity and effect of such instruments. Legislators might argue that divorces were not needed because these separations couples arranged for themselves took care of basic concerns such as dower rights and the maintenance of wife and children. But no document divorced a husband and wife or freed either of them to marry again. After his wife, Judith, agreed that their marriage should be dissolved, Joseph Cocke announced, "We will have a divorce and I shall consider myself from this day a free man." But whether Joseph and Judith Cocke or Elizabeth and George Whitfield or any other couple considered themselves liberated, until the legislature approved a divorce, the state regarded them as legally bound to each other. A frustrated Sally Carter argued that because the continuation of "a *legal union*" between herself and her husband served no useful objective, "the interests of society can not require it."[32] But most Virginians believed that matrimony involved something more than a legal contract and that the community did have a stake in marriage.

THE COMMON GOOD VERSUS PERSONAL HAPPINESS

The relative concerns of society as opposed to those of the individual became the focus of a major legislative debate in the 1804 assembly session. Conservative delegates agreed wholeheartedly with the sentiments of Thomas Randolph, who argued that marriage was a sacred institution subject to "injury . . . from the least incautious touch of the Legislative body." But how best should they safeguard this foundation block of society? More delegates seemed disposed to grant divorces than in the past. Would not threatened marriages be in less danger from incessant tinkering if the assembly calmly set forth narrow and precise grounds for granting divorces and then let district chancery courts hear the evidence and decide the issue in individual cases?

Littleton Tazewell, the future U.S. senator and governor, proposed such a measure and put himself at the head of an ineffectual crusade for a general divorce law. The brilliant young lawyer from Norfolk, thirty years old and serving his first term, wanted the assembly to establish "some fixed principles, for deciding all subsequent cases" and then, following European practice, turn the whole divorce business over to the courts. Up to this point the legislators had granted absolute divorces only to white men whose wives had engaged in sex across the color line. But Tazewell had at least one other principle in mind: adultery. In Virginia, he observed, where the legislature "occasionally resolved itself into a kind of ecclesiastical court, few precedents had been formed and few principles had been permanently established." The analogy to a church court might have worried some legislators. In recent years they had moved decisively to cut any connection between church and state by voiding all laws concerning religion, except Jefferson's Statute for Religious Freedom. The notion that in deciding divorce cases they were assuming an ecclesial function akin to the British Parliament would not appeal. Yet Tazewell failed to persuade his colleagues. As his biographer noted, he was "an extreme individualist, wholly unaffected by trends of social thought." But Virginia's culture opposed divorce, and the legislators saw themselves as custodians of its moral values.[33]

The petition that enlisted Tazewell's support in this debate came from Joseph Mettauer, a prominent physician in Prince Edward County. The saga of his multiple efforts to free himself legally from his spouse clarifies the reasons why many legislators were reluctant to give the courts jurisdiction over divorce and the skepticism with which they read individual petitions. After serving as a surgeon with Lafayette's army in the American Revolution, Mettauer, a native of France, settled in Virginia. During the 1780s he established a thriving medical practice in Prince Edward County. His younger brother, John Peter Mettauer, emigrated to join him there in 1790, shortly before their father's death. The senior Mettauer, who was also a doctor as well as mayor of Sultzbach in Alsace, had possessed substantial wealth. Taking his younger brother's power of attorney to act on his behalf, Joseph returned to France in October 1790 to claim their inheritance.[34]

John Peter remained in Prince Edward County. A young widow, Jemima Gaulding, was also living in the doctor's home at that time, and before his departure Joseph promised Jemima that he would marry her upon his return. Six months later he was back in Virginia. True to his word, the doctor had Drury Lacy, a Presbyterian minister and vice-president of nearby Hampden-Sydney College, perform their wedding in May 1791. According to his version of events, Joseph was soon horrified to discover that his bride was several months pregnant, courtesy of his brother. Six months later she gave birth to a full-term baby girl. John Peter quietly disappeared to Georgia, while Joseph separated from Jemima and prepared to seek a divorce.[35]

In the petition, which he submitted two years later, in 1793, Joseph explained how well he had treated Jemima. He had accepted her "into his home and family, from a life of wandering and Misery." Gradually, by "artful Contrivances and Insinuations," she wormed her way into his affections until he agreed to marry her if she maintained "Fidelity, Truth, and proper Behaviour" while he was in France. Because foreign travel carried risks, the doctor also arranged "for her comfortable Support in case of his Death." He left Jemima instead of John Peter in charge "of his house, family, and Estate" and told his brother "to do every thing in his power" to help her. He did not want to leave Jemima dependent on John Peter, he told the assembly, and so had instructed her to call on a neighbor, Samuel Venable, for help if his brother caused any problems. But all seemed well when Joseph came home, and believing in Jemima's "Fidelity," he went ahead with the marriage as planned.

Joseph Mettauer's petition vibrates with wounded innocence and moral indignation. Despite all he had done for her, Jemima had betrayed him. To consider her now "as the partner of his Bed" was "pollution." To live as man and wife would "mark your petitioner as depraved and abandoned to every feeling which distinguishes civilized man from the savage; or even the beasts." He informed the assembly that Jemima had "felt the Justice of these impressions" and agreed to the annulment of the marriage. He asked the legislature to fulfill "one of the great ends of society, the happiness of unoffending Individuals" by "releasing him." A legislative refusal would only increase his suffering if that "were possible." But he concluded with an appeal based on class. Referring to his previous behavior, he pointed out that his diligence and competence as a doctor and his "useful" service to the community set him apart from those "whom dissipated morals and dissolute Courses involve in Matrimonial Squabbles." In words that would come back to haunt him, Joseph told the assembly that the record of his life betrayed "no Instance of Disregard to the Sacred Obligations of Social Life or Inattention to the great duties of Morality." In contrast, his "unreformed" wife "continues to associate with the dissolute."[36]

After considering Mettauer's petition for more than a month, a legislative committee reported a resolution that summarized his argument, noted his good reputation in his community, and recommended a divorce bill. The House, however, first tabled the issue and then a week later rejected the committee's resolution. Three years passed before Joseph tried again with the same petition and the same result.[37] Affidavits from neighbors affirmed his recital of events. In a letter of introduction to Edmund Randolph in Richmond, ten leading citizens explained that soon after his arrival in Prince Edward County, the good doctor had been "unfortunately impos'd on by a designing woman, who by art, and Stratagem induced him to marry her." They asked Randolph, who had recently returned to his law practice after resigning as secretary of state, to use his good offices to help Mettauer gain a divorce or annulment, because otherwise he would probably return to France. Written between the lines is their anxious concern that their community might lose an excellent physician. Although the committee parroted the doctor's case for a divorce, the House postponed its consideration indefinitely.[38]

Although the assembly again refused his petition, the doctor did not leave Virginia. Instead throughout these years he continued to prosper economically while caring for the medical needs of his neighbors as well as people in nearby counties.[39] In 1804 he tried a fresh approach in his third attempt to gain a divorce. This time he claimed that John Peter had pressed the marriage upon him and assured him of Jemima's "virtuous character." When Joseph discovered that his brother had made her pregnant, he had fled the "incestuous" relationship. Since then Jemima had "abandoned herself to a course of profligacy and prostitution notorious to the whole neighbourhood in which she dwells." A bevy of affidavits verified her fallen state and named assorted men upon whom she had bestowed her "favours." The committee's resolution approved Joseph's petition, but the House refused to order a divorce bill by a roll-call vote of 95 to 66.[40]

The dispute over the Mettauer divorce attracted press attention. As the *Richmond Enquirer* obliquely reported, his petition was turned down "in spite of very cogent arguments" because of "peculiar circumstances."

A damning amendment to the committee report, published in the House *Journal,* showed that the good doctor had not been completely candid with the legislature. Mettauer had actually "seduced" the widow Gaulding by promising to marry her and then "kept her in a state of concubinage for some years, during which she bore two children." The assembly undoubtedly knew that Jemima had first appeared on Joseph's doorstep for treatment of an infected leg. She remained in his home and, during the years before their marriage, bore two sons whom the doctor acknowledged as his own and named John Peter and Francis Joseph.[41] So when Joseph told the assembly that he had left Jemima in charge of his "family" while he went to France, he meant their sons. In claiming that she had seduced him, he reversed their roles. Nor is it difficult to imagine that while Joseph was safely across the Atlantic, John Peter followed his brother's example in having his way with Jemima.[42] Critical legislators could also challenge the doctor's assertion that after he had discovered Jemima's condition, he had immediately separated from her. Her daughter was born in November 1791, but two years passed before he petitioned for a divorce. Some delegates must have raised the British principle of condonation. Joseph could hardly cite Jemima's adultery as grounds for divorce because he had continued to cohabit with her after he knew of her affair with his brother. Thus he had condoned the fault against which he now petitioned. In sum, opponents of Mettauer's divorce could punch gaping holes in his story and his claim to have upheld "the great duties of Morality."[43]

Yet in a striking example of the privileged place afforded the male head in domestic relations and the doctor's status in society, sixty-six House members supported his divorce, including the four delegates from Prince Edward and Lunenburg Counties, where he practiced medicine. Had his case been heard in a district chancery court there, the judge might well have ruled in his favor under pressure from local interests that wanted a husband's power affirmed and an excellent physician satisfied. Tazewell was prepared to decide the case in favor of Mettauer solely on the basis of the "abstract principle" that adultery was sufficient grounds for divorce "in the court of Doctor's Commons in England," a cluster of buildings in London that housed the principal church courts. Tazewell was wrong about English ecclesiastical law, but in addition to the problem raised by condonation, the House majority probably held back for the sake of two further considerations. In the first place, circumstances mattered. Whatever Jemima might have done, the doctor's treatment of her offended the moral values of Virginia society. Keeping a white mistress in one's home while she bore your children out of wedlock violated community standards the assembly was expected to uphold.[44]

Moreover, in the second place, by refusing to approve Joseph's divorce, the legislators served a closely related principle, the public or common good. The doctor had pleaded his right to happiness, a theme repeatedly sounded in petitions from both genders of every class. While these texts often acknowledged the sanctity of marriage and its importance to society's welfare, they emphasized their anticipation that wedded life would produce "Pleasures," "Enjoyments," and especially "happiness and bliss."[45] Happiness was the prime desideratum, but it meant different things to husbands and wives. In detailing their expectations, men commonly desired "allegiance" and "affection" from a virtuous wife, while women voiced a need for "protection" and "support" for themselves and their children from a provident husband.[46] When spouses failed to deliver what was expected, both men and women argued that justice entitled them to a divorce.

The legislators normally replied that a couple should remain married for the sake of the common good of society. Divorce destroyed the sanctity of the marriage bond and undermined the integrity of the family unit that formed the bedrock of Christian civilization. Therefore the assembly consistently privileged marriage and family life over the happiness of an individual, regardless of how important that person might be in the community. The common good mattered most. Staunchly sociocentric, this civic republicanism defined virtue in terms of a willingness to subordinate one's private, personal interests for the benefit of communal goals and values. Gordon Wood identified this concept, which informed the idealism of the Revolutionary generation, as "the essence of republicanism," and A. G. Roeber emphasized its importance for early-nineteenth-century Virginians. In the South more generally the concept found expression in what Richard Weaver called "'social bond' individualism," a freedom contextualized by antecedent social relations. In this society the larger entities of family and community helped to define and focus the person in terms of rights and responsibilities.[47]

In southern discourse, appeals to the common good repeatedly surfaced in debates over divorce law in the legislature and the press throughout the age of Jefferson and beyond. The relative weights assigned to the welfare of society as a whole compared with the personal happiness of individuals formed a central theme in the legislative and press discussion of divorce, as well as in the petitions submitted by dissatisfied spouses. To what extent were individuals entitled to marital satisfaction? Were they expected to sacrifice personal desires and familial comfort for the sake of preserving societal values? Ordinarily the assembly privileged marriage. Even when legislators granted a divorce, evidence suggests that they did so out of the conviction that continuing a particular marriage after one party had flagrantly violated normative societal values might damage the common good more than the dissolution of the union. The divorce records indicate that many southern women and men defied those values, rejected social restraint, and shed spouses and families in pursuit of personal happiness. But the societal consensus, as expressed especially by the assembly at the political center, rejected such behavior. Debating the merits of a case, one delegate summarized the prevailing sentiment in the legislature through most of these years: "The welfare of society" demanded "that divorces should be discouraged as much as possible."[48]

From a republican perspective, parties contracting marriage assumed social responsibilities. In exceptional circumstances the legislature might annul an individual marriage or provide a legal separation in order to protect a grossly abused wife. But to establish a divorce system that defined causes and specified court procedures for dissolving solemn, public relationships defied sound social policy. The assembly would threaten people's confidence in the institution of matrimony and permit purely private interests to determine community standards. Equally important for the southern mind, it would intrude into the domestic space of masculine prerogative and responsibility. This conservative ideology, so compatible with the slaveholding, hierarchical South, resisted a growing liberal discourse that privileged the autonomous individual free to choose personal happiness and self-fulfillment. For the next three decades southern white males who were restless to assert manly independence and liberate themselves from unwelcome marital and familial ties would find westward emigration a more realistic alternative than legislative divorce.[49]

In rejecting Mettauer's petition as well as a general divorce law, the legislative majority in 1804 had determined not to grant divorces simply on the basis of enumerated causes such as adultery or desertion. The context of each case counted, too. But Virginia's quarrel over the nature and purposes of matrimony and the proper basis for a divorce was just beginning. A few years later Tazewell's proposal surfaced again in the 1807 session when the legislature considered a bill to give jurisdiction over divorces for certain specified causes to chancery courts. The preamble leveled a broadside against the perspective enunciated earlier by traditionalists such as Thomas Randolph and pushed the possibilities for divorce into much broader grounds than previously proposed. In equating marriage with any other contractual obligation, the bill's preamble bluntly stated that "the marriage contract" should not be regarded as "indissoluble" in cases involving "gross fraud, or where one of the parties has so acted as to have disabled him or herself from promoting the happiness of the other." Fraud was obvious, but making "happiness" a ground for divorce would open the floodgates. The draft of the bill stated that in cases of desertion, either party could sue for divorce, but the rest of the proposal blatantly favored the male partner and exemplified the prevailing double standard of sexual morality. The court could end the marriage if the wife was pregnant before marriage by a man not her husband, produced a mulatto child, or committed adultery. The measure failed to pass a second reading.[50]

The next year the men got their comeuppance, however, when women submitted four of the seven divorce petitions and, for the first time since Anne Dantignac's petition twenty years earlier, the male legislators gave them a sympathetic, positive hearing. Impressed by their stories of desertion, bigamy, violence, and abuse, the lawmakers granted absolute divorces to all four women. Evidently a legislative majority that year agreed with petitioner Margaret Brough, who urged that divorce under circumstances "of extreme hardship" was so reasonable that the assembly should "forget a hoary prejudice . . . too stale to be eagerly embraced by the wisdom and liberality of modern times."[51] Numerous Virginians must have noticed the burst of legislative activity because unhappy spouses inundated the assembly's next session in 1809 with twenty-three petitions, a majority of which came from women.

Arguing over individual cases could have consumed much of that session. Instead, as the petitions poured in, the delegates appointed a committee, which included Tazewell, to produce a general bill "concerning divorces." The result was a limited measure designed solely to streamline the assembly's work. Anyone desiring a divorce must have a circuit court jury decide "the facts of the case" and forward the court transcript with the petition to the assembly. But even though this restricted proposal did not establish any grounds for divorce or authorize any court to grant them, the House tabled the bill.[52] The assembly swung back to a more cautious stance. Petitions that almost certainly would have merited divorces the year before were rejected outright. The reasons for this reversal are not immediately apparent, but the composition of the legislature changed significantly each year with a high turnover in the membership.

In 1808 Henry St. George Tucker, a young lawyer in Winchester, wrote to his father, St. George Tucker, expressing contempt for Virginia's assembly. Describing himself as "sated and disgusted with public life" after a single term in the House, he bemoaned the absence of "public virtue" in the legislators, which he equated with "public honour[,] public honesty[,] and independence of character." A year later he criticized their inconsistencies, which he attributed to their hunger for political office. What they approved one week they might easily reject the next. In particular, "the spirit of innovation" alarmed the future judge and law professor. "I am averse to change if it can be avoided," he wrote tellingly to the senior Tucker, a distinguished judge on Virginia's Court of Appeals. "Since I have grown up . . . I have been induced to think the greatest praise of the American patriots (particularly Virginians) was their aversion to change and the avoiding of all alteration in the system of things in existence" when the Revolution began unless absolutely necessary.[53]

In sturdily resisting change, whether political or social, Tucker spoke for his generation. If the printed copies of the proposed law provoked any reaction throughout the commonwealth, it reinforced the conservatives. Another fifteen years elapsed before the legislature gave the courts a role in divorce procedures. In the meantime, one disgusted constituent asked his representative if he did "not feel degraded in perpetually legislating on . . . divorce cases and other Tom Dick and Harry interests." In his view the lawmakers should divest themselves of this "mass of trash" by approving a general divorce law. Legislator and future governor David Campbell acknowledged the unsavory aspects involved in sifting through the cases that he thought hardly fit for polite society. On one occasion, he told a friend, a group of women had arrived in the gallery expecting to hear a debate over moving the state capital. Instead they almost heard a divorce case; but someone indicated to them the nature of the upcoming topic, and they beat a hasty exit.[54]

Several times over the years various delegates proposed vesting authority in the courts, but a majority always opposed that measure. While agreeing that divorce cases were "troublesome and difficult," most feared that local juries would be too lax in favoring the pleas of unhappy individuals instead of the common good.[55] During this period women received the larger portion of the few divorces the assembly granted, but these were generally legal separations on grounds of extreme cruelty and abusive treatment. Absolute divorces were rare and usually were granted only in clear-cut instances of fraud, impotence, or bigamy. In a case reminiscent of the Turnbull affair, Rebecca Sims cried "fraud," claiming that Hugh Sims had been "incapable of consummating the marriage, by reason of natural impotence." The assembly handed the issue over to a chancery court for investigation and mandated a decree of nullity if the charge was proved.[56] Occasionally a divorce bill provoked heated debates and concluded in a roll-call vote. Persistence on the part of petitioners was often needed, though not always rewarded. Tabitha Toler badgered the legislature for three years before the lawmakers permitted her to cast off her spouse on grounds of fraud and deception and resume her unmarried name.[57] Sometimes the delegates attempted to assign guilt and to chastise the erring partner. Mary Brady gained an absolute divorce in 1820 because the assembly agreed that she had been "deluded into matrimony by her husband . . . under the cloak of religion"; Thorton Brady was prohibited from remarrying.[58]

That year Thomas Ritchie's influential *Richmond Enquirer* discussed "this question of *divorce, a vexata questio* in our legislature, session after session." The editor did not object to legal separations "of two beings who are only a curse to each other, or one of whom brings nothing but unhappiness and persecution upon the other." But Ritchie cautioned against allowing easy remarriage. If they thought absolute divorces readily available, spouses anxious "to form a *new connection*" would focus on faults just as easily ignored and might even induce "one party to commit an outrage" to create justifiable grounds. "Throw as few temptations as possible in the way of married people," the editor urged. "Every thing before our eyes, the whole history of mankind, prove that the wisest part of the Lord's prayer is, *'Lead us not into temptation.'*"[59] Clearing a path for divorce, especially absolute divorce, would only tempt dissatisfied couples to tread it.

RATIONALIZING THE SYSTEM

While Ritchie watched anxiously from his press office, the annual influx of divorce petitions in the 1820s created legislative logjams. "We have done little else since we met but receive petitions," complained one delegate in December 1824; "there are more petitions for divorces than I ever knew offered at one Session." Examining these private marital disasters had become a time-consuming, expensive, and massive distraction from the public business. "I wish to get that subject out of the Legislature," insisted another representative.[60] Sixteen people asked for divorces in 1824, and for four of them it was a second request. Each one furnished a sheaf of documents that sometimes amounted to twenty or thirty pages of petitions and affidavits. The standing rules of the House did not permit a second petition unless new evidence was forthcoming, but rejected petitioners often fattened their files with new affidavits and tried again. The House clerk then produced the original documents from his office and added them to the pile of new data. Though the delegates dismissed some requests quickly, they labored over others, debating the evidence and considering possible bills. The assembly approved only three divorces in the 1824 session, but the process consumed an enormous amount of time. Each year the workload increased.

As petitions piled up, the 1825 assembly fumbled around the question. Finally General Samuel Blackburn bluntly proposed that all divorce cases be turned over to the judiciary. A respected lawyer from Staunton and a former Federalist candidate for Congress, the old politician was a forceful, persuasive orator. The House agree to his resolution, and within several weeks Blackburn's bill had inaugurated vigorous debates. A succinct preamble asserted pragmatically that "applications to the Legislature, in the first instance, for divorce, are equally unfavorable to economy, correct decision, the general weal, and the best interests of all concerned." Therefore the bill proposed that all petitioners apply to their respective district Superior Court of Chancery. There a jury could establish the facts of the case and the chancellor could issue a "final decree." Either spouse might appeal this decision to the assembly and submit a complete court transcript in evidence.[61]

One observer thought the exchange on this bill engaged the House's most competent members. The discussions also revealed the range of issues and sharp disagreement. When one delegate proposed that county courts be given divorce jurisdiction, others objected that local courts would grant divorces too easily and unevenly. Archibald Bryce complained that Blackburn's bill provided chancery courts with too much discretion. He thought that any law should enumerate the grounds for divorces, as other states did. Still another proposal sought to restrict the chancery courts to legal separations and reserve absolute divorces for the legislature. All these amendments failed to pass, but then an alternative bill added provisions for awarding child custody and dividing common property, concerns the delegates had not yet considered.[62]

Though he had retired from politics for the second time in 1824, Henry St. George Tucker, now a judge of the Superior Courts of Chancery, injected himself into the debate. In notes he printed for the students at his private law school in Winchester, he explained that the legislature regularly rejected most applicants because they sought divorces for reasons that "at common law" were unjustifiable. The former senator particularly praised the Senate for its "opposition to such petitions." A superb legal preparation under his father, his own legal and legislative experience, and now his vantage point on the bench fitted Tucker to write authoritatively on the Old Dominion's law and practice in 1826. State law, he pointed out, already authorized the Superior Courts of Law to grant absolute divorces in cases of consanguinity and affinity. Other legitimate grounds for divorce existed also. Tucker's operative principle was that once a "right" had been "recognized and established by the principles of the law," then "the *remedy* must be found somewhere." But he thought separation agreements to be of dubious legality.

Tucker proposed instead that either the General Court or the chancery courts grant absolute divorces in cases that would merit such treatment in an English church court, and that chancery courts grant legal separations with suitable provisions for alimony in cases of adultery and cruelty. "If marriage be in its nature a civil, as it is in its celebration a sacred contract," he wrote, "it seems consonant with the principles of equity, to give its aid to parties, if for want of another jurisdiction they cannot find it elsewhere." The chancellor of Virginia's fourth judicial circuit wanted the assembly to solve the problem "by some statutory provision."[63]

In 1826 the legislature acted. The House passed a substitute bill offered by Bryce. During the debates he had questioned whether the contract provisions of the Federal Constitution allowed state legislatures "to interfere in a marriage contract, by disturbing any marital right, except for causes anticedent to the contract and affecting its validity." His bill embodied this conservative posture by limiting judicial divorces to specified grounds in existence at the time of marriage. It also resurrected an old proposal. Anyone petitioning for a divorce must first have a jury decide the facts of the case in a Superior Court of Law and then submit the court transcript with the divorce petition to the assembly. The Senate amended the bill to include provision for *a mensa* divorces in certain instances, but the session concluded before the House could consider these amendments.[64]

The next year, in passing its first general law regarding divorce, the assembly stayed close to Bryce's amended proposal. It furnished two avenues for divorce. The first lay through the Superior Courts of Chancery, which had replaced the single High Court of Chancery and were located in nine districts across Virginia. These courts could grant absolute divorces in cases of "idiocy," "bigamy," and "natural or incurable" impotence at the time of marriage; they could decree divorces *a mensa* (legal separations without permission to remarry) for "adultery, cruelty and just cause of bodily fear." In the words of the new law, these were "causes which justify such divorces by the principles of the common law." As the assembly had done in the Turnbull case in 1791 and as Tucker suggested in his class notes, this statute treated the ecclesiastical law, which specified these same grounds for marriage annulments and legal separations, as if it were part of common law. The law also authorized the court to decide issues of property and child custody. Thus the lawmakers had finally given state courts a jurisdiction approaching but not quite matching that of English church courts.[65]

The second approach to divorce remained by way of the assembly after a stop in court. The petitioner, after notifying his or her spouse, would have to apply to a Superior Court of Law, which was a trial court, and file "a statement of the causes." After hearing the evidence, a jury would decide whether and to what extent the allegations in the petitioner's statement were true. A transcript of these proceedings and the verdict had to accompany each petition to the assembly. Either spouse in a divorce case retained the right to appeal this decision to the Court of Appeals, the supreme court in Virginia.[66] In cases of legislative divorce, this two-step process made it more likely that the assembly would receive an accurate account of the marriage and its problems than could be gleaned from the petition and whatever affidavits or supporting evidence the applicant offered the legislature.[67] It was also a vote of confidence that local juries would serve justice.

Though the new law temporarily reduced the number of petitions, the assembly continued to consider private divorce bills for more than two decades. At least in the beginning of this period most men and women preferred to attempt an absolute divorce in Richmond rather than settle for a legal separation provided by the courts. Obviously an absolute divorce normally allowed the option of another marriage. But its definitive nature also brought a clarity that a legal separation sometimes lacked. For example, Mary Cloud obtained an *a mensa* divorce from the Superior Court in 1838, but her husband refused to recognize the court decree. Asserting that "his marital rights" remained intact and that he was still entitled to whatever property she held, a "lawless and violent" William Cloud continued to harass her. Mary complained in her petition that because her neighbors did not understand "the nature and force" of the court's action, she remained "in constant danger of outrage" and the seizure of "her property and person." For the sake of "peace and quiet," she begged for an absolute divorce, and the assembly obliged. The lawmakers were generally strict, however, in requiring a jury's judgment on a petitioner's allegations. For example, Henry Warwick wanted a quick and very private divorce. He rested his case on seemingly unimpeachable evidence of incest and fraud prior to the marriage, but the assembly rejected his petition because Warwick had not established the facts in court.[68]

Several times in the 1840s the lawmakers expanded the grounds and loosened the restrictions imposed by the 1827 divorce law. Their caseload had been mounting steadily. Senator Robert Young Conrad compared life in the legislature to the monotony "of a blind horse in a thrashing machine." His complaints exaggerated the "hundreds" of requests. But anxious to escape from "this higher ward of the state penitentiary," Conrad successfully introduced a bill in 1841 to expand the grounds for divorce by explicitly incorporating the canon law of the Church of England. The new law provided that a Superior Court could now annul marriages in any case "for which marriage is annulled by the ecclesiastical law." Following the same logic, the court could grant legal separations in all the cases provided by the 1827 act as well as "abandonment and desertion" and "any other cause for which a limited divorce is authorized by the principles of the ecclesiastical law." Thus the General Assembly formally completed the process of transferring Anglican canon law on divorce into the commonwealth's statutes. The House wanted to go further by permitting a petitioner divorced *a mensa* to remarry after seven years just as if the decree had been *a vinculo*. But the Senate rejected this addition and passed the bill in its original form.[69]

Any easing of the strictures surrounding divorce always met resistance. The senators, as Tucker averred in the 1820s, were particularly tough on the issue, frequently denying divorces the House had approved.

Over the years the Senate rejected forty-seven divorces, or almost one-fourth of the bills passed by the House. No matter how rigorous the assembly might be, the petitions kept coming. Although they treated grim subjects, some appeals made hilarious reading. But on a spring day in 1841, when House members began roaring with laughter, not everyone in the chamber was amused. One irate delegate gravely advised his confreres against tampering with the "marriage contract." Another politician opined that if every unhappy spouse could be divorced, "it would be the better plan to introduce the radical doctrines of Fanny Wright . . . and dissolve all the marriages" immediately. A frustrated legislator suggested considering all divorce bills on one "divorce day" and establishing "some general principle" for dealing with them.[70] Though the law now provided judicial procedures for obtaining a legal separation, more and more people in the 1840s wanted an absolute divorce instead. The assembly increasingly acquiesced.

The mentality of Virginians toward marriage and divorce was changing. Arguments that the common good demanded that all couples stay together no matter what horrors home life held were not nearly so persuasive in an age that treasured a companionate relationship between husband and wife. Refusing a divorce when a marriage had been irretrievably destroyed made no sense to the next generation. As one young man wrote his mother, "Separation, of man and wife, is no romance, or a thing to be lightly spoken of—but a *sad reality* that should be met at once and decided summarily for the peace of both parties."[71] And legal separation was not nearly so psychologically satisfying or definitive as divorce. In another era people had dreaded the notoriety that accompanied divorce proceedings; now the very process became, at least for some, the vehicle for vindicating personal innocence and family reputation.

The assembly acknowledged this changed environment. After 1843 the number of divorces rose dramatically. Since the passage of the 1827 law, the lawmakers had granted just 20 percent of the petitions and approved 33 divorces, most of which were *a vinculo*. Men received 14 and women 19. Between 1844 and 1851 the assembly granted 52 percent of the petitions by passing 78 bills, 39 for men and 39 for women. The grounds for most of these absolute divorces was adultery, or what was called "criminal conversation." Up to this time fraud had been the most successful argument a petitioner could use, and courts had granted legal separations for adultery. Now adultery became an adequate reason for divorce *a vinculo*. The treatment of Benjamin Wright demonstrated the assembly's new mood.

After three failed attempts, Ben asked yet again in 1844 for a divorce from his wife, Mariam. Though a jury had agreed with his charges of adultery, it noted that following their separation Ben "occasionally cohabited with her at her separate residence." From a legal perspective this indicated that he had forgiven his wife's adultery. Still he had presented plausible reasons for visiting Mariam, and the jurors had petitioned on his behalf. William Ballard Preston, chairman of the committee on the courts of justice, thought the House could not possibly justify a divorce and described Wright's case as "the weakest appeal, of its kind, before the Legislature." But a roll-call vote of 86 to 30 approved his cause and his divorce bill passed that spring.[72]

THE DEMISE OF LEGISLATIVE DIVORCE

The dam had finally broken. Cases now sped through the legislature, sometimes by unanimous votes.[73] Given the new attitude toward divorce, Virginia's laws were out of date; in 1846 and 1847 legislators made further efforts to change them. One proposal was to give the courts all absolute divorce cases, an idea that the Senate, the more conservative body, advanced in 1848 as a new general divorce law was making its way through the legislature. The preamble explained that petitions for absolute divorces were numerous and time consuming and belonged "more properly" in the courts than in the legislature. This law authorized the Circuit Superior Courts of Law and Chancery to grant absolute divorces for adultery, to decide guilt and innocence, and to permit both parties or only one to remarry.[74] This act marked the first major break with English church court precedent, but its elaborate provisions demonstrate the assembly's concern to prevent easy or fraudulent divorces.

In his authoritative commentary on Virginia's laws in the 1830s, Henry St. George Tucker insisted on the importance of carefully defining "*jurisdiction*" and procedures in divorce cases. This 1848 law established, for the first time, explicit citizenship and residency requirements and assigned jurisdiction to the local court of one or both parties. It further mandated a five-year statute of limitations; that is, the application for divorce must take place within five years of the last known adulterous act. No divorce could be decreed in cases of condonation, collusion, or adultery by the petitioner during the marriage. Moreover, if the jury's task was to decide the facts of a petition for a subsequent legislative divorce, the court record must now include ironclad assurances to the assembly about all these matters and prove that the plaintiff had "well and truly discharged his or her conjugal obligations." Collusion was the biggest concern. In all divorce cases where the defendant did not appear either in person or represented by counsel, the commonwealth attorney, the local district attorney appointed by the county court, had to defend the marriage. If he decided that the evidence did not justify the jury's decision, he should ask the court "to set aside the verdict, and to award a new trial." It must have kept them busy. One commonwealth attorney, Samuel Bassett French of Chesterfield County, soon complained about the lack of "compensation" for managing divorce petitions before the court and asked the legislature for a pay raise.[75]

Despite the expanded jurisdiction of the judicial system, Virginians continued to petition the assembly in increased numbers. For some a legislative divorce appeared quicker, cheaper, and more private.[76] Perhaps because of the enlarged caseload, the assembly occasionally seemed complaisant and even careless. For example, Martha Allison in Fairfax County said she was too embarrassed to face a local jury. Married at seventeen, she stated that her husband had never "consummated" the "connubial rites" and became "peevish, fretful and discontented" when she was around him. A single affidavit from her sister's husband supported Martha's petition. Based on what his wife had told him, Walter Powell asserted that James Allison could not "accomplish that which nature prompts," while he described Martha as "of robust health and very comely." Martha told the assembly that she did not want a trial "where she would be subject to the taunts and perhaps reproaches for thus making public the infirmities of her husband." Despite the procedural violation and the hearsay evidence, the assembly approved her divorce.[77]

The legislators could also be unyielding, however, especially if a case attracted public notice. Samuel Zinn had approached the assembly because the law did not include insanity as a grounds for judicial divorce or separation. His first, simple petition in 1839 explained that his marriage to Nancy Weaver had been happy until she became mentally ill and "reckless what she done." After she scalded one of their children to death and tried to drown another, Samuel sent the surviving offspring to live with friends. Finally, fearing she might murder him, he had moved out of his home. Though he had spent his few resources "to restore her mind," her hopeless condition destroyed "any comfort or satisfaction with her." But the assembly turned him down because, though he included several affidavits, the court transcript was missing. He tried again in 1849. Nancy was now hospitalized at the Eastern Asylum in Williamsburg, and the superintendent verified her condition as "Dementia" and held out little hope of recovery. Samuel described his wife as a "raving lunatic" whose condition for seventeen years had cost him "much of the happiness of life." A community petition supported his story and character, and his bill passed two readings before the debate boiled over into the press. New York had recently made "incurable insanity" a basis for divorce. After the *New Orleans Picayune* roundly criticized that action and characterized anyone who used it as "heartless" and worthy of "universal contempt," the *Richmond Whig* picked up the story and attacked both the insanity grounds and those House members who supported it. Samuel Zinn's happiness was pitted against "in sickness or in health," and the assembly turned him down, probably because of the public furor.[78]

That same newspaper article castigated "this Locofoco Legislature" for passing divorce bills "with race horse speed." The next assembly in 1850–51, facing the largest number of petitions in any single year, approved sixteen of thirty-seven requests for divorce. As the legislators finished their work, a state convention drafted a new constitution. It forbade the assembly from passing private divorce bills.[79] Some cheered the demise of legislative divorce as an important social reform. In terms of regularizing the process, it certainly appeared to be that. The reality, however, was more complicated. For decades legislators had wrestled with the seemingly intractable problem of balancing concern for the common good with the demand for personal happiness by victims of bad marriages. Even in extreme cases nervous lawmakers had hesitated to sever matrimonial bonds. They granted authority to the courts only after enormously painstaking deliberations. Even then, when judicial divorce was in place, legislators themselves continued to act on private petitions and to afford relief in instances that would never have satisfied a church court in England or a chancery court in Virginia. One could never be sure how the assembly might respond. By the 1840s its judgments had become highly idiosyncratic. Increasingly the press and some legislators complained about slipshod procedures and faulty decisions. A legislature did not function well as a court. Busy about many things, it could make mistakes, even grievous ones.[80]

As the pace of dissolutions quickened after 1844, demands to permit absolute divorce for adultery were accompanied by calls to streamline the entire process.[81] Virginia's leaders responded. In 1849 the assembly approved a revised legal code that authorized the courts to grant absolute divorces in cases of adultery or confinement to the penitentiary for seven or more years. The delegates to the constitutional convention of 1850–51 took the definitive step by ending legislative divorce. They were a body different from the assembly, not only in authority but also in composition. Lawyers comprised over 70 percent of the convention membership, 98 of 138 delegates. By contrast only 34 percent of the assembly of 1850 belonged to the legal profession.[82] The constitution these lawyers approved did not expand the grounds for divorce or change the statutory procedures under which courts would evaluate cases. But it forced a differentiation of governmental roles by separating the duties of legislators from the functions of judges, juries, and attorneys.

At least superficially, ending legislative divorce appeared to mark a progressive moment in Virginia and, by extension, in southern legal history. But was this liberal or conservative reform? Was it designed to facilitate divorce, to make it more difficult, or simply to rationalize the process and free the assembly for other, more pressing responsibilities? To understand more fully the reasons behind this transferal of authority, we must examine the religious values that undergirded perspectives on marriage and divorce in southern society.

CHAPTER 2

This Holy Relation

Shortly before he immigrated to the United States from Great Britain in 1835, William Bartlam had married Temperance Cook. Nine years later when he asked the Virginia assembly for a divorce, Bartlam was a co-owner of the Etna iron pits in Chesterfield County across the James River from Richmond and a highly respected member of his community. In the petition his lawyer drafted, William asserted that he had once loved his wife "with all the affection which should exist in this holy relation" of matrimony. But she had behaved immodestly and acted too freely toward "the rougher sex." Despite repeated warnings that such conduct compromised her reputation, Temperance refused amendment and instead grew ever bolder. Eventually, when his wife neglected him during a protracted illness, the suspicious husband decided to discover exactly what "pleasures had seduced her." Though still quite sick, he dragged himself about the house until he found his wife in a locked room with her lover hiding beneath the bed. He considered an immediate separation, but memories of "the joys of days gone by" led him to pardon Temperance if she promised to "sin no more."

Forgiveness, however, brought only fresh infidelities. While visiting her family in New York, and much to their horror, as her own brother informed her husband, Temperance had written shameful letters to various paramours in Virginia. In his petition William claimed that "by the grace of God" he had done everything possible, but the time had finally come to seek a divorce. "Would to God this cup had passed," he exclaimed to his attorney. After hearing a dozen witnesses, a jury agreed that Temperance had behaved as her husband charged and had been "unfaithful to the nuptial bed." In elaborate detail the verdict described how on one occasion when she was visiting Richmond, she had climbed into a man's bed while he was sleeping and attempted to arouse him sexually. In the jury's judgment she had committed adultery and William deserved a divorce. What made this case unusual was William Bartlam's position as a Methodist minister "in good standing" with his denomination.[1]

For decades preachers had been making valiant efforts to stem the tide of marital failures that rose slowly but inexorably in the Old Dominion. By the time Bartlam prepared his petition in 1844, however, a noticeable change that paralleled the new receptivity toward judicial divorce in the state's assembly had occurred in the churches. That year a group of Methodist ministers in Wytheville, in the western part of Virginia, testified that Leonard Bailey, who was asking for a divorce from his wife on grounds of adultery and desertion, was a reputable member of their church. They supported his case. From Nelson County, John J. Campbell sought a divorce on grounds that his young wife had turned out to be "a Common prostitute." He believed that, in addition to "the best feelings of the human heart" and "the sympathetic feelings and enlightened views" of the legislature, "the Laws of God" entitled him to a divorce. Campbell asked the lawmakers to pause and to "do unto your petitioner as they would be done unto." The assembly ultimately granted absolute divorces to Bartlam, Bailey, and Campbell.[2]

The request for a legislative divorce by a respected minister, the open clerical endorsement of a divorce petition, and the explicit reference to a gospel warrant for divorce offer tantalizing evidence of a significant shift taking place within the mentality of the evangelical clergy and laity who heavily influenced the religiously based culture of the Old Dominion. Writing in Richmond in the mid-1840s, Presbyterian minister, lawyer, and historian Robert Howison enthusiastically proclaimed, "Those who are most competent to judge, have believed that in no one of the United States, has Christianity had more vital power than in Virginia." Given the level of cultural influence held by the state's religious leaders, their acceptance of divorce, at least in certain situations, represented an important development in the slow and halting transformation of attitudes toward divorce in much of the antebellum South.[3]

A century ago, in his monumental study of marriage and divorce, George Elliott Howard pointed to the significance of religion in forming cultural values and the impact of the Reformation in producing divergent perspectives in British North America. Writing as an anthropologist in the 1960s, Clifford Geertz explored how religion functions as "a cultural system" and pointed to the power of religious beliefs, practices, and symbols "to synthesize a people's ethos . . . and their worldview."[4]

Recently David Hackett Fischer developed this theme in his argument that four British "folkways"—sets of "values, customs, and meanings" —formed American society. Among these he included "*marriage ways, ideas of the marriage-bond, and cultural processes of courtship, marriage and divorce.*" Of the formative influences on American culture, Fischer concluded that religion proved "the most powerful" determinant.[5] This chapter will explore the evolving religious perspective on marriage and divorce that informed southern culture, provided grist for legislative debate, and guided the formulations of divorce law in Virginia at least until the middle of the nineteenth century.

THE ANGLICAN COMMONWEALTH TRADITION

From its foundation in 1607, Virginia adhered to the religious perspective and canon law of the established Church of England. As in the mother country, colonial laws invested marriage with religious significance by requiring that it be solemnized by an ordained minister according to the ritual of the Book of Common Prayer after the publication of banns in the parish church. By the eighteenth century the Church of England was established throughout the southern colonies. Everywhere the statutes preferred its ministers and rituals, though civil and other religious services were sometimes tolerated, particularly where clergymen of the established church were not available. Virginia had the strictest laws in this respect. In the Old Dominion, the largest and most populous of the British colonies in North America, the Church of England maintained a dominant presence supported by the elite families who controlled all civil and religious institutions. From Maryland south to Georgia, divorce, even by the legislature, was unknown, though the county courts, as we have seen, occasionally provided separation agreements for troubled spouses.[6]

The failure to provide divorce expressed a distinct perspective on marriage. Although formally rejecting matrimony as a sacrament, the English church retained the central Catholic teaching on the indissolubility of marriage and treated it "as sacramental in nature." The canons approved by the church convocation in 1604 interpreted the scriptural permission for divorce to allow legal separation. Seventeenth-century theologians sang the praises of marital love as they waxed eloquent on the sanctity of marriage and the permanent nature of marriage vows. Developing the thought of continental reformers as well as earlier Catholic writers, they elaborated on a new perspective that John Witte Jr. has termed "the commonwealth model of marriage." It rationalized the prohibition of absolute divorce in terms of the social utility of marriage. In this analysis both the natural order of creation and the Hebrew and Christian scriptures demonstrate that God designed marriage for the common good of spouses and children. It formed the family, a "domestic commonwealth" hierarchically structured and bound together by a network of reciprocal duties and obligations. The family in turn provided the foundation for the religious and political commonwealths of England.

"In Anglican commonwealth theology," Witte writes, "marriage was presumed permanent because God had chosen this instrument to convey his law for the Commonwealth." The good order of society required that families be well regulated and, of course, that husbands and wives stay together. The men and women who settled the Anglican colonies thought of marriage in these terms. Their statutes embodied the values of this theology. Their descendants echoed its sentiments and concerns in their debates over divorce. After all, this Anglican cultural perspective dovetailed nicely with the legislative arguments for encouraging virtue and promoting society's common good in the young republic.[7]

In his study of divorce in Western society, Kevin Phillips highlights the importance of secularization in the process of liberalizing divorce law. When the Virginia assembly first considered divorce legislation in the 1790s, the principal opposition to the traditional outlook on marriage came from rationalist devotees of the Enlightenment. Regarding religion as a completely private matter, they had strongly backed the passage of Thomas Jefferson's Statute for Religious Freedom in 1786. As his notes for the Blair divorce trial in 1774 make clear, Jefferson had familiarized himself with the arguments on both sides of the divorce issue. We cannot be certain whether he would have regarded divorce as a legitimate avenue in the pursuit of happiness or an assault on society. On one hand, the revision of Virginia's laws that he helped to draft during the Revolution did not provide for divorce. Yet on the other hand, at the beginning of the 1790s a majority of legislators had no great quarrel with divorce, especially in proven cases of adultery and desertion. Jefferson might well have taken their side.[8]

How did rationalists view marriage? Within a range of variations, a rationalist perspective presented marriage in purely contractual terms as a legal arrangement between two parties. Starting with human beings in a state of nature, it privileged the instinctive qualities found there. According to one early-nineteenth-century writer who approached marriage from this horizon, human beings tended not only to group together but to separate into pairs. Marriage could, therefore, be considered as "natural" to human beings—that is, dictated by human nature. Rationalist apologists for divorce reform found much to praise in the virtuous love of husband and wife and the role of parenting, but given their starting point, it was not necessary to inquire about the duration of marriage, its permanence, or the legitimacy of divorce. Civil government was responsible for regulating those areas of the marriage state. Some divorce petitions, particularly in the late eighteenth and early nineteenth centuries, followed this line of thought and argued for marriage as a contract that might end whenever the parties involved chose to terminate it. Drury Fletcher, for example, argued in his divorce petition that the "essence" of the marital agreement involved "the moral rectitude of the parties generally and the chastity of the parties particularly." If that "ceases to exist or is destroyed, the legal ties of the contract ought to be dissolved too."[9]

Tucker's edition of *Blackstone's Commentaries* summarized the common law for Virginia's legal community at the beginning of the nineteenth century. It established marriage simply as a "civil contract" between two parties who were capable of entering the relationship, who wished to do so, and who completed the process the law stipulated.[10] Tucker pointed out the limitations of Virginia law in the area of divorce. As we have seen, Littleton Tazewell proposed a solution during the debates over Joseph Mettauer's divorce and later in presenting his own bill concerning divorce. Yet despite his legal acumen, the Norfolk attorney failed to persuade the majority of the assembly to establish judicial procedures for granting divorces in specified cases.

Instead the Anglican position on the indissolubility of marriage retained its hegemonic position well into the fourth decade of the nineteenth century. Despite the assault on the church establishment after the Revolution, the colonial period had embedded this perspective within the culture. It had become integral to the way Virginians and other southerners thought about marriage, whatever their religious affiliation. Because their society had never had divorce, it was unthinkable. In this respect the southern colonies proved even more conservative than Britain, which changed over time in the eighteenth century. After the Revolution the South Atlantic states were the most difficult venues for divorce. For example, in 1807 a convention of Maryland's Episcopal Church formally opposed divorce except in cases of female adultery, and the state did not pass its first general divorce act until 1841. It dropped legislative divorce right after Virginia in 1851. North Carolina approved a modest divorce law in 1814 and eliminated legislative divorce in 1835, but it kept grounds for absolute divorce more rigorous than those in Virginia. Georgia required a court trial plus a two-thirds vote in both houses of the assembly until 1833. South Carolina never allowed divorce before the Civil War.[11] All these states and the South generally kept one eye on English precedent and especially the canon law operative in the church courts.

Eventually, as we have seen, the Virginia legislature wrote English canon law on annulment and legal separation into the state's civil code. But only when evangelical churchmen, lay and clerical, became convinced of the need to ease the law did the assembly permit judicial decrees of absolute divorce. Support for this hard-line position did not come simply or even principally from members of what had been the Church of England in Virginia or from the Episcopal clergy. Anglican cultural values on marriage and divorce perdured in the old South because members of other denominations—Baptists, Methodists, and Presbyterians—absorbed and supported them. The relationship of these traditions, however, was symbiotic, and as they grew together in the nineteenth century, the South solidified its support behind the indissolubility of marriage. If Norma Basch is correct in stating that "the decision to accept formal rules for divorce . . . constituted the true legal revolution in marriage," then the South's revolution was decidedly retarded.[12]

EVANGELICAL VIRGINIA

To appreciate the impact of evangelical communities on divorce legislation, we need to survey the development of these groups in Virginia. By the beginning of the nineteenth century, evangelical Christians were already a potent force on the politico-religious scene. The Presbyterians had been a familiar presence since before the mid-eighteenth century. The Scotch-Irish represented them well in the Valley of Virginia. Later in the Piedmont under the revivalistic leadership of Samuel Davies, Presbyterians offered the earliest challenge to the religious monopoly enjoyed by the established church. One major irritant they faced with other emerging groups of religious "dissenters" was the law that all marriages be witnessed before Anglican clergy, a requirement that did not ease until after the Revolution. Although their insistence on an educated clergy destined them to remain relatively few in number, the urban presence, publications, and commitment of their church to higher education through institutions such as Hampden-Sydney and Washington Colleges gave it a high profile in the Old Dominion and throughout the South. In the nineteenth century several presbyteries formed the synod of Virginia, the chief governing body of the church.[13]

By the Revolutionary era the revivals that spurred Presbyterian growth were transforming the religious landscape of the Old Dominion, and the Baptists quickly became a significant religious presence. Their New Light preachers encouraged an enthusiastic, deeply emotional religious experience that touched human lives more profoundly that the formal ritual of Anglican parish liturgies. Baptist churches offered a sense of group identity that gave definition to people's lives while frequently rebuking the lifestyles and values of the larger society. They had come together, a typical church covenant proclaimed, "to Keep up and maintain a Christian discipline amongst us agreable to the Holy Scriptures." Marital fidelity and restrained sexual relations figured prominently among the disciplinary matters. Fiercely democratic in church polity, the local church was the normative agency with the authority to ordain clergy and admit, correct, and expel members. Groups of local churches formed associations for mutual support and advice. In Virginia a general committee of representatives from these associations coordinated statewide cooperative activity in matters of general concern, and by 1800 Baptists formed one of the two largest denominations in Virginia.[14]

Like the Baptists the Methodists grew by leaps and bounds in the years after the Revolution. Originally a reform movement started by John Wesley within the Church of England, Methodism spread widely through lay itinerant preachers who applied Wesley's techniques of practical piety, discipline, and Christian fellowship to the work of evangelization. Along with large numbers of white converts, most of whom were women, the Methodists attracted African Americans, both slave and free, into communities that emphasized free will in the process of sanctification. At a Christmas conference held in Baltimore in 1784, the preachers separated formally from the Episcopalians and organized the Methodist Episcopal Church. They devised a hybrid polity that contained a flexible ministry of circuit-riding preachers within a tightly organized hierarchical structure presided over by a superintendent or bishop. The regional governing body was the conference. Two of these, the Baltimore Conference and the Virginia Conference, took responsibility for northern and southern Virginia, respectively.[15]

Though polar opposites in church polity, Methodists and Baptists held a similar appeal, mainly to the lower classes, white and black, though they also attracted converts from among the gentry. As a rule, however, the middle and especially the upper classes generally gravitated toward the Presbyterians and Episcopalians. The former established church had suffered significant losses in clergy and laity during and after the Revolution. A century and a half as a state church, wholly dependent on the legislature, had crippled initiative. A spiritually enervating rationalism gripped many of its lay and ordained leaders, though a viable Episcopalian presence perdured in urban areas such as Norfolk and Fredericksburg. Then, after the War of 1812, the dynamic guidance of Bishops Richard Channing Moore and his successor William Meade renewed the Protestant Episcopal Church in Virginia. Vigorous churchmen, Moore and Meade advocated a moderate Calvinist doctrine and a strict personal code of conduct that conformed to the evangelical ethos of Presbyterians, Baptists, and Methodists.[16]

Meanwhile in the so-called age of Jefferson, rational religion declined sharply in influence and prestige, while the Second Great Awakening launched evangelical Protestantism into a period of extraordinary growth. This relatively new force on the religious landscape called for the personal conversion of individual believers and the transformation of society through the message of the Christian gospel. Preaching proved the most valuable weapon for spreading their message. Although the seacoast South did not experience a Cane Ridge, the revivals there swelled evangelical ranks. This led over the years to the institutionalization of the revival as a technique deliberately designed to whip up religious sentiment. The outdoor camp meeting provides the best-known example. The *Virginia Argus* reported typically in 1809 that a five-day meeting outside Richmond had drawn more than 4,000 people and sixteen ministers. At such gatherings preachers of various denominations took turns appealing to the congregation, though one cynic observed that when the Methodists were preaching, the Baptists were baptizing the Methodist converts, while the Presbyterians stood on the sidelines wringing their hands at the lack of solid Christian instruction.[17]

Less discussed by historians but probably more important forums for evangelization were the preaching marathons that occurred at the meetings of Baptist associations, Methodist conferences, Presbyterian synods, and Episcopal conventions. The lay and clerical leaders of each denomination met at least annually for as long as a week in cities and towns across the state. In addition to conducting church business, the ministers fanned out to the various churches and meetinghouses for extensive preaching to the local population as well as interested persons from nearby counties. When a Baptist association met in Richmond in 1810, a local newspaper reported the presence of 800 "strangers" in the city with "between 30 and 40" preachers, some of whom were from other associations. An admiring press writer praised "the respectability of the sect, the simplicity of their principles, and the enthusiasm with which their ministers propagate their tenets." The event gave "a new air to the occupations of the city." Sunday crowds thronged the chamber of the House of Delegates as well as the city's churches to hear the preachers. In Lynchburg a typical eight-day Methodist conference in the 1820s pulled in 125 ministers and two bishops. Between 30 and 40 Episcopal ministers attended an 1828 convention in Petersburg and preached in all the city's churches to sizable crowds. Widely reported in the secular as well as religious press, these denominational assemblies of church leaders demonstrated the growing vitality of the evangelical presence and the cooperative work of the Protestant churches.[18]

To assist the work of evangelization, the churches engaged all the forces at their disposal. Tracts, published sermons, and religious books had long been popular items, and circular letters were a prominent feature of Baptist life. Presbyterian minister John Holt Rice produced the *Virginia Religious Magazine,* the first religious periodical in the South, in 1804 with the avowed purposes of promoting "Religious Knowledge" and spreading "the influence of Christianity." That effort lasted only three years; then in 1815 he published the *Christian Monitor,* a weekly, which was succeeded by the *Virginia Evangelical and Literary Magazine.* Rice wanted his publications to attract the widest possible audience. With an ecumenical outreach he included news of Baptist associations and Episcopal conventions and promoted "religious intelligence," emphasizing the achievements of tract, missionary, and Bible societies.[19]

These agencies were yet another instrument in the transformation of America into the "Christian Kingdom." Voluntary societies are a well-known part of American religious life. The first two decades of the nineteenth century saw a host of them founded in Virginia: societies to distribute the Bible and religious tracts; organizations to support foreign as well as domestic missionaries; Sunday schools to spread "the doctrines of religion, and the precepts of morality"; and a variety of other societies for which evangelicals provided both leaders and members. Through them like-minded women and men from different churches could participate in common efforts without compromising doctrinal positions. The key to the long-term success of Protestant evangelization was not the frenzy of revivalistic preaching or the outpouring of emotional religion but organization. The Second Great Awakening became, as Donald Mathews has pointed out, an organizing process, a time of both renewed order and creativity. Evangelicals organized people—clergy and laity—and involved them directly in the work of evangelization. They reached out to the unchurched and indifferent, recruited them by the tens of thousands, and organized local churches that remained after the revivals had ended. As the Baptist General Meeting pointed out in 1817, the rapid expansion of Bible and missionary societies indicated "the dawn of that glorious day, . . . when the knowledge of God shall cover the earth as the waters cover the great deep."[20]

During the early decades of the nineteenth century, evangelical religion transformed many of the ideas, values, and attitudes of Virginians. In 1828 John Pendleton Kennedy, author of *Swallow Barn*, wrote disdainfully to his fiancée of the "*churchly* morality" that had invaded the state. What had been "the seat of noblemen" was now controlled by "penny-saving presbyterians." When Nathaniel Beverley Tucker, the evangelical son of rationalist St. George Tucker, was called upon to preach a funeral sermon on the death of John Adams and Thomas Jefferson, he cast his words in a theological context that would have sent both men revolving in their graves. Tucker portrayed Jefferson as the unwitting instrument of God's providence. By his Statute of Religious Freedom, Jefferson imagined that "he was inflicting a death-blow on . . . the errors[,] false doctrines and superstitions of Christianity." He exuded a confidence that truth would prevail, and indeed it had. In Tucker's view the subsequent expansion of evangelical faith showed that Jefferson had done more to spread Christianity than its "warmest advocates." Tucker himself exemplifies a striking development in the early nineteenth century: how one individual after another accepted religion in later life. Edmund Randolph, William Wirt, John Randolph—these men and others of their class who had been skeptical about religion or flirted with deism all became serious Christians. The next generation of southern leaders fit solidly into that pew.[21]

WHOM GOD HATH JOINED TOGETHER

Most evangelicals embraced a common outlook on Christian morality. At the top of their agenda was the preservation and enhancement of the domestic institutions of marriage, home, and family. They based their attitudes toward marriage on Christian moral teaching about the nature and purposes of marriage as a sacred institution designed by God. The heavy investment in religious language in the public discussion of divorce demonstrates how pervasively their thought permeated the commonwealth in the nineteenth century. Whether or not men and women believed what they wrote about the holiness of marriage and the sacred character of their vows, they knew what the lawmakers expected to read in Richmond. James and Maryanne Settle had entered "the holy state of Matrimony" and now asked to be freed from it. Should legislators separate "those whom God hath joined together"? Elizabeth Waterfield thought so, but only because her husband had destroyed "every object for which marriage was intended." Osbourne Parker appealed to "justice, morality, and Religion" in a vain effort to justify a divorce on both rational and religious grounds.[22]

Clerical and lay writers of various denominations stoutly opposed divorce. On the basic level of scripture, the creation story of Adam and Eve informed their outlook on the permanence of the marriage state. "By making them one flesh," wrote George Bourne, the secretary for the Virginia Religious Tract Society, God "condemned Divorce." This Presbyterian minister urged the most comprehensive and conservative view of any Virginia writer. In 1813 he published a tidy volume titled *Marriage Indissoluble and Divorce Unscriptural.* From Bourne's rigidly framed perspective, civil government could not dissolve a marriage for any cause whatsoever. Extremely difficult cases might regrettably require a "temporary" separation, but Bourne regarded absolute divorce as never permissible. Adultery and desertion were insufficient grounds, and he suggested that rather than sanctioning divorces in these cases, the government consider punishing the offenders along gendered lines. Women who committed adultery should suffer "imprisonment, private whipping, and an exhibition in the pillory," while for male transgressors he recommended "confiscation of property, accompanied by imprisonment, labour, corporeal punishment, public disgrace, and the total deprivation for life of all the privileges" of citizenship.[23]

Bourne also denied that most commonly accepted impediments invalidated marriages. The only one he would acknowledge was a previously existing marriage. Legislatures and courts might free the parties from the marriage contract, he argued, but that contradicted the divine dispensation. Ignoring such patriarchal practices as polygamy, he insisted that all divine laws including those in force before the Mosaic code remained fully operative. Stretching the biblical evidence back to the children of Adam and Eve, he pointed out that even consanguinity, although it should not be done and laws against it were appropriate, did not render a marriage "*ipso facto*" void; "to separate even these offenders, by an act which would permit them subsequently to marry other persons, legalizes incest, fornication and adultery, and therefore cannot be justified." Even the most extreme example he could conceive, interracial adultery resulting in the birth of a mulatto child, did not validate divorce.[24]

This tough-minded minister, whose rigorous opposition to slavery would later render him persona non grata in the South, based his case on the Bible. But he also emphasized repeatedly the destructive social effects of divorce on the community, family life, and women and children in particular, themes that even nonreligious persons could accept. Society as a whole suffered when the marriage state was rendered impermanent, as apologists for the Anglican commonwealth tradition had argued two centuries earlier. The common good demanded that couples stay together for the sake of the "happiness of the community." These arguments carried a great deal of weight among Virginia legislators who had lapped them up as children. With great regularity they echoed them during debates over divorce bills in the assembly. Marriage was the foundation stone of republican society. As Barry Shain has cogently argued from the perspective of the Reformed tradition, Protestant thought adjusted well to civic republicanism with its insistence that individual needs and desires must yield to the welfare of the larger society. The family as well as the community shaped the individual, and each person bore responsibility for society's welfare. From Bourne's perspective, better a few wretched individuals than any weakening of matrimonial ties.[25]

The wretched in Bourne's treatise are generally women, because unlike some writers, he thought that marriage was essential to their happiness and protection. The minister could not abide the existence of an unmarried woman. "The constitutional timidity, the corporeal weakness, and the natural reliance of the female sex upon man," he wrote, "indicate that her enjoyment materially results from the marriage connection." Divorce was therefore much more injurious to the dependent female. Deprived of security and without family or even her children, the castoff woman had few options in life beyond prostitution. Bourne concluded his book with a sweeping, vigorous summation: "Divorce is the child of hell; the parent of lust; the destroyer of female chastity; the enemy of virtue and religion; ruin to families; death to nations; extinction to the church; and universal extermination."[26]

Although few clergy shared Bourne's extreme position, they embraced many of his attitudes and arguments. From the perspective of all Christian churches, God had instituted marriage as a sacred union for the sake of raising children and the mutual support of husband and wife. Ministers of every denomination regarded marriage and family life as the foundation of the social and religious order. Home and family provided "nurseries for the church" where conscientious parents educated their children in religious and moral virtues. There parents sowed the seeds of Christian life, and faith took root. A Virginia Methodist referred to the home as a "domestic sanctuary" that existed to promote "progress in intelligence, refinement, and religion." Presbyterian Bourne agreed: "The most agreeable scene which we can survey upon earth, is a peaceful and happy family."[27]

Evangelicals could endorse Isaac Hite's definition of marriage as "a Covenant between a Man and a Woman about perpetual and faithful Cohabitation, and joint Care of a common offspring." A student at William and Mary at the outbreak of the Revolution, Hite fought in the war and married the sister of James Madison, the future president. After her death, he married the daughter of an Episcopal clergyman. In his commonplace book this layman enumerated three points he considered crucial in a Christian marriage: the absolute fidelity of the spouses to each other; a primary concern for the well-being of the family, particularly "Right Education of their Children"; and a permanent union until death.[28]

Among all the threats to marriage, extramarital relations held pride of place. Preachers seldom missed an opportunity to denounce them. Betsy Watts, a Bedford County housewife, described to her daughter a local camp meeting in 1807 as "the same old scene with a few variations." The high point was the rousing attack one preacher launched against "fornication and adultery." Although the speaker had not identified anyone in particular, Watts reported that "a great number got a severe box on the ear especially the Gentlemen who have never in any age or country been remarkable at being wholley *immaculate*." She thought the minister was on target and treated his topic with all due propriety, but when he named the sins "a general alarm" sounded among the women present. "The ladies rose in a body spread their umbrellas looked at a little cloud and showed evident apprehensions of an instantaneous thunderstorm."

The preacher paused, took stock of the women's alarm and the possibility of rain, and let them remain under the campground tents until the threat passed and their "exquisite m[odest]y" subsided. He then resumed his sermon.

With evident satisfaction Betsy noted the male discomfort, but the women's prudishness disgusted her. Men believed the minister "had no business with vices which custom had so long made familiar," while the women expected the preacher to spare "their feelings a little more." But Betsy observed shrewdly, "The truth is the more true the more offence." She took some comfort, however, in witnessing "a number of married Ladies who were very much pleased as well as single ones whose heads contained a little ballast and took the liberty of thinking for themselves instead of adopting the sentiments of their beaux." In Watts's view, sexual relations outside marriage were a serious moral evil and a common occurrence, and the minister had done well to denounce the sin by name.[29]

Baptist associations, Episcopalian conventions, Methodist conferences, and Presbyterian synods inveighed against this threat to marriage and family life in sermons, exhortations, and addresses. Houses of prostitution were common enough in Richmond, Norfolk, Charlottesville, and other cities and towns to make a popular target for Virginia's religious leaders. A Methodist preacher warned his hearers against "that burning hell which awaits the licentious profligate! . . . Listen not to the lying words of the foolish woman. . . . Her house is the way to hell, going down to the chambers of death."[30] In a formal "address to the churches" in 1814, the Presbyterian Synod of Virginia decried "the extent to which it is apprehended that fornication, and even adultery, are practiced among us."[31] The next year Parson Mason L. Weems published a small pamphlet titled *God's Revenge against Adultery*, which recounted in juicy detail two stories of adultery and the devastating effect it had on people's lives.[32] Episcopalian minister Jared Rice threatened his congregation in 1830 that God's judgment on "Whoremongers and adulterers" would exclude them from heaven.[33]

Some clergy decided to punish the transgressors on earth. Baptist churches routinely excluded from fellowship members judged guilty of adultery.[34] But when the rector of the Episcopal church in Fredericksburg publicly refused Communion to Hugh Mercer, a prominent member of his congregation who was widely suspected of adultery, the outraged planter wrote Bishop Moore demanding satisfaction. Moore coolly replied that Mercer had been forewarned and would have to live with the consequences. The planter's wife and children had been terribly distraught. But sin was sin, regardless of class or station. The public could be as unyielding as the church. When rumors implicated a judge in an adulterous affair, some lawyers expected him to lose his seat on the bench.[35] Writers depicted the results of a husband's adultery as relentless tragedy. Infidelity would ultimately force the husband out of the house "to find relief in the maddening excitement of the bacchanalian revel." Meanwhile the "pure-minded and loving" wife, "united for life" to an unfaithful husband, led a miserable existence until death took one of them or, even worse, she became a fellow traveler in sin and "in a spirit of retaliation and revenge" trod "forbidden paths" to "disgrace and ruin." In a series of lectures given at his wife's school and later published, politician and planter James Garnett argued that women were in great danger if they became tied to "men of bad morals, bad habits, or bad tempers," which he called the "heaviest, most afflicting curse of wedded life!" He urged his female readers to "call no one *husband*, whose temper is ungovernable,— whose habits are vicious, and whose principles are depraved." Thus they would save themselves from many a "hysterical fit afterwards."[36]

Desertion and bigamy followed closely behind adultery, and they were common enough in a society where divorces were so difficult to obtain. A celebrated case involved a member of the General Assembly. Elected to the House of Delegates in 1810 from Lee County, in the western part of the state, John McKeon married Fanny Glenn in Richmond that summer in a ceremony performed by the local Presbyterian minister, John Blair. When the assembly convened in December, McKeon was charged with bigamy. Multiple witnesses testified that for about eight years he had been living in the west with another woman whom he had sometimes represented to be his wife. Because the evidence of a first marriage was murky, the allegation of bigamy remained unproven, but after a full dress review and roll-call vote the House expelled McKeon for "conduct grossly immoral, disgraceful and highly reprehensible."[37] The assembly may have moved cautiously in McKeon's case because the marriage law of 1792 made bigamy a felony punishable by death, a sentence later reduced to one to ten years in the state penitentiary.[38] But even if civil society failed to condemn a bigamist, the churches did not tolerate members who remarried without benefit of divorce. Frying Pan Spring Baptist Church, for example, excommunicated Charles Helm for "marrying a second wife in his first wife's lifetime."[39]

Prolonged separations of spouses increased the possibilities of serious lapses in right conduct. A French traveler observed that Virginia males made "good husbands, and good fathers" but were absent from home more than other American men. He blamed their "love of dissipation." The Reverend Jared Rice agreed and thought the devil found an opening in the separations that occurred in so many marriages. Husbands and wives spent far too much time away from each other for the good of their souls, he argued, and noted the entering wedge that the separation of Adam and Eve provided the serpent in the Garden of Eden. The churches maintained a sharp eye. When a Baptist community in Bedford County heard a report that one of its members, while on a western trip, had brought a "base" woman into his house, the church ordered an investigation.[40]

In an abusive situation churches and clergy could also serve as powerful forces to check the behavior of a husband who rode roughshod over a wife or ignored her needs or desires. For a husband physically to assault his wife jeopardized his standing in the religious community. When Joseph Drury whipped his wife, his Baptist church "deeply censured" him and condemned his conduct as "scandalous." The church members agreed that "for a husband to beat his wife we judge to be a practice contrary both to Scripture and Reason, to the law and Gospel. And as such, not to be once named among Christians" or tolerated "on any pretence whatever."[41] Even being "truly sorry" for assaulting his wife did not keep a husband from being disbarred from church fellowship. Local churches watched carefully over the marriages and family lives of their members. When another Baptist "used violence toward his family," the local church sent an investigating committee to interview the couple. It reported that "harmony had been restored" and recommended that the male offender be allowed to remain in church fellowship.[42] Husbands and wives were expected to live together rather than apart, and the church punished spouses who did not do so peaceably. When a continually brawling couple in Bedford County failed to reconcile their differences, their church finally excommunicated them both "for not living as becomes the gospel."[43]

Writers repeatedly cautioned women against being deceived by men. The male of the species, Garnett advised his readers, was "a very imperfect animal." Male vices were generally more vicious. Warning women against marrying a man on the basis of his appearance, Methodist preacher John Bayley summarized the problem: "He may be a fine-

Frontispiece from Marriage As It Is and As It Should Be, *by John Bayley. This work idealized domestic life. (Courtesy of The Library of Virginia)*

looking man, equal to Absolom in beauty, and of noble bearing among his fellows, but at the same time be an empty, conceited coxcomb, or a lazy, drunken, worthless member of society." Presbyterian Bourne went even further in arguing that the husband was much more often the offending rather than the offended party in situations of marital strife and infidelity. If the southern lady was not already on her pedestal, Bourne was trying to put her there. A wife's failure to be chaste, he argued, was "almost always" the responsibility of "an intriguing seducer" or the earlier adulterous behavior of her husband. In fact, Bourne speculated that unfaithful husbands sometimes conspired to produce similar conduct by their wives in order to justify a separation.[44]

Marriages also failed, various writers argued, because young, immature couples rushed into wedlock with insufficient reflection and for the wrong motives. Societal pressures to *"at all hazards get married,"* Garnett observed, pushed too many women into marriage. This destructive error that had ruined many lives was rooted in the popular belief that a woman could find fulfillment only in marriage and that her value depended on her husband. "Grammatically speaking, these very provident matrimonisers, will not even allow *woman* to be a *noun-substantive,* but only a miserable conjunction, *'having no signification of herself,'* unless coupled in wedlock to a *man.*" Pointing out that Virginia provided abundant examples of widows whose management of affairs was much better than that of their deceased husbands, Garnett insisted that women were more capable than popular opinion recognized.

Taking exception to another widespread viewpoint that Bourne embraced, Garnett disputed the belief that a woman's identity depended on a husband and marital status. Instead he argued that single women were often happier than their miserably married counterparts. While from a theoretical standpoint a person could achieve "more happiness" in the married than in the single state, "more wretchedness" was found there, too. Better a contented celibacy than a flawed marriage. Women would be wiser not to marry at all, he insisted, than to attach themselves to a man whose vices and failings would blast their chances for happiness. They should calculate what they were selecting when picking out a husband and consider objectively what kind of marriage would result from their choice. From Garnett's perspective it was "as true as the gospel, that there are many more blanks than prizes *in this lottery of matrimony.*" The headlong rush into marriage showed that people were just "blind as bats to everything but the gratification of the moment" and oblivious to the deplorable fate awaiting them.[45]

In the same way, Betsy Watts urged her teenage daughter studying in Williamsburg to be extremely careful about choosing friends and to stay "an old maid . . . for six years at least." In another letter she reported with approval on the fate of a cousin's erstwhile swain. Although the young man was rich, "washed in lotion and highly perfumed with bergumot," the relative had wisely discarded him. Her suitor turned out to have "no real brain . . . but wind and froth." Moreover, "the ogling muscles are very much worn and decayed" from overuse.[46] Beauty was not enough to ensure a successful match. Nor was wealth all important. Money would not make a marriage happy, warned Bishop James Madison in a letter to his daughter at the time of her wedding. Bayley further asserted that choosing a spouse for the sake of her wealth was "sordid, unmanly, and wicked." Furthermore, "whenever it be done, either by man or woman, the bitter fruits will be seen by all who have not been blinded by the love of gain."[47] The "bitter fruits" were marital unhappiness, quarreling, fighting, adultery, desertion, and ultimately divorce.

Underlying the advice of most writers, religious and lay, was the shared premise that the matrimonial choice was absolutely crucial because the decision was irrevocable, "a contract to endure until death." They wrote within a society in which divorce was a scandal that tainted not only the parties directly involved but also their families. One petitioner put it bluntly when he acknowledged the "unfavorable impressions which are generally made on the Public mind, against both Parties, when a separation takes place, between Persons plighted to each other in the most solemn manner, for life." Couples remained married not only for the sake of the children but for their own reputation and that of their relations. Often simple endurance, rather than personal happiness, was the only or at least the main consideration. James Garnett's lectures to young women may have been designed to scare them into caution in picking marriage partners, but he reiterated the idea that many or even most marriages were not particularly happy and that many couples were *paired, not matched.*[48] They lived together not for love or happiness but because the alternative was worse.

THE EVANGELICAL ROAD TO DIVORCE

But what was the alternative to remaining in an unhappy union? If a marriage collapsed, what could one do? For John Wesley, the English founder of Methodism, the only ground for divorce was adultery, and only in that case could a person remarry. But in the immediate post-Revolutionary era the concluding prayer for the marriage service in the Methodist Episcopal Church signaled a more rigorous position. It began, "O God, who . . . didst teach that it should never be lawful to put asunder those whom thou by Matrimony hadst made one; . . . Look mercifully upon this man and this woman." A Methodist conference in 1796 expressed that prayer in law by adopting a resolution not to accept into the church anyone who had remarried after separating from a spouse "no matter what the Crime was that caused them to part." Virginia newspapers, even those not necessarily in the hands of evangelicals, echoed the clergy's concerns and reprinted northern laments against easy divorce laws. In 1805 a Richmond paper contained a warning from the *Vermont Post-Boy* against "opening Pandora's Box, and giving wings to every evil that can poison the felicity and morals of society."[49]

Yet at least some evangelicals began to adjust their thinking during the early years of the nineteenth century. While continuing to hold up the Christian ideal of permanence in marriage and to denounce any rupture in "Hymen's bonds" or stains on the "nuptial bed," in practice they mitigated that perspective and began to tolerate divorce among church members. There was, after all, a great difference between abstract principle and its application in ordinary lives. When a divorce case involved someone you knew, especially a family member or a friend, whose pain elicited your sympathy, then it became a different matter. You could contrast principle and application. This was not unique to the South, and it hit home in the fellowship of church communities, especially those of mixed race.

In Virginia one of the first verifiable issues that breached the dike against divorce involved slave marriages. Ever since the revivals of the 1760s, African Americans in ever increasing numbers had been joining evangelical churches. Local congregations, particularly of Baptists and Methodists in the Tidewater and Piedmont, were normally composed of black and white members, and in some cases the slaves made up the majority of the flock. Black ministers and exhorters, sometimes but not always free, commonly preached to both black and mixed assemblies. The baptism of slaves did not raise a significant problem, even for slaveholders who were not particularly religious. Preachers could be expected to insist on St. Paul's dictum that servants obey their masters. But marriage between slaves or between a slave and a free black person presented major difficulties for ministers and churches intent on upholding the sanctity and permanence of the marriage state.

The chief concern was inherent to the structure of a slaveholding society that countenanced the sale and consequent separation of spouses and the division of families. This could happen for a variety of reasons. Slaves might be sold at any time or, upon the death of a slaveholder, willed to different persons. Slaves who were husband and wife often belonged to different masters, one of whom might relocate and take his slaves. These situations destroyed marriages and dispersed families. As early as 1788 the state's Baptist leaders expressed their strong opposition to the practice of separating husbands and wives and urged church members under pain of excommunication to exert the "utmost endeavours to keep man and wife together." But since each church was sole judge of its own members, not all Baptists accepted that decision.[50]

Christopher Collins was one slaveholder who did agree with the judgment of his church. He would later become a Baptist minister, but that lay in the future when he faced the problems of keeping slave families together during a move to the West. Collins owned a slave woman named Indy and her two children, but her husband, Tobit, belonged to Robert Carter of Nomini Hall. Indy preferred to remain with Collins lest she lose her children, so before the move Tobit repeatedly begged Collins to purchase him in order to keep the family together. On the day set for the departure, Collins wrote Carter asking to purchase Tobit. "There has no circumstance attending my removal been so grievous and distressing to me as the separation of men and wives and I have laboured to prevent it as much as possible," he observed. He had already purchased the husband of one woman and agreed to leave "one of my best hands" in the area so he could be with his wife. The business of buying and selling slaves was distasteful for the "conscientious" Baptist, but he saw no other way except freeing the slaves. That, he averred, was not "in my power."[51]

Traveling through Virginia in 1759, Quaker itinerant John Woolman noted that although the slaves "marry after their own way," these marriages meant nothing to some whites who easily separated couples at slave sales, particularly when estates were settled. A Frenchman touring Virginia noted that most slaves were Baptists or Methodists and pointed out, "They are baptized, but not married."[52] Virginia did not recognize the legality of slave marriages, and state law strictly forbade ministers from witnessing weddings involving a slave without the written consent of the owner. Of course a Christian master might import a local clergyman for a plantation ceremony, and black preachers in the neighborhood could perform the service with or without the permission of the slaveowner or the local church. But often enough, even without the presence of a minister, the slaves would "come together according to their custom as Man and Wife."[53]

Gradually the churches recognized these slave marriages as valid despite their informal nature. The Presbyterians were among the first to do so. In 1791 Hanover Presbytery, the governing body of ministers and church elders east of the Blue Ridge, wrestled for some months with the issue of accepting into the church slaves who were living together without benefit of a religious service. The Presbyterian leaders finally decided the question by appealing to the nature of marriage itself. Marriage was constituted "in the sight of God," they declared, by the "mutual consent of the Parties." Enough people ordinarily witnessed this ceremony to make the couple generally known as husband and wife. Therefore as long as the two remained together and lived Christian lives, the church should accept them in full membership. The presbytery further determined that in cases where the couple had been forcibly separated by the sale or removal of one of the spouses, the slave who was left behind might take "another Companion" and remain in religious fellowship. In effect the result was "as if the other was dead."[54]

Thus Virginia's Presbyterians quickly settled for themselves the marriage and divorce questions for slave members. They possessed a central governing body to decide such matters and, more to the point, relatively few African American members. On both counts Baptists faced the opposite situation. During the decades that followed the Revolution, local churches and regional associations agonized over the "perplexing question" of slave marriages. After several years of discussion the Dover Baptist Association, a grouping of Tidewater churches, finally counseled in 1789 that "the state of the slaves . . . was of so singular and delicate a nature, that no general rule could apply." Each church would have to decide for itself. Four years later when the problem of forcible separations of spouses was raised, the ministers could not agree and weakly suggested that the member churches "act discretionarily." Similarly, the Virginia Portsmouth Association debated for two years before the chagrined clergymen decided that the question was "so difficult, that no answer could be given it." Meanwhile the Baptist General Committee refused to touch the issue, claiming that it was delegated to oversee the "*external* interest and concerns *only*" of Virginia's Baptists. A majority of Baptist ministers from the Strawberry Baptist Association proved more bold. In 1793 they advised that a "negroe sister" separated involuntarily from her husband did not commit adultery if she took a new husband.[55]

Associations might recommend, but the local church made the ultimate decision. Buck Marsh Church in upper King and Queen County offers a case in point. In October 1791 the members discussed "black Members parting with former Wives and Taking of others" and reprimanded those who had remarried as well as those who had encouraged it. The issue resurfaced, however, the next month and was postponed. Then in March 1792 the church decided it was "Sinfull." The question appeared again in 1794, and again the members disapproved of remarriage. But this hard-line solution did not end the problem for the Buck Marsh Baptists. Time passed, and fifteen years later they were asking the Ketocton Association for advice on what to do "with a Baptist slave, whose wife was taken from him and carried to such a distance, that in all human probability, he will never see her again, and has taken another wife." The ministers responded with a plea for understanding "the peculiar situation of slaves." At the whim of a master their marriages could be destroyed, and these "unhappy people are forcibly se[parated]." The association thought that the church "would do well to bear with such as fin[d it ne]cessary to take another wife or husband."[56]

But could the same principle of freeing the innocent party from a marriage that had been destroyed operate on behalf of white Christians? Some preachers thought so, particularly in cases involving adultery. The scriptures, after all, offered warrant for this. As early as 1811 Joel Johns, the foremost Baptist minister in Lunenburg County, signed a community petition in support of a woman who sought a divorce on grounds of her husband's adultery. After Johns's signature and that of another subscriber, Matthew Goodwin, the phrase "Minister of the Gospel" is written, so the assembly would recognize the support that came from clergymen. A Baptist association proposed in 1813 that a wife should be allowed to remarry when her husband ran off with another woman, provided that he had been gone seven years and she did not know whether he was dead or alive.[57]

Another group of preachers advised in 1819 that white church members legally divorced "for fornication" could marry again. In the case of slaves the local church might "judge the fornication" itself, and if it was "clearly proven, they may then pronounce them divorced, and permit such to marry again." Two years earlier, noting that state law did not cover slave marriages, the same association had recommended that member churches "adopt some rule by which it may be known, when any one of them who is a member, takes a husband or wife; thereby preventing many unpleasant things, that sometimes take place" among church members who were slaves. Keeping pace with public opinion and legislative activity, at least some ministers and churches had begun to accept divorce in certain cases for adultery and desertion. Six clergymen, for example, prominently identified themselves among the signers of a petition to support a legislative divorce in 1826 for Benjamin Sewell, whose wife had eloped with another man.[58] Their experience underscores the potential dissidence inherent in democratic societies. The same individuals might assume disparate, even opposing perspectives, depending on their relationship to the situation, the people involved, and their own commitments. A legislator inclined to rigidity might assume a much more sympathetic posture toward a troubled marriage in which he, his friends, or his class interests were personally invested.

Some Episcopalians, years before Bishop Moore had begun his reform of the church, had already broken with Anglican tradition and made peace with divorce in a spectacular case involving one of their own ministers. St. George's Parish in Fredericksburg was an exception to the general decline of the former established church after the Revolution. There the lay vestry met regularly, collected funds, hired the clergy, and even enlarged the church. Several ministers served the parish during this period, but the vestry had trouble finding a suitable one. Competent clergymen were scare. So they considered themselves fortunate when they finally hired Samuel Low, a New Yorker who had studied theology and could preach up a storm but was not yet ordained to the ministry. Then some disquieting news surfaced. In April 1809 reports rippled through Fredericksburg that Low, who was living with a woman he presented as his wife, also possessed a wife and family in New York. At a vestry meeting Low vehemently denied the accusation. He must have offered a convincing explanation, because in dispatching Low to the church convention at Richmond the next month the vestry declared that they were completely satisfied with his "correct and most exemplary" behavior. But a few weeks later the whole story came out. Low had indeed been married but had left his wife some six years earlier and remarried. He returned to New York and procured a legal divorce in May.[59]

Back in Virginia Bishop Madison was about to proceed with Low's ordination, but he wanted the vestry's approval. They demurred. Low's multiple excuses for his marital problems and his denunciation of "a revengeful woman, who is altogether unworthy of me" did not persuade the Episcopalian laymen. They took a dim view of bigamy. Low's "habitual adultery" had outraged "the most sacred obligation." Nor did his efforts at self-justification sway the vestrymen, who told him bluntly, "We differ

greatly from you." Yet despite their resolute disapproval of the dangerous tendency of Low's behavior—"a practice of renouncing the conjugal
vows at pleasure would wound social and domestic happiness in their
most vital parts"—the laymen left open a door for divorce: "Great occasions may exist for the absolving power of the Law and a legal separation
in rare and extraordinary cases is compatible with the ends of the marriage state. It is believed however that the legality of the divorce is essential to the justification of it." No doubt because of the extreme shortage of
Episcopal clergymen the vestry continued to employ Low as a preacher,
and two years later they "sincerely and cheerfully" recommended that
Bishop Madison ordain him.[60]

Writing several decades later, evangelical Bishop Meade described
Low as "a person of disreputable character" whose ministry must have
been "disastrous to the Church." But St. George's vestry would have disagreed with Meade's judgment, once the New York divorce had regularized Low's marital situation. They approved of his preaching as "*Ortho-
dox, Scriptural, rational, and edifying.*" Virginia's Episcopalians may not
have entirely approved of divorce, but they accommodated it. Meanwhile, their Maryland brethren wrestled with the same issue. Meeting in
Baltimore in 1807, an Episcopal convention urged the legislature to refuse
all divorces except when a court had convicted a woman of adultery.[61]

Lay Episcopalian Isaac Hite represented the other extreme from the
rigor of Presbyterian minister George Bourne. Hite accepted a series of
natural and moral impediments. Among the former were those "grievous Disorders and miserable incurable Distempers, inconsistent with a
friendly Society, or excluding all Hopes of Offspring, such as Idiotism,
perpetual Madness, Leprosy, and some other Diseases." He also claimed
underage persons were incapable of marriage. Consanguinity was the
chief moral impediment, though he was not sure how far that extended.
Hite was also willing to accept the legality of divorce for those grounds
that violated what he considered the essentials of marriage: adultery, desertion, impotence, extreme alienation, and "gross Outrages" that destroyed any possibility of an amicable marital relationship. Hite accepted
the prevailing belief that in granting a divorce, the state should decide
guilt and dispense punishment and permit the innocent spouse to remarry. Only a "strangely inhuman" society, he thought, further penal-
ized someone who had been injured in one marriage by not permitting
that person to marry again and have children. Moreover, in an effort to
make the punishment fit the crime, Hite offered the novel suggestion

that "guilty Parties" in a divorce proceeding should be forced to remarry "Persons equally infamous with themselves."[62]

What Hite shared with Bourne, the clerical rigorist, and with so many others in Jeffersonian Virginia was a concern for the common good. For Bourne the damage divorce inflicted on society was so great that no exceptions could be made. Concern for individual happiness must yield to the common welfare of the whole body politic. To permit divorce, even in rare cases, would ultimately open the floodgates and destroy the institution of marriage. Better that a few should suffer "than that dissension, debauchery, and wretchedness should overflow the universe." Bourne's perspective was not unique. But Hite, from the liberal camp, took a different tack. He argued that a marriage incapable of producing a "friendly" relationship should end. Others took an intermediate, more centrist position between these two extremes. While not forbidding divorce in Bourne's absolutist terms, they urged couples in unhappy marriages to try to stay together, since the "remedy . . . would be worse than the disease."[63]

Henry St. George Tucker argued against divorce in a similar vein in the 1830s. The assembly elected Tucker in 1831 to preside over the Court of Appeals, the highest judicial position in the state. That year he published his *Commentaries on the Laws of Virginia,* an expanded version of the notes he had prepared for his law students. Expressing his approval Tucker summarized the provisions of the new divorce law he himself had urged. Given this statute's impact on Virginia's chancery courts, Tucker thought that "the decisions of the spiritual courts of Great Britain" and of state courts "where judges had occasion for judicial legislation" became immediately relevant. Ignoring the other states, however, he turned his attention to New York. The strict divorce law there, reminiscent of its Anglican cultural heritage, approximated Tucker's desired policy. In a discussion of divorce Tucker relied on the work of Joseph Chitty, an English legal writer, who in turn had quoted extensively from Sir William Scott. Perhaps the foremost authority on English canon law, Scott headed London's diocesan court and the Court of Arches, the supreme ecclesiastical tribunal in Britain. Drawing on Chitty's published notes, Tucker reproduced Scott's warning against facile divorce laws:

The general happiness of the married life is secured by its indissolubility. When people understand that they *must* live together, except for a few reasons known to the law, they learn to soften, by mutual accommodation, that yoke which they know they cannot shake off; they become good husbands and good wives from the necessity of remaining husbands and wives; for necessity is a powerful master in teaching the duties it imposes. If it were once understood, that upon mutual disgust married persons might be legally separated, many couples, who now pass through the world with mutual comfort, with attention to their common offspring, and to the moral order of civil society, might have been at this moment living in a state of mutual unkindness—in a state of estrangement from their common offspring—and in a state of the most licentious and unreserved immorality. In this case, as in many others, the happiness of some individuals must be sacrificed to the greater and more general good.

Tucker's two-volume commentary, republished in 1836–37, was the most authoritative source for Virginia's legal community until the revision of the laws in 1849. Writing about marriage, the judge again quoted Scott on the solemnity of the marriage contract and its importance not just for the couple but for their children and "the moral order of civil society." Marriage was more than a contract for Scott and, presumably, for Tucker as well. "To this contract is superadded the sanctity of a religious vow." Scott expressed the Anglican commonwealth tradition with which Tucker was both conversant and comfortable.[64]

Lawyers, judges, and legislators also listened to the clergy. From within their moderate ranks, William Swan Plumer offered yet another perspective on divorce. By the beginning of the 1840s Plumer was arguably the most important minister and best preacher in Richmond, if not the state. As pastor of the elite First Presbyterian Church and editor of a major religious newspaper, the *Watchman of the South,* Plumer commanded attention whenever he spoke or wrote on issues of religion and morality. In an editorial he published in 1840 the minister commented approvingly on a secular newspaper's strictures against casual divorce, but he then used the occasion to edge the discussion toward the center by attacking the attitude "that divorces should *never* be granted." He thought that viewpoint "contrary to good morals" and just as reprehensible as granting them too easily. New Testament writers Matthew and Paul had justified divorce on the grounds of "adultery and permanent wilful desertion," he wrote. While he believed the country as a whole was much too lax in granting divorces, still, if the legitimate purposes of marriage—mutual love and support, the procreation of children, and "the prevention of lawless impurity"—were "entirely lost" by the behavior of one spouse, then the innocent victim should not have to suffer.[65]

The Presbyterians' Westminster Confession of Faith of 1647 permitted divorce on grounds of adultery and allowed the innocent party to remarry, though some Presbyterians took a more rigorous view. Plumer's leadership role in the Virginia synod practically guaranteed that he did not speak for himself alone, and his support for a biblical warrant for divorce in cases of adultery and desertion probably pushed some legislators in the direction of greater liberality when the assembly began easing the divorce laws in the 1840s. Certainly he was on close terms with state senator Robert Young Conrad, who regularly attended Plumer's church when the legislature was in session. A committed churchman, Conrad knew, as he wrote his wife in 1841, that the legislation he supported to stop the flood of divorce petitions threatened "to undo all the clergy have been doing for years." But Conrad believed that divorce had to be regularized through the courts for the sake of an ever more complex society.[66] The marriage ideal that he shared with other evangelical Christians clashed with the solid evidence of failed marriages and broken families.

Yet the path of moderate reform advocated by Plumer and Conrad faced strong, consistent opposition. In a series of articles titled "The Influence of Morals on the Happiness of Man, and the Stability of Institutions," published by the *Southern Literary Messenger* in 1838, an anonymous writer laid out the guiding political principle in capital letters: "It is the FIRST DUTY OF EVERY CHRISTIAN AND OF EVERY PATRIOT TO OPPOSE EVERY THING WHICH TENDS TO CORRUPT PUBLIC MORALS OR TO PROMOTE LICENTIOUSNESS OF OPINION." Divorce provided an obvious target. Many a legislator undoubtedly believed he had upheld public morality when he refused someone such as Watkins Harper from Essex County. In 1842 Harper asked to be released from "the Holy bonds of Matrimony" because of the adultery of his wife. She had run off with a local "known profligate and rake" and borne his child. He had proven the facts before a jury in the circuit court. The "Supreme Law," he reminded the lawmakers, "the law of God" allowed him "to put away his wife for adultery." When the committee of the courts of justice recommended rejecting Harper's petition, James Garnett, a delegate from Essex who had probably sponsored the measure, objected. But his motion to accept was defeated 38 to 57. The angry legislator then pushed the issue further by introducing a resolution that would instruct the committee "to enquire into the expediency of amending the law concerning divorces, so that the superior courts of law and chancery may grant divorces *a vinculo matri-monii*, in cases of adultery." The House postponed consideration. Harper would try twice more before he gained his divorce in 1846.[67]

The social prejudice against divorce remained unyielding on the part of many. In 1847 Robert Balls wrote Edmund Jennings Lee, a lawyer in northern Virginia, about the procedures for divorcing his wife, Octavia, for drunkenness. The dumbfounded attorney, who was Octavia's cousin, responded bluntly that a divorce was impossible on such grounds. The petition would likely fail in the assembly and only serve to publicly humiliate them, their families, and their friends. Robert offered all sorts of excuses for the mistaken marriage and claimed to have "deserted her bed" a week after the wedding. But Lee, a devout Episcopal vestry-man, proved unsympathetic. Marriage was indissoluble. Grounds such as "condition rank *fortune* or *character*," he wrote, were unacceptable "for impeaching or dissolving the *tie*." Lee urged Robert to honor his mar-riage vows. But if they could not live together, then he advised them to hire a qualified attorney, "who can consult *both parties*," to draft a separa-tion agreement and send it for Lee's inspection before signing it. Octavia wrote Lee, blaming herself entirely. Her lawyer-cousin disagreed. Hus-band and wife bore joint responsibility for the failure of their marriage, but Lee thought Octavia would suffer most. He urged her retirement to a "respectable boarding house . . . in some pleasant village." He also offered his help, as a family member, because in her "calamitous condition" she had no one else to turn to.[68]

The couple had been separated two years when Lee wrote Robert on Octavia's behalf. She was living in Loudoun County and wanted to sell a piece of land. But she would not do so if Robert took the money. So Lee asked his intentions. The correspondence between the lawyer and the unhappy husband and wife exposes the legal disabilities that bound even couples who formally separated. Only a divorce finalized a wife's status as a *feme sole* capable of owning property in her own right. Evi-dently Robert did not respond to Lee's satisfaction. Octavia finally peti-tioned the legislature in January 1851, claiming desertion. When they had married in Alexandria, it was part of the District of Columbia. They had then moved to New York and separated there. Because they had never cohabited in Virginia, the courts had no jurisdiction over their marriage. She asked for "the unlimited right to dispose of her own property which she had before marriage." The legislature, untrammeled by restrictions on domain, voted an absolute divorce.[69]

In passing general divorce laws, the assembly had only granted chancery courts roughly the same jurisdiction and scope of activity possessed by English church courts. In effect, outside the arena of legislative divorce, Virginia operated strictly according to the ecclesiastical laws of the Church of England until March 1848, when the proposal offered by James Garnett five years earlier finally became law. While this significant amendment to the divorce laws moved through the legislative process, Conway Robinson and John Mercer Patton, two of Virginia's most distinguished lawyers, were drawing up a revision of the state's civil code, the first since 1819. A successful lawyer before his entrance into politics and election to Virginia's Council of State, Patton had served briefly as acting governor. Robinson, born in 1805 and seven years Patton's junior, was the scholar. He had established his reputation with a three-volume work *Practice in the Courts of Law and Equity in Virginia,* published in the 1830s, and had been admitted to practice before the U.S. Supreme Court. In the early 1840s he put out two volumes of *Virginia Reports* in his capacity as the official reporter for the state court of appeals.[70]

For the segment on divorce the two revisors brought together and folded into one chapter the various laws the state had passed between 1827 and 1848. Much of the work consisted of organizing the material and eliminating duplication and unnecessary verbiage. They also suggested corrections where the law appeared inconsistent or unclear. The most interesting segment of the printed revision of the chapter on divorce, as Robinson and Patton presented it, is in their footnotes. Here they repeatedly invoke English canon law as the ultimate authority on which both statute and practice depend. For example, while recognizing that the 1848 statute made adultery a cause for *a vinculo* divorce that did not exist in England, they presumed that in every other respect the ecclesiastical law controls the outcome. As a revised legal text they proposed, "For adultery, the decree may either be *a vinculo matrimonii* or *a mensa et thoro,* as under the circumstances may seem most proper. For any other cause, the court shall make such decree as ought to be made by the ecclesiastical law of *England,* annulling the marriage where by that law it ought to be annulled, and decreeing a divorce *a mensa et thoro* if by that law the same be proper."

In discussing court fees they criticized the injustice of the canon law courts that required the husband always to pay the wife's court costs. Virginia law left open the question of whom to charge, a policy they approved as less likely to produce nuisance suits. The work of Robinson and Patton demonstrates that divorce legislation as late as the 1840s rested on Anglican church precedent. Though Virginia was now religiously pluralistic, the laws of the Church of England still undergirded civil law in a matter so sensitive as divorce.[71]

More change, however, was in the air. When the legislators discussed the revised code, they radically altered the presentation throughout the section on divorce. In the final version, "Of Divorces," they rearranged the revisors' work, placing the different reasons for voiding marriage or divorcing couples in diverse sections. Significantly, the revised code included a new ground for *a vinculo* divorce: "where either of the parties is sentenced to confinement in any penitentiary for life or for seven years or more." But perhaps most telling, while it contained various references to the age of spouses, residency, cohabitation, condonation, collusion, alimony, maintenance, custody, property, and punishment of the guilty, the revised code of 1849 dropped all explicit references to English canon law.[72] Marriage and divorce now depended ostensibly on the laws and culture of Virginia.

As the assembly's amendment of Patton and Robinson's work makes clear, the direction that divorce legislation would take was in doubt at the end of the 1840s. More Virginians had begun to rethink the nature and purposes of the marital relationship and the wisdom of obstructing divorces for those who wanted them. But no consensus existed. As the caseload of petitions mounted steadily through the 1840s and some members tried to rush bills through the assembly, debates over individual divorce cases grew increasingly acrimonious. The Senate in particular offered a forum for sharp disagreement. Concerned by the increased number of divorces, some senators wanted further precautions and more extensive discussions. Thomas Moseley Bondurant, a Presbyterian elder and owner of the *Richmond Whig,* opined that he opposed all divorces "except in cases of fraud before marriage." His perspective had prevailed forty years earlier. But from the other side John G. Stringer echoed a growing sentiment when he called marriage simply "a civil contract—which could and ought to be dissolved, for the sake of adultery." Stringer further separated the scriptural warrant for marriage from its contractual nature in society. There was nothing inherently holy or sacred in this particular union that forbade its dissolution. Although "ordained by God," marriage was, "when entered into, . . . simply a conventional agreement between the parties." Divorces could therefore be given "for good cause."[73]

Reform-minded ministers would not have gone that far, but the matter lay outside their control. Even the revised code's expansion of grounds for absolute divorce failed to satisfy everyone. Anticipating modern no-fault divorce, James Ferguson, a western member of the House of Delegates, suggested in 1850 that any couple who wished a divorce should receive one immediately. A horrified Senator Robert Stanard from Richmond City decried this trend and vowed to oppose those who behaved as if "the highest and most solemn contract that a man could enter into under God, could be as easily annulled or set aside as a contract for a horse." The legislature, he thought, was simply encouraging "unmitigated licentiousness and dissoluteness on the part of persons who wished to separate" and mocked the "sacredness of the marriage tie."[74] There matters rested when the constitution of 1851 went into effect. Virginia's legislators were at loggerheads over the permanence of the marriage bond.

Ending legislative divorce achieved multiple purposes. It eliminated the assembly's burdensome workload of divorce cases, the acrimonious debates over individual suits, and the real possibility that a divorce could be rushed through the process without a court trial of the facts or be granted for reasons that in the abstract would never have been approved. Legislators were susceptible to pressure from political and kinship connections. A majority could be swayed by a particularly heart-rending tale of woe. For example, James Stevens told the legislature that he could not afford the cost of a court suit to divorce his wife, who had left him and married in Ohio. Without a court transcript and on the basis of his petition and a single affidavit, the legislature obliged. When Huldah Heiskell had complained bitterly about the abuse she had sustained at the hands of her husband, Ferdinand, a court had provided an *a mensa* divorce. Now the legislature made it absolute, freeing the parties—including Ferdinand the batterer—to marry again. William Rucker from Allegany County could barely scratch out his petition, but he wanted a "devours" from his wife, Elizabeth, claiming miscegenation on her part. As a legal note in his petition file explained, the 1848 divorce law, which authorized chancery courts to grant absolute divorces in cases of adultery, did not apply in William's case because Elizabeth's "offense" had occurred before their marriage and the five-year statute of limitations had been exceeded. But the assembly produced an absolute divorce for William.[75] In recent sessions a majority of the assembly had responded affirmatively in such situations, much to the dismay of those who held a traditional view of the marriage bond and believed divorce would destroy Christian society.

Conservatives thought the legislature had become far too lenient. They had once feared the courts, but no longer. Now the judicial system appeared to be the last bastion of marriage and family life. The Senate, which was notoriously stricter than the House in rejecting divorce bills, tried without success in 1848 to give judges authority over all divorce cases. Where earlier the legislators had feared local juries sympathetic to their neighbors, they now saw them as potential allies, provided that the grounds for divorce were limited and specific. Empowering the courts not only insulated the assembly from a mass of essentially private concerns; more significantly, it made the divorce process more formidable. The law bound the courts by stricter rules for dissolving marriages than the assembly had recently followed. Moreover, the commonwealth's attorney could ask the judge to overrule a jury decision and order a new trial, or the judge could do that himself. Ending legislative divorce, therefore, was not designed to liberalize and facilitate the dissolution of marriages in Virginia, much less to open up the possibilities of divorce for poorer men and women. By the late 1840s legislative divorce fulfilled those purposes. Instead, the constitution of 1851 stopped this trend and made it both more difficult and more expensive to shed a spouse.[76]

The lawyer-dominated constitutional convention may also have had one eye cocked on Charlottesville, where a new professor of law had already begun training the next generation for Virginia's bar and bench. John Barbee Minor had arrived at Mr. Jefferson's university in 1845 at age thirty-two to succeed Henry St. George Tucker. For almost twenty years Tucker's *Commentaries on the Laws of Virginia* had defined the perspectives of the Old Dominion's legal establishment, and the author had been as solidly opposed to divorce as any reasonable clergyman. Now a devout Episcopalian and rigorous pedagogue filled his chair. Virginians concerned with upholding marriage and the moral values of their society could rest assured that the formation of the legal profession would continue to rest in Christian hands. Minor would remain for fifty years, teaching the law and Sunday school. In his spare time he pushed the causes of temperance and public education, opposed secession, and helped his university avoid bankruptcy after the Civil War.

Like his predecessor, Minor wrote books out of his classroom preparation. His blackboard notes, laboriously copied each day, eventually became the *Institutes of Common and Statute Law*. A masterful four-volume compendium of virtually every aspect of the law, it functioned as the legal bible for every Virginia judge and lawyer and was widely used across the nation. The prologue to the section on divorce law did not mince words. "Religion, reason and experience combine to enforce the sanctity of the marriage tie," he began. It is "in the interests of society and of the true happiness of mankind that it should be dissolved only in rare and extreme cases." The South's most distinguished nineteenth-century legal scholar considered divorce both "a sign and a cause of moral degeneracy" and damaging to society. Even legal separations, he argued, should be severely restricted, though he admitted that the grounds for *a mensa* divorces in the Old Dominion basically expressed "the common law as always administered in England in the spiritual courts."

Minor dismissed as unacceptable some of the grounds the state accepted for *a vinculo* divorces. For example, to allow one party a divorce because the spouse had been sentenced to the penitentiary or had been indicted for a felony and become a fugitive from justice was not only bad "policy," but it violated the "scriptures." For the benefit of his students he quoted the Matthean gospel text against divorce as he explained his guiding principle: "It is vain to expect that individuals will conform their conduct to even the coarser rules of morality and virtue, when the laws of the land admit and encourage a license at variance with the *spirit* of Christian teaching, and hardly to be reconciled to its letter."[77] The Bible, rather than English canon law or Virginia's statutes, was Minor's ultimate authority. His *Institutes* expressed the commanding influence of nineteenth-century evangelical Christianity in southern legal culture and its outlook on marriage and divorce.

CHAPTER 3

Respects to Grandmother

THE COMMUNAL SETTING

Writing as the matriarch of an extensive clan, Martha Walton implored the Virginia assembly in 1809 to grant a divorce to two of her grandchildren. Though she and other relatives had tried to help the troubled marriage of Walton Knight and his first cousin, Nancy Yarbrough, their fighting and bickering had divided her progeny into warring camps and "almost brought me to my grave several times." This chapter examines, first, this kinship marriage as it unraveled in its local setting. Historians have discussed the significance of extended families and kinship groups, especially within the planter class, for the South's social structure.[1] As divorce petitions demonstrate, these same relational patterns also existed within the middle and lower classes. Family networks, neighborhoods, and local communities frequently provided critical support for marriage and family life. They could also breed hell. The Old South witnessed both.

As in so many divorce cases, family relationships and interventions contextualized Walton and Nancy Knight's matrimonial disaster. But their story also demonstrates the limitations a determined woman could place on what men and women might regard as male prerogatives and the potential for shifting power from husband to wife when family members take sides. In virtually every divorce case the extended as well as immediate family, the neighbors, and the local community form essential background elements. So, second, this chapter focuses explicitly on these presences and how they exercised agency in conflicted marriages and the divorce process. Interventions varied. Sometimes relatives and especially parents attempted to save a marriage; at other times they worked to end one. When family honor was at stake, divorce could also function as a means of asserting or reclaiming it. Moreover, families, neighbors, and communities played critical roles in conflicts between husband and wife, even to the extent of freeing an innocent party no matter what Richmond decided. This chapter explores the multiple dimensions of kinship and neighborhood involvement. Finally, by way of conclusion, it examines cases of legal incest as Virginia law defined it to forbid certain marriages on the basis of affinity. Here the state assumed responsibility to keep apart or to divorce couples who wanted to be married. Their successful resistance reinforces a major conclusion of this study, namely, that local authority lodged in families, neighborhoods, and communities held the preponderance of social power in the Old South.

AN ENEMY AND A STRANGER

Large families were not unusual in the Revolutionary era. Patrick Henry had been one of eighteen children, and between his two wives he fathered seventeen of his own. Three wives presented Tidewater planter Thomas Whiting with a total of fifteen children, one of whom, Anne Whiting Pryor, we will meet later. In Southside Virginia the Waltons also contributed to the population explosion. A descendent of early settlers, George Walton had married Martha Hughes in 1749 and eventually become a substantial planter and slaveholder in Prince Edward County and an elder in Briery Presbyterian Church. During the first quarter-century of their marriage Martha bore five boys and eight girls. When George died in 1796, he left his wife the sole executrix of a large estate to divide among their nine living children and more than forty grandchildren.[2]

The Waltons' seventh child, Martha, or Patsy, as she was familiarly called, married Woodson Knight a few months before General Charles Cornwallis surrendered at Yorktown. The scion of another old Virginia family, Knight had been wounded while fighting for the patriot cause at Guilford Court House. John Billups, a contemporary who knew the old soldier well, described his personality in terms reminiscent of the classic southern male accustomed to command. Knight could be pleasant and likable "when cool and in a good humour," but "if crossed, he is very turbulent." He owned enough land and slaves to be considered a lesser planter. The oldest of Woodson and Patsy Walton Knight's six children was named Walton for his mother's family.[3]

Temperance Walton, Patsy's younger sister, married Joseph Yarbrough, a well-to-do farmer and slaveholder who served many years as a Lunenburg County justice.[4] They named their firstborn Nancy Hughes Yarbrough. Martha Walton raised her grandchildren Walton Knight and Nancy Yarbrough at her home in Prince Edward County. Within ex-

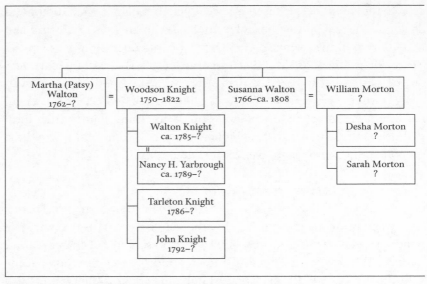

Some descendants of Martha and George Walton

tended southern families, children often spent lengthy periods with relatives. Undoubtedly the two children kept their grandmother occupied while providing her with company and emotional support after her husband's death. A few miles away in Lunenburg County the Knight and Yarbrough families lived near each other on amicable terms.

Among the various branches of the extensive Walton clan into which he married, Joseph Yarbrough enjoyed a particularly good relationship with Woodson Knight and his son Walton. As Walton and his brother Tarleton reached maturity, they spent more than a year in Richmond learning how to run a business under the watchful eye of another uncle, John Walton, who lived there with his family. Joseph Yarbrough visited his nephews in the city and regularly wrote Walton encouraging letters of advice. He obviously enjoyed helping the young man, and Walton reciprocated by handling some of Yarbrough's legal business. In early 1805, when a Lunenburg neighbor offered Yarbrough an option to buy 300 acres of land, he suggested that Walton purchase it, obviously hoping that his nephew would settle near him.[5]

Yarbrough apparently knew of Walton's interest in his daughter Nancy. The two cousins were married on 20 May 1805 by Archibald McRobert, a local Presbyterian minister. The bride was fifteen or sixteen years old, and the groom was also under age; so both Woodson Knight

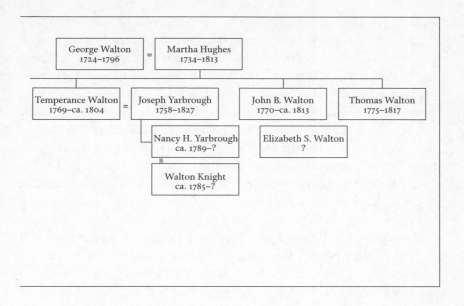

and Joseph Yarbrough had to consent to the wedding. Knight assented reluctantly. He may have gone along with the marriage in order to avoid a rupture with Yarbrough or possibly with his son, but a neighbor later testified that the senior Knight "did everything in his Power to Prevent" the wedding. Though his reasons are unknown, he may have thought the couple too young to marry, or perhaps he disliked his prospective daughter-in-law. The close family connection probably did not concern him, because marriages between first cousins occurred frequently in the South, especially given the size of families and the close proximity in which so many relatives lived. Kinfolk often comprised much of the neighborhood. A quarter-century later Judge Henry St. George Tucker complained to his wife about the number of weddings between first cousins. He thought the matches "a very bad fashion." As Richard Beeman points out in his study of Lunenburg County, family ties increased dramatically there during the post-Revolutionary era, with an ever increasing percentage of households sharing the surnames of other families in the county. Two other weddings between first cousins united four more of Martha Walton's grandchildren.[6] The marriage of Walton Knight and Nancy Yarbrough, however, would would rip apart the extended Walton clan.

At first the newlyweds lived with Walton's parents, a common practice for couples who were not yet financially established. Within a year or so, however, they set up their own home and farm, and with his father's financial assistance, Walton operated a store at Double Bridge, a small hamlet in Lunenburg.[7] Kinship ties remained typically close as relatives visited back and forth, and the older generations sought to support the younger. Martha Walton in particular tried to help her grandchildren, especially after she discovered that marital life was proving rocky. She first suspected problems when one of her slaves, a cooper whom she had sent to make some barrels for Walton, returned home extremely hungry. Martha asked why Nancy had not fed him. It was not her fault, the man replied, because Walton did not allow her to carry out the normal duties of the mistress of the house. Walton was denying his wife power and responsibility within the domestic sphere. The concerned grandmother decided to visit her grandchildren. When she told Walton that she thought that he and Nancy were not "happy together," her grandson replied that "he had firmed in his mind before he married how he meant to Conduct himself toward his business and that he lived as happy as he wished to live." This became his stock response whenever his grandmother questioned him.[8]

A later incident exemplifies Walton Knight's arbitrary authoritarian style. His mother, Patsy, and younger brothers, Tarleton and Jack, were staying at his home, and grandmother Martha had come for a visit. At noon Tarleton felt sick and unable to eat dinner. Though Walton had also been ill, he came to the meal. That evening Tarleton wanted to eat at least some bread, and when Jack arrived, the two brothers began supper together. Then Walton came into the room, inspected the meal, and announced that if there was anything eatable in the house, he would eat it. He then ordered the table cleared, "for there was nothing to eat." His mother observed that there was enough food "for four hungry work men," but Walton's insulting retort reduced her to tears. He then complained that she provided a bad model for his wife. Nancy cried whenever he spoke to her, he said, and now she would feel justified in doing so. His mother continued to weep until finally Walton got up from the table and tried to embrace her; but she pushed him away, saying that she and Jack would leave in the morning and eat no more of his food.

With a perverse and fiendish glee, Walton delighted in bullying and humiliating his wife. On one occasion, when they were staying at Martha Walton's home and got into her carriage with some other cousins to visit another relative, Walton insisted that Nancy should not sit next to him. According to his grandmother's account, he then began "Cursing and abusing" his wife and vowed that he would soon leave her if she did not go first. After they arrived at their destination, he demanded that Nancy kiss him in front of everyone. She did so, and he ordered her to do it again, until an uncle told him to stop. His grandmother feared that Walton's gross behavior was destroying the marriage. Alarmed by his conduct and hoping to "Reconcile" her grandchildren, Martha Walton spent more time at their house. During one of these visits Nancy was sick, possibly pregnant, and Martha came to take her back to her own home and nurse her. Walton berated his wife and cursed her father, who was absent, until finally his grandmother remarked that she would give "five of the best Negroes" she owned if only it would rectify the situation. Walton thought a bit and then said that if Martha gave him those slaves, "He would never curse his wife again." But the shrewd old lady retorted that "there was ways to treat a woman ill without Curseing" her.

The next morning, before Martha Walton left with her granddaughter, her grandson told Nancy "he had a good mind to kill her." Thinking that a slave girl was laughing at him, Walton felled her with a single blow. He then punched Nancy and practically "Kicked her out of the door." Walton then told his grandmother to take his wife because "he Could do better without her than with her." This time Nancy remained away for an extended period, probably through the birth of the first of her two children. The child died, however, and both Martha Walton and Joseph Yarbrough urged her to return to her husband and try to make the marriage work. She did so, and the result was a second pregnancy. That child also died, but in the midst of a painful labor Nancy told her grandmother that this would never have happened a second time if she and her father had not insisted on a reconciliation with Walton.[9]

Why did Nancy Knight accept this situation? She was not replicating the pattern of a battered wife. Any love she had once felt for her husband had died with the hope that his behavior might change, and she no longer wanted to remain with him. But Nancy was not yet twenty-one. Her mother was dead, her father had remarried, and he and her grandmother heavily influenced her course of action. They were her only resources. Southern society expected marriages to last and women to assume a position subordinate to and dependent on their husbands. Both women and men reinforced those values in family members. Whether women accepted this situation willingly or not remains a disputed matter among historians.[10] In this particular case John Billups, who had known Nancy and Walton from their infancy, remarked tellingly that Nancy possessed "a mild Passive disposition." In southern parlance such a description was intended as a compliment when attributed to a woman. But Billups and other neighbors had not yet seen her capacity for action. The very appearance of passivity, however, added to Nancy's vulnerability until her grandmother and other relatives finally supported her decision not to return to her husband.

In contrast Billups described Walton's temperament as "morose, Peevish, and inclined to suspicion and Jealousy." His ill treatment of his wife eventually became notorious in the neighborhood and among the extended family. In a society where kin frequently visited for lengthy periods, marital problems could not remain private affairs. Family members uniformly denounced Walton's behavior, and Nancy's female cousins came forward to offer her their support. Elizabeth Walton, after spending almost two months at the Knights' home, reported that virtually every time he came into his wife's presence, "Walton would Curse and abuse her in a most violent manner and . . . Call her a lude woman but in more vulgar terms." Venting his jealous suspicions when Nancy was in the kitchen, he told Elizabeth to see whether Thomas Farmer, a neighbor, was out there with her. After an inspection Elizabeth told him that Farmer was not there, but Walton refused to believe her.[11] Another cousin, Sarah Morton, described her visit to the Knights. Nancy had killed and cooked a chicken, but when she served it for dinner, Walton began vilifying her, saying she would "ruin him" and that "he had a good mind to throw it in her face." He then thought better of it, however, and sat down and ate the meal. That night he was away in Petersburg, and when he returned the next day, Walton asked Sarah if Meriweather Hunt, the owner of a nearby ordinary, had slept with Nancy in his absence. Sarah's sister, Desha Morton, witnessed similar incidents of Walton's jealousy and abusive behavior shortly after the couple had been married. These women as well as most of the other people who ultimately gave depositions in the divorce case supported Nancy's suit.[12]

Walton's father and friends, however, came to his defense by charging Nancy with adultery. An "aged and infirm" Elizabeth Atkins had lived in Woodson Knight's household as a dependent for many years. She testified that when Walton and Nancy had stayed there, Nancy was decidedly cool toward her husband but showed great affection toward a man named Samuel Crump. Atkins claimed that the two "were as fond as man and Wife" and spent extended periods alone. She was convinced they had enjoyed "improper and unjustifiable intercourse." Woodson Knight had earlier opposed his son's marriage; now he denounced both Nancy and Crump. Patsy Knight, however, told Crump to ignore her husband's drunken accusations. Walton's behavior replicated his father's. As one witness noted, Woodson Knight had leveled the same charges against Patsy that his son made against Nancy, but both were "women of Strict Virtue."[13]

Relationships within the extended clan became strained as family members chose sides. From Martha Walton's perspective, all had been "peace and harmony" among her vast brood until Nancy and Walton's marriage. Now the Knight and Yarbrough families lived on hostile terms, and Woodson Knight dragged his brother-in-law Thomas Walton into the county court on charges of "tresspass, assault and battery." Nancy's uncle, undoubtedly fed up with Woodson's verbal abuse of his niece, had decided to punish the slanderer. The jury found him guilty, but the amount of the twelve-and-a-half-cent fine made clear where their sympathies lay. The next year Thomas Walton brought a civil suit against Woodson Knight over the estate left to his sister Susannah Walton Morton and her children. This case would drag on for several years. Meanwhile Walton Knight sued his uncle Thomas Walton.[14]

A heartsick seventy-four-year-old Martha Walton viewed these court cases and quarrels as the direct result of her grandchildren's disastrous marriage. In May 1808, three years after their wedding and while Walton's litigation against his uncle was in arbitration, Nancy left her husband and returned to her grandmother's home. She did not tell Walton, however, that she would never return to him, nor did she write to him. A few weeks later he scribbled a brief note, expressing surprise that she had not yet come home. He expected her soon, he wrote, and if she could not arrange transportation, he would send his gig. In other news he also reported the increase in the number of turkeys, ducks, and chickens. He signed the letter tersely, "Respects to Grandmother."[15]

Nancy did not respond, and his grandmother failed to write. By July Walton was becoming concerned. In a long, rambling letter to Nancy he recounted household events and asked when she planned to come home. If Martha's carriage was not available, Walton offered to bring his gig and come for her himself. This letter was signed "yours ever loving and affectionate Husb[an]d." His uneasiness was evident in the postscript, for Walton told Nancy that neighbors had inquired when she would be back, and he had to explain that he did not know because she had not written him. "Please comply with my request," Walton asked. Her continued absence challenged his authority over his family and undermined his position in the neighborhood. The anxious husband noted that he had seen his father-in-law the day before. Joseph Yarbrough had told him that "he asked you to send me word when you was comeing home and you did not tell him."[16] Her father apparently hoped for a reconciliation, but Martha Walton was on Nancy's side now. Walton Knight had lost control of his marriage and his wife.

Two days later he quickly discovered the extent of the breach in their relationship when, still lacking a response from Nancy, he went to his grandmother's house. It was Friday, and he planned to spend the weekend and bring Nancy home with him on Sunday. He left that first night, however, after discovering that she would not share his bed. "If I am at a home where my wife is I think I ought to Sleep with her," he wrote Nancy, explaining his premature departure. Amazed that she would "deny me laying with you," Walton reminded her, "you must know we are married" and urged his wife to "reflect and pray." He wanted her home "as soon as possible." By now the panicking husband realized something was dreadfully wrong, and he promised that "if I have done Any thing that injures your feelings," he would "never . . . be guilty" of such conduct in the future. Rambling from one thought to another, he wrote of plans for the future; of fixing up their home "as well as most people's"; of opening the store, though "every thing appears to be against me"; and of his need for her to place her trust in him as her "nearest friend."[17]

Walton had Charles, a household slave, carry a letter to Nancy along with a new bonnet as a present. When Charles returned with the bonnet and no letter or note from Nancy, Walton wrote her, "These thing hurts my feelings." She had been away for "upwards of Three Months." Was that not long enough? And he begged for "the happiness of being admitted to your friendship." Two days later he was wondering if she planned ever "to live with me again," and he promised that if only she would come home, he would always treat her "well." She had told him she did not believe his promises. By now Walton was desperate to get her back and was ready to "do any thing that you will ask." If only Nancy would come home to him, Walton vowed, "if I ever give you Occasion to leave me again, I will then forever give you up to live as you please." Again and again, line after line, he begged her to return.[18]

Later in August Walton planned another visit to Nancy, but after a trip to Petersburg he became sick and could not leave the house. Using Charles again as courier, he sent his wife several presents and told her he had gotten rid of the old $50 buggy and purchased a new one—"one of the nicest Gigs your Eyes ever beheld"—for $200. If she would only come home, he promised to buy her a pair of shoes, too. By September Walton was immersed in traveling to Petersburg on business and supervising carpenters and bricklayers working on his farm. "Many things trouble me," he wrote, "but our liveing gives me much more pain." He wanted her back with him, to "lay aside what is past and agree to come home. . . . Write me That you will come home—it is all I want to be in friends with you."[19]

Nothing worked. By the following spring Nancy was still at their grandmother's home, had sent back his presents, and had failed to answer his letters. She refused even to acknowledge his "howdy" in public places or speak to him when he visited the house. Walton had finally begun to think Nancy "Cared but little for" him. In a March 1809 letter—the longest in the collection—he renewed his entreaties and promises of amendment, pledged his love "till Death," and confessed his anguish at her treatment of him and her refusal to return home. Walton also tried a religious tack, appealing to "God's ordinance" which "particularly bound" them. Reflecting on their wedding when they stood before the minister, "I assured myself of the happiness we should enjoy," he wrote, and in an rare moment of candor he added, "however, in part it has been otherwise."[20]

In early July Nancy finally broke her silence and wrote to Walton. She had heard that he wanted a divorce. If he would give her back her property, she said, "I will tell you my reasons for leaving you wich [sic] you very well know." She had brought to the marriage two young women slaves and other assets. Now she refused to speak to him until he returned the two slaves and other possessions she regarded as her own. But she also told him that she would never live with him again. By the end of the summer, realizing that their marriage had effectively ended, Walton hired an attorney and notified his wife that he was beginning the process for a legislative divorce. Nancy responded swiftly by announcing by mail that her father would serve as her "attorney in fact." Joseph Yarbrough informed Walton that he would depose witnesses in Tennessee and Georgia as well as Prince Edward County.[21]

That December Walton Knight submitted a petition that suggested his wife had committed adultery. Despite the "love and regard" he expected from Nancy in the "hymenial State," he had encountered an affective alienation to the point "that she preferred the society of and intercourse with other men." Although he had made strenuous efforts to reclaim her, she had definitively left him and refused to "cohabit with him as her husband." In an affidavit drawn up to support Walton's case, Anderson Bagley claimed that "a Certain Lady" told him that she had spent an evening in the Knights' home while Walton was away and overheard Nancy in bed with another man, telling him "she loved him and never did like her husband and never would." On Walton Knight's request, however, the justices who deposed Bagley in November rejected this "hearsay" testimony.[22]

On the same day that the assembly received Walton's petition, Nancy's counterpetition arrived in Richmond. She had always intended, she told the legislators, to be a "dutiful, affectionate Wife according to the Sacred Obligations of the Married State." But instead of the "Kindness" properly owed her and commonly expected "in every Civilized Country," she had encountered her husband's cruel treatment, which had forced her out of his home and into a "State of exile," where she had taken "Refuge" with "friends." Now he had come forward with a brazen assault on her virtuous character that demanded response. She had no objection to the divorce, but she wanted it "placed on its true ground." She was the innocent party, she claimed. The legislative committee agreed with her. The summary of their investigation characterized Nancy as of "mild temper and disposition," cleared her of any "unchastity," and found Walton frequently drunk and in such a condition "very turbulent." The assembly turned down his divorce application in early January.[23]

A month later Walton Knight eloped with a young woman named Frances Stokes. According to a neighbor, he had been "Courting" her for almost a year. The couple did not reappear until October, when Walton suddenly showed up in the neighborhood with a very pregnant Frances, and they began living openly as if they were married.[24] The next autumn Nancy applied for a divorce with a petition that detailed Walton's "cruelty" in "breaking a heart that knew no sin but loving" and accused him of adultery with Frances Stokes. Multiple affidavits corroborated Nancy's charges. The whole neighborhood was now agog with the scandal as rumors circulated that Walton had wed Frances in North Carolina. A separate petition, signed by forty-seven men, including two ministers and some of the most prominent people in the area, supported Nancy's divorce application. They testified to her "fair amiable and unblemished character," the respectability of her parents and family, and the need for both "pity" and "substantial relief." The assembly's resolution stated that

Walton had inflicted "blows and stripes" on Nancy and lived "in a state of concubinage with a woman of bad fame," but a divorce bill was defeated on the first reading.[25]

The next year Nancy tried a different tactic with the legislature. Her property and future financial security now became the major concerns. Walton had gained "two valuable slaves" by their marriage and held "considerable wealth." Yet he failed to support her, she lived off the charity of relatives and friends, and he could seize anything she might acquire or inherit. Nancy asked for a law returning her property and allowing her to own and acquire as "if she were an unmarried woman." Once again family and neighbors rallied behind her petition, and the assembly responded partially in her favor. It approved a bill permitting her "to hold and enjoy such property as she may hereafter acquire . . . as if she were an unmarried woman." But the House committee rejected a proposal to return to Nancy the property Walton had acquired by their marriage.[26]

The couple renewed the battle for the fourth and last time in 1813. Again Walton petitioned for a divorce, or at least to have the same kind of law passed in his favor that Nancy had received in the previous session. In an extraordinary newspaper announcement published before the assembly met, he spelled out his plan to prevent her from ever "claiming" any "dower or maintenance, as my Wife, as you conduct yourself towards me not as a Wife, but as an enemy and a stranger." Nancy also asked for a divorce and attacked the slurs his petition cast on her character. The legislature rejected both petitions. The hatred between the cousins who were still legally husband and wife was palpable. As Nancy bluntly declared in her fifth and final petition, she remained "the wife of one whom she must ever dispise and abominate."[27]

The marital tragedy of Nancy Yarbrough and Walton Knight continued to poison family relationships after Martha Walton's death in September 1813. In siding with her granddaughter, Martha had alienated other relations. She left slaves and furniture to Nancy Hughes Knight, but her will expressly excluded some of her descendants, including daughter Patsy Knight and her children. A battle royal followed in the courts as Patsy's husband, Woodson, and his children sued Joseph Yarbrough, Martha's executor, and the rest of the extended family in the Superior Court of Chancery in Richmond. Thus an unhappy marriage between cousins metastasized into a family feud of epic proportions that lasted into the 1820s as the younger generations fought over property and estates. By then Nancy Knight had moved to North Carolina. She apparently never remarried. Walton Knight relocated to Georgia, probably with Frances as his common-law wife. Many other relatives scattered across the South.[28]

Family networks such as that formed by the Waltons and their in-laws represent an important type of community in the antebellum South. Such face-to-face, intimate relationships based on blood and marriage could be intensely affectionate and supportive, and family members often felt a strong sense of direct responsibility for one another. But they could also cause the worst heartaches. Martha Walton did everything possible to help her grandchildren, and other close relations—parents, siblings, aunts, uncles, and cousins—appear to have been on the scene for extended periods in various assisting roles. Thus, though Nancy and Walton Knight resided on their own farm without other permanent residents except a few slaves who probably lived in a separate cabin, they hardly comprised a nuclear family. Contact with near relatives was constant, and relationships were both intense and intrusive.

FAMILY TIES

Nancy and Walton Knight's situation was not exceptional. In the tightly woven fabric of southern society, families typically saw the well-being of one member as intimately bound up in the happiness of all. Whether in the countryside or in town, the constant visiting back and forth provided plenty of opportunities for kinfolk to observe their relatives' domestic lives. Even when unrelated by blood, members of the families of the bride and groom often knew one another, and especially in rural areas, they frequently occupied nearby farms. Thus a marital failure, particular one as bitter as the Knights', could have severe repercussions on patterns of social and economic reciprocity within neighborhoods as well as families. Applications for divorce regularly opened fissures in a local community as family members, friends, and neighbors composed affidavits and signed petitions on behalf of opposing spouses.

No class was immune. Even elite families became entangled in bitter fights that ruptured long-standing relationships. For example, years before their children became joined by marriage, the Brookes and Hamiltons had been well acquainted. Judge Francis Brooke, a distinguished member of the Virginia Court of Appeals, had built St. Julien, as he styled his plantation home, outside Fredericksburg and only a few miles from Forest Hill, the Hamilton seat. Though Francis and Mary Brooke had strongly opposed the marriage of their daughter to Robert Hamilton, they relented when an infatuated Helen pleaded that "she should never be happy unless she was permitted to marry him." Parental concern may have been economic, because the groom was not yet settled in the legal profession, though Robert Brooke, Helen's older brother, thought Hamilton "very promising" and approved of the match.[29]

But problems surfaced almost at once. After the wedding in May 1843, the young couple moved into the same Richmond rooming house where Helen's parents boarded during the court session. The judge observed at first hand Hamilton's unkindness to his daughter but "hoped for the best." After the session ended, the Brookes retired to St. Julien. When Mary Brooke returned the following spring to assist her daughter with the birth of her child, however, she noticed that her son-in-law was "coarse and harsh" toward Helen and spoke to her severely. In part this may have reflected Robert's intense dislike for his mother-in-law. He knew of her opposition to the marriage, but she had also persuaded her daughter that, for health reasons, she should abstain from sexual intercourse during the last five months of her pregnancy. When Robert admitted, about six weeks after his wife gave birth, that he had gotten Helen's mulatto maid, Louise, pregnant during the interval, an outraged Mary Brooke stonily told her son-in-law to "look to a higher power for forgiveness." Later, fearing for his daughter's personal safety after Helen intimated that Robert had treated her roughly, Judge Brooke confronted Robert and said that he "could not conceive how any man of courage could abuse any woman especially his wife."[30]

After the couple separated within a year of their wedding, Helen wrote an extraordinary letter to her father-in-law, accusing her husband of cruelty, lying, and religious infidelity. "I have heard him curse his maker," she asserted. In the face of such charges, Robert Hamilton's five sisters leaped to his defense and replied in a group to Helen, "We Brothers, sisters and all were quite as much opposed to your union with our Brother, as your parents could have possibly been." Professing absolute confidence in Robert's "honour and rectitude" and outrage at Helen's allegations against him, they expressed their delight at finally having him return "to the bosom of his own family, and to the paths of comparative peace and happiness, and in closing our intercourse with your family."[31]

But neither the marriage nor the families' feud had yet ended. Moreover, Robert was sure that his mother-in-law did not want marital "harmony" restored. That was not true, however, of either Robert's or Helen's father. When the young couple reunited and moved into a house that

Robert bought in Richmond, Francis Brooke provided both household slaves and most of the furniture and restored cordial relations with his son-in-law. George Hamilton gave his son and daughter-in-law a book that Robert Hamilton later praised for its "excellent advice" and admitted to his father, "Had we both followed it, our union would no doubt have been more harmonious." Within a few months of their reunion, Robert was writing to his father of his hopes that "relations" between the two families would improve, even though two of his sisters had refused to speak to Mary Brooke when they collided in a Fredericksburg store. Yet an ominous sentence in that letter portended marital wreckage. Exuding male superiority, he pointed out that he had refused to discuss problems or conflicts with his wife and told his father, "I have no doubt . . . it will not be very long before Helen will be made to feel most sensibly the impropriety of her recent course."[32]

Silence and emotional manipulation, however, only drove a final wedge in their relationship. About ten months later Helen and Robert Hamilton separated permanently. As the latter had once presciently counseled his future wife, "Ere you marry me, tune your notes for the last requiem to your happiness and on your bridal day sing 'Mozart's last requiem'." He had then decried his "most unfortunate eccentricities" that made him demand total compliance to his will at all times, even in the most "trifling" matter. By his own admission, Robert Hamilton was unfit for marriage. Yet when it ended, he did not want to drag either family into the issue, and he urged his siblings not to write or speak against Helen's parents but to follow his lead in keeping quiet. "I did not marry [Judge Brooke] or his wife—but his daughter." Still, personal and family vindication were ultimately entwined. "I ardently desire," Robert wrote his sister, "that the immense superiority of myself and my family in this unfortunate affair may be seen in our moderation and forbearance." When Helen proposed yet another reunion, Robert told his "Papa" it was "madness" to take it seriously, consulted his brother, and finally wrote Helen that he was unwilling to trust her again with his "happiness and character." In his view she had "sported with both" and slandered his reputation in Fredericksburg and Richmond.[33]

Devastated by the collapse of Helen's marriage, Francis Brooke moved to help his daughter obtain a legislative divorce. Robert Brooke served as her "next friend" in the legal proceedings, a messy, sordid business that produced a transcript of 161 pages of statements, testimony, and evidence in the Superior Court of Chancery for the Richmond Circuit. Helen received the divorce as well as custody of her infant child in early 1847. But as Judge Brooke told his son-in-law in one blistering interview, this marriage had "destroyed the happiness of one of the happiest families in the world."[34]

As the Hamilton and Knight divorce cases demonstrate, a marriage's success or failure clearly affected not only the couple but the entire extended family. In both instances family members, particularly the fathers, encouraged efforts at reconciliation and endeavored to smooth the bumpy relationship with financial support and friendly advice. Divorce presented a blight that families despised, but in the end some found it preferable to a loveless, hostile, tortured relationship or social disgrace. If the Hamilton and Knight marriages exemplify the loveless relationship, the Cauffman marriage represents the social disgrace. Rachel Cardozo was seventeen when she married Simon Cauffman, a German immigrant, in 1816. Rachel's father, Isaac Cardozo, was a gentleman's tailor. As founding members of Richmond's small but well-established Jewish community, he and his wife, Sarah, must have been pleased that their new son-in-law shared their religious faith. Simon was twenty-nine and a peddler, an occupation that frequently developed into a successful career as a merchant, but he would not follow that professional path. Instead all prospects for a happy marriage and prosperous business were soon blasted by Simon's propensity for liquor. After three years and three children, he "violently expelled" Rachel from their home in Philadelphia. She returned with the children to her parents in Virginia. A short time later Simon scribbled a brief letter to his wife, offering to support the children and give her a divorce. Rachel had chosen to leave him, Simon claimed, "without any cause." But what "most" bothered him, he continued, was the impact of their marital troubles on Rachel's parents, to whom he sent his "best respects."[35]

A few months later he was convicted of theft and wrote to Rachel to explain the "unlucky circumstances" that had landed him in prison. "Drinking . . . to excess I have brought myself to trouble," he confessed. He promised to reform and begged forgiveness not just from his wife but, significantly, from "all of you." Again he expressed concern that his behavior "offended" Rachel's parents, but this time he did not offer a divorce. Instead he hoped that Rachel would live with him when he got out of jail and that her father would lend him "a little money to begin anew."[36] Simon was released from the Philadelphia penitentiary in September 1820 after completing his sentence, but by December he was back behind bars in New York. This time he claimed innocence, regretted the "disgrace" he had brought on the family, and asked Rachel's intercession with her father to send him "fifty or sixty Dollars" to get him out of this "horrid place." No money was forthcoming. Instead, through an emissary from the local Jewish community, Isaac Cardozo asked his son-in-law "to sign a bill of divorcement." In Jewish law only the husband could initiate a divorce. Cardozo wanted Simon Cauffman to sign a *get,* a document of divorce prepared by a Jewish religious court. Once Rachel had accepted it, observant Jews would regard the divorce as final. Only then could one of the parties sue for a civil divorce. But Simon refused; he wanted to resume married life and promised sobriety and "honest and industrious living."[37]

The next spring Simon escaped from the New York prison before completing his term. Writing to Rachel of his hopes "that the Past may be buried in Oblivion," he dedicated "My Future Life" to "*God* . . . and the Peace and Happiness of my Family." Sending affectionate greetings "to our Fond Parents and the Family," he announced his intention to flee to Baltimore, or anyplace else she desired where, they could reestablish their lives together.[38] Less than a month after he penned that missive, Simon was convicted in the Baltimore City Court of stealing a box of ribbons worth eighteen dollars. Rachel had written to her husband earlier, but not until August did a deeply remorseful Simon respond to her letter and explain how he had been sentenced not just for theft but "for Cursing and Swearing and indecorous Language to the Court." He had been on his way to Richmond, he explained, when he fell into "bad Company and this led me to Drinken and Dishonesty and at last cast into Prison." His term was eight years. He acknowledged to "Dear Rachel" his "Folly" for not heeding her "Counsels" and bringing such humiliation upon her "and the rest of the family" and again begged forgiveness.

In her divorce petition three years later, Rachel Cauffman included her husband's letters as evidence of his "utter unworthiness." Simon was "irreclaimable," and his conduct had "brought ruin and disgrace on the family." Her concluding statement spoke for more than herself and her children when she wrote, "Nothing but infamy can attach to a family in which he is an associate, or over which he has any control."[39] The honor of a family mattered. In this case legislative divorce became the process by which the offense was confessed, the offender was removed from familial relations, and honor was reclaimed.

A similar situation preoccupied the children of Moody and Olympia Blood. Olympia Meridith had been only fourteen in 1836 when she married Moody Blood, a laborer who had emigrated from New England to Tidewater Virginia. So abusive was his behavior that Olympia got a peace warrant from the local county court and eventually fled with her two children to her mother's home for support and protection. Meanwhile, after running through the assets he had acquired by the marriage, Moody was jailed for receiving stolen property. Olympia petitioned for a divorce in 1841 and again in 1843. Both times the Senate rejected the divorce bill; but Moody disappeared from the scene, and Olympia's mother, Ann Meridith, cared for her daughter and grandchildren, Fleming and Friendless Blood. When they were barely in their teens, Fleming and Friendless petitioned the assembly through an adult "friend" to change their surnames from Blood to Meridith. They explained that their mother's family and particularly their grandmother had supported them. But more important, they lived in a county where their surname represented "a legacy of reproach and disgrace."[40]

For Olympia Blood, Rachel Cauffman, Helen Hamilton, and Nancy Knight, as for so many other women snared by disastrous marriages, family was the place of ultimate refuge and security. The vast majority of women in similar circumstances returned to their parents' homes and sought their assistance. The battle then often shifted from a contest between husband and wife to a clash between rival males, as the husband claimed legal rights over a wife under coverture while the father attempted to extend to a daughter the protection and support denied by her spouse. If the husband had deserted his family or been incarcerated, like Simon Cauffman, the situation was somewhat eased. A father or widowed mother might take in a daughter and grandchildren and support them without challenge. Sometimes in-laws also reached out to care for an abandoned wife and her family.[41]

In some cases, despite a husband's legal rights, a male parent held the upper hand, particularly if he had the support of the neighborhood and the husband was an outsider. On the morning after his marriage to Betsy Clise in September 1809, David Dryden was charged with already having a wife in Kentucky. When he discovered that Christopher Clise, Betsy's father, planned to have him jailed until the matter could be investigated, David quickly quit Rockbridge County, leaving his bags at Clise's home. From a safe distance a few weeks later David sent his "complements" to his father-in-law and his regrets over the "delicate" position in which he had left father and daughter. He claimed that the Kentucky marriage, due to that wife's "Brothers and Fathers treatment," had failed before they even lived together, and that she had received a divorce. David urged Clise to drop the prosecution, "for it is certain I never Will be taken alive on that Subject and my Dead Body will not answer you, or any Other person any purpose." For the sake of the "happiness" of everyone concerned, he asked his father-in-law to forward Betsy as well as his clothes and papers to Abingdon in southwest Virginia and deduct "any charges against me" from the money he found in his luggage. Instead, Clise obtained an affidavit from the brother of David's first wife that she awaited her husband at her father's home in Kentucky, and in December Betsy filed for divorce.[42]

Families frequently became closely involved in divorce proceedings. While some fathers, such as Joseph Yarbrough, represented their married daughters in the court and assembly proceedings, that task could also be filled by a brother or other male relative or friend, or even by another woman, provided she was unmarried. When Catherine Hillary sought a divorce, her sister served as her "next friend." After the assembly granted his wife a divorce, an outraged John Robertson claimed that his brother-in-law had composed the petition. Family members also sought whatever connections in Richmond or the legislature that might help their relations gain divorces.[43] Some fathers even went so far as to submit the divorce petition themselves on behalf of their daughters. For example, John Harris had fought against the wedding of his daughter Martha "as long as opposition was available," but ultimately John Hemmings, "a most artful and designing villain," deluded her into marriage in 1835. Two years later Harris asked the legislature to divorce his daughter from Hemmings. A thief and a swindler, Hemmings had already been driven from the community. Martha's contribution to the process was a sworn statement before a justice of the peace that she subscribed to her father's petition. But despite three attempts, the Senate rejected the divorce.[44] She had married the man. Now she was stuck with him.

Virginia Crawford's story was similar. The belle of Wheeling on the Ohio River had been seduced by the elegant manners and suave bearing of William Crawford, a New Orleans businessman whose talent for forgery finally earned him five years in a Kentucky prison. The jury's verdict in the marriage case noted William's vow that once he was out of jail, he would return to his father-in-law's home to claim his wife and son. If she refused to go with him, he had promised to "kill her." Despite the family's "high standing and respectability" in Wheeling, the assembly rejected Job Stanbery's petition for his daughter's divorce in 1839. He had hired two first-rate lawyers in Ohio County, Daniel Lamb and David Wheat, to prepare the case. The next year Virginia herself applied in florid terms: "A daughter of Virginia appeals to *you* . . . fathers brothers and sons, assembled at Richmond as the Legislature of Virginia." She and her father even planned to travel to the capitol to appeal in person. John Tyler, as the vice-president-elect, wrote on her behalf to James Lyons, a state senator, asking his "kind intercession" if he was satisfied "that a divorce ought to be granted." During a recent visit to Wheeling, Tyler had promised to use his good offices to help the divorce along.[45] But nothing worked. The assembly seldom ruled against a husband's right to control his wife and children, no matter the challenge his behavior or lifestyle presented to a family's honor. Virginia had made an unfortunate marriage; now she must make the best of it.

Yet though a divorce be denied, a family supported by the local community might successfully defy a husband's claims. Polly Toomes's husband wanted to return to his wife but feared her brothers "would shoot him, on account of his conduct to her." He had also gotten another woman pregnant. Family quarrels sometimes exploded in violence. Elizabeth Kimberlin claimed that her husband had shot her father and burned down his barn before running off to Kentucky. Elizabeth Corbin and Nancy Lane successfully petitioned for divorces on grounds that their husbands had murdered their brothers, while Mary Burke received her freedom because her spouse had killed his sister's husband and fled the state.[46] None of these particular divorce petitions fully explore the context, but frequently in the collection there is a sense of local entitlement already at work—first, to assert the justice of a claim and then, if denied in Richmond, to apply equity within a family and neighborhood. The petition of the injured party, the depositions of witnesses, the collection of supportive signatures, and after 1827, the Superior Court verdict after a trial of facts—all these steps involved multiple agencies, interactions, and public encounters. The process operated discursively to end the marriage so far as the community was concerned, regardless of what the assembly ultimately decided.

It was more difficult, however, for a parent to assure a daughter's financial independence from her husband. The real possibility that he might eventually return to claim whatever property his wife inherited led some parents to refuse to give their daughters anything or to set conditions for their estates. For example, at her death in 1809 Judith Lyon's mother left her daughter a "considerable estate" on the express condition that she have no "further intercourse" with Alexander Lyon, her husband. He had already "squandered" the property Judith had inherited from her father before deserting her in 1795. She had not seen him since then, and her mother had been the sole support of Judith and her four children. An affidavit from Polly Smith in North Carolina stated that Lyon had done the same thing to her.[47]

Outside a divorce, which the assembly denied Judith Lyon, the only legal option that would render a married woman economically independent of her husband was a separate estate. In his guide for justices of the peace, William Waller Hening suggested a precise form for these documents. Sometimes a parent made such an arrangement for a daughter either before or during her marriage. While still unmarried, a woman could also set up a separate estate for herself and select a trustee, normally a male family member or trusted friend, to administer her property on her behalf after her marriage. As early as the 1780s Anne Dantignac had made such a disposition with her future husband in a formal agreement they signed in the presence of a justice of the peace. Elizabeth Dowdall, a widow, had done the same before her second marriage in order to ensure her entire control over a slave girl and three horses as well as the cattle, hogs, furniture, and farming implements she brought to the marriage.[48]

Worried that his daughter Evelina's life would be miserably insecure because of her unfortunate marriage, William Gregory planned to set up a separate estate for her in his will. A wealthy planter, Gregory arranged to leave her a plantation, slaves, and a fund from which the trustees would pay her a regular income until her husband died, when she would receive full title to all the real and personal property in the trust. Ultimately a divorce solved Evelina Gregory Roane's marital troubles, but she had learned to protect herself by legal means. Before her third and fourth marriages she established a separate estate to secure her property for herself and her children against the claims and creditors of her future husbands and their families. A wealthy Norfolk woman, Martha Massenburg, worked out an elaborate arrangement in her will that provided regular support for her daughter and granddaughters but cut her son-in-law, Edwin Walke, completely out of any share or control of the estate or even the use of her pew in Christ Church. A few months after her mother's death in 1839, an economically secure Sarah Walke left her husband. A decade later an angry, frustrated Edwin Walke bitterly complained about the destruction wrought on his marriage and asked the assembly to ensure that his wife would never receive a widow's dower if he predeceased her.[49]

In all these cases, property control was vested in a trustee or trustees who managed the assets on behalf of the beneficiary. Whether this worked well or not depended on a number of variables. The executor of Josiah Parker's will had great difficulties administering the estate and paying Ann Parker Cowper's annuity because her husband grabbed control of the property, and local authorities appeared more disposed to drag out the issue than to resolve it in Ann's favor. Trustees also might become incapacitated, die, or move away. Thus the system of separate trusts was clearly second best to a divorce that would render the woman legally independent and free from the restrictions of coverture. Nancy Saunders had suffered enormous abuse from her husband, who had eventually abandoned her and their four children. In a story repeated dozens of times by deserted wives, Nancy told the legislature that her aging father wanted to accommodate his daughter and grandchildren "provided it could be done so as to keep it from the controul of her said husband, and . . . free it from the trammels of a trustee."[50]

The instinctual response for most families and particularly immediate relatives such as Martha Walton and Joseph Yarbrough was to support and preserve marriages, even when they were embroiled in turmoil and violence. When Francina Falkler walked out on her husband, her brothers did everything possible to persuade her to return to him. Divorce only became a serious consideration in Rachel Cauffman's family after Simon's crimes put him in jail. In Virginia the bias of law, religion, and custom strongly favored matrimony as a permanent institution, for better or worse. Yet at other times family members appear in the records as instruments of marital breakup. When, for example, John Peyton's in-laws emigrated from Virginia to Arkansas, they took his wife and left him behind. Polly Cooper's parents were so anxious to have their daughter leave her husband that her mother helped her pack and demanded Polly go with them.[51] Nor was Robert Hamilton the only husband who believed his mother-in-law was gunning for him. Ferdinand Heiskell thought the discord between himself and his wife, Huldah, stemmed from her mother, a "misguided and ill tempered Woman" who blamed him for the couple's childlessness and wanted to separate them. She "poisoned" Huldah "with hostility," and on frequent visits she would belittle him and magnify his faults. Given Ferdinand's propensity for strong liquor and domestic violence, his mother-in-law probably made some valid points. But it especially galled Ferdinand, who had inherited a respectable estate, when the old lady remarked that Huldah "could have married a much richer man."[52]

The assembly could become intractable if the lawmakers suspected that a parent had intervened to destroy the marriage. The only child of Dibdral Tally, a planter in Hanover County, Judith Tally married Joseph Anderson Cocke, who turned out to be an alcoholic ne'er-do-well. Two years and one child later, their relationship dissolved when he took Judith back to her father's home and moved himself in with his father, William Cocke. Fifteen years passed, and they were still living on their respective parents' farms when Judith petitioned for a divorce. The objection was raised—and vigorously but ineffectually refuted—that her father had been instrumental in separating the young couple. No divorce was forthcoming, although Joseph Cocke died in 1823 and Judith later remarried. In the case of James Pollack and Fanny Gibson, the bride's mother had both made and unmade the marriage. Fanny had been sixteen and James a year older when they were wed in 1808 at the instigation of Fanny's mother. She mistakenly thought that James, whose parents were deceased, owned sufficient resources to support herself and her husband in addition to his wife. Within a few months, however, she realized her error and separated the couple. Fanny asked for a divorce on the grounds that she needed to marry someone who would provide for her, while James petitioned separately that he had been tricked into the marriage. The legislature was unimpressed.[53]

In some divorce cases family members completed the triangle that destroyed the marriage. William Cloud brought his niece, the daughter of his sister, into the house provided by his father-in-law, set her up as "mistress," and had several children by her while reducing his wife's role to that of a servant. Peter Davis's wife ran off with his uncle and bore him two children. Henry Carty discovered his wife in bed "with his own brothers son." And Taylor Noel initiated an incestuous liaison with his own daughter, which he continued even after her marriage to John Fogg. First cousins feature even more prominently as home-wreckers. Elizabeth Bourn's husband ran off with her cousin. Abraham Leatherman was nineteen when he married twenty-seven-year-old Mary Ellen Hull. Both he and the entire neighborhood thought she was "chaste," but Mary Ellen had deceived them. Before the marriage she had enjoyed the sexual favors of her first cousin and bore his child three months after the wedding. Robert Moran's wife, on the other hand, had committed adultery with her husband's cousin.[54]

In the vast majority of divorce petitions, parents, other family members, friends, and neighbors form an essential backdrop to the composition. Would marriages have worked better and been more successful if couples had been left alone, if families had been less complex and more nuclear, and if communities had been less intrusive? In the domestic situation of Walton and Nancy Knight, any argument favoring this proposition must recognize the abusive treatment Walton meted out to Nancy and her need for protection and support. Yet the pervasive family presence may have contributed to their marital problems. As an adult and husband, Walton Knight attempted to live up to a distorted image of manhood constructed for him primarily by his father. More than anything else, he feared Woodson Knight's scorn and rejection if he treated his wife in a manner different from the example his father had set. Since Walton felt he had to act out this identity, the presence of family members may have encouraged his violent speech and actions. When his grandmother rebuked his behavior, Walton replied "that he treated his wife as his father would wish, for that his father told him never to give up in the least degree to a wife, and that he should be glad to please you all but he was dam'd if he did not please his father at the Resque of his life."

The threat to Walton's life stemmed not from physical danger, however, but from exposure to shame and loss of personal honor. Treating his wife with love and respect, showing consideration for her feelings and wishes, and identifying her as the mistress of their home would, in Walton's twisted mind, render him weak and inferior and thus violate masculine behavior patterns learned from his father. When Martha reported Walton's response to her son-in-law, Woodson Knight "Swore it was a dam'd lye." She then asked Woodson "upon his honour" whether he had ever witnessed his son's ill treatment of Nancy. The father replied that "he had seen him behave like a Raskul." No doubt he had approved of it as well, because he acted that way himself. Although the senior Knight condemned his son's conduct to his mother-in-law, his wife, Patsy, pointed out the similarities in the alcoholic behavior of father and son.[55]

If Nancy and Walton Knight had been left alone, however, their marriage would have been an anomaly. Families, neighbors, and local communities were notoriously intrusive. Relatives and close neighbors provided the bulk of the testimony in the initial efforts to obtain a divorce, but after Walton ran off with Frances Stokes and then returned and began openly living with her, the larger community in Lunenburg County became involved. Despite the rural environment, their adulterous relationship was widely observed. Walton had once accused Meriweather Hunt of a dalliance with Nancy. Hunt signed a group petition in support of Nancy's divorce and later testified that Walton and Frances "lived together in one house . . . as man and wife." John Jordan, who had cared for Walton's stock while he and Frances were gone, watched the couple sharing farm duties after they came home. Elizabeth Hightower had observed even more, for she claimed to have "seen the Said Walton bed with the said Frances." Had she been peeking through the window? [56]

If the testimony in most divorce cases is credible, Virginians took great liberties at all hours of day and night. They looked through open doors and windows, walked into other persons' homes and farm buildings, and wandered through their neighbors' property. This was a society that lived in the open even when most closely closeted. Eyewitness accounts of adultery were common. Divorce petitions regularly included affidavits from people outside the family circle who claimed they had seen a couple "beded together." [57] Robert Gonoe in Monroe County happened by Abby Norman's house and "saw her in bed with two men"; he also observed that they were still there in the morning. A poor but industrious mechanic who made wheat-threshing machines in the Northern Neck's Loudoun County, William Yonson suspected that the friendship of his wife, Eliza Jane, with neighbor William Smith had blossomed into adultery. But he needed proof. Pretending to be away from home, Yonson and some friends laid a trap and awakened "the guilty parties . . . in his own bed." Smith was permitted to pull on his clothes and depart; on the way out he apologized to Yonson and ungallantly blamed Eliza Jane. As we will see, the African American community enjoyed the least protection from curious eyes, particularly when the latter belonged to a white master. A slave could not bar the door at night or refuse a master's command to share his bed even though others were watching.[58]

Observers could be family members, neighbors, or friends, but they collectively formed what Thomas Bender has defined as a community:

"a limited number of people in a somewhat restricted social space or network held together by shared understandings and a sense of obligation." Something more than simple physical proximity marked their relationships in community, namely, "mutuality and emotional bonds."[59] For the generations of southerners between the Revolution and the Civil War, society was decentralized. Identities and values were primarily localist. Individuals lived within multiple, varied communities: families, neighborhoods, churches, voluntary associations, lodges, and economic, political, and social networks. Because the intimate world was local, many unhappy spouses preferred to seek divorces in the legislative halls of the state capital rather than in a district courtroom. A distant Richmond promised a degree of anonymity for the process, while nearby courts were more public and so more embarrassing.

Yet local communities were almost invariably drawn into the marital traumas of their members. William and Nancy Dinwiddie's opposing petitions in 1826 illustrate how family and friends could choose sides. Six years earlier, according to William's account, Nancy's allies had forced him into a shotgun wedding. He had been courting her at the time; but his weak financial situation made marriage impossible, so they had limited their relationship to "the exchange of ordinary civilities." Then one of Nancy's friends told him that Nancy had borne a child, named him as its father, and was close to death. When he arrived to refute the change, William found Nancy in excellent health, surrounded by a crowd of her family and friends, and with a clergyman present and marriage license in hand. Thus "menaced, intimidated and threatened with death," he went through the ceremony; later when he confronted his new wife, she explained that her "friends" had forced the issue. He told the legislature that he had never lived with Nancy and wanted a divorce. He also rallied his allies. Two weeks before the assembly received his petition in Richmond, almost seventy of his supporters in the central Piedmont agreed that the marriage had been "a fraud and imposition" upon William. A smaller group signed a second affidavit asserting his "Unimpeachable Character."[60]

Nancy Dinwiddie's counterpetition, however, presented a sharply different picture of their relationship. According to her narrative, a two-year courtship had resulted in a formal engagement in 1818, but they delayed their wedding for two more years before William finally announced that it would take place in "a few weeks at most." At that point she "yielded to the seducing arts of her intended husband, and proved pregnant." Her uncle's family, with whom she was living, took a dim view of her unwed condition. But William continued to be attentive, and the day after the baby was born, he acknowledged the child as his own and married Nancy voluntarily. He then wrote to "his friends" expressing his pleasure in the marriage. Within two months, however, he became "indifferent" toward wife and child and soon separated from them. Nancy asked the assembly to reject the petition of "a perfideous and unfeeling husband."[61] Although no one else wrote or signed a petition on Nancy's behalf, the lawmakers took her side against the male subscribers to William's cause. In all likelihood the wedding had possessed a certain coercive quality, but six years had elapsed before the groom had seen fit to complain. What he had been doing in the interim was anybody's guess.

Despite the setting of male dominance or perhaps to preserve the values it enshrined, a community's moral sense limited a husband's domestic authority over wife and children. Neighbors became particularly active in cases of extreme spousal abuse when a woman needed physical protection from a violent husband and no male relatives were on hand to intervene. For example, Pamelia Cole's father was deceased, so local male leaders became involved in a concerted effort, first, to prevent her from being murdered and, later, to gain her a divorce. From a "respectable family" in Chesterfield County across the James River from Richmond, Pamelia Wooldridge had married John Cole in 1814. He turned out to be a severe alcoholic who regularly assaulted his wife, and in many respects she appeared as a classic example of a battered spouse. Boarders in the Cole home early in the couple's married life later recalled John's drunken threats against his wife and the screams that emanated from their bedroom at night. On numerous occasions John threw Pamelia bodily out of their home. As the brutality escalated, several neighbors intervened. Robert Wilkinson once locked Pamelia in his house to protect her from John. A close neighbor, Elam Cheatham, later remembered that one night when he was about to go to bed, he "heard Mrs. Cole screaming and her little daughter crying out that her Father was killing her Mother." Cheatham ran next door and discovered Pamelia "prostrate on the floor" with her husband "kicking her." Cheatham stopped the assault.[62]

The violence reached new heights on an evening in 1820. James Gates, one of the more prosperous farmers in the community, was traveling down the road when he spied John brandishing a huge knife and chasing his wife "with her clothes very much torn." She had two of her babies with her, and John was swearing "he would kill her." Gates intervened and "asked what he meant to do and demanded the knife." The two men exchanged words, and Gates grabbed John's arm, "triped his feet from under him and took the knife." Meanwhile Pamelia fled into Cheatham's home and quickly climbed into the loft. Cheatham sent to Edward Bass's ordinary for help, and Bass and several others rode to Cheatham's home. The men found John "somewhat intoxicated" in his house and Pamelia afraid to leave Cheatham's loft. They finally coaxed her down, and a couple of the men stayed all night to protect her. The next day she and her children moved to Bass's house for a while. John appeared there one day with a huge stick and demanded to see his wife. She was reluctant and finally agreed only when Bass told her that he would prevent her husband from doing anything violent. When John became "Very angry," Bass ended the interview and forced him to leave.[63]

In 1821 Pamelia applied for a court order restraining her husband only to have him soon violate its terms. She moved into her brother's house and in 1824 petitioned for a divorce. By this time John had become a penniless "vagabond" roaming the countryside in rags "full of vermin" and "Begging something to drink."[64] Nineteen men, most of whom were prosperous farmers and slaveholders and who included in their ranks the local sheriff, a justice of the peace, a doctor, and two tavern keepers, testified to Pamelia's excellent character and John's wretched behavior. Clearly they had acted together, because as Philip Turpin, one of the wealthiest men in the neighborhood, pointed out, "Mrs. Cole's Relations and Friends take a most lively Interest in her Welfare, and are extremely anxious she should be divorced." James Gates stated the community consensus that a divorce would be an "act of justice." The assembly granted an *a mensa* divorce that "forever abolished" John Cole's "rights and authority . . . over the person and property of . . . Pamelia and her children."[65]

In Pamelia Cole's situation male neighbors and community leaders first tried to persuade John Cole to treat his wife and family better; then they restrained him from acts of brutality and, finally, offered Pamelia and her children physical protection and shelter. Later they were prime movers in helping her to obtain a divorce. This same pattern of community intervention was repeated again and again in cases of spousal abuse throughout the antebellum decades. The support of close neighbors also proved critical when mental illness threatened a family's safety. When, for example, Moses Dixon seemed mentally deranged at times due to excessive drinking and verbally threatened to kill his wife and children, his friends moved into his house to safeguard the family.[66]

At times community support could be overwhelming. In Lynchburg, for example, after Samuel Rose Irvine's wife left him and eventually became a prostitute, 344 people signed a petition to support his divorce so "that his family may be released from such a disgusting connection."[67] The lawmakers in Richmond turned Irvine down. But while the assembly held the line against divorce in the name of the common good and the damage it would inflict on marriages and families, neighborhoods and local communities regularly privileged the injured spouse. Persons closest to the scene of injustice could most easily recognize themselves in the victim's stead. Thus as the center upheld the republican ideal, the margins pushed the cause of individual freedom and autonomy. The contest between civic republicanism and individualism as localism repeated itself in case after case of divorce.

Susan Bell's situation presented a particularly dramatic instance of a community's endorsement of justice for an individual and her right to happiness in the married state. Susan's husband, a Baptist minister, had deserted her and his church flock in Sussex County in 1827. On the pretext of taking a short business trip, he had borrowed a horse from her father, but neither horse nor rider had since been seen. Five years later he wrote from St. Louis, inquiring about the kind of reception he might receive should he decide to return. More than 200 people who claimed to have known Susan from her infancy signed a petition supporting her request for a divorce. Some may well have been part of the congregation that the preacher had deserted along with his wife. "*We know* her worth," they told the assembly. "She deserved a more prosperous, and happy fate." They testified further to the overwhelming support she received not only from the jury when the facts of the case were tried but also from the judge and everyone present. From their perspective, "to grant her a divorce, . . . will not only be an act of sheer *justice* in itself but will be gratifying to every person in Sussex County who has ever seen, or even heard, of this unfortunate marriage."[68]

Not every community expressed such unanimity. Neighbors could also muddy the waters with conflicting testimony. Anna Roane Woolfolk seemed at the mercy of her husband until several old friends intervened to help her obtain a divorce. The daughter of Spencer Roane, one of Virginia's premier judges in the early national period, Anna was about fifty years old and living comfortably on her inherited plantation in Hanover County when she married her overseer, Bentley Woolfolk, in April 1849. Unfortunately Anna apparently inherited a Roane family tendency toward eccentricity that sometimes shaded into mental illness. A doctor friend who lived nearby and knew her well testified in 1851 that she was "of unsound, and insane mind, and incapable of entering into the marriage contract." Two days after the wedding, complaining of Bentley's brutality toward her and his public professions of love for Lucy, a slave girl, Anna left her home and sought refuge with nearby friends. By June she was petitioning Judge John B. Clopton of the county's Circuit Superior Court of Law and Chancery for an absolute divorce on grounds of adultery. She also wanted her property back. But her husband occupied the plantation, said he wanted her to come home, and published a notice that he would not pay her debts.[69]

As September began, Bentley responded to Anna's suit. He had obviously hired a good lawyer. Vigorously proclaiming his innocence, his answer pointed out that the wedding festivities had lasted several days in a house full of people. Thus he could hardly have committed the crimes she charged. Instead he blamed Anna's sudden departure on his "unwillingness to make a post nuptial settlement" that others for their own mercenary purposes had urged. Having disposed of the particulars of the case against him, Bentley turned to the Bible. He reminded the court of the indissolubility of marriage and "its foundation deep in the first principles of our nature." Most important, "the policy of our law in common with the jurisprudence of every christian state, recognizes and enforces as the great bond of our social system, the scripture truth, 'what God hath joined together let not man put asunder.'" He wanted Anna home "to realize those fond anticipations of domestic happiness, that prompted their union, in the sacred bonds of matrimony."[70] His response sounded reasonable.

The depositions did not help Anna's case. Through the fall and again in February, lawyers for Anna and Bentley deposed thirteen neighbors in the presence of justices at various sites in Hanover County. The questions revolved around Anna's sanity, Bentley's fondness for booze and Lucy, and the quality of the corn crop on the plantation. The overseer had lived in Anna's house for two or three years prior to the marriage and apparently worked the farm well. After Anna's departure, he had let his work slide, sold the horse, and enjoyed life with his sister, his niece, and Lucy. A deputy sheriff had sold the movable property to pay Anna's debts. But much of the testimony about the overseer was hearsay evidence and hence inadmissible. As the case dragged on in court, Bentley felt "Triumphantly Vindicated" from Anna's "foul aspersions."[71]

A legislative divorce remained her only alternative. Through James and William Taylor, her "next friends," she petitioned for a divorce in January 1851, repeating in more lurid detail the charges against Bentley she had first made to Judge Clopton. Bentley counterpetitioned the next month, objecting to the divorce and accusing "certain designing men" of luring his wife away. He no doubt had the Taylors in mind. He also complained that he had known nothing of Anna's petition or the deposition of two witnesses in January 1851 until someone wrote him from the capital that a divorce bill had been reported out of the House committee. He wanted the bill recommitted until he could gather evidence and defend himself. There matters stood as Anna's attorneys notified her husband that they would gather fresh affidavits. The legislative divorce might well have failed, but the revelation that he had been arrested in another county for theft and then escaped from jail after setting fire to it confirmed any questions about Bentley's character. If he was ever caught, his crimes merited a lengthy confinement in the penitentiary, a situation the legislature had recently approved as grounds for absolute divorce. The assembly ended Anna and Bentley's marriage in March 1851, the last month the Virginia legislature granted divorces.[72]

THE LAW OF ARTIFICIAL INCEST

The capacity for community involvement, the desire for local control, and the closeness of extended family ties are all exemplified by the way Virginians responded to cases of incest as defined by statute. All states forbade certain marriages on the basis of consanguinity, a blood relationship such as that between a parent and a child or a brother and a sister. In contrast to New England, however, all southern states except Georgia allowed marriage between persons as closely related as first cousins. In addition many states passed laws that defined certain marriages as incestuous because of affinity, a relationship created by the previous marriage of one of the parties. In this respect the Old Dominion ranked among the more restrictive states in the South. Following the English precedent set in concrete by Henry VIII's divorce of Catherine of Aragon, his deceased brother's widow, Virginia law forbade a person to marry the sister or brother of a deceased spouse or the widow of an uncle or nephew. The marriage act of 1792 provided that the state attorney general could indict such couples in the High Court of Chancery. The court could declare the marriage null, fine the couple, and order them to separate and post bond with securities for its payment should they violate the court's decision.[73] Despite this law, such marriages occurred, and families and local communities quietly accepted and sometime even endorsed them.

In the second decade of the nineteenth century, however, the marriage of a prominent Tidewater clergyman to his sister-in-law created consternation within the elites of both church and state. The youngest of twelve children of a devout Anglican father, Andrew Broaddus had disappointed his parent by his conversion and ordination as a Baptist minister. He distressed his religious confreres even more when he wed his deceased wife's sister. She was actually his third wife. He had first married Fanny Temple, who lived in Caroline County, where Andrew cared for various Baptist communities as well as the Baptist church in nearby Fredericksburg. When Fanny died after the birth of their fifth child, he wed Lucy Honeyman. This marriage produced no children and ended with Lucy's death. Then, for his third wife, Andrew took Lucy's sister, Jane, who was also the widow of his nephew. Contracted in December 1815, this marriage resulted in three children and a major scandal.

Andrew Broaddus knew that he violated church sentiment as well as state law. Even before the Revolution, Virginia's Baptist leaders had disapproved of marriage between a man and his deceased wife's sister. Later, when a Baptist woman married her brother-in-law after her husband's death, a regional associational meeting in 1792 decided she should be left alone, but the ministers refused to "commend" her second marriage. The Baptist clergy in Andrew's own Dover Association had gone on record twice in opposition to such marriages. In an association letter of 1808, after noting the objections of some members to Virginia's prohibition of such marriages as "incestuous," the preachers had argued in support of the law and urged their churches that "at least for the sake of example, we ought to obey our mild and moderate institutions." They repeated that advice in 1813.[74] Presbyterians agreed. Some had evaded the law by being wed in Maryland, but ministers and church members frowned on such subterfuges.[75] Just the month before Andrew Broaddus married his sister-in-law, a couple in Norfolk had publicly agreed "to separate and live apart" because the church regarded their marriage as "unlawful."[76]

Andrew was one of the most eloquent and best-known preachers in Virginia, and his defiance of the marriage law created a popular stir that could not be ignored, particularly after he and his new wife went to Washington, D.C., in March 1816 and got remarried. As the Fredericksburg press account pointed out, "The connection, which has made so much noise in Virginia, is now completely legalized, according to the law of Maryland, and that part of the District of Columbia which formerly belonged to Maryland." In 1817 an obviously mortified Dover Association published a long circular letter on Christian marriage that insisted that a "professor of our Holy Religion" ought to obey the law. Andrew had evidently claimed the right to seek happiness and follow the demands of his heart, but he failed to convince his Baptist colleagues. Sinful human beings needed restraint, they argued, precisely for the sake of "safety and happiness." A prominent Presbyterian minister chimed in with two articles that argued that such marriages not only violated God's law but were immoral because they violated "an express law of the land."[77]

The state concurred. Virginia's attorney general, Philip Norborne Nicholas, prosecuted Andrew and Jane Broaddus in the Richmond District Superior Court of Chancery for violating the marriage act. But two distinguished attorneys, William Wirt and Benjamin Watkins Leigh, argued on behalf of the minister and his wife that the 1792 law was unconstitutional because it violated Virginia's Declaration of Rights, which guaranteed trial by jury in criminal cases. The section of the marriage law dealing with incestuous marriages was a "penal statute authorizing a criminal prosecution," but it gave jurisdiction to the chancery court, which was an equity court for civil rather than criminal proceedings. When the judge agreed with the defense, Nicholas took the case to the Supreme Court of Appeals. Speaking for the bench, Spencer Roane agreed with the lower court and dismissed the appeal.[78]

Despite this verdict, however, Roane publicly decried the Broaddus marriage as "highly" offensive to "the laws and public morals of the country." By laws, he meant English precedent; by country, he meant Virginia. Roane believed in a vigorous, independent judiciary. He could hardly turn down the opportunity to lecture the legislature from the bench. This "crime," Roane noted, was "a growing one" in the Old Dominion, and he encouraged the assembly to take steps "for preventing and suppressing it in future."[79] The lawmakers leaped at his suggestion. Within a few days after the Supreme Court of Appeals decision became public in February 1818, they amended the marriage law to provide for a grand jury indictment and changed the venue from a chancery to a criminal court, "the superior court of law in which the offenders may reside," which could nullify the marriage, decree a separation of the couple, and impose a fine. In a further slap at Broaddus, the lawmakers added still another category to the legal incest list: the marriage of a man and his deceased nephew's wife.[80]

Reaction to the verdict and the newly amended marriage law came swiftly. After a local grand jury presented them in court in 1818, John Moore and Jesse Parker, from the Southside's Southampton County, submitted virtually identical petitions to the assembly asking for relief. Both men had married sisters of their deceased spouses in 1817, before the assembly had amended the law, and thus at a time when, according to the verdict in the Broaddus case, no law existed under which they could be separated. Their petitions claimed that, although similar marriages had frequently occurred since the passage of the law of 1792, not a single case had ever been prosecuted. Nor did such a marriage, they argued, violate "the natural, divine or moral law." Most important, Moore and Parker complained that the amended marriage act of 1818 was an "ex post facto law" and hence "unconstitutional," because it criminalized couples who had married before its passage. Grand juries agreed, they noted, and were refusing to cooperate with the law even though there were numerous couples who could be indicted. Pleading their obligations to their wives and "the unfortunate and helpless offsprings . . . the tender pledges of their parents love," who were destined to be "torn by the unrelenting power of the law, from the bosom of [their] mother," the petitioners asked that the law be changed.[81]

Realizing the error of its hasty action the previous year, the legislature re-amended the act to end prosecutions of marriages that had taken place before the passage of the 1818 law. But the criticism did not stop. The grand jury of Northampton County on the Eastern Shore offered a blistering critique of the assembly's actions. Obliged by oath to uphold the law, the jury had presented two couples in court. One man had married a deceased uncle's widow; the other, the sister of a deceased wife. The jury used the occasion, however, to condemn not the couples but the law. Their text is noteworthy:

The grand jury in making the foregoing presentments have not been actuated by a desire to censure the conduct of the individuals who are the subjects of those presentment, because they can discern nothing in what they have done either vicious or immoral; but they are impelled to it by a sense of their obligation to support and enforce the laws of the land however impolitic or improper. They do therefore present the laws of the commonwealth of Virginia, so far as they will support the foregoing presentments, as highly oppressive and contrary to the principles of a free government. And the grand jury seize this opportunity of expressing to this honourable court and to the community at large their entire disapprobation of so much of the laws aforesaid as subjects these individuals to censure, and will take the liberty to say, that they cannot perceive any thing in [their] conduct . . . contrary to the laws of God or the principles of morality.

In his prologue to this published text, the foreman of the grand jury blamed the "private opinions" that Judge Roane had attached to his decision in the Broaddus case for unduly influencing the assembly to pass such "unjust, oppressive and impolitic" legislation. So much for state judicial supremacy.[82]

Four years later the Northampton grand jury fired off yet another salvo, attacking and urging the repeal of those sections of the law that criminalized the marriage of a man and his deceased wife's sister or deceased uncle's wife. The newly elected Northampton County delegate, Abel P. Upshur, quickly assumed the leadership of the repeal forces. Meanwhile other petitions from both married couples and county groups appeared in Richmond protesting the laws on incest.[83] Beginning in 1822 the assembly routinely entertained repeal bills only to defeat them. Reporting the House debates and the strenuous efforts of Upshur in the 1824 session, the *Richmond Enquirer* resurrected the case of Henry VIII and Catherine of Aragon and editorialized against the repeal efforts recently defeated by a vote of 87 to 108: "Ought not a man to consider his wife's sister as his own?" the writer asked. To allow marriages to evolve from such relationships would corrupt and deprave society.[84]

The press was not dealing in abstractions. A huge scandal involving just such a relationship had recently rocked the upper reaches of Virginia society and destroyed both a family's happiness and a promising career. Henry Lee, the eldest son of Revolutionary War hero Light Horse Harry Lee, had married Anne McCarty in the spring of 1817 and established his home at Stratford, the ancestral Lee plantation on the Potomac. An 1809 graduate of William and Mary, Henry had already served three terms in the Virginia assembly and commanded troops in the War of 1812. He seemed destined for a prominent role in Virginia's and even the nation's affairs. Nearby lived Anne's younger sister, Elizabeth. The two girls were orphans. Lonesome for her sister's company, Elizabeth arranged to move to Stratford and have Henry Lee serve as her guardian until she came of age. The threesome lived happily together, and in 1818 Anne gave birth to a daughter named Margaret. Two years later the child wandered out on the front porch, fell down a steep flight of stone steps, and died. The terribly distraught mother went into severe depression, secluded herself, and found escape in morphine. The bereaved father and aunt turned to each other for consolation, and Elizabeth became pregnant. The tragedy played itself out when Elizabeth returned to her stepfather's home and gave birth to a stillborn child. Years later she married Henry Storke and eventually returned to Stratford after her husband bought the plantation at auction.

Henry Lee, profoundly repentant for what he termed "the enormity of my sin," begged his wife's forgiveness. They eventually reconciled, but in the meantime he suffered severe financial reverses and lost Stratford to his creditors. Finding it impossible to secure a government position despite Andrew Jackson's friendship and patronage, a bitter Henry Lee turned to writing history. He and Anne were living as expatriates in Paris when he died in 1837 at age forty-nine.

A few years earlier he had expressed his thoughts about the nature of his "offence." He had not just engaged in adultery. He had violated his responsibilities as Elizabeth's guardian and committed what Virginia law criminalized as incest. Lee thought that the incest "diminished" the adultery. Ignoring English precedent, he reasoned that in an effort "to extend the sphere of fraternal affection in families," the state had tried to create a natural impediment where none actually existed. The result, Lee argued, was that in Virginia a man related to his wife's sister "with all the unguarded intimacy which he would observe toward his own sister," but without the instinctual "barrier" set up by a "blood connection." Thus he could more easily be "surprised into adultery."[85] One can only wonder what Judge Roane would have made of that argument.

Upshur probably had Lee's situation in mind when he renewed the struggle in the 1825 assembly session. Rather than protecting public morals, the law of "artificial incest," he argued, actually encouraged adultery, particularly within Virginia's gentry class. But if couples related as sister- and brother-in-law were allowed to marry, then "the usual reserves of discretion" would intervene. Some of his auditors thought his four-hour speech had won the debate.[86] The Northampton delegate had obviously prepared a solid case. But when Samuel Blackburn, one of the oratorical warhorses, led the charge against Upshur's "filthy bill," he regretted the "time, talent, and research, thrown away on a cause so unworthy." The conservative Blackburn, who had earlier proposed a general divorce law, based his argument on Virginia tradition and the potential dangers of introducing "novelty." Repealing "this salutary law," he said, would transform the lawmakers into "pimps for the *devil*." He further suggested that the only reason some delegates repeatedly pressed for repeal was because a few ministers, judges, and "would-be-great-men" had violated the law. Another legislator spoke long and learnedly against this assault on "the Levitical laws," much to the disgust of John Campbell, who thought the Hebrew scriptures did not belong in the debate. Regardless of what the Bible said, Campbell favored the law because it contributed to "the good order and well being of society." The next day the House rejected repeal by an even larger margin than the previous year's, 70 to 125. Henry Lee was undoubtedly correct when he wrote that "aversion to change" rather than "force of argument" had carried the day.[87]

The assembly had clearly set its face against repeal, so Upshur and his allies tried a new tack. They would modify the penalty and strike a blow for localism. Late in the same session they brought in a bill to reduce the crime involved in the marriage of a man and his deceased wife's sister to a "misdemeanor" punishable "by such fine and imprisonment" as a jury saw fit. The proposal also eliminated the provision requiring a separation of the couple and pardoned past offenders. As one delegate noted, in Pittsylvania County alone this meant freedom for ten couples and their children. In a spirit of liberality the bill sailed through the House by a vote of 106 to 59, only to be defeated in the Senate. The next year, however, it passed with a close House victory, 85 to 76, and an equally thin margin in the Senate, 11 to 8. However narrowly won, the result was yet another triumph for local self-determination. Each community could now establish its own standards. As one legislator remarked during debate, such marriages would occur only in counties that supported them. If enthusiastic magistrates or zealous commonwealth attorneys chose to prosecute, juries would levy only token fines.[88]

One immediate beneficiary was Augustine Leftwich from Bedford County. He had married Hulda Hackworth, his deceased wife's sister. In April 1822 a grand jury had presented him in court for violating the incest law. A desperate Augustine had begged the assembly to legalize his marriage, but the lawmakers refused. The next year a jury convicted him, and in 1824 he had again applied in vain to the legislature. Augustine then appealed the court verdict on the grounds that the court had separated him from his wife but that Hulda had never been prosecuted. In effect she had been convicted and punished without a jury trial. The case made its way to the Supreme Court of Appeals in the June term of 1827. Judge Roane had died in 1822. The eight-member bench, which included newly elected Judge Abel Upshur, unanimously agreed that the new law passed a few months earlier had repealed the old law without proving any penalties for those who had violated the previous one. Therefore Leftwich could not be punished.[89]

Virginia law, however, held no more consistency on the state than on the county or local level. A few years later, for example, the Supreme Court of Appeals let stand a lower court's separation decree in the case of a man who had married his deceased brother's wife, and occasionally the courts prosecuted other violators of the laws dealing with incestuous relationships.[90] As late as 1847 the assembly still refused to repeal the laws that criminalized a man's marriage to a sister-in-law or a "brother's widow," though a general revision of the laws two years later quietly dropped the prohibition against marriage to the sister of a deceased spouse.[91] Long before that date, however, local communities had made up their own minds. In the western part of the state, for example, in the 1830s several hundred church members who openly identified themselves as Baptists, Methodists, Presbyterians, and Lutherans signed a petition in support of a man who had married his sister-in-law and wanted to be exempted from the punishment for incestuous marriages. Baptist churches, in particular, proved notoriously independent in tolerating violations of the marriage law.[92]

The legal entanglements that arose because of Virginia's efforts to define and forbid certain marriages as incestuous demonstrate the same conclusions about southern life that can be drawn from the antebellum divorce cases. Considered together, the evidence is overwhelming that families, neighborhoods, and local communities retained ultimate control, even in the face of laws to the contrary, over marriage arrangements and social relationships in the Old South. What Richmond accepted or rejected was not nearly as important as the decisions reached in church fellowship or on county court days each month.

The directness and intimacy of face-to-face encounters with kinfolk and neighbors counted far more in establishing the rules and customs by which people lived than decisions made in a remote, anonymous state legislature. Most southerners lived in rural areas, not towns or even villages. Even county authorities could be too distant when crises suddenly arose. These people had to look out for themselves, their families, and neighbors over the next creek or across the fence line. In thousands of locales throughout the South they set their own public standards. Individuals or couples who defied a strong community consensus were probably well advised to move along. Cheap land was plentiful on the other side of the mountains, and social dissenters would be happier there.

II Causes

CHAPTER 4

The Greatest Lewdness

CROSSING THE COLOR LINE

Business was booming for Isaac Fouch in expanding Loudoun County in 1805. The millwright could afford to hire Jane Campbell, a white woman, to assist his wife in the house. Three years earlier, when he had wed Elizabeth Beach, the twenty-two-year-old groom had been completely smitten. Isaac later recalled that from the first time they met, he had been head over heels in love and that the "strictest Love, Friendship, and happiness" marked the initial idyllic years of their married life. But Isaac's skill in erecting the machinery for mills kept him away from home much of the time. Jane would not only ease Elizabeth's housework and keep her company; she might also keep track of visitors in Isaac's absence.

By the time Jane began working in the Fouchs' home, the young husband may already have suspected his wife's infidelity. Though Isaac did not confide in Jane during the five months he employed her, she observed that he often seemed troubled and frequently paced the floor. Elizabeth's behavior also struck her as odd. Despite Isaac's "kind and affectionate" treatment of his wife, whenever the millwright was away from home, James Watt visited Elizabeth. Jane heard the neighbors' gossip and noticed that James and Elizabeth often spent time together upstairs in the loft. Her suspicions aroused, she decided to play detective. Later she testified that when "Mrs. Fouch would send me to the Spring, and sometimes to milk the Cow, I would go to the end of the house and look through a hole and have seen them several times in the very Act." Jane thought the couple suspected that she had been watching them when the hole got plugged. Meanwhile Isaac finally confronted Elizabeth. Still desperately in love, he pointed out the scandalous path that her life had been taking in hope that she would reform. He later claimed that he had "repeatedly" reproved Elizabeth for her "Wickedness" and threatened to leave her if it continued. But instead of repenting, Elizabeth grew bolder. At last after twice catching her "in bed" with Watt, the irate husband moved out and petitioned the General Assembly for a divorce.[1]

What made Isaac Fouch's complaint noteworthy was the fact that while he and Elizabeth were white, James Watt was a "man of caulor." Adultery was serious, but when it involved white women and black men, the situation became explosive. In the slaveholding South, race was the taproot of a society that officially denied intimacy, especially sexual intimacy, between blacks and whites. Elizabeth Fouch had violated more than her marriage vows. At stake in her conduct was not only the image of the white woman as the repository of purity, virtue, and religion but the identity of a white male as a member of the master race. That an African American, whether slave or free, could compete successfully against a white man for the affection of a white woman challenged foundational values of white society. One way Virginia law asserted white male supremacy was by denying even the possibility that African Americans could be responsible parties in interracial liaisons. Presumably black men were incapable of initiating such relationships, so they were innocent parties. Thus the marriage statute of 1792 forbade white persons from marrying "negroes or mulattoes." Should an interracial couple marry, the county court could imprison the white lawbreaker for six months without bail and levy a fine of thirty dollars; no punishment or fine was prescribed, however, for the African American participant.[2]

Moreover, any clergyman who performed such a marriage was liable to a $250 fine. Despite their egalitarian stance in forming biracial congregations, the evangelical churches did not scruple at this restriction. For decades after the Revolution, southern Baptist churches commonly held black and white members, but they did not tolerate interracial relationships that began in the spirit and ended in the flesh. Shortly after the conclusion of the war and before the Virginia legislature codified the marriage laws, Baptist leaders in the Old Dominion advised their congregations that they were not to permit marriages between black and white members. Of course, this statement did not settle the issue for the independent-minded Baptists. Early in the nineteenth century a local church queried the Dover association: "In case a white man and black woman (slave) should live together as man and wife, are they fit subjects to be received into the church?" The answer was a resounding negative.

The ministers were not speculating on moral abstractions. A question from a church indicates that sex across the color line was a live issue.[3] It had been a reality almost from the beginning of the colonial period. Some argued that precisely through this means, slavery could be eradicated. During the Revolutionary era one Virginian told New Englander Timothy Pickering that the southern black population would eventually *"mingle their blood with the whites."*[4] This involved more than white men and black women. The image of the white slaveholder and his sons creeping around the slave cabins, forcing black women to become unwilling victims of their sexual aggression, is a familiar one in historical writing as well as folklore, film, and novels. The involvement of white women in liaisons and even marriages with black men is not so well known, in part because interracial sex involving white women has been largely ignored or minimized until recently.[5] Yet they formed permanent as well as transient relationships with African American men. This can be documented not just from occasional references in letters, travel narratives, or census records but from the divorce petitions of ordinary Virginians.

Patterns in these petitions challenge us to rethink historical generalizations and traditional stereotypes about gender roles, class values, and race relations in the slaveholding South. During the era of legislative divorce in Virginia, at least 53 petitions from 23 men and 19 women accused spouses of adultery across the color line. The assembly granted divorces to 16 men (70 percent) and 11 women (58 percent). Since the lawmakers only granted divorces to 33 percent of all applicants, both men and women, proof of interracial sex clearly helped male petitioners. Cases involving women petitioners prove more difficult to analyze because factors such as battery may have determined the assembly's vote.

In terms of class, the male petitioners reflected the mass of the white population. Their ranks included a storekeeper, a miller, and a shoemaker. Three men owned large farms of several hundred acres or more; one-third had smaller holdings, and another third owned no land at all. A few appear to have been related to well-to-do families in the counties in which they lived. At least a third owned from one to six slaves.

The class background of the white women who accused their husbands of adultery with black women was even more diverse. Three represented Virginia's elite families; the husband of one was a slave-trader, while another practiced medicine. But most spouses were middling farmers, and some had little or no land and no slaves. The overwhelming majority, whether they owned a few slaves or not, fit Stephanie McCurry's definition of yeoman farmers, men who "worked the land with their own hands."[6] Thus we can safely conclude that interracial sex occurred among white men and women of all classes, not just a neighborhood's poor whites.

More important, apart from those poor whites on the bottom of the socioeconomic heap, class divisions ended at this issue. The petitions from white males, even those who owned little or no land, reflect a sameness about their expectations of white women's behavior. If their texts accurately reflect values, not just elite white women occupied the pedestal. White men of laboring, trade, and yeoman farming classes also thought their wives should be chaste and modest. Certainly they expressed those expectations to the white male elite who sat in judgment on their divorce petitions. Some years ago Edmund Morgan argued that slavery created a common identity among white men. Whiteness, in effect, leveled the playing field.[7] That principle held true at the political center, but less so on the margins. By responding positively to divorce on the grounds of female adultery across the color line when they rejected almost every other argument for marital dissolution, the lawmakers privileged racial solidarity among white males and ignored class differences. White women shared a common racial identity as well and often expressed a sense of being degraded by their husbands' sexual liaisons with black women. But the legislature responded quite differently to their petitions.

This chapter will first examine the complaints from white men, then those from white women. Finally, we need to consider, as far as the evidence allows, the position of persons on the other side of the racial divide.

CONSTRUCTING THE HUSBAND'S CASE

As the nineteenth century opened, white women who engaged in interracial sex posed a significant threat to a society increasingly concerned about the growth of the free black community. It was bad enough that lack of sexual restraint by white males increased the black population. At least the offspring of slave mothers added to the labor force and remained enslaved. In a break with the common-law tradition, the status of the child followed that of the mother. The reproductive systems of slave women increased the slave population whether the paternity be black or white. But the children of free women were free also, regardless of the father's status.[8] Thus Elizabeth Fouch and other white women involved in sexual relations across the color line threatened to en-large the free black population just when the state was moving to restrict manumission and the drive to export free blacks was gathering steam. The revelation of Gabriel's plan to launch a slave rebellion in 1800 sent shivers down the spines of white Virginians and led to a great outcry to tighten the laws designed to control the activities of both slaves and free blacks. The uproar increased in 1802 when authorities claimed to have uncovered more plots. Even vigorous opponents of the "infernal System of Slavery" urged the removal of the free black and mulatto population, a proposal that would give birth to the American Colonization Society in the next decade.[9]

Amid this controversy over the increasing numbers of free blacks in Virginia, the lawmakers suddenly reversed their stubborn opposition to divorce. After a decade of denying divorces for all reasons, they began granting them to husbands who could prove that their wives had en-gaged in sexual relations with black men. They allowed Dabney Pettus to divorce his wife on this basis in January 1803 after having rejected his petition the previous session. Undoubtedly they knew that the Maryland assembly had approved several absolute divorces in similar cases. During the next six years before Fouch's complaint, the assembly approved three more absolute divorces on the same grounds. All fulfilled certain require-ments. When Isaac Fouch requested a divorce, it was important, first, to prove that James Watt was black. Sworn affidavits stated that he was the son of Mary Watt, a "woman of colour," and that while Mary's mother had been white, her father had been black. Even if James Watt's father, whoever he was, had been a white man, having one black grandparent classified Watt as an African American in Virginia law. But two other facts were crucial for Isaac's case: Elizabeth's adultery and Isaac's good treatment of her. Jane Campbell was the star witness on these points, and seven subscribers to her affidavit attested to her honesty. The committee considered all these elements before recommending that Isaac receive a divorce. His bill passed easily.[10]

From then until the 1840s, when divorce restrictions eased, proof of a wife's sexual liaison with an African American, whether slave or free, be-came the most successful grounds, along with fraud, for husbands seek-ing a divorce. Sixteen of the twenty-three male petitioners who alleged this activity received divorces, usually on their first attempt. No doubt guided by lawyers, the men carefully constructed a self-identity designed to appeal to their male counterparts in the assembly. Their petitions usually followed a pattern, and this pattern, plus the wording of the bills granting divorces, reveals not only the prevailing attitudes of white Virginians toward interracial sexual relations between white women and black men but also the requirements the legislature set for divorces.

Of critical importance was the husband's belief before the marriage that his prospective bride was a woman of chaste virtue. Isaac Fouch was typical when he stated at the outset that he had married Elizabeth Beach because he thought her a woman "of fair Character and unsullied Reputation." Other petitions followed suit. According to Dabney Pettus, Elizabeth Morris had "an unspoiled Character." Several neighbors of James Burch testified that his daughter Rebecca had always appeared to be "a proper and Reputable" woman, and they thought William Bayliss had "married her supposing her to be a Virgin" and "a virtuous woman." Benjamin Butt swore that his motives in marrying Lydia Bailey had been "affectionate, pure, and honorable" and that he had trusted in her "Chastity and Virtue." Daniel Rose thought that his wife, Henrietta, was "worthy of his affections" and expected that marriage would bring "that happiness which awaits a virtuous connection." Sometimes the husband's expectations of his wife's virtue rested on her family's reputation. Dabney Pettus described his prospective bride as "descended from honest industrious parents." Richard Hall claimed that his wife, Sarah Paul, was "of respectable parentage" and held "a respectable standing in society" when he married her.[11]

The assembly was also concerned about the reputation of the husband and the way he had treated his wife during their marriage. More than sixty neighbors helped Daniel Rose's case when they vouched for him as "a young man of good character." Sometimes husbands contrasted their mental state after they had discovered their wives' infidelity with their previous joys they experienced as married men. Within such narratives they frequently sought to justify their own performances as husbands in companionate terms. Their self-descriptions are not those of patriarchs. Dabney Pettus, for example, described his first months of marriage as marked by "all the affection and tenderness that could possibly exist between husband and wife." Ayres Tatham, self-identified as "a plain labouring man seeking his subsistence by honest industry," claimed that throughout a dozen years of married life he had "cherished" Tabitha as his wife. Joseph Gresham swore that he had "rigidly, and faithfully" performed a husband's responsibilities. In fact, he considered himself "liberal in supplying all the *wants* of his wife" and behaved in a "peaceable, kind, and affectionate" manner. Sarah Gresham's evil behavior had not been "induced, by *want, severity* or unkindness" on his part, he asserted. Hezekiah Mosby may have been illiterate, but he told the assembly that he knew the "correct moral conduct" expected in marriage.[12] The birth of a mulatto child usually provided the centerpiece of the husband's case for a divorce, proof positive that a wife had engaged in sexual relations across the color line. Often the child was born within a few months after the marriage, as for example, in the case of Henrietta Rose, who married in February and gave birth in September. Midwives' testimonies proved helpful because accusations had to be certified, not simply asserted. Elizabeth Merryman attended the birth of Elizabeth Pettus's child and told the legislature that immediately after the birth, she had asked Dabney's wife "how she came to do so." Hezekiah Mosby was suspicious that his wife, Betsy, had "bestowed her favors on men of a different colour than herself" and thought that she might destroy the child at birth. When Betsy went into labor, he sent for some "highly respectable ladies . . . that they might see and judge" whether or not the child was white "before any accident could happen to it."[13]

Although the mulatto child was normally conceived before the marriage, in some cases the couple had been married for several years and even had other children. Ayres and Tabitha Tatham had lived together harmoniously for almost twelve years and had three children when she gave birth to "the issue of an illicit intercourse with a black man." John Cook had been married for quite a while when his wife produced "two Molatoe Children" in 1810. David Parker had enjoyed a fruitful first marriage with six children and almost ten years of "uninterrupted connubial pleasure and happiness." But after his wife's death, he had unfortunately gotten remarried to a woman who grossly embarrassed both him and his children. The identities these men constructed for their wives are significant. "Degraded" was a favorite adjective for the fallen spouse. In Parker's case he charged his second wife with "acts of the greatest lewdness, immorality and vice" by her frequent "criminal intercourse with slaves or persons of color." Richard Jones wrote that his wife had deserted "every principle of virtue and chastity which ought to govern the conduct of a woman and a wife."[14]

Sometimes the petitions named the paramour, and frequently he was a slave in the neighborhood, even one owned by another member of the petitioner's family. He might also be, as in the Fouch case, a free black or mulatto who lived nearby. The notoriety a mulatto birth occasioned in the local community was frequently mentioned as an added reason for a husband's embarrassment. Petitions argued that the public scandal doomed the marriage. For William Bayliss it was a matter of "that happiness and self respect, which every rational being *has a right to seek.*" Not to ask for a divorce, he informed the legislature, would be "a lame and shameful submission on his part to a personal degradation scarcely before equalled in the annals of domestic life." As might be expected, race figured prominently in the shock these petitions expressed. Virtually all the husbands emphasized their horror at the discovery of their wives' conduct. For Benjamin Butt the birth of a mulatto child produced "inexpressible Grief and astonishment," and from that moment he felt "totally alienated" from his wife. Daniel Rose experienced such "heart-rending mortification" that he left it to others to describe. The fact that his wife continued in her adultery made them "feel for his situation." Leonard Owens described it as a "horrid violation of the marriage bed."[15]

Almost invariably the cuckolded husband is depicted as so repulsed by his wife's infidelity that he ended the marital relationship as soon as her fall from grace was discovered. At least in part, he had to do so in order to maintain his honor and position in society. But the legal dimension was more crucial. The legislature was on guard for the slightest hint of condonation on the part of a husband. The petition and accompanying affidavits could not suggest that he had known of the adulterous relationship and forgiven it. To do so meant rejection. So the men waxed eloquent. Isaac Fouch expressed his outrage by his typical resolve "never more to have any further connection with a Woman, who had so basely degraded herself and dishonoured a Husband, whose Misfortune it was to have been attached to her." Although it took a while for Richard Jones to realize that the child was not his, eventually "the darkness of its colour and its unusual appearance" convinced both him and the whole neighborhood that the baby girl was not white. Peggy Jones confessed her crime, and Richard told the assembly that marriage in this situation was "impossible to continue with her on those terms of harmony and affection which ought to subsist between those united by such intimate ties."[16]

The husband's subsequent conduct measured the degree of alienation that had taken place. It also verified his own good character. One witness testified that Leonard Owens had lived with him and had not "cohabitated" with Nancy Owens from the time she gave birth to a mulatto child and that Leonard "hath behaved himself orderly." A jury certified Bryant Rawls to be "not a man of loose and dissolute habits." Seldom were husbands willing, as Isaac Fouch had been, to try to recall their wives to fidelity before it was too late. And in most cases the legislature refused divorces to men who forgave their wives. William Howard petitioned three sessions of the legislature and submitted affidavits to bolster the charge in his second petition that he had caught his wife "in Bed with . . . a man of coular" and "an immediate separation" had taken place. But he changed his story between petitions. In his first attempt he did not mention any interracial sexual activity but simply accused his wife, Betsy, of leaving him despite his forgiveness of her "habits of adultery." He eventually learned how to prepare the proper case, but it was too late. The assembly rejected his pleas.[17]

THE WIVES RESPOND

The women's reactions to their husbands' accusations varied enormously. In a few cases, such as Elizabeth Pettus's, they confessed what they had done, blamed their African American paramour, and hoped for forgiveness. Elizabeth claimed that Bob, one of her grandfather's slaves, had threatened to break up her proposed marriage to Dabney "if she did not conform to his humours." Lydia Butt acknowledged that her conduct was reprehensible but asked her father-in-law to intercede on her behalf, telling him a slave named "Robin had overcome her by saying that he wou'd Conger her to get Benjamin Butt Junr. to be her Husband." David Parker thought that his wife's "sense of shame and a consciousness of guilt" drove her to remove with her black child to North Carolina. But sometimes the wife renounced the mulatto baby. Elizabeth Pettus, for example, wanted to give her infant to another woman to raise.[18]

Frequently the wife consented to a formal separation before a justice of the peace before the husband asked the legislature for a divorce. This data then became part of the petition. After she realized that a reconciliation was impossible, Elizabeth Pettus signed a statement that since "we shall never more live together as Man and Wife," Dabney was "no longer my husband" and was free to marry "any other Woman Without molestation of myself." She abdicated all legal claims as his wife. Benjamin Butt considered his marriage ended "in the Sight of God and Man" and claimed that he was "justly absolved from every Matrimonial engagement." He and Lydia signed a notarized agreement "never to come together" for either "assistance" or "mintainance" for the rest of their lives. Ayres and Tabitha Tatham formally agreed "never more to be man and wife" after a division of property in which she received her dower of "one third of his Personal Estate." The couple sold their ninety-acre farm on the Eastern Shore but reserved part of the land as a residence for Tabitha. After a few months, however, according to Ayres's version of events, "shame and confusion" forced her to leave Virginia and move to Philadelphia with her mulatto child. A year later the new owner sold the land back to Ayres.[19]

Other wives were defiant and, like Elizabeth Fouch, Henrietta Rose, Sarah Hall, Rebecca Bayliss, and Betsy Mosby, apparently cared little for society's opinion. They present an image of southern womanhood at striking variance with the prescription literature as well as some historians' views. An affidavit for the Mosby divorce reported Betsy as saying "that she saw no more harm in a white woman's having a black child than in a white man's having one though the latter was more frequent." And it must have set Fairfax County tongues wagging when the "notoriously infamous" Rebecca Bayliss moved in with her lover, Wilfred Mortimer, and had another baby. Sarah Hall had her first mulatto child six or seven months after Richard Hall married her in 1829. He had not been near her since then, but by the time he finally petitioned for a divorce almost ten years later, she had borne two other "coloured" children.[20]

After Isaac Fouch left the house, Elizabeth told Jane, the white servant girl, that she doubted he would return. Jane had not witnessed the final scene between Elizabeth and Isaac, but the husband and wife had talked a bit before he went off. Although Elizabeth asked Jane "if I did not pity her," she acted "very cheerful and easy on the occasion." Soon afterward someone arrived to pick up Isaac's belongings. Elizabeth then loaded up a wagon and departed toward the west "with much apparent satisfaction"; James Watt trailed behind her. Jane heard later that a constable had caught up with the couple near Leesburg and had taken some of Isaac's property from them.[21]

Not every woman quit without a fight, however, and several challenged their husbands in court. The 1827 law required a jury to find the facts of the case before submitting a petition to the assembly. Joseph and Sarah Gresham had been married for eleven years when on 14 November 1832 Joseph filed his written intention to divorce Sarah in the Circuit Superior Court of Law and Chancery for James City County. Following procedure, the judge instructed the sheriff to order Sarah to appear and answer the charges in the December court or pay a fine of £100. The next day the sheriff swore an oath at the clerk's office that he had personally delivered the summons to Sarah. She was not prepared, however, when the case came to trial in April, so it was postponed at her expense. Finally, on 25 October 1833, Sarah, Joseph, and their attorneys appeared at the Williamsburg Court House. A jury of twelve men, drawn from the town as well as the surrounding county, was selected, and the trial opened.

The bystanders got a good show. According to the record, "numerous witnesses" verified Joseph's lurid accusations that Sarah had committed adultery with "a man of colour" and bore a "mulatto child" in September 1831. But Sarah did not let Joseph's statement go unanswered. She did not contest his charges but filed a "bill of exceptions." Joseph had claimed in his sweeping statement that he liberally supplied every one of his wife's "*wants.*" Sarah demurred. She promised that, if permitted to cross-examine one of her husband's witnesses, she could prove that when they were married, Joseph had been incapable of fulfilling his "marital duties, of sexual intercourse." If this were true, then by the law of 1827 the court could immediately grant her an absolute divorce on grounds of impotence at the time of marriage. Joseph would need no petition to the legislature; the marriage could end now. One can only imagine his face as he confronted his wife before his friends and neighbors. The humiliated and probably enraged man countered that his "incompetence" was not at issue in the proceedings. The judge agreed. But Sarah objected to this ruling and formally asked that her bill "be signed and sealed by the Court." This guaranteed that the clerk would include her accusation against Joseph in the trial record and send it to Richmond for the perusal of the lawmakers. The assembly awarded Joseph a divorce. But Sarah had left some bruises.[22]

Thomas Culpeper's day in court was even more difficult. In his list of accusations, Thomas stated that his wife, Caroline, had left him six or seven months after their marriage in 1831 and, over the next four years, committed adultery numerous times. Most damning, she "repeatedly associated with negroes and . . . had carnal intercourse with black men or negroes." Her conduct had therefore made her "infamous and bankrupt in reputation, and unworthy of associating with the decent and respectable in the community." Ultimately Thomas wanted his divorce on the grounds that Caroline had become a prostitute and adulteress. Caroline, however, struck back. She claimed that she had never been legally married to Culpeper and that his charges were "false[,] scandalous and defamatory." If the court permitted her, she was ready to prove, among other things, that Thomas had seduced her prior to their "supposed marriage" and that he now lived "in a state of illicit intercourse" with another woman. The court, however, was not interested in Caroline's charges because the 1827 law merely asked the jury "to ascertain the facts" of the plaintiff's accusation. Ultimately it agreed that the marriage had taken place and that Caroline had lived "a most abandoned life." But although the verdict stated that she had committed adultery with various "white" men, it said nothing about sexual relations with blacks or mulattos. Culpeper lost his case in Richmond. Adultery and desertion were insufficient grounds for absolute divorce in the 1830s.[23]

The court record names Carter Moore Braxton as Caroline Culpeper's attorney. He managed the case and spoke on her behalf. Grandson of Carter Braxton, a Virginia signer of the Declaration of Independence, the forty-year-old lawyer was known as "an elegant gentlemen" in Norfolk County. A Virginia blueblood, Braxton would seem, at first blush, out of place representing a woman who had clearly fallen off her pedestal. Yet the petition files show that divorce cases, even from the lowest ranks in society, drew outstanding members of the bar. Because the law was an enormously popular career in Virginia through the first half of the nineteenth century, making a decent living as a lawyer proved challenging even to the best barristers. In 1803, his first year of practice, Henry St. George Tucker wrote regularly to his father in Williamsburg to report his income and caseload. He found the competition intense from the overabundance of attorneys in Frederick and neighboring counties. Seven years later he had to support his family by farming in addition to his legal practice. By 1820 he pointed out that Frederick County had twenty resident lawyers plus "Foreign lawyers" from other counties who showed up on court days in hopes of getting some business. A successful career at the bar required more than a solid knowledge of the law. An attorney also needed forensic eloquence, influential friends, and a network of local supporters. Even then, after more than fifteen years of practice in Winchester, Tucker spent most of his time in the higher courts. Much as he loved his profession, he told his father, a reliance on the county court business would not "make salt to my bread."[24]

The law set the fees and regulated legal practice in Virginia courts well into the nineteenth century. Lawyers who practiced before the General Court could charge the most for their services. The revised code of 1819 specified that legal advice for litigants there was worth $3.58. If the case went to trial, the fee jumped to $8.33, and if the conflict involved land ownership or boundaries, that bill doubled. Property law was always more complicated. At the opposite end of the legal spectrum, lawyers at the county courts earned $1.66 for advice (in helping, perhaps, draw up a divorce petition), $2.50 for a common lawsuit, and twice that if it involved land. Braxton's fee for his services to Caroline Culpeper in a Superior Court suit was $2.50. Because remuneration was independent of the financial worth of the parties, it is not surprising that a lawyer took whatever cases walked into his office. The law had teeth. Attorneys charging more than the prescribed fee could be fined $150, half of which went to the state's public education fund and "the other half to the informer."[25]

Braxton had earned his fee by demolishing the crucial section of Thomas Culpeper's case about sex across the color line. Lewis Bourne's efforts to shed his consort met a similar fate. His case is instructive on several counts. First, it demonstrates the difficulty a contested divorce could face even when the evidence against a spouse seemed overwhelming. Second, the neighborhood's involvement shows how such divorce cases could engage the local community. The Bournes obviously provided a delicious scandal for rural Louisa County as dozens of people scurried off to magistrates to relate stories of adultery and interracial sex or to testify to Lewis's good character. Most important, however, the Bourne case illustrates the legal status and property rights of married women.

When he married Doratha Woodall about 1811, Lewis Bourne was much older than his bride. According to his account their early married years were happy. Dolly, as she was familiarly known, "conducted herself like a dutiful affectionate and faithful wife," and Lewis reciprocated "with all the tenderness affection and respect which could have been asked . . . as a husband and a man." Dolly gave Lewis two children, a son and a daughter. Then, six or seven years before Lewis applied for a divorce, Dolly's behavior changed, and she began "to live in open adultery." Although Lewis only mentioned one slave, the affidavits indicate that Dolly's adventures involved two or more. She kept "the Company of Negroe slaves" and gave birth to a child who was very obviously black, probably fathered by a slave named Jack. This child lived only about three years. Meanwhile Dolly switched her affections to another slave named Edmund, who like Jack belonged to John Richardson but was variously described as "a white slave," "a very bright mulato," and "white as she is." She bore Edmund's child, who seemed "to all appearances white," and Edmund and Dolly lived together "almost as man and wife."[26]

Dolly had long since left her husband's home and moved into a cottage on one corner of his property. Richardson thought that her sole reason for leaving Lewis was the age difference between them, but the growing tension between husband and wife may also have dictated the move. Rumors circulated that Lewis had beaten his wife or ordered her whipped for her infidelity, charges that many of the affidavits take pains to deny. Lewis Bourne was also "old and infirm," and after Dolly left him, he turned to William Bourne, a relative and neighbor, for assistance. According to William's narrative Dolly had given away most of Lewis's supplies and provisions to her slave friends and "reduced him almost to a state of necessity." So impaired was his health that at least one neighbor expected him to die in early 1823, but after William took charge, Lewis's condition improved significantly.

By this time the local community was fully aware of the Bournes' domestic problems, and in June 1823 John Fleming asked Lewis to visit him at the home of George Fleming, a wealthy justice of the peace in Louisa County and probably a close relative. When Lewis and William Bourne arrived, John invited Lewis into a back room and offered to help him obtain a divorce. His services would cost $100, he said, but only $50 if he was unsuccessful, because the "expenses" would still be quite high. When Lewis told John Fleming he could not afford the money, George Fleming remarked, "You had better do it Lewis. Otherwise you will have them mulatto children to support all your life." But Lewis still refused, and he and William went home.[27]

William Bourne then decided to take matters into his own hands. Early one November morning he and another man named Pleasants Proffit went to Dolly's cabin and surprised her in bed with Edmund. The two white men then found a magistrate and swore to Dolly's adultery. This roused Lewis to write his own divorce petition castigating Dolly for having "no regard for himself" and "no respect for the laws of God or of man." He expressed his confidence that the assembly "will look indignantly upon such a course of conduct . . . and that they will embrace every opportunity to shew their disapprobation of a practice and a state of things so directly against the spirit and policy of our laws; so injurious to the morality of the country." Accompanied by multiple affidavits verifying Lewis's story, this petition arrived at the assembly in December 1823.

The divorce bill passed easily enough through the House that winter but then foundered in the Senate after Dolly roused herself and visited the legislature.[28] Accompanied by at least one woman friend and with her babe in arms, she presented herself at the capital with her own petition, written by none other than John Fleming. Her memorial added a new dimension to the divorce case. The entire business, she pointed out, was the work of William Bourne, "the inner mover and instigator of this prosecution." He and her husband had struck an agreement extremely beneficial to William's interests, which effectively squeezed Dolly out of any rights, even her dower. Lewis had sold William all of his land until Lewis and Dolly's eight-year-old son, Thomas, came of age. If Lewis was still alive then, William could keep the property until Lewis died. In addition, Lewis had sold William "all his personal property of every description," and William had taken possession of the house, the furniture, and the farm stock. The only payment for all this was William Bourne's agreement "to maintain Lewis Bourne during his life and our son Thomas till he is of age." Lewis also agreed to give William permanent title to 150 acres, or half of his land, if he would take care of Lewis and Dolly's nine-year-old daughter, Fanny, until she was twenty-one.

Dolly argued that William was so personally invested in her marital trauma that the legislature should disregard his entire testimony. She further informed the assembly that his sidekick Pleasants Proffit was "a poor labouring dependant" under William Bourne's control. Her petition also implied that she had been forced out of her home. She came before the legislature "houseless and unprotected caring [sic] the youngest [child] in Her arms relying with confidence on the justice and humanity of the tribunal . . . and trusting your decree will be that Her husband living she shall not be unprovided nor dying unendowed."[29] What legislator could fail to be touched by such an appeal? Lewis and William Bourne tried to discredit Dolly's petition by telling the story of John Fleming's attempts to extract money for his services in obtaining a divorce, but the damage to their case was irreparable.

Further evidence in late January 1824 from two of Dolly's friends threw doubt on the accuracy of the neighborhood gossip. A woman who claimed to have served as Dolly's midwife every time she gave birth declared she had "never delivered her of a coloured child." Lewis's allies submitted fresh affidavits for his side, but to no avail. Confronted by a mass of conflicting testimony, the assembly hesitated, and no divorce bill passed that session. The next autumn Lewis Bourne prepared to try again and enlisted some neighbors to gather direct evidence. One early November night four men slipped into John Richardson's slave quarters and surprised Dolly in bed with a slave. In the resulting melee she escaped briefly, but they caught her and forced her to make her mark on a statement acknowledging that she had been detected "in Bead With one of [Richardson's] Negroes." Even this confession of guilt, however, did not convince the legislature to grant Lewis Bourne his coveted divorce. The bill failed on its first reading.[30]

Despite strong evidence from some of Louisa County's most respectable citizens that Dolly Bourne had repeatedly committed adultery with slaves and given birth to mulatto children, several points registered strongly against Lewis's case. First, if he had sold all his property to William Bourne, he had violated Dolly's rights under Virginia law, which specified that a husband could not sell property without his wife's permission. He had furthermore ignored her future legal claims because the sale stripped Dolly of her dower in both land and personal property. These actions rendered Lewis and William Bourne liable for a major lawsuit on Dolly's part. They may have hoped that an absolute divorce bill would eliminate this possibility by ending the legal claims that spouses had on each other. But Virginia's lawmakers took a dim view of this assault on the rights of a wife and widow. Dolly's claim that William Bourne influenced Lewis to pursue the divorce explains a second concern in the case that might have troubled the legislature. By his own admission Lewis had tolerated Dolly's conduct for six or seven years without seeking a divorce. For part of that time they were living together in the same house, presumably as man and wife. Lewis would certainly have known that he had a strong case for a divorce as soon as Dolly gave birth to her first mulatto child. Yet he waited at least three years before submitting his petition. In effect, he gave his tacit consent to, or at least an indication of forgiveness of, Dolly's misdeeds; in other words, he exhibited condonation. When the legislature in 1848 finally authorized the courts to grant absolute divorces in adultery cases, the law specifically excluded situations in which the injured spouse had forgiven the guilty one.[31] Lewis's later change of heart toward his wife demonstrated the hold William Bourne exerted after he became an interested party in the affair. This in turn may have convinced the legislature of the truth of Dolly Bourne's assertions. Thus Lewis Bourne failed to gain his divorce despite strong testimony that his wife had engaged in interracial sex.

The lawmakers generally proved to be sticklers in demanding ironclad evidence. They knew the schemes that plaintiffs were liable to cook up. In the allegations made against wives, the racial identification of their children proved to be a crucial point. In one notorious case that did not involve divorce, the husband went insane, and the courts ultimately determined the child's race. Several years before his death John Carlton of King and Queen County wrote a will that left his entire estate to a son and daughter. He made no reference to his wife, Sarah, who was pregnant at the time with a son she bore six months later and named William. John became mentally deranged, perhaps when he discovered his wife's infidelity, and died in that condition. After John's death the county court awarded Sarah Carlton her widow's dower. The rest of the estate was divided in thirds for the three children. But the portion assigned to William Carlton came under litigation in 1829 when John's daughter, Mary, and her husband, William Watkins, alleged that William Carlton was a mulatto and therefore illegitimate and not entitled to any inheritance. John Carlton, they maintained, could not have been William's father, since both he and Sarah were white.

The case ultimately made its way to the Court of Appeals, where Benjamin Watkins Leigh, one of Virginia's most distinguished lawyers, argued that "if the white wife of a white man brought forth a mulatto child, that child was begotten by a negro man in illicit intercourse with her." The issue was a matter of factual evidence, since blacks and whites were "distinguished by natural marks not to be mistaken." It would be impossible, Leigh concluded, for a white husband to "beget a mulatto child" by his white wife. In rebuttal William Carlton's lawyer proposed that despite the views of natural philosophy, "the general opinion of mankind" agreed that a child might have the "appearance" of a mulatto because of "impressions made on the mother at the time of conception, or during pregnancy." Thus two white parents could produce a child that looked like a mulatto. Speaking for the court, Judge Henry St. George Tucker agreed with his old college friend Leigh that the "physiological question" should be settled by scientific opinion. If John Carlton could not have been the father because he was white and William was a mulatto, then William was illegitimate. Tucker also added that he believed it was "a law of nature, that a white couple cannot produce a negro or mulatto child."[32]

By the time Judge Tucker rendered this decision, the assembly was demanding that every divorce proceeding submit a court record proving the facts alleged by the petitioner. The House turned down William Bayliss in 1831 for not supplying this transcript despite his eloquent petition and multiple affidavits that his wife, Rebecca, had been engaged in interracial sex. The next year, after a jury judged his facts to be true, the lawmakers gave Bayliss an absolute divorce. Every rule had its exception, however, and in the minds of the legislators sex across the color line occasionally warranted one. When Richard Hall asked for a divorce on those grounds, he argued that "the notoriety of the facts is such as to leave no doubt." Someone had advised him that "it was wholly unnecessary to incur the cost or to bring the matter before two different tribunals." Evidently the legislators in the 1837 session agreed, because they speedily dissolved his marriage.[33] Wives who committed adultery with African Americans rubbed the most tender spot in the southern white male psyche.

THE DOUBLE STANDARD

The situation was different, however, if the sexual relationship involved a white man and a black woman. The cases alleging adultery across the color line furnish an unusual opportunity to assess the different behavioral expectations of southern white men and women regarding what is now known as the double standard. Briefly, women are held to much higher and stricter norms of chastity than are men, and the same conduct that would define a woman as "fallen" and forever beyond the pale of respectability may be regarded in a man as regrettable and reprehensible but still pardonable. Though this mentality was national in character and existed apart from questions of race, the divorce petitions demonstrate how it was applied in southern society and internalized by the white people there.[34]

Compare the response of the legislature to male as opposed to female allegations of their spouse's interracial infidelity. Explaining the reason for David Parker's absolute divorce bill in 1827, a Lynchburg newspaper pointed out, "It was proved that the woman had lived in adultery and had had a colored child." But when Sarah Robinson's case came up in 1841 and one legislator argued for the divorce on the grounds that Samuel Robinson lived "in open adultery with white and black," Briscoe Baldwin objected. The other legislators were about to elect this highly respected lawyer to the Supreme Court of Appeals. During his career Baldwin had successfully represented at least one women plaintiff in divorce proceedings. But now he retorted, "If the House undertook to grant the petition for a divorce of every lady, who had a worthless husband, it would establish a very bad precedent. There was a law on the subject to which aggreved parties might have recourse." In his view Sarah Robinson should settle for a legal separation. Baldwin called for a vote, and her divorce bill was defeated 37 to 69.[35]

Any respectable white woman of any class—and they were present in virtually every class—who carried on an adulterous affair with a black man fatally compromised her social standing. But the attitude toward a male dalliance was much more tolerant, provided that it did not challenge the fundamental ethos of a slave society. This does not mean that white men could flaunt their affairs or that white southerners accepted sex across the color line without demur. During the Revolutionary era a foreign visitor, noting the disapproval of interracial sex, observed that white males had to "satisfy their desires" secretly and that "no white man is known to live regularly with a black woman." But a French traveler surely exaggerated when he wrote, "Woe to the white man who would have the most secret love affair with a Negress. . . . He would be scorned, dishonored; every house would be closed to him; he would be detested." Certainly Thomas Jefferson was deeply embarrassed by the charges made against him on this account.[36] But in fact some white men did get away with long-standing liaisons, and white women found it much more difficult to obtain divorces from husbands who had black mistresses than did white men whose wives had engaged in interracial sex.

First of all, wives had a major problem proving their husbands were having sexual relationships with black women, slave or free. The presence of mulatto children at a plantation or farm, even if they resembled the master, could always be blamed on a neighbor or overseer. After the plantation or farmhouse door closed for the night, what the neighbors knew about the intimate details of a couple's family life or sexual relationship was generally hearsay, and rumors or a ruined reputation were not sufficient evidence for a divorce. Moreover, white males were permitted and, at least in some circles, even expected to form casual liaisons with black women. A measure of discretion was demanded, of course. The black mistress or concubine could never have the public status of a white woman or be treated as a wife. Sexual desire might cross the color line, but it dared not try to erase it.

Thus, for example, the 1836 vice-presidential candidacy of Richard Johnson on the Democratic ticket with Martin Van Buren caused such strong revulsion in Virginia that party leaders refused to place his name on the state's ballots. Defying convention, the Kentucky politician had flaunted his mulatto mistresses and sought white husbands for his mulatto daughters. In a family letter written while she was visiting Washington in 1836, a young Virginia girl reflected the loathing of Johnson she had undoubtedly learned at her parents' knees. The niece of Senator Thomas Hart Benton and daughter of a prominent Virginia Democrat, Sally McDowell was invited to a White House reception, where she admired the ladies' dresses, the splendid supper, and the brilliance of the gathering. Then, after meeting President Andrew Jackson and being squired about the East Room for an hour by Vice-President Martin Van Buren, "the little Magician," she suddenly spied "Dick Johnson." The "thunderstruck" girl reported to her mother that she "was ready to puke over every thing I saw, whichever ever way I turned Dick Johnson was before me." She wanted to "vomit at every thing even oysters." Sex across the color line, however common it might be in Virginia, did not sit well in polite society.[37]

The double standard in expectations, the difficulty in obtaining proof, and the distinction between casual sex with black women and open violations of racial convention are all evident in how the assembly treated divorce petitions from white women who accused their husbands of sexual relations with black women. The legislature had already begun granting divorces to men on such grounds when a women first leveled similar charges against her husband in 1806. Charlotte Ball's accusations included adultery with both black and white women, but her witnesses mainly repeated what they had heard her tell them. One man testified that when playing host to Charlotte's husband, he discovered him at supper time "behind an out house with a negroe girl," but as near as he could make out in the dark, "they were not near enough together to *touch*." That was not close enough to count for much with the legislature.[38]

Samuel Hunter, according to his wife, brought home "the vilest blacks in town" to engage in sex and "openly boasted of the number of his black wives." But the assembly required more than a spouse's allegations. Nancy Rowland told the assembly that soon after her marriage she watched her husband's nightly romp with the cook. "Before her eyes and in the very room in which your petitioner slept," he would "go to bed to said slave or cause said slave to come in and go to bed to him." The neighbors certainly pitied Nancy and testified that she was a "moral chaste and respected woman," but they could only swear to what Nancy had told them. No one else had actually witnessed it.

Even eyewitness corroboration did not necessarily suffice. When Robert Dunlap married his wife, Ellen, he gained legal title to Milly, Ellen's slave. Ellen's divorce petition charged her husband with being "criminally unlawfully and Carnally Intamate" with Milly. Affidavits supported her allegations, but the assembly rejected Ellen's petition. White women who discovered their husbands' affairs with slaves expressed no less repugnance than white men whose wives crossed the color line. Nancy Rowland could not begin to express the "pain" she experienced at her husband's infidelity. Describing the "horror of her unhappy state," Elizabeth Harwell characterized her husband as "vile and profligate." She had left him and rejected his pleas to return unless he promised to get rid of Betsy, his slave mistress.[39]

Elizabeth's behavior, however, was unusual. Although wives might be revolted by their mates' adultery with blacks or mulattos, there was a critical difference between men and women after the discovery had been made. Despite their abhorrence at their husbands' infidelity, women appeared much more tolerant of male philandering and were more willing to forgive and to remain in the marriage if their spouses promised reformation. The double standard was not only expressed in male words and actions. Many women internalized its values and made it a constituent element of their own identities. No doubt economic and familial realities shaped this reaction. What options did a wronged wife possess? Except in the relatively rare case of a woman, normally from the planter, merchant, or professional elite, who held a separate estate, the husband controlled all property and wealth in a marriage. If she walked out the door, how could she support herself? Some women returned to their parents or moved in with siblings. But if male relatives accepted the double standard, what reception could women expect? Other women struck out on their own and strove to construct a new life. Some succeeded in that effort, but it was always an uphill struggle. Others stayed with an adulterous husband and looked the other way when a spouse headed toward the slave quarters or a slave mistress appeared on the doorstep. Inside they must have been filled with rage.

The divorce petitions reflect the anger, hurt, and disgrace white wives experienced because of the infidelity of their husbands. At the same time, they demonstrate the vast gap in power between white men and women in southern society. For example, when John Brewer notified his wife, Delilah, that he would be applying for a divorce, he accused her of adultery. She denied the charge but also decided to give the assembly her version of their marriage. According to Delilah, not long after the wedding she discovered her bridegroom's affection for one of his slaves: "He could not, nor did not forbear to bestow his caresses on her in my presence, with loud encomiums on her accomplishments, charms, etc. declaring her the handsomest woman in the world." After a year or so of this nonsense, Delilah had had enough. She took her three-month-old baby and went to live with friends, but she told the legislature, "I do not wish any otherwise than to live with him, but I wish to live with him as God has commanded and to fulfil the duties of a wife and mother." She did not want a divorce. Instead her petition expressed a need for the "protection" that a husband and father could offer.[40]

The legislature agreed. Whether Delilah Brewer or her husband was the chief offender in the marriage was immaterial. The social order expected husbands and wives to stay together, mainly for the benefit of the women and children. Only truly extraordinary circumstances permitted divorce. Run-of-the-mill male infidelity, even across the color line, did not justify the destructive effects that separation brought to individuals, families, and society. By itself interracial sex on the husband's part did not merit a legislative divorce. Other factors had to be present. Jonah Dobyns boasted to his wife, Sopha, within the hearing of at least one witness, that he had enjoyed sexual relations with a slave woman in Sopha's bed and "would do so again whenever it suited him." But in granting Sopha a divorce *a mensa,* the assembly was moved more by the descriptions of Jonas's extreme cruelty and the repeated whippings he had given her.[41] By the time Sopha gained her freedom, the legislature was providing legal separations for women in cases of physical battery.

When the lawmakers in 1820 passed the first absolute divorce for a woman who alleged adultery across the color line, abuse figured largely in her petition. Barbara Price came from a respectable Hanover family when she married Hugh Pettus from neighboring Louisa County in 1809. Shortly after the wedding, she discovered that Hugh was involved in the slave trade. He would disappear for months on end and then come home with slave women, "*his kept mistresses,*" who would share Barbara's home. When she remonstrated, Hugh beat her. His conduct became notorious in the community. Perhaps for that reason, after one child and almost ten years of marriage, Hugh sold his Virginia property and prepared to move his operation to Georgia. But his wife and baby were not included in the transition. Hugh had instead picked out a new wife from a "respectable family" in Louisa County. They had gone south together, leaving Barbara and child "without a home or the means of support." Her friends and the law helped out, but she wanted a divorce from the "monster" she had unwittingly married. Three affidavits and a court record verified her story, and Barbara got her divorce.[42]

Five years later another case involving a slave mistress also merited an absolute divorce. But again the husband's conduct defied societal norms on several counts. Evelina Gregory's marriage to Newman Roane in 1823 had joined two prominent planter families in King William County. But even before the wedding, rumors circulated that Newman kept a black mistress on his plantation. When Evelina's brother confronted the prospective bridegroom with the story, Newman denied any relationship and promised to send the slave woman Biney and her mulatto child away. The wedding took place on schedule, but several months later Biney surfaced at the plantation with two mulatto children in tow. Newman bluntly told Evelina the children were his and that he planned to raise them himself. Her petition described the scene to the assembly: Newman would put the older child "upon his knee, and instruct it to abuse your unhappy supplicant, and place her under the most positive and threatening injunction not to correct it; declaring his strong attachment for the mother and stating that the two children were his and that he meant upon principle, to do more for them, than for his lawful children." Evelina was forced to become their tutor, and Newman bragged about his plans for their education to both her and his friends.[43]

The role reversal was complete. Under orders from Newman, Evelina worked in the kitchen, hauled water from the well, and suffered "the situation of a Slave," while Biney enjoyed "an easy situation, . . . happy and cheerful in idleness and the undisguised friendship of her master." The slave woman had been "adopted . . . as the more eligible companion and wife." When word of this situation got around the neighborhood and one of his wife's relatives protested, Newman told him that Biney's "fidelity was essential to him and he felt for her and her children what was natural." If Evelina's family pressed him, he would sell his estate and move "to the Ohio and . . . settle this woman and children in an independent situation." Evelina remained with her husband for a year and gave birth to one child, but after Newman beat her severely one day, she fled for safety to her family and petitioned for a divorce. Her petition, one of the longest in the legislative files and drawn up with the help of her lawyer-brother, graphically describes her treatment under Newman's ministrations and her deep resentment at Biney's supremacy in her husband's affections. The competition between the two women is palpable in Evelina's memorial. The slave knew how to please Newman. Evelina did not. He responded to Biney's every whim, and she became, in effect, the plantation's mistress. For her part Evelina detested "the sight, the presence, and the presuming behaviour of a worthless, ignorant, and un-principled negroe woman," with "her system of insolence and offence."

Amid all the allegations of ill treatment and cruelty, the assembly paid particular attention to Newman Roane's behavior toward his slaves and his views on race relations. Evelina and her supporting witnesses argued that both in speech and conduct Newman repudiated the mores of a society based on white supremacy and black slavery. The master who educated his slaves and failed to discipline them properly was not well regarded by his peers. But the most damaging accusation was that Newman had reversed the proper roles within a culture based on slavery by demoting his white wife to the rank of a servant and elevating his black concubine to the status of mistress in the house. Evelina's charges of physical brutality and psychological cruelty were serious but not unusual. The legislators heard these cases virtually every year without granting absolute divorces. But the race issue challenged the foundation of southern society. Undoubtedly this also factored into the unusual punishment Virginia's legislators inflicted on Newman. The divorce bill gave Evelina Roane custody of her son, an exceptional breach of paternal control, and forbade Newman Roane to marry again.[44]

Two years after approving Evelina Roane's divorce, the assembly passed the law requiring a court trial of the facts before submission of a divorce petition. For the last quarter-century of legislative divorce, the lawmakers were much more evenhanded in approving bills for wives whose husbands had engaged in interracial sexual relations. Even more graphically than in earlier petitions, these court documents set up the conflict between white and black women for white male affection and included sometimes harrowing stories of physical brutality and desertion. They also detail the incidence of runaway husbands. For example, Mary Alvis's husband had deserted both her and another woman that he had subsequently married in New York and was back in Richmond living "with a colored woman in a state of open adultery." Desertion was also part of the pattern in Lucy Watts's troubled marriage. Her husband had bolted twice and at one point moved in with a free black woman and "claimed her as his wife." The jury who heard Ann Eliza Eubank's case accepted her claim that her spouse had "frequently left the marriage Bed to seek the Bed of a colored woman." Elizabeth Pannill's husband had tried to run away with Grace, his black paramour in King William County. The assembly gave all these women absolute divorces.[45]

The Pannill case also demonstrates how a jury might examine the evidence and reach a varied decision. Elizabeth was not yet nineteen when she applied for a divorce from Edmund Pannill. According to the story her attorney Benjamin Dabney presented to the court, her two years of married life had been hell. In addition to wasting all the property she brought to the marriage, Edmund regularly whipped her, tried to have her poisoned, and fornicated with "white and coloured" women, especially a hired slave named Grace, whom he egged on to abuse and beat Elizabeth. But when he and Grace attempted to exit the scene, neighbors caught them. Grace, after all, was someone else's slave. Elizabeth's parents were evidently dead, because "friends" were now protecting her from Edmund. He did not show up for the trial in November 1836, having skipped out of the county to avoid another trial on felony charges. But a jury heard the evidence for Elizabeth's case and rendered a mixed verdict. Reviewing the charges item by item, they found the bulk of them "substantially proven," but they were not convinced that Edmund had whipped or poisoned her.[46]

Edmund Pannill had run away. Yet not every male who formed an adulterous liaison across the color line coupled it with desertion. Control over the home marked a critical difference in the legal status of men and women. Wives might be responsible for domestic arrangements, but ultimate authority rested with their husbands. Thus wives could be put out on the street for sexual infidelity, while husbands could dictate the guest list regardless of their spouses' wishes. Actual practice varied widely, depending on the companionate style of their marriage, the relative strength of the personalities involved, and the issues at stake in a particular circumstance. Many males preferred to escape with a paramour rather than face an outraged wife reinforced by her family and neighbors. Yet law and custom led other men to regard themselves as utterly supreme within their own little worlds. Newman Roane's behavior was bizarre but not unique.

Men such as Robert Hamilton and James Norman prided themselves on their vaunted abilities to control both people and events. As we have seen, the Hamilton-Brooke marriage was a disaster. It is obvious that Helen had never taken to heart James Garnett's lectures to young ladies, if she ever bothered to read them. In a long letter a few months before the wedding, the prospective groom warned her of his "most unfortunate eccentricities" and "peculiar disposition" and advised her that any plans for marital happiness were doomed from the outset. "No woman could be happy with me," he predicted accurately, because he insisted on having his wishes completely satisfied in every respect. He would tolerate no opposition nor be denied anything he wanted. This "insane principle of my nature," he advised his bride-to-be, was bound to "destroy our happiness forever." She must yield to him in everything. What the infatuated Helen never expected, however, was that Robert's desires included sexual relations with her mulatto slave, Louisa. Married in June 1843, the couple separated after a pregnant Louisa named Robert as the responsible agent and he admitted it to Helen. As he naively informed his father-in-law, he thought this confession "would reconcile" his wife; "his passions controlled his moral sense," he explained. A brief reunion forestalled talk of divorce. Helen had borne a child and, ever the optimist, entertained fair hopes of her husband's "reformation." But in 1845, after enduring treatment that she described as "Harsh and cruel," Helen retreated to her parents' home. Louisa was already there. The relationship between their children, if they grew up together, must have been interesting.[47]

If Robert Hamilton had indulged his adultery in private, James Norman preferred to enjoy his illicit relationship in the presence of his wife, Lucy, and their boarders and guests. The marriage had been rocky practically from the start. Within a year James told Lucy he had only married her for her property, which was considerable and now his, and would like her out of his life. He had no intention of leaving and wanted her to go, hoping the neighbors would think the separation was Lucy's idea. But neither his "indifference" and "contempt" nor "the most abusive violent and indecent language" could force Lucy from her home. Instead she petitioned for a divorce. Her memorial, the depositions, and the court record focused on James's affair with a black slave named Maria. Humiliated to make her troubles public but determined to regain her freedom and to keep her property, Lucy told the assembly that at night James brought a woman "*not of his own color*" into her bedroom. When she protested, her husband remarked that "if she did not like it she might look out for other quarters." While his wife watched from the bed, James "slept" with Maria on a nearby cot. Nor did he hide his affection from their houseguests. "He often embraced and kissed her in my presence," one guest testified, "and appeared to be passionately attached to her." The dining room became a battleground. Lucy objected to having a slave share their meals, but James demanded Maria join them at dinner. When Lucy protested and told the woman she would be "severely punished,"

James threatened Lucy with the same "punishment" if the slave was touched. A visitor reported that Lucy then "burst into tears and asked me if it was not too much for her to stand." James retorted that "it was nothing to what he intended to inflict upon her." Ultimately James and Maria found lodging elsewhere. Lucy received her divorce in 1849 after a legislator argued that James "had grossly outraged public decency" and deserted his wife.[48] By then the racial aspects of the case were not the determining factor. Solid proof of adultery and desertion was sufficient.

ON THE AFRICAN AMERICAN SIDE OF THE LINE

One can only speculate what Louisa or Bob or James Watt or any of the other slaves and free blacks enmeshed in these domestic triangles thought about their situations. They emerge from the pages of the petitions, affidavits, and court records as shadowy figures at best with only limited power to structure their own lives. For slaves that power depended almost entirely on their facility in pleasing their white masters or mistresses. Affection undoubtedly played a part in some relationships, but in a slave society force and the threat of violence remained ever present realities. For free blacks and mulattos the burden was somewhat different. As members of an underclass based on race, they had to be continually concerned for their own survival in a white-dominated society. Agency and choice could never belong entirely to them. Those who engaged in interracial sex played a dangerous game that incited the worst fears and antagonism of the whites.

The real or imagined authority of particular blacks surfaces in a number of the divorce files. Whites sometimes imputed power to blacks in order to divert blame from themselves. We have no way of knowing their sincerity. Elizabeth Pettus, for example, alleged that before her wedding to Dabney Pettus a slave had threatened to destroy the engagement unless she yielded to his sexual advances. Lydia Butt claimed that "Robin had overcome her" by promising "to get Benjamin Butt Junr. to be her Husband." A few white women cited their fears that their husbands' paramours would attempt to kill them. Evelina Roane only took the food prepared in the kitchen if Newman Roane ate some first. Fried chicken made Elizabeth Pannill so desperately sick that she was convinced either her husband or his slave mistress had put poison in it.[49]

No doubt a wife forced to compete with a slave for the love and affection of a husband experienced profound humiliation. In a race-based society a husband who maintained a black mistress effectively ranked his white wife below a slave. For women caught in such circumstances, the idealization of white womanhood, so common in public and literary discourse, must have sounded hollow. But their ability to lash out at the men invested in this system was severely circumscribed by cultural inhibitions. It is not surprising, therefore, that in their petitions white wives frequently characterized the slave women as brazen, disrespectful, and undisciplined, as if they were chiefly responsible. Delilah Brewer, for example, complained about the "contempt" she received from her husband's black paramour. But black women were trapped in a situation not necessarily of their own making and without the freedom white women retained, at least theoretically, to walk out the door and seek refuge elsewhere.[50]

Sometimes life offered other options. A white owner, for example, possessed enormous power over a slave woman, but it was another story if the white man making the advances on a slave woman was not the master. Then she might be able to assert her own bodily integrity. When Charlotte Ball's husband, who was generally out of control, "attempted an improper connection" with one of his host's slaves, the woman doused Ball with a pitcher of water and fled the scene. Freedom also brought at least a limited degree of empowerment. Free African American women could haul men who attacked them into county courts on charges of trespass, assault, and battery.[51] Even under slavery, a religiously based household possessed another authority available to all, slave and free. Buckingham Baptist Church, for example, expelled a church member who attempted to induce a slave belonging to Steven Garrett to have "carnal intercourse" with him. Late one night Agee Bounderant had entered Garrett's kitchen and made sexual advances toward the woman. When she refused his overtures, he offered her money, which the woman took and then woke her master to complain that Bounderant was badgering her. Garrett "ordered him off with roughness" and set his dogs after him to speed his departure. Garrett reported that Bounderant had later begged him not to reveal his behavior to the church because he would be dismissed and his good name destroyed. When Garrett informed the church, the membership voted "unanimously" to expel the man.[52]

African American men and women, slave and free, sometimes asserted what appears to be a surprising degree of personal freedom in a culture based on slavery. The bonds of affection across racial lines could run deep enough that some individuals simply thumbed their noses at the rules of white society. Henrietta Rose's slave lover continued his affair with her even after her marriage. Free blacks such as James Watt and Wilfred Mortimer set up housekeeping with white women, and Mortimer and Rebecca Bayliss had a child. Whether white or black, single women who bore children and unmarried couples who lived together were liable to be presented at a county court and fined. In county order books, entries such as the following occasionally appear: "Against Hezekiah Johnson, Mulatto, and Sarah Taylor, white woman for unlawfully cohabiting together, by information of William Watts, Isaac Holland, and Ralph Jenkins three of the Grand jury." In Isle of Wight the grand jury presented Elizabeth Gray in 1815 "for cohabitating with negroes."[53] But presentation in court did not necessarily mean the couple separated or were even punished.

What did the local community think? An extraordinary divorce petition from Campbell County in 1816 indicates the views of one group of white neighbors and demonstrates a level of interracial acceptance that counters all stereotypes of the Old South. In his memorial to the assembly, Robert Wright described himself as "a free man of color" who married "a free white woman" named Mary Godsey in 1806. In itself that was a remarkable event because the county clerk had furnished the marriage license and Mary's mother had consented to the marriage for her underage daughter. Then, according to Wright, a clergyman had defied the law by performing the ceremony. It is not difficult to imagine the minister arriving for the ceremony, only to discover that the bride and groom were an interracial couple, but proceeding with the wedding under the pressure of the situation.

What makes such a scenario plausible is the place Robert Wright occupied in Campbell County and the respect he commanded among his neighbors. In fact, he was one of the more prosperous small planters in the area, having managed well the property he inherited from his father. More than thirty years before, Thomas Wright, a white man, had formed a permanent relationship with Robert's mother, a slave woman named Sylvee. The senior Wright had died in 1805, leaving an extraordinary will. In it he gave "the sole and exclusive use and enjoyment" of his plantation house and two acres around it to "Sylvee a woman of colour formerly my slave but since emancipated and with whom I have had child." In her later years Sylvee would treat their relationship as if it had in fact been a marriage and an economic partnership. To his "natural son," Robert, Thomas Wright left 377 acres of prime land, his slaves, and his stock, as well as the house and land in Sylvee's possession after her death.[54]

When Robert married a white woman the next year, apparently no one blinked an eye. All the evidence indicates that the local community accepted the match between Robert and Mary. Neither in his reported exchanges with his neighbors nor in his divorce petition did Robert apologize for his behavior, display embarrassment, or express concern for violating a supposed taboo. Indeed, his petition defiantly asserted that as a "free man of color" he wanted a divorce from his "free white wife," who had eloped with a "free white man." This implied assertion of equality with whites by virtue of his free condition could not have escaped the legislators. They discarded his petition. But though Wright's status meant nothing in Richmond, the local response differed dramatically. In Campbell County, where enslaved African Americans comprised approximately 50 percent of the population, everyone immediately concerned in family and neighborhood behaved as if the legislation prohibiting interracial marriage did not or should not exist. Although the locals clearly knew Robert was a mulatto, they chose not to construct his identity on that basis.

Thomas Wright successfully transferred his respected position in the community to his son. Robert's closest friends and associates were white men who shared his socioeconomic background. Slaveholders and lesser planters like himself, some had been schoolmates and boyhood chums. In addition to doing business with one another, they hunted, gambled, and drank together. As he shared their values, the mulatto farmer moved easily and naturally in their society. When his wife abandoned him, he turned to them for the assistance and support they readily provided. His father's friends and neighbors had became his, and one of Thomas Wright's three executors in 1805 signed the affidavit eleven years later supporting Robert Wright's divorce petition. Class counted more than race.

Although the community in which he lived knew he was black, for most practical purposes during these years Robert Wright passed as white, and when Mary had a baby, they named him Thomas Pryor Wright for his paternal grandfather. According to the divorce petition the marriage was a happy one until Mary met William Arthur, a white man, who gradually wooed her away from her husband. The pair ran off in 1815. When Robert petitioned for a divorce a year later, he reported that his wife and her paramour were "living in a state of adultery" in Nashville. His memorial correctly pointed out that although at the wedding both his white wife and the minister had broken the law and were liable for punishment, the marriage was still "valid and binding between the parties."

Hence he wanted a divorce. Three men signed an affidavit verifying the truth of his allegations, and more than fifty others affixed their signatures to a statement that they had known Wright "for many years past and do with pleasure certify that we consider him an honest, upright man, and good citizen and . . . from the best information we have been able to collect on the subject his petition contains the truth."

The assembly immediately rejected Robert's petition, true or not. Testimonials from Campbell County counted for little in Richmond, and the marriage, however valid, had been blatantly illegal. Robert did not petition again for a divorce, but like so many other Virginians of his time and circumstances, he formed a new relationship with a white woman. With the assistance of her father and brother, Polly Davidson moved into Robert's home and lived with him until his death in 1818. Thomas Wright's white relatives then surfaced to claim Robert's estate; but after a protracted trial the court denied their suit, and the property went in trust to his son. Their subsequent legislative petitions were also denied, though multiple lawsuits from black and mulatto members of Wright's family kept lawyers and courts engaged until after the Civil War.[55]

The relationship between Thomas Wright and Sylvee, the ten-year marriage of Robert Wright and Mary Godsey, and Robert's subsequent liaison with Polly Davidson suggest an openness in interracial sexual relationships and a degree of white acceptance of sex across the color line that challenges historical generalizations and traditional stereotypes of both free blacks and the slaveholding society of the early-nineteenth-century South. These conclusions in turn reinforce the evidence from the divorce petitions that interracial sexual liaisons involved white women from every class in society and were far more common and more tolerated, particularly in local communities, than historians until recently have noticed. In the ultimate analysis, however, what emerges from the pages of these divorce petitions is not the capacity of certain individuals, black and white, to surmount the values and accepted mores of the antebellum South, but the resilience of those very values and mores in the face of their overt rejection. As the years passed, the attitudes of the majority race grew ever more fixed, and resistance to change stiffened, even though in fact that meant divorce was easier to obtain and another traditional southern ideal, a stable family life, was threatened.

Meanwhile the double standard for sexual conduct thrived throughout the antebellum period. For a man to receive an absolute divorce, it was generally sufficient for him to prove conclusively that his wife had engaged in interracial sex without his knowledge prior to the marriage or without his consent afterward. Before the assembly granted a divorce to a woman, she needed to prove something more. Generally her case included a harrowing recital of grievous physical abuse. As the evidence considered in this chapter suggests, most women who charged their husbands with adultery across the color line and received a divorce were also battered wives.

CHAPTER 5

Private Disputes in Families

THE BATTERED WIFE

Male Virginians living in or near Isle of Wight County in the early nineteenth century greatly admired Ann Pierce Parker Cowper. In the view of a local doctor, she ranked among "the most accomplished of her sex." James Johnson, a planter-lawyer and congressman, described her in 1816 as "a lady of great respectability, integrity and virtue. She possesses a very highly improved and cultivated mind," he wrote, "and is certainly one of the most intelligent females with whom I have the pleasure of an acquaintance." The only child of Revolutionary War colonel and later congressman Josiah Parker, she had received an education uncommon for women of her time, "as if she had been a son, in the languages and in all manly arts," boasted the family historian.[1] But native intelligence, academic training, and social position did not save Ann Cowper from becoming a battered wife.

The abundant documentation surrounding her efforts for a legislative divorce provides graphic evidence of a viciously abusive marital situation. Scholars in the fields of psychology, sociology, and feminist theory have addressed the contemporary reality of wife abuse, at times quite heatedly and from sharply opposing points of view.[2] The historical literature on battered women, however, remains relatively sparse, particularly for the first half of the nineteenth century.[3] Yet Virginia's records provide detailed material for examining these women's lives and experiences, the power context in which marital violence occurred, types of abusive male behavior, women's strategies in response, and the reactions of family, neighbors, and society. Battered women did not necessarily suffer in silence. Wives who refused to tolerate a violent spouse possessed several alternatives. They could, and often did, vote with their feet by returning to their families or relocating elsewhere away from a vicious husband, in some cases taking their children with them. Flight might prove, however, to be only a temporary solution. Common law privileged the husband with ultimate control over his wife and children, if he chose to exercise it and adult family members or neighbors failed to intervene.

But legal remedies also existed. A woman in an abusive relationship could obtain a restraining order requiring her husband to keep the peace. William Waller Hening's useful handbook for county justices, which he drew up in 1795 and periodically revised, included an extensive section on "preventive justice." If a wife expected domestic violence, she could ask a local justice to require her husband to offer public assurances of peaceable behavior. The court would require him to find sureties, people who would vouch for his future good conduct. He and his sureties would then sign a recognizance, a bond that obliged each of them to pay a hefty fine if he failed to "keep the peace." The sheriff could seize and sell whatever property they possessed to raise that money. John Marshall thought that this system performed an extremely useful service by maintaining "internal quiet" in Virginia's communities.[4]

A wife could also sue in a chancery court for a separate maintenance or alimony arrangement, even without obtaining a divorce or legal separation. A husband who threw his wife out of the house or forced her to flee to escape his cruelty had to pay her support—so Hening argued in his compilation of precedents for the benefit of county justices. Later in *Almond v Almond*, Judge Dabney Carr argued for the Court of Appeals that an "outcast" wife was entitled to "the protection of the law." A chancery court should decree her maintenance apart from her husband. But what if the husband offered to take her home? As "a general rule," the court would then not award a settlement. However, Carr presented a hypothetical exception: "Suppose it fully proved to the Court, that the husband was in the constant habit of intoxication; that when drunk, he was a madman, and his anger particularly pointed at his wife. Surely, the Court would not, because of the offer to take her back, refuse a support, and thus force her either to hazard her life, or depend on charity."[5]

Ordinary men and women, as well as lawyers and justices, knew these legal recourses that Hening explained and the *Almond* decision reinforced. Yet the assurances of security afforded by the law were not always fulfilled in real life. At times legislative divorce provided a final, necessary resort. Legislators learned this reality as they read the petitions and supporting affidavits that flowed into Richmond. It helped move them toward the law of 1827 that established cruelty and fear of bodily injury as reasons for a judicial divorce *a mensa*. In Virginia battery became, after desertion, the most frequent grounds women presented in their divorce petitions. In addition to actual physical violence, this included psychological and verbal cruelty, economic deprivation, and other forms of coercion designed to enhance the power and control of one marriage partner over the other.

The discussion in this chapter, however, is confined to those petitioners who alleged actual bodily assault and whose files offer corroborating evidence for their charges. Sir William Scott, the English legal authority, argued that more than harsh words were needed to justify divorce. Only physical violence and a "*reasonable apprehension of bodily* hurt" warranted the state's intervention.[6] As noted earlier, relatively few women or men caught in an unhappy marriage approached the legislature for relief. The vast majority either put up with their lot or separated by mutual agreement, and undoubtedly most battered wives suffered silently in the privacy of their homes, as their modern counterparts do today. Thus this chapter focuses on a set of unusual women who determined to liberate themselves legally from a physically abusive marriage. It first presents a case study of Ann Parker Cowper as a battered wife and William Cowper as a battering husband; second, it surveys the cases of other abused women and abusive men in the divorce petitions for patterns and divergences; and finally, it investigates the social structure within which battery occurred and, in particular, the values and attitudes of families, neighborhoods, and Virginia society toward wife abuse.

A DISTRESSED AND UNFORTUNATE FEMALE

Ann Parker Cowper's marriage reveals the pressures inherent in the gendered power relationships of Virginia's society. The evidence from her divorce files includes eight legislation petitions, numerous letters and affidavits from third parties, the testimony of two physicians, and court documents and decisions. Considered as a whole, these records offer irrefutable proof of the truthfulness of her charges against her husband. At the same time she writes in a style deliberately designed to evoke the sympathy and support of the male lawmakers. Like other petitioners, her primary objective is to make such a persuasive case that the assembly will grant her request. Her petition exemplifies the style emulated by other battered wives. Writing to the assembly in November 1816, she identified herself as "a distressed and unfortunate female, who has fallen, from prosperity, and affluence."

Ann's original status derived from her father, Colonel Josiah Parker.

She took pains to remind her readers that he had been a hero of the Revolution who later served in the state assembly and the House of Representatives. In the latter capacity, Parker chaired the Committee on Naval Affairs, where the career of William Cowper must have drawn his admiration. During the undeclared naval war with France, young Lieutenant Cowper had distinguished himself and earned a promotion to captain of the U.S. frigate *Baltimore*. After the war Cowper retired to Norfolk, joined a business partnership with his brothers, and married Ann Pierce Parker in 1802. Gallantry in battle did not guarantee commercial acumen, however, and a few months after their wedding, the Cowper firm failed. Ann moved back to Macclesfield, her father's plantation home on the James River, while her husband returned to the sea. Several years later, after turning a nice profit in the Santo Domingo trade, William attempted to make a fresh start. Josiah Parker helped set him up with a store, home, and servants. But once again the navy captain showed no talent for business.[7]

As this new venture declined, family tensions rose, and the couple quarreled. As Ann discovered, her husband possessed a violent "temper." In 1806 he was charged with assault and battery and faced a trial in the county court. Josiah Parker served as his surety to guarantee his son-in-law's court appearance. But then Ann experienced his wrath also. Up to that point William had showed her nothing but "fondness and affection," she told the legislators. Now he behaved "in the most dissolute manner," insulted and threatened his father-in-law, and treated Ann "with the most unfeeling barbarity," charging her with "crimes, at which *humanity* sickens." She fled to "Pappa" for "protection." When the collapse of his store once again rendered William destitute, he begged "forgiveness" of Ann and Josiah Parker. By now the old colonel had nothing but scorn for his son-in-law and proposed to use his considerable political leverage in Richmond to gain his daughter a divorce. Ann, however, rejected the offer. Like so many other women in her circumstances, she dreaded the inevitable notoriety. Given the financial security afforded by her father, the step seemed unnecessary.[8]

When Colonel Parker died in 1810, he left Ann seven slaves, household furniture, livestock, and the use of Macclesfield for as long as she chose to live there. His executor, Joseph Baker, was to pay her $250 and then an annuity of £100 per year in quarterly installments for the rest of her life. He bequeathed the bulk of his estate to his eldest grandson, Josiah Cowper, with the proviso that he assume the surname of Parker.

William was at sea when his father-in-law died, but in three months he returned to Virginia, assumed the guardianship of young Josiah, and maneuvered to gain control of the legacy. A lawyer informed him that with an immediate change of names, Josiah would come into his inheritance. Then, if the boy died, William would be his son's heir. Otherwise, if anything happened to Josiah, Ann was his heir. According to Ann, William proposed that they petition the legislature to change Josiah's surname at once. They would then pack their son off to a Portuguese "Convent" and seize the management of the estate from Baker. If Josiah dared to interfere, William told Ann, "he would cut his throat from ear to ear." Horrified by this "*inhuman* proposition," Ann resisted his plans, and William retreated for a time. But he returned from a quick trip to London more determined than ever to grab his oldest son's inheritance.[9]

The doctors who cared for Ann later testified to William's increased physical brutality toward his wife and the impact of his beatings on her body. She refused to reveal to the legislature the precise nature of the "irregularities, and immoralities" of her husband except to say that she found them "disagreable and distressing . . . mortifying and grating." Only concern for her "poor little children" kept Ann from leaving him that spring of 1811, she said. That decision almost cost her her life. She was pregnant with her fourth child when William tried to push her out of a carriage one evening. He then openly urged her to have an abortion, threatening to "murder" her if she refused. "I gave him my penknife," Ann reported, "and offered my bosom to his stroke." Her husband turned down that invitation, but evidently in an attempt to produce a miscarriage, he increased the levels of battery. His violence put Ann in bed for several weeks, and the child was born prematurely. She was still convalescing when William came to her bedroom "knocked me down, draged me by the feet, all over the room; and treated me so cruelly, that I was not able to turn myself in bed; and spit blood for several weeks." When he attempted to starve her, the servants brought her food secretly.[10]

Ann had finally determined to leave when suddenly William appeared a changed man and urged her friends to effect a "reconciliation." She later admitted she was duped: "his promises appeared so fair, that I agreed to it." In April 1811, by a trust deed to Thomas Pierce, Ann's uncle, William turned over for her use all of the property left her by her father. That summer, however, he returned to his old ways, ordered his wife out of Macclesfield, and threatened her with death if she refused to destroy the trust deed. His rage at Ann may have been related to a defeat he had suffered that day in court. After a jury determined that he had broken his recognizance, the justices ordered him to pay $100 to the state.[11] He came home and vented his wrath at Ann. Because the weather was foul, Ann locked herself in her room. Two days later she emerged to visit a friend. William insisted on accompanying her, then abandoned her there and drove home alone. That winter the legislature entertained petitions from both husband and wife. William asked the assembly to change his oldest son's surname to Parker in conformity with the terms of Josiah Parker's will. Ann counterpetitioned with a closely reasoned argument that effectively blocked her husband. At the same time she also petitioned for a divorce. She withdrew that request, however, when the couple reconciled again in December.[12]

To get his "beloved wife" back to Macclesfield, the captain signed a formal agreement with Ann that he would not attempt to change their son's name and would act as "the best of husbands . . . to promote both her happiness and Welfare and that of our dear children." To achieve this goal William promised that he would provide for his family by returning to the sea, allow Ann to be "complete mistress of her family and domestick Concerns," and educate Josiah at nearby Smithfield academy. The terms were those of a companionate marriage that respected the separate spheres of husband and wife. In raising their children he further agreed to "advise and Consult with my dear wife and pay all the respect to her opinion and wishes which a fond and affectionate husband ought to do." In any disagreement, "which God forbid," each would select a friend to mediate the issues. For her part Ann promised to return home, to use her influence with her father's executor to secure estate funds for Josiah's education, and to help her husband, "so that both of us may as much as possible do away the remembrance of what is past."[13]

But past was prologue. Ann was scarcely home before marital relations resumed their familiar violent pattern. William had dispatched his legislative petition with an accompanying letter to James Johnson, a delegate from Isle of Wight County. In response, probably after reading Ann's petition in opposition to her husband's, Johnson castigated William's "improper conduct" in seeking to have his son's name changed and told him never to call upon his services again. The enraged husband now "*choaked*" his wife and threatened to kill her. A few weeks later, still furious at being thwarted, he whipped her severely. When Sally Copeland, a relative who lived at Macclesfield at Ann's request, tried to intervene, she felt the lash also.[14]

In March 1812 Ann finally approached the courts for help. Over the next five months she would learn their limitations. She first sought a peace restraint from the county court. At the instigation of some of her friends, James Johnson acted as her lawyer. He later wrote that William's "confessions" in court proved that he had committed "the most wanton and outrageous acts of cruelty toward his wife." The justices forced him to find a surety and make a recognizance that he would keep the peace for one year, so William and a friend, Robert Newman, each had a bond of $200. But the peace warrant proved ineffective. William first tried to pay a neighbor to beat Ann, but the man refused. Finally one night he attempted to break into her bedroom and assault her with a kitchen knife. Ann barricaded the door and warned him that she had a pistol. He withdrew, but the next day when she discovered he was trying to purchase some guns, she took her youngest child and fled to the home of her uncle, Thomas Pierce, in nearby Smithfield.[15]

From that safe haven Ann asked the county's Superior Court of Law in May 1812 to intervene and give her further "security of the peace." But William successfully opposed the motion, pointing out that the county court's March peace order was still applicable. Two months later she filed suit in the Chancery District Court of Williamsburg to ask for the return of property her father had left her, the use of Macclesfield, and a separate maintenance from either the trust estate William had signed over on her behalf to Pierce or its profits. With the help of her uncle, Ann drew up a long statement to the court, much of which she would repeat to the legislature four years later. Andrew Woodley, a local magistrate who befriended Ann throughout her troubles, took the depositions for the trial. Despite Woodley's characterization of William Cowper as a man without "honour," he could still call on powerful friends from his days as a sea captain. He counted St. George Tucker of Williamsburg among them. To plead his defense in the Chancery District Court, William enlisted Littleton Tazewell. The Norfolk attorney successfully defanged the court. Judge Robert Nelson briefly ordered William and "his agents and attorneys" to cease "exercising any sort of ownership over any of the property" left to Ann in her father's will. But the decree had no teeth. William ignored it with impunity.[16]

Three courts had failed to give Ann justice. For the next five years she lived with relatives while William occupied Macclesfield with three of their four children. Thomas Hancock, a neighborhood planter, had signed the bond as surety when Joseph Baker became executor of Josiah

To the Honorable the Speaker and Members of both Houses of the General
Assembly of Virginia

The Petition of Ann P. P. Cowper

A distress'd and unfortunate female, who has fallen, from prosperity, and affluence, humbly
represents, unto your honorable body, (who she is informed has power to afford her that justice,
and redress of her greevances, which humanity requires.— She was the only child, of a fond
and affectionate parent, the late Col. Josiah Parker, who I hope deserved well of
his country, for his life was devoted to her service. He was among the first, who espoused
her cause in her greatest difficulty, and danger, and was one of that convention, who formed
our State constitution. he entered the army, drew his sword, and fought in defence of those
rights; he had asserted in her councils— He was one of that little band of hero's, who after
retreating through the Jerseys; recross'd the Delaware in the night, and obtained the victory at
Trenton; I have always understood he received the sword of the expiring British Commander
(Col. Rawle) A few days afterwards, at the same place; when a little creek seperated the
American & British Armies; he commanded a party that defended an important pass over
the creek, while engaged with the enemy General Mercer called to him "to defend the pass,
at every hazard for the safety of America depended on it"— My Father did his duty—
He was next day. feild Officer of the day; at the battle of Princeton — and was in most of
the important actions which followed; while he remained in the Army— He retired from
the regular service, some time prior to the invasion of Virginia; by Arnold & Cornwallis;
during the greater part of this time, he commanded that division of the Militia; which
defended the south side of James River.— His military services ceased with the capture
of the British army in York.— When the war was ended, he was appointed to an important
Office, which he fill'd; untill the adoption of the Federal Goverment— he was then chose
by his fellow citizens their Representative in Congress, which he continued to be during the
administration, of General Washington and Mr Adams— (My fathers merits are not mine
but I hope they may excite some sympathy, for the unfortunate & only offspring of an
old soldier) He then retired from publick life, to the bosom of his family, wishing to enjoy
in his old age; that happiness which arises from the reflection of a life well spent;
sweetened by the endearments of my mother, and myself; of whom he was so dotingly fond
that he spared neither trouble or expence; for my improvement or gratification.
Shortly after this in 1802. I married Cap. William Cowper, who had commanded the
United States Sloop of War Baltimore.— Here commences the sad narrative of
my misfortunes— In a few months after my marriage, the house of John Cowper & Co
failed, in which house my husband was a joint partner. he made no exertions for my
support, and I was left destitute— my father touched with my situation took me
again to his house; where he declared he would support me, and divide with me his
th

Parker's estate. Nervous over William's obvious control of the property, he asked the county court in the late summer of 1812 to relieve him and to name a "counter-security."[17] Baker did his best to administer the estate by collecting monies due to it, and he tried in the county court to regain Macclesfield for Ann. But the justices repeatedly postponed Baker's suit to have William evicted until the case abated upon the executor's death in 1816. The press of other business may have forced this delay, but some magistrates clearly reflected the popular male attitude that disapproved of a woman holding property independent of her husband.[18]

Over the years the estate's value declined sharply under William's inept management. He rented out the land and sold virtually all the movable property, including Josiah Parker's bequests to his daughter. In blatant violation of the law, he "secretly and clandestinely" attempted to sell several slaves to Thomas Hancock with an understanding that they would be spirited out of Virginia. A disgusted Hancock refused and reported the offer to Ann and her uncle. William also tried various strategies to change his son's name in order to gain authority to sell the estate's lands. In the Superior Court of Law he produced a written statement that he was changing his son's name to Josiah C. Parker because of his "natural love and affection" for the boy and "by virtue of the authority which natural rights gives me as the father" to name his son whatever he chose. But legally that did not work, nor did the press release advertising his son's new name effect the change. William needed the assembly to act, but four times the legislators rebuffed his petitions. At one point he again approached Tazewell for assistance, but to no avail. Meanwhile his securities as his son's guardian watched William's conduct with growing alarm. Finally in August 1815 they asked the county court to force him to give an account of his guardianship and to provide additional security for young Josiah's inheritance.[19]

At first Ann stayed nearby with her uncle, but after William tried to shoot Pierce, she moved some forty miles to the home of a half-sister. Visiting her sons became impossible. To complicate matters, no one was willing to replace Baker as executor when he died in the spring of 1816. That November Ann petitioned for an *a mensa* divorce. The next month she wrote Joseph Cabell, the senator representing her district in Richmond, that she found the legislative divorce process "most painful," but she had no other alternative. The court orders had had "no effect." Almost the entire personal estate was gone, except for a few slaves, and William was renting out the land a year at a time. So she had decided "to apply to a *higher Tribunal.*" Possibly criticizing her experiences in court, she pointed out that she acted without a lawyer, having "neither inclination or ability" to hire one. She trusted the Senate would treat her fairly. Toward the close of her lengthy, dramatic petition to the assembly, Ann appealed to the legislators for "justice" and "mercy": "You who have *daughters* that are blooming, think of my *Father;* You who have *darling infants* think of *me*!" Eleven affidavits supported her case, including a statement from James Johnson and another from seven magistrates. In January 1817 the General Assembly obliged with a bill that "forever dissolved and annulled" the marriage. Both parties were forbidden to marry again during the lifetime of the other.[20]

William Cowper offers a classic profile of a battering husband. To understand that dynamic, we need to look at those elements in his adult life that were most crucial to the construction of his identity. We know virtually nothing of his childhood, but when he retired from the navy in 1801, the captain was a young man of twenty-eight whose military achievements had been rewarded by promotion and public recognition. Thus far his adult life exemplified the emerging nineteenth-century masculine ideal of aggressive, self-directed activity. The natural locus for that engagement now shifted to commercial enterprise, precisely at the time when the self-made man of business was coming to epitomize male involvement in the world.[21]

Memories of naval exploits, however, were soon overshadowed by the realities of failure. First the firm Cowper entered with his brothers went bankrupt. Then the store he set up with Parker's assistance collapsed. Between these twin defeats the young man returned to the sea reluctantly, urged by his father-in-law. Ann wrote that after the failure of her husband's first business venture, her father insisted that William "make some exertions for himself," since he possessed "youth, health, and a lucrative profession." William, however, turned out to be a diffident sailor, "compell'd to resort to his profession." For whatever reasons, a ship captain's occupation did not appeal to him. As soon as he earned a tidy profit of $5,000 in the West Indies trade, William Cowper quickly abandoned his vessel, hurried back to Southside Virginia, and again tried his hand at business. But a second financial setback confirmed his inability to attain the status of an independent entrepreneur.

William's need to resort to Parker for funds to support this second venture deepened his sense of inadequacy. Incapable of self-achievement, he depended on the very man against whom he competed for the affection and respect of his wife. The contrast between the two males was striking. Josiah Parker's prestige within Virginia's gentry class rested on his accomplishments as patriot, politician, planter, and business investor. At one time William might have dreamed of following the same career path, but those hopes faded within a few years. The son-in-law could not measure up. As a man William Cowper was a failure. He lacked the independence that he expected to possess and the community presumed. Perhaps most embarrassing, he could not even support his wife and growing family of boys. Instead they returned to Parker's care at Macclesfield, and whenever he was not at sea, William resided in his father-in-law's home on the latter's indulgence. Ann acknowledged that in her first eight years of marriage she spent a total of only six months under her husband's "entire controul." His powerless situation displayed the utter absence of the personal liberty and self-sufficiency expected of the American male.[22]

When the frustrated sea captain exploded with anger and rage, a disgusted Josiah Parker ordered him out of his home, effectively separating William from his wife and children. Though Ann rejected her father's suggestion of a divorce, she and her children remained under "Pappa's" care. Even from the grave Parker tried to guarantee their security by giving Ann considerable personal property and slaves, the use of Macclesfield as long as she wished, and a steady income from an annuity designed to last for the rest of her life. William could not legally touch a penny. Ann's position clearly frustrated her husband's need for gender superiority. It also defied the limitations that Virginia law placed on a married woman as a *feme covert*. A husband typically expected to own and control all property. But William Cowper had no property of his own, while his wife possessed considerable economic assets and the financial independence he lacked. To add insult to injury, Parker's will instructed his executor to consult only Ann in the disposition of his estate. In addition, houses and lots that Parker had owned in Norfolk, Portsmouth, and elsewhere could be sold only with Ann's and Thomas Pierce's approval. In short, Parker left his son-in-law economically emasculated. Most galling of all to William must have been Parker's provision giving his entire estate to his oldest grandson and namesake on the condition that he legally change his surname from Cowper to Parker.

Utterly humiliated by his father-in-law, William later acted out his fury by ordering the slaves to exhume the bodies of Ann's parents and other relatives and "scatter them over the marshes." He also vented his frustration at home by treating Ann harshly and exploding violently whenever she asserted any authority within the family. Sally Copeland described a dinner scene shortly after Ann returned to the plantation in December 1811. When she "mildly" corrected one of her sons for fighting with his younger brother, "Capt. Cowper jumpt up from the table seized the knife he was eating with, and swore he would stab her as he knew . . . that she intended the rebuke for him."[23] Ignoring Parker's will and the Chancery District Court's decree, William commandeered complete control of the house, slaves, and plantation; harassed the executor; drove Ann from her home and children on several occasions; and finally forced her to live apart.

Contemporary sociologists who have analyzed the social environment of domestic abusers are helpful in discerning the reasons for William Cowper's violent conduct. Resource theorists, for example, argue that violence occurs when people do not have the social, economic, and personal assets they require to maintain control. William Cowper demanded dominance over his family in order to fulfill his gendered identity within a male-dominated society, but he lacked the resources that were available to his wife and father-in-law. Violence became his way of dealing with the stresses that developed from his own inadequacies in marriage and career. To assert a power and authority that he in fact lacked, William lashed out at his wife. Ann became the focal point for his frustrations and failures. "If one of my children or a servant offended him, after correcting them he would punish me," she wrote; "if at a public place he was slighted by any one, or had a dispute (*which often happened*) he would on his return home, wreak on me his vengeance."[24]

William's behavior can also be understood in terms of exchange theory, which postulates that "the principle of costs and rewards" governs domestic abusers. A batterer uses violence when it results in the achievement of power and control, and society in terms of the family, community, and the law either ignores or condones it. If the price for violence is too high, however, the abuser will moderate such conduct. William acted violently unless and until the costs outweighed the benefits. For example, after Josiah Parker ordered him to quit Macclesfield and after his business failed the second time, he appeared to be sincerely penitent in hopes of gaining financial support. Later, after Ann had gotten a court order requiring him to keep the peace, William closely inquired whether his wife could testify against him if he beat her without any witnesses present. He wanted to assault her physically but refrained—at least for a time—because the law might punish him. Ultimately, however, she saved herself only by flight.[25]

Throughout the early years of Ann Cowper's ordeal her behavior followed the classic pattern of a battered wife. Her petitions and the affidavits of numerous witnesses suggest six major episodes between 1807 and 1812, with some of them taking place over several weeks or months. As Leonore Walker has proposed, each episode moved in three stages. First came a period of rising tension between the couple, usually because Ann blocked her husband's attempts to control her property and seize their son's inheritance. Then came the battery. William beat, choked, and horse-whipped Ann. He knocked her down, dragged her around a room, and attempted on various occasions to starve her and to throw her out of a carriage. He also abused her verbally, threatened her with bodily harm and even death, destroyed her furniture, burned her clothes, and expelled her from Macclesfield. Each incident was followed by a third period of contrition, promises of amendment, efforts at reconciliation, and quiet. Sometimes this stage lasted for months; once it endured for only sixteen hours.[26]

The most immediately arresting reality in this case is Ann Cowper's efforts to conciliate her husband and continue their marriage. Her strategy was to use "every tender, and, soothing method; to produce an alteration in his conduct: [she] promised to be obedient to his wishes." Thus she endured periods of abusive treatment and returned to Macclesfield after serious, even life-threatening incidents. She also attempted to conceal her marital troubles. Ann did not tell the assembly, for example, that she had rejected her father's proposal for a divorce. Witnesses, including a doctor who examined her, noted that she was embarrassed by the injuries her husband inflicted and tried to hide the evidence of his assaults. Despite her best efforts, however, she could not keep the violent episodes from the household, relatives, or neighbors. William Cowper's cruelty toward his wife became notorious in the community.[27]

Ann was also torn by conflicting emotions. Of the two principal men in her life, the one she called "Pappa" was her rock of support. His role in the construction of her identity is evident from the long introduction to her divorce petition, which details his military exploits and political offices in hopes that "they may excite some sympathy, for the unfortunate and *only offspring* of an old *soldier*." But despite William's failings, Ann still loved her husband and the father of her children. After Josiah Parker

The cruel catastrophe of MARY FINLEY.

Frontispiece from God's Revenge against Murder, *by Parson Weems.*
This pamphlet told the story of Polly Middleton and Ned Findley. Findley,
a drunkard, married Middleton for her money. Eight weeks later, after battering
her repeatedly, he drowned her while they were crossing a river in a canoe.
He was quickly caught and hanged. (Courtesy of Virginia Historical Society)

expelled him from Macclesfield, she secretly sent him money from the allowance her father provided her. With a desperate urgency she wanted to believe that he was capable of reformation, that his repeated protestations of change and promises of love were sincere and would be effectual. From her perspective his battery was due to an "intolerable temper" that for far too long she thought he could correct.

In the final analysis, however, Ann Cowper submitted to an abusive husband for as long as she did for the same reason she ultimately sought a divorce: for the sake of her children. On the inheritance rights of young Josiah, Ann was unyielding. When William Cowper suggested he might murder the boy, "all the instinctive fears of a Mother, rushed at once on my heart; and trembled for the safety of her darling child." She returned to Macclesfield because "the welfare of my poor little children was at stake." She utterly rejected William's proposal that she abort her fourth son, even when he threatened to murder her if she refused. In Ann's eyes William was an "unnatural father" to keep this youngest child from her when she was breastfeeding him. Then, after she finally took the baby and left, "*the instinctive love of a mother*" compelled her to return to see her other sons.

As multiple eyewitnesses testified, William did everything possible to block Ann's visits, threatened to kill anyone who brought her to see the boys, and raised them "to hate" their mother. The justices as well as friends and family members who wrote on her behalf warned the legislature that William "entirely neglected" his sons. She rested her case for a divorce on the fate of her children: "My life I could resign, but the love I bear my children entwines around my heart, and irresistably impels me to exert myself for them." Writing in the third person, she proclaimed, "Her wish is to *support* and *educate* her children, to resque them from *vice* and ignorance (to which they are now exposed under their father) and bring them up in *piety* and *virtue*." The identity she constructed for herself is that of a mother whose first concern is for the health and welfare of her children. In that respect she modeled closely the maternal image of southern women that Sally McMillen has described.[28] More important in terms of presenting a successful petition, Ann Cowper exemplified the American mother of whom antebellum male Virginians approved.

PATTERNS IN ABUSIVE RELATIONSHIPS

To what extent was Ann Parker Cowper's situation typical of that of battered women who sought legislative divorces in antebellum Virginia? Of the 204 women whose grievances are known, 86 (42 percent) pleaded physical battery. Of this group 32 (37 percent) received divorces, with 23 (72 percent) of these being absolute divorces. Of the total number of 242 women petitioners, 81 (33 percent) received divorces, with 62 (77 percent) of these granted absolutely. Some of these were undoubtedly battery cases, but their petitions have been lost or removed from the assembly's files. In contrast, 218 men petitioned for divorce, and the legislature passed private bills for 72 (33 percent) of them, the same percentage of successful women petitioners. Thus women who asserted battery as grounds for divorce received more favorable attention from the lawmakers than the other women or the men seeking divorces. Apart from this general conclusion, however, statistical comparisons are impossible to make. The divorce files vary enormously in content, size, and detail, as do the collateral tax, property, and estate records.

Given the volume of battery cases, however, we can make significant generalizations about the situations of battered women and the men who beat them. Available records indicate, for example, that women from across Virginia and from every class and rank in society sought divorces on the grounds of battery. Equally significant, battering husbands tended to come from lower socioeconomic levels than their wives, and like William Cowper, they frequently appear to have been incompetent or unlucky in managing property, personal finances, and business affairs. For example, at his death in 1827 John Kirk of Lancaster County left his wife, Ann, with an extensive plantation and at least seven slaves. About two years later she married John Edmonds, who bore, in Ann's words, "a fair character" but possessed few if any resources. Within a short time he began "to squander her property by the most scandalous and profligate course of life until he had reduced her from comparative affluence to almost abject poverty." Turning on his wife, John introduced his mistress into the house, installed her in Ann's bed and place at table, and forced his wife to work in the garden. On several occasions he flogged Ann into consenting to legal deeds that would have bartered away her widow's dower. This event was forestalled only when the authorities imprisoned John for raping Ann's twelve-year-old niece, who was also his ward. Before the trial he escaped from jail and disappeared. The assembly gave Ann Edmonds an absolute divorce.[29]

Though the accusation is not explicit in the records, John may well have married Ann for her property. Many battering husbands appear to have this motive, and financial and property considerations loom large in the assembly files. Some brides wed against the advice of family and friends, but many more married with parental consent only to discover that they had been beguiled by grooms who were only interested in tangible assets. Some deceptions were reciprocal and identify both parties as naive. When Ann Fisher married Abner Rankin in 1826, she did not know that he was afflicted with venereal disease, although he appeared in "feeble" health and was unable to work. After he infected her and she bore a stillborn child, Ann realized the problem. Meanwhile Abner abused her, wasted her dower, and absconded after voicing his disappointment that she had brought him less property than he had expected.[30] Both parties felt deceived by each other.

Young James Norman, on the other hand, knew the fortune he acquired when in November 1842 he wed a thirty-six-year-old widow, Lucy Harris Price. Earlier that year she had married a wealthy widower, John Price, but he soon died and left his widow the bulk of his substantial estate. Hungry for "a life of contentment and happiness," Lucy rushed heedlessly back to the altar and got a fortune hunter not yet twenty-one. Too late she realized her error. In classic understatement she later described her marriage as "an unfortunate connection." James Norman, as we saw in the last chapter, preferred to sleep with a slave girl on a pallet in his wife's bedroom. Lucy's family and friends may have forced him out, because within a few years James left and ultimately agreed to a separate maintenance with Lucy that gave him the larger half of the economic loaf. Two years later the assembly granted her a divorce.[31]

Battering husbands such as James Norman typically anticipated great economic benefits that failed to materialize. Joseph Anderson Cocke married the only daughter of wealthy Dibdal Talley, fully expecting that his father-in-law would give him the whole plantation and everything on it. Joseph told a third party he never would have wed Judith Talley otherwise. Alfred Eubank, enraged at the discovery that his wife's estate was not all that he had expected, eventually departed after months of beating and choking her. But such was the law that even husbands who had deserted their wives could reappear at any time and claim whatever property their wife possessed or inherited, unless a farsighted relative had placed it in a trust with specific restrictions. Polly Stone's situation was typical. She had finally fled back to her father's home after her husband had tried to kill her several times. Jeremiah Stone had relocated out west, but Polly begged for a divorce because he threatened to return to Virginia and seize whatever estate her father left her and her child.[32]

Many battered women found themselves in Polly Stone's situation and sought a divorce in order to maintain or regain control over whatever property they possessed or hoped to inherit. Margaret Combs's plight was typical. Her father had left her a handsome estate, but her husband, Benjamin, had squandered it and then violently expelled her from their home. A rich uncle provided financial support while she lived with her grandparents. Twenty years later only her aged grandmother was left, and her uncle's legacy was payable to Margaret upon the elder woman's death. Benjamin, living nearby with his paramour and their two children, now threatened to demand his "marital rights" and seize Margaret's inheritance. Only a divorce would eliminate that danger, and the assembly responded.[33]

As in William Cowper's case, absolute male control over all marital property was continually asserted in multiple ways. Battering husbands typically forced wives out of their homes. This happened repeatedly to Jane Godwin, who lived near the Cowpers. Evening brandy "frolicks" brought out the worst in Edmund Godwin, and his brutality repeatedly forced Jane to flee to the swamps along the James River. Later in the night she might sneak back into the kitchen in search of some protection against the weather, but if he discovered her, Edmund attacked her "with his fists and with sticks." Sally Powell lived in the Godwin house and once was ordered off the plantation along with Jane. The next day Edmund "sent his horse and gig after us," but when they returned, he ordered them to leave. For seven years Martha Barnett regularly escaped to the woods when her husband kicked her out of their cottage. Thomas Boling eventually "took the bed from under" Susannah and expelled her from the house. Jonah Dobyns repeatedly whipped his wife and threw her and their four young children out of their home. One witness testified that "he had heard the said Dobyns boast to his wife that in her absence he had taken one of his own negroe Women into her bed and that he would do it again whenever it suited him."[34]

Many battered women, like Ann Cowper, left their husbands only when they finally realized that their lives were endangered. Though she discovered shortly after her marriage to Uriah that he had infected her with "a Loathsome and distressing disease," Sarah Grantham stayed through six years of physical and psychological violence. Such brutality was not unusual for battering husbands. A legislative committee found that Elizabeth Robertson's husband had given her venereal disease, beaten her until she was physically incapacitated for the rest of her life, and attempted to kill her, all of which he denied.[35] Henry Rollins knocked his wife to the floor with the fireplace tongs and then "stamped" on her body until he broke her ribs. Juliana Baker witnessed William Ball dragging his wife Charlotte "around the house by the hair of her head" and heard him "cursing and threatening to kill" her. Ball ultimately drew a pistol, but it misfired. Nathaniel Roberts knocked his wife down the staircase, broke her ribs, and caused her to suffer a life-threatening miscarriage. Often he forced her to sleep on the floor and "beat her head against the bed post and wall till her sense had nearly left her." She finally left him, and the court found she had "Just cause to apprehend bodily injury."[36]

Enormous verbal and psychological abuse almost invariably accompanied physical battery, and one could never be sure what would result. Long before he finally assaulted his wife with an axe, Newman Roane delighted in suggesting that he would do to Evelina what his cousin had done to his wife. That murder in a prominent gentry family created a sensation. Writing to her sister, Eliza Thomson reported that John Roane Jr. had slit his wife's "throat and pulled out the sinews." That was only one item in Eliza's catalog of marital violence. She reported that another husband had hung his wife and a third was in jail for murdering his spouse. "The Devil has broken loose among the Husbands in this part of the world," Eliza concluded. The particular devil in question may have been demon rum. The petitions overwhelmingly identify alcoholism as a major problem. As one wife testified, "The brandy bottle raised his frenzy to its highest state."[37]

Huldah Graham's case for a legal separation from husband, Ferdinand, in 1846 presents a typically graphic picture of wedded life on the rocks. Married eighteen years earlier, the couple first lived happily with his parents before moving into their own home. Then Ferdinand's indulgence in "ardent spirits" made him "harsh and unkind." One Sunday he pushed and pulled Huldah around the porch and hit her so hard that she fell down "Senseless." She then returned to her mother, resolving "never again to put herself in his power." For the next two and half years Ferdinand begged her to return and demonstrated his repentance by abstaining from alcohol and joining the Methodist Church. Huldah relented and lived to regret it. As she described her husband "like the dog returning to his vomit, and the Sow to Wallowing in the Mire, he again became more and more intemperate and more and more Morose in disposition, and harsh and unkind." Finally he became so drunk one August day that he "vomited over the bed, until it was alas entirely unfit for [Huldah] to sleep upon." While he was unconscious on the bed, she fell asleep in the adjoining room. About midnight Ferdinand woke up, stormed into her room, and demanded to know why she was there. Before Huldah could respond, he began to slug her "on her side and breast, some three or four severe and violent blows with his fist." He dragged her out of the house, still clobbering her, and Huldah thought she would have been killed had not two young men, awakened by her cries, intervened. In his response Ferdinand admitted a drinking problem but denied that he had done anything more than "played Roughly with her." Later he confessed his violent conduct but offered a simple reason: "It was liquor set me crazy."[38]

Not all abused wives accepted that facile explanation for the violent behavior of their husbands. Elizabeth Waterfield, for example, offered a more perceptive analysis. Describing the savage behavior of her spouse, she told the assembly, "At first his harsh treatment was ascribed to the too free use of ardent Spirits, but the lapse of time convinced your petitioner of the fallacy of this opinion and that it arose solely from an insensibility and savageness of heart." Throughout the petitions and supporting affidavits, women and witnesses testify to "violent and vindictive" tempers, "morose" behavior, "harsh and cruel" dispositions, and men "devoid of feeling." Susan Whitlow lived with Alfred and Mildred Wingo and noticed that, drunk or sober, Alfred normally entered the house "cursing his wife" and often threatened to kill her. Susan saw him "slap his wife's jaws, pinch and Kick her, and all this without any provication on her part." A male boarder who stayed with the Wingos for several years concluded, "He was the most ill natured man I ever saw towards his wife."[39]

Male jealousy and insecurity often enhanced a husband's brutality. What destroyed his sobriety, according to Ferdinand Heiskell, was his suspicion that Huldah entertained a "forbidden love" for another man. But drunk or sober, battering husbands frequently unjustly accused their wives of infidelity. While this tactic may have reflected male insecurity and psychological weakness, it served more importantly as yet another method of control. For example, on their wedding night Griffin Bayne suggested that his sixteen-year-old bride had been unchaste, and the next day he accused Nancy of having had an abortion. He was sure of this, he told her, because he possessed "superior Knowledge of the female Sex." After that he gave her "no Rest" on the issue but promised that if she admitted her guilt, he would forgive and forget. Convinced finally that

"Nothing but a Lye would satisfy him," Nancy remarked, "Silence gives Consent." Of course that failed to mollify Griffin. He leveled even more wild charges, accused her of incest, and drove her from their home.[40]

As in the case of Ann Cowper, pregnancy and the birth of a child often brought out the worst in battering husbands. David Hutchings was so insanely jealous of his wife, Elizabeth, over her conversations with visitors to their home that he attempted to kill her on several occasions. When she became pregnant, David forced her "to ride a wild and dangerous horse in a violent storm," and she miscarried. When his wife, Susannah, was far advanced in pregnancy, a drunken Thomas Boling tied her hands behind her back, put a rope around her waist and threw the other end around a beam. He then hoisted Susannah up until her toes barely touched the ground and beat her senseless. After extreme suffering, she lost the child. Charlotte Ball was in an advanced stage of pregnancy at the time of one of the worst attacks by her husband, William. Newman Roane was particularly cruel to Evelina during the last stages of her pregnancy and shortly after the birth of their son.[41]

When they were not torturing their wives for supposed infidelities, many battering husbands engaged in adulterous and/or interracial liaisons. Griffin Bayne contracted a venereal disease and tried to infect Nancy. Thomas Boling kept "a harlot" in his wife's bedroom. Both William Ball and Newman Roane engaged in long-term sexual relationships with household slaves. Ball bragged to one of his male friends that he slept with both white and black woman, including one of his mother's servants. Roane openly established a slave girl in his home "as the more eligible companion and wife." Such affairs were mentioned frequently in the divorce petitions. Sally Ballinger bore her husband, Richard, six children while he had one child by a first mistress and three by a second. Finally he drove Sally and her six out of the house and established his lover with "all the power or privileges" of "his lawful wife." Barbara Pettus unhappily tolerated her slave-trading husband's beatings and interracial affairs in her home for nine years. He then sold his property, left Barbara and her child, and relocated in Georgia with his mother, slaves, and a young woman he persuaded to elope with him.[42]

Like Sally Ballinger and Barbara Pettus, many battered wives remained in a violent marriage far longer than would seem humanly possible. Hoping their husbands would change, the women tried to reform them and returned to them when they promised amendment. All the well-known patterns prevalent in abusive relationships today occurred then and represent an important continuity between past and present dispositions in battered women and battering husbands. Credulity repeatedly triumphed over knowledge and reason. Like Ann Cowper, Polly Stone believed her brutal husband's "many fair promises" and went back only to suffer more punishment. Even though he had lashed her repeatedly, Sopha Dobyns returned to Jonah when he appeared at her father's plantation and apologized "in the most imposing manner, expressed his contrition and deep felt sorrow, for the numerous insults and injuries offered to her feelings and person." Later she could only explain her foolish decision as an "infatuation." Two weeks later their marriage resumed its normal course when Jonah whipped Sopha, threatened her life, and chased her around the farm with a loaded pistol.[43]

Elizabeth Maxwell finally left an alcoholic husband who frequently assaulted her mercilessly. But then she returned to him, she told the assembly, "when she was urged and pressed by fervent and repeated letters from him, written in the most artfull, feigned, and insinuating manner, and pointedly addressed to, and intended to work upon, and bias the feelings and passions of your Petitioner." Alas it was all a trick to get her back into his clutches. Ultimately she and her three children fled "for safety and protection." Mary Lowry, responding to her husband's "importunities" and "fair promises of future good conduct," returned to a brutal marriage that she had resolved to quit. Though she soon discovered that Aaron Lowry had changed not a whit, she still "unremittingly endeavoured by every method in her power to reclaim and reform him" while he proceeded to abuse her. Many women tried, like Pamelia Cole, to appease a brutal husband by a "dutiful and affectionate course of conduct toward him," hoping to "soften his temper and conduct toward her."[44]

The same scenario played itself out in marriage after marriage. Wives, believing that a separation would somehow hurt their offspring, frequently remained with brutal husbands for the sake of their children. Catherine Wells endured years of vicious treatment from an alcoholic husband who beat, kicked, and bloodied and bruised her on numerous occasions—so much so that she was confined to her bed. But until her own life was immediately threatened, she told the legislature, she remained with him because of her three children. Only when he warned her to make her "peace with heaven" did she finally flee to her father's home. Sometimes battered wives, like Ann Cowper and Pamelia Cole, attempted to hide their plight from family and friends until their situation became insupportable. For six years Pamelia kept her marital troubles to herself, but far from responding to her blandishments, John Cole's "temper" worsened. Eventually she could no longer hide the physical evidence of his brutality.[45]

The divorce files demonstrate that Ann Parker Cowper's situation was typical of that of battered women who ultimately sought divorces. The data are sufficient to provide composite pictures of battering husbands and battered wives that bear striking similarities to the profiles in modern-day studies.[46] Antebellum Virginia's abusive husbands tended to come from poorer socioeconomic backgrounds than their wives and frequently married with hopes of riches that did not materialize. Even when they profited economically from their marriages, battering husbands often proved to be poor managers of money and property. Whether lacking in talent, luck, or both, they normally dissipated their assets and wound up as poor or poorer than when they started, unable or unwilling to provide for their wives and children. Frustrated by their defeat in the competitive male world, they exploded in anger at home. As resource theorists suggest, material disappointment and ineptitude fed a rage they took out on their spouses. The privacy of the family circle allowed them the latitude to assert the power and control denied them in the public arena. Since they were economic and social failures, the only superiority left them was race and gender. These circumstances in turn legitimized and reinforced the tendency to batter wives, as well as children, servants, and slaves. Sometimes the battery began on the day of the marriage, but it might be delayed for months or even years until the men experienced frustration at the lack of those social, economic, or political resources they demanded as constitutive elements of male dominance.

In terms of personal characteristics, abusive husbands overwhelmingly demonstrated classic alcoholic behavior. But as some perceptive wives noted, their tempers and moody dispositions appeared more responsible for their violent conduct than liquor, which tended to release inhibition rather than cause the battery. Abusive behavior sprang from more deep-seated causes; drinking simply exacerbated it. Drunk or not, male batterers almost always threatened to kill their wives before or during a battering incident. Sometimes the battery took place during pregnancy or shortly after childbirth. Frequently suspicious of their wives, jealous husbands would accuse them of infidelity. Battery could then take the form of explicit sexual dominance—rape—which sometimes left a wife seriously and permanently injured. Yet these same men were often unfaithful themselves. Some formed sexual liaisons with servants or slaves, and a majority eventually deserted their spouses to live in adultery or bigamy.

Before desertion or a final separation, a series of battering incidents normally occurred, generally in increasing stages of violence. After each incident, particularly if the wife had sought refuge with her family or neighbors, the husband typically begged her to come home and promised to change his behavior, amend his life, and treat her well. Too many women went back, hoping for a reformation and thinking that they could change their husband's behavior by their own submission and obedience. They also returned to their battering husbands for the sake of their children. In this respect they were trapped by laws that ordinarily entrusted children to the father's custody. Moreover, the treatment they had received was a source of deep humiliation, which many wives attempted to hide as long as they could.

GENDERED EXPECTATIONS

Women's efforts to conceal their abuse resulted from the fact that battered women were often too embarrassed and ashamed by the failure of their marriages and blamed themselves. They had learned this response. Practically without exception the religious and lay prescription literature mandated a family structure in which the husband headed the household and the wife subjected herself to his direction. Marital shipwreck awaited spouses who attempted to alter the respective positions assigned them by both nature and the Bible. The same authorities, however, also wrote in warm, expansive terms of the desirability of mutual love and respect between the spouses. Some historians of gender relations have recently examined the inherent dissidence in literature and practice. In her study of the conflicted marriage of William and Elizabeth Wirt, Anya Jabour argued that the reality of domestic male control clashed with the mutuality and reciprocity expected in a companionate marriage. Yet as Stephen Frank has pointed out, "Companionate ideals were advanced in a patriarchal context."[47] While the values attached to each perspective on marriage and family life coexisted, albeit uneasily, the aspirations for companionate marriage reflected the increasing consensus of informed opinion.

Whether religious or secular, matrimonial experts focused more on the gendered expectations for a wife than for a husband. Bodily stature and strength dictated that the woman was the dependent party—a follower, not a leader. The wife who attempted to control her husband not only acted contrary to the proper nature and order of creation; she was also destined to make herself miserable and destroy her own happiness. As president of William and Mary from the Revolution until his death in 1812, Episcopal bishop James Madison, the cousin of the president, helped shape the views and values of two generations of southerners. Writing to his daughter Susan on the eve of her marriage in 1811, the bishop advised her "never to attempt to controul your husband by opposition of any kind." She should never "take from him the freedom of acting as his own judgment shall direct; but . . . place such confidence in him, as to believe that his prudence is his best guide." Madison was certain that a wife's happiness depended entirely on the love bestowed upon her by her husband, and he wrote as if the responsibility rested entirely on her shoulders. He warned his daughter, "A difference with your husband ought to be considered as the greatest calamity, as one that is to be the most studiously guarded against." The frequent republication of Madison's letter in the secular and religious press demonstrates that his advice accurately reflected the perspective of the antebellum South.[48]

In the mid-1830s, for example, the *Southern Literary Messenger* urged "the softer sex," especially women recently married, to heed Madison's "wholesome advice." Women naturally occupied a subordinate position in marriage, explained another writer, because they formed "the second grade in the order of created beings." Men came first.[49] Therefore, proposed a clergyman, even if the wife was the more intelligent and wiser partner—an "incongruous union," from his perspective—she should never "expose her husband to the pity and contempt of others" by an obvious display of her superiority. "Feminine minds in men and masculine minds in women are both deviations from the ordinary course of nature, and unfortunate for the subjects. And when the woman of masculine mind is married to the man of feminine mind, of course the former will strive for and generally gain the mastery." Nevertheless, "the faithful wife will not refuse to obey her husband, in all matters where he may rightfully claim her subjection." Lay writers agreed that the wife made a fatal error if she attempted to gain the superior position in a marriage. James Garnett argued that the wife who dominated her husband would be respected by neither men nor women, and he advised the girls who heard or read his lectures, "Be content, when you marry, to let the chief control of family concerns remain where the laws both of God and man have placed it."[50]

All marital experts recommended lists of virtues appropriate to the dutiful wife. "The great desiderata," Garnett wrote, "are a tolerably good understanding, moderation, forbearance, goodness of heart, self-control, and incorruptible morals." What marriage demanded was "qualities for *use*, rather than for *show*." The clergy concurred. Methodist John Bayley thought that a successful wife regarded her husband with "*reverence*," dressed modestly, and cultivated "mildness, softness, sweetness of temper," and "CHEERFULNESS." When he returned home, the husband should be "soothed and encouraged by the gentle words and cheerful smiles of a true-hearted, loving wife." The true wife was an asylum from the world for her husband as well as the domestic repository of chastity. It belonged to her as "the better sex" to cultivate the "passive virtues."[51] She bore chief responsibility for a happy home, a satisfied husband, and the rearing of dutiful and obedient children. Given this mandate, failure to produce the anticipated results reflected poorly on women. While some women obviously rejected or ignored the role prescribed by preachers, educators, writers, and politicians, it was embedded in women's upbringing. When a marriage failed, the wife could blame herself and minimize her husband's responsibility.

At the same time, the culture of domesticity taught women and their attorneys the most effective way to present their cases in Richmond. Lawyers knew what formulas were most likely to succeed. Thus women invariably appeared weak, pitiable, completely helpless, and utterly dependent. Even when they had other resources, such as strong family support, their petitions tended to omit or minimize them. Instead their documents were crafted to appeal to the protective instincts of the male lawmakers. The supporting affidavits from other women as well as men often provide balance to the petitions while they fill in the pictures of domestic violence and tragedy.

From time to time, however, a woman petitioner could break loose from this role and still succeed in gaining a divorce. Scotty Catherine Brown wed Orlando Brown in 1834. Five months later, after abusing her and threatening her life, Orlando abandoned his wife. She had more cause to leave him but did not do so or publicize his behavior. Thirteen years passed before she explained her silence: "Notwithstanding all the wrong and injury I have received, I still possessed a womans heart, still endure the frowns of some, still feel the poignant grief resulting from such conduct." Going public with her situation would have been too humiliating, until she learned that Orlando had surfaced in another county, announced that Scotty had died, "wore crape upon his hat and arm," and shortly thereafter married again and fathered a child. A male correspondent urged her to "Let it pass off as the wind that Blows By you" and be grateful that Orlando had not left her with any children to support. But fed up with her lot in life, Scotty was outraged. "Is not the crime of bigamy alone sufficient to procure my release?" she challenged the assembly. The legislature agreed.[52] Bigamy, after all, violated the law.

SOCIAL SUPPORTS FOR BATTERY

Community attitudes and legal and governing structures reinforced the gender subordination that undergirded a society structured to support battery against women. For many if not most antebellum males, violence was a socially acceptable and even expected means of controlling a wife. The operative common-law text of Blackstone acknowledged the husband's right to chastise his wife for "misbehavior . . . in the same moderation" he might use "to correct his servants or children."[53] In this context society took for granted family privacy and male domination of the home. The institution of marriage had to be upheld regardless of the suffering of individuals. Family members, neighbors, and local authorities worked cooperatively to maintain this absolute value, even in extreme cases.

As a result relations and friends sometimes strove mightily to reconcile a couple who belonged apart. William Ball had beaten his wife, Charlotte, badly and chased her with a tomahawk until she finally got a court order requiring him to keep the peace. This meant jail for William, since he was without funds to give security and no one else would guarantee his conduct. At this juncture a neighbor intervened to persuade a reluctant Charlotte that she should return to William lest he be locked up. Margaret Combs's parents were both dead, so her grandfather coached her to use "submission, kindness and a careful discharge of all her duties" to gain at least civil care from her husband, Benjamin. When her uncle learned of the "cruel treatment" she was receiving, he only recommended that she "bear up" as best she could. Nancy Bayne's parents had attempted to dissuade her from marrying Griffin Bayne, arguing that he was "the worst of men," but the infatuated teenager had insisted. When Griffin threw her out of the house a month or so later, they took her back "like the Prodigal of old." But then a male delegation, including Nancy's father, a neighborhood lawyer, and a state legislator, called on Griffin to effect a reconciliation. The men agreed that Nancy "should return, and that no Blame should be attached to her," so back to Griffin she went.

The same pattern of abuse was renewed, despite her father's efforts "to procure her better treatment," until Griffin finally tossed her out of the house.[54]

Fathers, family, friends, and neighbors supported the value system that underlay the proposition that the husband was the head of the wife. But while society endorsed male domination, continuing high levels of abuse and excessive violence in marital relations were unacceptable because such conduct threatened other values considered desirable. The authorities at the University of Virginia summarily dismissed Professor George Blaettermann from the faculty in 1840 because he publicly beat his wife.[55] In the Cowper case, relatives and other members of the local community submitted numerous and detailed affidavits. Their texts reveal the responsibility men felt to preserve the gendered hierarchy that sustained their own prerogative and the investment that both men and women had in maintaining stable, comfortable marriages in which reciprocity marked familial and social discourses.

Kinship and community proved crucial. When a situation had become unbearable, the first acceptable refuge of many battered women was with a father who could extend male protection. Despite the husband's legal authority over a wife, a male parent, particularly one well known and respected in the community, might offer sanctuary to his daughter and grandchildren and attempt to provide for her financially after his death, as Ann Cowper's father did. This was not always successful, however, because of the status the common law afforded the husband. Happening by the Dobyns's farm one day, Sopha's father, Major Thomas Leftwich, tried to protect his daughter from a beating by her husband and wound up "beaten and mangled" himself when Jonah turned on him, whip in hand. Eventually, older and wiser after six years of marriage, Sopha took her three children and "threw herself on the protection of her father." Jonah then threatened a lawsuit against Leftwich "for the protection afforded her."[56]

Sometimes, when spousal abuse grossly violated community standards of behavior and a father's presence provided insufficient protection, neighbors intervened extralegally to stop the battery. Eleanor Neff was a schoolgirl when Lemuel Allison moved into her neighborhood in Hampshire County. Foolishly she fell in love, and he persuaded her to elope with him to Maryland. But soon after their marriage Lemuel's conduct changed abruptly. After leaving Eleanor for a year, he reappeared, became "ferocious in the extreme," and publicly whipped his wife mercilessly. When her father intervened and took her home, Lemuel threatened to kill him. The neighborhood had had enough of this interloper. After beating and tarring him, the locals tied Lemuel to a "Gondola" and shipped him "down the river." He did not reappear in Hampshire County, and Eleanor received her divorce. In this case both the neighborhood and the legislators had reinforced, not diminished, male prerogative. Excessive domestic violence threatened the values of family life and good order that assembly, courts, and communities were determined to uphold.[57]

The Cowper case exemplifies the balance between community opposition to excessive violence and the responsibility men felt to preserve male dominance. Multiple testimonials by magistrates, neighbors, and relatives corroborated Ann Cowper's version of events, and an unusual declaration of support signed by seven justices of the county court accompanied her petition. William Cowper's "brutal treatment to his wife" and "turbulent conduct" had been a matter of court concern for some time. His temper appears to have become uncontrollable. Interrupting a church camp meeting attended by more than a thousand people, he had attacked the ministers, beaten up a member of the assemblage, and yelled "the most Shocking blasphemies of the Almighty God." For this conduct Justice Andrew Woodley had ordered him to keep the peace and appear in court. But when he showed up at the courthouse and before his case was heard, he started a brawl. The court made him and his securities pay their fines for the campground scenes and then bound him by an even stiffer recognizance. Finally, William tried to shoot Thomas Pierce, Ann's uncle, but missed. Andrew Woodley had the sheriff throw William in jail, but Pierce withdrew the complaint on condition that William swear "that he would never again molest either himself or any of his family." James Johnson, who had rebuked William and represented Ann before the county court, occupied Josiah Parker's old congressional seat in 1816. In his affidavit supporting the divorce, Johnson called William Cowper "a base mean unprincipled and contemptible being."[58]

But despite widespread community support for Ann's divorce, local males would not acquiesce in any attack on the masculine prerogatives of absolute control over property and children, regardless of the law or the legislature. The divorce restored Ann to the status of a *feme sole* with the right to own and manage her own property. In early April 1817 the county court named Ann, at her request and with her friends Andrew Woodley and Arthur Smith as her securities, as the administrator of her father's estate. William, however, still occupied Macclesfield as well as the other

Parker lands. So Ann revived the suit that Joseph Baker had brought before the county court to evict him from the plantation. The trial lasted a full day before, in a stunning decision, the jury determined that she had no "right of possession" to the property. So much for the verdict of the Chancery District Court. The two presiding justices, who happened to be Andrew Woodley and Samuel Woodley, immediately set the verdict aside as "contrary to law and the evidence." But almost a year passed before the same two magistrates presided over a retrial with a brand new jury that decided in Ann's favor.[59]

The jury system Ann faced lay at the heart of local government in Virginia. In continuing the common-law tradition, the state guaranteed the right to a trial by a jury of twelve of one's peers in criminal and civil proceedings. To be eligible to serve on a county court jury, one had to be a white male citizen of a minimum age of twenty-one with property holdings worth at least $150. For a Superior Court trial, the freehold had to be $300 or more. In advance of court days the sheriff would draw up a list of potential jurors and summon them to attend. At the beginning of a trial court officials would call them forward, publicly examine them, and make the selection with the participation of attorneys for the plaintiff and defendant. If necessary the court could complete the panel by calling on bystanders. In the effort to secure an honest verdict by impartial jurors, the law laid down an extensive list of possible challenges and rules to govern jury deliberations. The jury's task was to examine the facts of a case, come to a verdict, and in civil suits, award damages. As a manifestation of local government the jury system provided citizens with the opportunity to exercise their liberty in determining the kind of society in which they would live. In the Old Dominion, as F. Thorton Miller has argued, it provided "the legal dimension to the Virginia Doctrine" of limited government and local control.

A jury could obstruct judges, ignore judicial precedents, and contradict the assembly and its laws.[60] So this jury did in *Cowper v Cowper* in Isle of Wight County in 1817. One can only speculate about what was in the minds of the men who sat in this body and its successor a year later. In economic terms the first jury was composed of wealthier individuals. These men owned an average of almost 6 slaves, in contrast to 2.5 slaves for the second jury. The first jury owned more land as well, though none of the members held as much as the 2,000 acres of the Parker estate that William Cowper occupied. Most of the second jury were simple farmers, and only two members owned carriages, compared with seven members of the first jury. But perhaps a more telling difference is the location of their residences. Isle of Wight County was divided into two districts for the sake of tax assessment. Ten members of the jury that sided with William Cowper resided in his district. One could presume, therefore, that they lived closer to him, and perhaps that made them more sympathetic to a friend, wary of a potential enemy, or self-interested as renters of the land he controlled. Nine jurors in the second trial came from the other district. Perhaps living farther from William Cowper gave them greater perspective or more freedom in their deliberations.[61]

What questions did the magistrates and lawyers pose in the preliminary examination of potential jurors? At least one member of the first jury, Edmund Godwin, was a battering husband or the father of a batterer. The next year Jane Godwin would petition for a divorce, but her efforts were thwarted when her husband objected to legislative interference in his family life. Two other Godwins joined Edmund Godwin on the jury in the Cowper trial. Did the kinfolk hang together to support another male who shared their values about a husband's rights to own and control all the property in his home, including his wife? Did other male jurors resent the very idea that a woman might hold so much property? If so, their feelings paled in comparison with the antagonism they felt toward the assembly's restriction on the guardianship of the Cowper children. In fact, the jurors in this trial at the end of May 1817 may have reached their decision because of the county court's custody decree earlier that month.

While the Cowper divorce bill was passing through the assembly, a Senate amendment stipulated that the county court should select a guardian for the children, but it could not appoint their father. That proviso led to what the *Richmond Enquirer* called an "animated discussion" in the House. Some delegates wanted the county court to have the discretion to choose William Cowper if the local justices thought best. But the House majority agreed with the Senate restriction.[62] So after being appointed to administer her father's estate, Ann asked the county court in May 1817 to designate her as the guardian of her son, Josiah Cowper. William knew this was coming, and his lawyer James Trezvant was on hand to contest Ann's motion. Challenging the assembly's action as "unconstitutional," the able attorney argued that the court had no right to deprive a father of his "natural" right to be the guardian of his son. By a 3-2 decision the magistrates appointed Ann, though two justices formally dissented. The matter was not settled, however. In August fifteen-year-old Josiah appeared in court to request that his father be appointed his guardian. His mother was present, brandishing the assembly's act. But the majority of the justices approved Josiah's "choice." In blunt terms they insisted that the provision forbidding William Cowper to be his children's "guardian" was "unconstitutional and void." In effect a local government was nullifying an act of the state legislature. Even apart from that argument, however, the magistrates thought that a "fair construction" of the divorce act allowed them "to confirm" Josiah's "election" of his father. Ann immediately appealed to the Williamsburg Chancery Court.[63]

While this suit was pending, William Cowper petitioned the assembly to repeal the provision of the divorce act that removed him as "the Guardian and protector of his own children." More than a hundred men, including ten justices and congressman James Johnson, signed their names in support of the proposition that in depriving a man from being "the Guardian and protector of his own Children" the assembly had acted contrary to the "Natural rights we have rec[ieve]d from our Maker, and our Constitutional rights." Though the legislature ultimately defeated a repeal bill, the widespread support for William Cowper's position in the community indicates that the assembly's act had struck a raw nerve. The constitution invoked first by Trezvant, then by the magistrates, and now by a broad range of citizens was not the written document that Virginia had drawn up in 1776 or that of the federal government. Rather, it was the ancient constitution of the common law. It privileged the familial role of husband and father and, in the Virginia context, the power of the local gentry at the county courthouse against the central government in Richmond.[64]

Other battery cases demonstrate the shared perspective that supported a husband's dominance over his wife. Observing her neighbor Ann Cowper gain a divorce may have induced Jane Godwin to petition for one in 1818. Eyewitnesses offered sworn testimonies of her husband's drunken brutality. Nathaniel Gray had seen Edmund Godwin, as he set out to whip his wife, grab and push Jane down. "I asked him if he meant to kill her[;] he answered . . . he meant to break her dam neck." Gray maintained that no wife "could live with him without danger of her life." But after drawing up a divorce bill, the legislators ultimately turned Jane down. Perhaps they expected her to try to gain relief from the local courts. But they may also have been swayed by Edmund's letter to his delegate. In his crude scrawl Edmund strongly protested against his wife's divorce petition, denied the charges, and demanded "a copy of her allegations." He was, after all, "a free Man and in a free Country hard would be to divource me from my wife without my conzent for mere trivials." That was the crux of the matter. In a society based on slavery, he believed that his status as a free white male conferred on him absolute power over his wife. Whatever conflicts occurred in his marital relationship were, in his own words, "private disputes in families."[65]

Both the assembly and society at large tended to exalt such privacy claims as part of the male prerogative and to minimize, as Godwin did, wife beating. After considering Elizabeth Dowdall's petition in 1809, the legislative committee agreed that her husband, John, was a drunk, "idle and disorderly . . . of profligate manners, and a quarrelsome and bad husband." A bevy of witnesses, men and women, testified to Elizabeth's good character, the "esteem" in which she was held locally, and John's attempts to shoot her on several occasions. He himself also favored a divorce. But the committee urged rejection of Elizabeth's request. The language is significant. Elizabeth Dowdall and the neighbors wrote in terms of serious attempts on her life, but the legislators found her husband merely "disorderly" and "quarrelsome."[66]

Forty years later Harriet Mallory testified that in his drunken rages her husband, Garland, had "struck her, choked, threatened her life, and put it in imminent peril, . . . wantonly deformed her and maliciously endeavored to destroy her reputation." She finally left him after he whipped her with a cowhide. Harriet hired a first-rate attorney, William Macfarland. Memorably described in the secession convention of 1861 as "the curly headed poodle from Richmond, nearly overcome with dignity and fat," he had represented Helen Brooke Hamilton five years earlier in her successful divorce suit against her husband, Robert. Macfarland assembled a huge file of affidavits verifying Harriet's charges. But Garland Mallory counterpetitioned, denying everything but the intoxication. Harriet had taken refuge in her brother-in-law's home, and a legislative committee ultimately decided a divorce was "Inexpedient."[67] No doubt the legislators thought Harriet should be satisfied with an *a mensa* divorce and alimony from a Superior Court. Even extreme battery by itself did not merit anything further in the minds of the legislators.

The press reinforced the tendency to minimize wife beating. After reporting the status of one extreme battery case, the *Richmond Enquirer* in 1820 cautioned against allowing the injured party in a divorce to remarry. The possibility of a second marriage, the editor thought, "very frequently . . . prevents a married couple from overlooking a great many acts in each other which they would otherwise contrive to make up." Given this social context it is hardly surprising that many battered wives did not seek a divorce until their husbands were irretrievably gone and their own future economic security demanded it.[68] Rebecca Trueman offers a case in point. Her husband, John, far from being the "industrious, sober and respectable man" she thought she had married, turned out to be a drunken wastrel who quickly dissipated Rebecca's $1,200 dowry. Promising to reform, he persuaded her to move west. But en route John abandoned his wife and child by the roadside without supplies or money. Afraid that he might reappear to claim the inheritance she would receive upon her mother's death, Rebecca petitioned for a divorce. The jury that certified the facts in 1828 also discovered that John had vulgarly abused Rebecca, "slapping her jaws and otherwise maltreating her."[69] But despite such abuse, she probably never would have sought the divorce if John had not abandoned her. Of the 204 women whose petitions have been located, 139 (68 percent) claimed that their husbands had abandoned them. Of the 86 wives alleging battery, 52 (60 percent) also claimed desertion. That lower percentage provides yet another measure of the desperate straits in which battered wives found themselves. Some simply could not wait until their husbands left them. Ann Cowper, after all, never asserted desertion. She had been forced to flee for her life.

The prevailing gendered mentality in Virginia becomes even more apparent in the legislative debate during the 1840s over a married woman's property act. As the contest was reaching a climax in 1849, a newspaper editorialized against "this invasion of the family circle—this interference between man and wife—between the father and his children—which annihilates that salutary subordination of the one sex to the other, which has made American and English women the purest specimens of humanity." While acknowledging that "some hard cases" existed in which "a sweet and virtuous woman" unfortunately married "a gambler, or drunkard, or spendthrift," the writer concluded with a classic example of blaming the victim. It was really "her own fault—and is it not better that the individual should expiate her own wrong, than that the whole of society should be made to suffer for it?" The "dependence" of women upon their husbands, he insisted, "inspires affection, generates confidence, and promotes domestic felicity."[70]

Ultimately the responsible legislative committee advised that Virginia would do well to reject the example of other states that had passed such acts. The "principles of the common law, which regarded man and wife as one person, and the legal existence and authority of the wife, as in a great degree merged and suspended during the marriage" best fitted "the purposes of nature" and "the character and constitution of the sexes." Allowing married women separate property rights could only create "domestic discord and unhappiness" and "mar the harmony which now reigns throughout the domestic circles of Virginia."[71] "Let well enough alone," the *Richmond Whig* enthused after the bill went down to defeat. "The old Common Law is good enough for us—notwithstanding Lord Mansfield's interpretation of it, that a man might correct his wife with a rod *not larger than his thumb*. It has produced the finest women in the world: and we would not have them corrupted by Red Republicanism and French morality."[72] There, as the debate ended, was the answer. In the Old Dominion, gynecolatry provided the ultimate justification for wife beating.

Ann Parker Cowper recovered from her traumatic marriage to live a productive, satisfying life. As Leonore Walker suggests from her contemporary research on battered women, this was probably due to her early upbringing and the personal strengths she developed before her ill treatment at the hands of her husband. William Cowper's death in 1819 ended any further challenge from that quarter, but once in secure possession of her home and estate, she found herself repeatedly in court pursuing its debtors and defending it against various claims resulting from her husband's mismanagement.[73] When he reached age twenty-one in 1823, Josiah Cowper successfully petitioned the legislature to change his name to Josiah Cowper Parker. Then, to free himself of all past and future annuities due to his mother according to his grandfather's will, he signed over Macclesfield and its 500 acres to her. He and his wife lived a few miles away at White Marsh, an even more valuable plantation left him by his grandfather.[74] Ann Parker Cowper apparently enjoyed a good relationship with her four sons. Until her death at Macclesfield on 21 March 1849, they lived either with her or nearby. Her youngest son, Leopold, was the executor of her estate.[75] For Ann Parker Cowper, family mattered most.

CHAPTER 6

A Monster in Female Form

As spring advanced through Virginia in the last year of the eighteenth century, John Pryor described to a friend his newfound comfort in "the Estate of Matrimony." Two and a half years earlier the Revolutionary War veteran and prosperous Richmond entrepreneur had married the vivacious Anne Whiting from Tidewater's Gloucester County. Though the bride had been seventeen and the bachelor groom some thirty years her senior, John sagaciously informed his old companion in dignified terms that "matrimonial happiness depends not so much on equality of age but on similarity of sentiments and virtuous endeavors to promote the happiness of each other." Even the failure thus far to produce "issue" had not ruffled their "repose." John described himself as "happy" and Anne as "an amiable and agreeable wife." He could include her "good wishes" with his own because she "has learned to respect those I like."[1] No doubt her husband had tutored her in that process, and the operative words in their relationship were "learned" and "respect."

John Pryor was considerate of his wife. When Anne suffered a bout of illness that summer, he contemplated taking her for a treatment to Virginia's springs in the Blue Ridge, but a doctor's regime kept them at home in Richmond and restored her health. His own condition, he reported in December 1799, had never been better, although he found 225 pounds "a burthensome" weight. A few years later, however, "Rheumatism" had attacked the aging veteran, and shortly afterward he complained that he was "torn to pieces." The accomplished horseman had not been in the saddle for two years and could "scarcely move my arms." Yet he evinced no problems in his marriage.[2]

Anne Pryor cared for her husband. As she later wrote to her family, she "respected, and esteemed him as a father." Her own father, Thomas Whiting, a wealthy planter, had died shortly after Anne's birth. She had been his fifteenth child by his third wife, Elizabeth Seawell, and her mother whom she loved intensely had soon remarried to Major Samuel Cary. Cary proved improvident in business affairs and careless about the resources that rightfully belonged to his Whiting stepchildren. A court suit on their behalf placed Anne, who lived with her mother and step-father, in an awkward situation, and she moved to the home of a married sister. This arrangement, however, proved unsatisfactory on a long-term basis, and the older sibling decided to play matchmaker.

For Anne's sister, as for her mother and stepfather who gave their con-sent for Anne to be wed, romantic attraction was not considered a pre-requisite. From the purely socioeconomic perspective that determined so much of eighteenth-century family arrangements, John Pryor made a fine catch. Besides a decent home in Richmond, he owned the city's largest livery stable and its chief amusement park, Haymarket Garden. The suc-cessful entrepreneur also possessed sizable chunks of urban rental prop-erty as well as lands in western Virginia, Kentucky, and the Northwest Territories. Well connected socially because of his Revolutionary War career, he served as vice-president of the Virginia branch of the Society of the Cincinnati and as secretary of the local horsemen's Jockey Club. Per-haps Anne's married sister thought it advantageous to attach her family to someone at the center of Virginia's economic and political world. De-spite the assertions of her relatives more than a half-century later, Anne may have been easily persuaded. She was young and impressionable. Marriage to John promised economic security in place of dependence on family charity, and it removed her from the drab routine of rural living to the excitement and glitter of Richmond society.[3]

The union did not bring love, however. Later Anne tried to explain that in her immaturity she had married too quickly without realizing how im-portant love would be to a marriage or how miserable she would be in its absence. "The heart requires some object, on which to rest its affections," she wrote; "I had none." Her expectations of companionate marriage re-flect an emotional world light years from the one inhabited by her elderly husband and older sister. In John Pryor's view he and Anne "lived hap-pily together . . . enjoying all the mutual affection, and confidence in each other, that could have attended the connubial state." But never in private letters or public documents did he describe their relationship in terms of love, the emotion his wife found most lacking. She later wrote that she had never discovered "that love for him to whom I was united; without which the marriage state of all others is the most wretched." She grew so desperate that after her mother died, she even contemplated suicide. As Anne turned thirty and remained childless, John aged and became infirm. While husband and wife may have later exaggerated their contradictory perspectives on the marriage in order to win a sympathetic audience, Anne was emotionally unsatisfied.[4]

Charles Fremon did not steal her affections. He filled a void. The handsome young schoolteacher had emigrated during the French Revolution and eventually landed in Virginia, where he found employment as an instructor of French. After a stint at William and Mary College, he joined the faculty of a prestigious Richmond academy operated by Louis Girardin. Anne met Charles when he arranged with her husband in June 1810 to rent a little house next to the Pryor home. Private French lessons with his landlord's wife blossomed into what Anne called love and her husband styled "criminal intercourse." Their adultery was revealed in early July 1811 when Girardin saw a letter Anne had written to Charles and confronted his French teacher. Fremon admitted the seduction, and Girardin notified John Pryor.[5]

The outraged old soldier then visited Major Robert Quarles, his sister's husband, and related Girardin's information. When the two men parted, Quarles rushed to Pryor's house, met Anne, and told her that he wanted to warn Charles to avoid his landlord because the latter would likely kill him "on sight." Anne wanted to know the reason, and Quarles reported that Girardin had informed her husband of her relationship with Fremon. Weeping and terribly distraught, Anne denied everything. But then, according to Quarles's account, she announced "that she would stay no longer in the house." A grim-faced John Pryor finally arrived, entered the room where Quarles and Anne were talking, and began loading a gun. He told his wife not to fear for her life. Though "she had treated him basely," he would not injure her. In response to her queries, he claimed to possess "evidence of her guilt." In Quarles's presence she again denied Girardin's assertions. John Pryor later told his friend Archibald Blair that he had considered "flogging" his wife but decided against it.[6]

The next day Anne prepared to leave Richmond. About six weeks later she wrote her family that John had "threatened me with the most cruel and violent treatment if I remained in the house another night." When she asked him where she should go, he suggested "Hell" but then decided that she should return to her sister's home. She would travel by coach to Williamsburg and then to Gloucester. Quarles was sitting outside on

There! G—d d—n you, take that!

Frontispiece from God's Revenge against Adultery, *by Parson Weems. This work implicitly excused the murder of a wife's lover. (Courtesy of The Library of Virginia)*

the veranda with John when Anne asked permission to take Sally, one of seven slaves she had inherited when her father's estate had been settled the previous year. John consented. Later Quarles heard Anne "sobing and crying" as she walked about in another room; she then returned and asked also to take Hannah, Sally's mother, as her husband would still have more slaves than he needed. She further promised "to go where you shall never more hear from me" and requested "that you will try to forget that you even knew such a creature as me." After consulting Quarles, John agreed to give her Hannah too.[7]

Meanwhile Girardin had warned Charles to avoid John Pryor, so the Frenchman sent someone to pick up his possessions and went to stay with John Lataste, a friend to whom he had earlier confided his love for Anne and their plans to marry after her husband's death. Now he determined to leave Richmond with Anne and insisted that he would kill John or anyone else who tried to stop them or hurt Anne because of their relationship. That night Fremon and Lataste met her at the stagecoach offices, and the next morning Charles and Anne left with Hannah, Sally, and their luggage for Williamsburg. Instead of continuing to Gloucester, however, as John had supposedly directed his wife, they proceeded to Norfolk and from there sailed to Charleston, South Carolina.[8]

Within a few days John Pryor published an announcement in the Richmond press that blamed "an execrable Monster of Baseness and Depravity" for alienating his wife's "affections." Because Anne had "abandoned my bed and board, for the protection of her seducer" and, John believed, had departed with Charles, she forfeited "all claims to my support." He would pay none of her bills or take responsibility "for any debts she may contract." In short, John was giving public notice that Anne had deserted him and therefore yielded any legal rights as his wife to alimony or a separate maintenance. English common law required a husband to maintain a wife unless she left him freely. Just the year before in a celebrated alimony case, Virginia's Supreme Court of Appeals had agreed with that principle. *Purcell v Purcell* settled several important matters. First, jurisdiction in disputes between husband and wife normally belonged in a chancery court that dealt with equity or fairness. A wife's legal condition of coverture meant that for most purposes the law regarded husband and wife as a single person. So marital conflicts could rarely be heard in a civil or criminal court. Second, the issue of alimony hinged on whether the husband was willing to support his wife at home or had expelled her from the house. A divorce was not necessary. Thus if John had forced Anne to leave, she was entitled to a separate maintenance and, after his death, to her dower rights, which amounted to a third of John's personal property and the use of one-third of his real estate and slaves. John's notice was specifically designed to place all blame on Anne and absolve himself of all financial obligations, present and future.[9]

When Anne read what she called his "cruel" notice, she realized its import and responded in August with a long letter to John Lowry, her sister Susanna's husband, that detailed her version of events and denied Pryor's allegations. She had not "run away but was turned out of doors at night and in an approaching Storm." In the face of her husband's wrath she had written a quick note to a lawyer, explaining that John "refused" to provide for her "future support." In reply he had advised her not to leave the house until John forced her out in the presence of witnesses, but she had been too afraid to remain.[10]

After Anne told her husband that she feared becoming a burden on her sister's family, John had allowed Hannah and Sally to go with her and had given "forty dollars" for her support. But he had also requested that Anne, while she was on her way to Gloucester, relinquish in writing "all future claim on him." She had asked him for "a part of my Negroes," the inheritance from her father, so that by their labors she might maintain herself "in some retirement." John rejected this appeal, though he knew, Anne asserted, that she would rather die than return as a rejected wife to her Gloucester relatives. Anne thought the people around her husband had stiffened his anger and made him more cruel and tightfisted than he would have been on his own. She may well have meant Robert Quarles. He served as John's principal witness that she had left her husband's home of her own accord. He also arranged, at John's request, for the divorce petition. With Anne's removal and the forfeit of her dower and a separate maintenance, his immediate family and John's other relations stood to gain a much greater inheritance. She may have underestimated, however, the utter humiliation and shame her elderly husband was experiencing. Anne and her paramour had made a cuckold of him before his friends and associates and the entire city. They had outraged male honor.[11]

If indeed, as Anne stated in August, John had cast her off, then she could sue for alimony. She informed Lowry that she intended to go to court to acquire whatever she might be entitled to. But property or money was not that important to her now. "We are poor," she acknowledged, "but we can be content with little, for I have found that happiness consist not in riches." She also welcomed her husband's petition for a legislative divorce and wished him success and marriage to someone able to make him "happier than it was in my power to do." But Anne's Tidewater relatives did not sympathize with her or perhaps even understand her position. She had repudiated their values and upended traditional mores by leaving her wealthy husband and going away with Charles. Such a pursuit of individual happiness in the face of corporate values shocked their refined sensibilities. Never again would Anne be accepted as part of their family. In fact they forwarded to John Pryor excerpts from her personal letters that he later used in his divorce application to foil a possible alimony suit.[12]

From Charleston Anne and Charles moved to Savannah, Georgia. They were living there in December when John submitted his petition to the Virginia assembly. The embittered old man lashed out at Charles for "basely and perfidiously" seducing his wife. The Frenchman had stolen her love and lured her into an adulterous relationship that the major believed had begun soon after they first met. The couple had "ardently desired my death," he asserted. He also told a melodramatic story that Girardin had related to him as coming from Fremon. One evening after John and his wife had retired for the night, Charles heard a racket. Thinking Anne's husband was mistreating her, the young man had taken his guns, entered their house through a door that happened to be left open, and crept upstairs to listen outside the bedroom with the intention of shooting John if he was beating his wife. But hearing nothing more, the Frenchman decided he was wrong and retired to his own house next door. John must have regarded Charles's actions on this occasion as a particularly gross affront. In addition to the implied threat to his life, the younger man had not only supplanted the older in his wife's affections; he had also usurped his role as her male protector. John Pryor's identity as a husband, which he had waited until well into midlife to construct, had been shattered.

According to the major's version of events, when her crime was exposed, Anne had freely left his home and "protection" but only pretended to go to her sister's plantation. The old soldier claimed that he would have supported her financially if she had actually gone to Gloucester "or to any other respectable abode to hide herself in retirement from the infamy that awaited her." Instead, John pointed out, she lived in an adulterous relationship in Georgia. The House of Delegates received his petition in early December and four days later rejected it on the recommendation of the committee. But the legislators accepted the committee verdict that agreed with John Pryor in all essential elements. Anne had "voluntarily left him" and committed "adultery."[13] Thus they effectively blocked any court appeal she might make for alimony.

John's proof of Anne's infidelity was irrefutable, but the assembly did not then grant divorces solely on that basis. It might have helped Pryor's case, however, if he possessed solid evidence that his wife and Charles had been married in Charleston or Savannah or elsewhere. Proven bigamy might have enhanced his chance for a divorce. In at least two earlier cases the assembly had granted divorces for such a reason, first to Robert Campbell, whose wife left him for another man she subsequently married in Connecticut, and then a few years later to Charles Bosher, a carriage maker, after his wife, Susan, eloped with a journeyman employee whom she married in North Carolina. Like John Pryor, both Campbell and Bosher lived in Richmond and so may have known and even done business with members of the assembly.[14] By the time John Pryor petitioned, however, the legislature had stiffened its back against divorces, and nothing may have furthered his cause.

What the assembly accepted as Anne's crime, adultery and desertion, was the complaint of almost 60 percent of the 171 men whose divorce petitions have been located. If adultery alone was the complaint, then 138 men (76 percent) who asked for divorce leveled that charge against their wives. In sum, infidelity within marriage was the most common reason men in search of a divorce petitioned the assembly. This chapter explores, first, the reactions of these men to their wives' adultery and their male perspectives on marriage and its responsibilities. Second, the conduct of the "fallen woman," frequently defiant and sometimes ferocious, provides a crucial dimension to our understanding of why husbands sought divorce. Also, as the example of Anne Pryor indicates, important monetary and property considerations complicated the rupture of domestic relations. Thus a third consideration of this chapter is the legal status of women revealed by such marital crises. Finally, their wives' adultery brought these men the shattering experience of betrayal, of loss of status, and of shame. At its center adultery by women defied male domination. If in any sense these cuckolds might be called patriarchs, at best they were deviant ones.

MALE REACTIONS AND PERSPECTIVES

The divorce process offered men the opportunity not only to express outrage, betrayal, and dismay but also to detail to other men who sat in judgment in the legislature their own expectations of marriage and the desired behaviors of husband and wife. For John Pryor as for 80 percent of male divorce petitioners whose wives had committed adultery, the challenge to the male ego aroused profound anger and bitterness. In describing their reaction to the discovery of their wives' infidelity, they used words such as disgust, pain, mortification, ignominy, disgrace, and dishonor. Alexander Mills wrote that "his bed had been polluted." "The discontent of his own mind," exclaimed Samuel Ritchie, could "only be imagined and not described." For Nathaniel Needles, "the Plans of his paridise was Converted into scenes of sorrow, and distress."[15] Frequently, as with Fremon, the paramour was well known to the husband. Often he was a neighbor, an employee, or even a lodger in the husband's own home.[16] A husband's extended absence from home sometimes provided the occasion for another man to seduce a willing wife. Business or a trip to the West could take a man away for many weeks. William and Esther Hobbs had several children and were happily married, at least from his perspective, until work called him away. While he was gone, Esther "formed a strong attachment" to another man that proved unbreakable.[17]

The War of 1812 evidently destroyed some marriages. A wagon maker in Martinsburg in the lower Shenandoah Valley, Matthias Kenney had been "happily" married for eight years and had four children when his company of artillery was mustered into service in 1813 and sent to Norfolk. Seven months later he returned to a pregnant wife who later gave birth to a child conceived in his absence. During the hot summer months while her husband was away, Ann Kenney had invited his apprentices "to sleep downstairs with herself." One of them, a twenty-year-old man, started keeping Ann company every evening and gradually began to assert new prerogatives, helping himself to her husband's clothes and even his watch. On the other hand the marriage may have been problematic when Matthias left. War offered an excuse for others. Nathaniel Needles joined the army during the war to get away from his wife, Sarah, whose adultery with George Pickenpaw had made life unbearable. When Nathaniel returned home, he found that Sarah and George had eloped and left the children behind as wards of the county.[18]

Sometimes the husband himself discovered the couple in adultery, in which case the consequences could be violent. Wyatt Hare caught his wife, Sarah, with his lawyer Clayton Harris "at the foot of the bed standing and flaps of his breaches down." The outraged husband "struck him with a Cain [sic] and drew a Bowey Knife." Clayton got away when Sarah grabbed her husband's arm, but Wyatt took his gun, followed Clayton, and killed him "in a neutral combat." When Kirchen Turner found his wife and her lover engaged in sexual intercourse in his own home, he became so "highly excited" that he "shot" the paramour. Significantly the local justices, after an investigation, refused to return an indictment, and Kirchen went free. No doubt the men agreed with the sentiments of another cuckold who reported that he had "inflicted" on his wife's Casanova "the chastisement which his perfidy deserved."[19] After Girardin had revealed Charles's affair with Anne, the young man had been wise to stay out of John Pryor's way and to leave Richmond as soon as possible, because the justice system probably would have tolerated whatever action the old soldier of the Revolution had taken against his wife's foreign lover.

John Pryor went public immediately, but many husbands did not. Acknowledging their marital situation to the world was acutely embarrassing, so much so that men often did everything possible to hide it. While some husbands immediately separated themselves from their spouse as soon as the adultery was discovered, others cast about for ways to shield both themselves and their relations from the inevitable gossip and noto-riety. A wife's misconduct reflected poorly not only on her husband but on her whole family. Nathaniel Hart was humiliated when the adultery of his wife, Eliza, became "the Publick Talk of the Neighbourhood." Henry Carty responded to his wife's infidelity with desperate attempts "to keep his family together and to prevent its public exposure."[20]

Yet other scorned husbands, realizing that they could not keep their domestic trauma hidden, saw the divorce process as a way to cut their losses and provide themselves and their families with a fresh start. William Hobbs viewed divorce as the only avenue left "for the promotion of his own peace and happiness and for the preservation of his reputation and that of his children." He claimed that his intentions were those of "an honest heart and an affectionate parent." His community agreed with that self-evaluation. At September court in Lee County in 1841, jurors considered the divorce petitions of two men and one woman. Nothing forbade a juror from hearing more than one case, so that day seven men served on three cases, six sat on two cases, and only one man heard one case. Hobbs himself was a member of the other two juries. These friends and neighbors verified the facts in all three cases, but the assembly passed only one divorce bill, for James Martin, who was petitioning for the second time.[21]

Like Hobbs, the overwhelming majority of men considered personal happiness their first priority. They accepted the companionate marriage ideal extolled by the prescription literature. In 1809 Judge St. George Tucker composed a poem titled "On Domestic Happiness"; the opening lines celebrated the equality and mutuality of married love:

Thrice happy they! The happiest of their Kind!
    Whom equal Stars in Hymen's Bands unite;
Whose constant Hearts, by mutual Love entwin'd,
    In sweet Endearment live, and calm delight.
Who in each tender Look can read the Heart,
    And every Hope, and Fear, and Wish, forestall;
In pain, and pleasure, bear an equal part,
    And in each other find their earthly *All*!

Though secular and religious writers in books, newspapers, and tracts agreed that women should be followers rather than leaders, the appro-priate relationship, one minister pointed out, was not one of "master and servant, or slave, as some enemies of matrimony affirm, but . . . the dependence of one true friend upon another." It was "a union of the oak and the vine, the latter clinging to the former, and supported by it, and compelled to some extent to follow its humors and inclinations."[22]

Whether oak and vine or elm and ivy, the image subordinated the woman. But the degree of compulsion varied tremendously, depending on the personalities and the assets of the spouses. Examples of potential or real conflict between husbands and wives abound, even as couples aspired to form a companionate marriage. Writing to Louisa Holmes, who would soon become his second wife, wealthy planter John Hartwell Cocke described the various roles he expected her to fill. In addition to managing the entire household, Louisa would oversee his children's education, improve the situation of the plantation's slaves, and care for the spiritual and material needs of the local poor. But most important for Cocke was that she would reciprocate "all the affection" he gave her. Was he asking too much of a wife, the planter wondered. Louisa's piety had first attracted John, and he was sure her religious convictions would enable her to fulfill whatever she determined to be her "duty." Louisa responded playfully that she would not be "so domestic" right away. She would need "to have my own way for a little while, and if I should fret and vex you a little, you must e'en make the best of it." John could accept that and promised "obedience to your desire," but when Louisa told his cousin that she would not try to sway her husband's judgment, John thought she had spoken "injudiciously . . . for a *modern ambitious* wife." He depended on her advice. "Indeed my beloved Louisa, I count very largely upon your Counsel, for dictated as it will be by good sense and purified by affection, where can be found so faithful an adviser as the wife of my bosom?"[23] John Cocke was generations away from John Pryor.

Not every marriage found the spouses in such universal sympathy and agreement. During the tenure of her husband, Henry Wise, in Congress, Anne Wise commented freely on his speeches and votes. When in an address he criticized the "ladies" for meddling in political affairs, she retorted that women generally possessed "as much sense and good judgment as you lords of the creation." After they disagreed about the route she should take to Washington, she replied to his "*angry, unkind* letter" by denying his charges as "unmerited and of course unjust" and ironically signed her letter "[your] dutiful, *obedient* wife." Ann then added a playful postscript: "Oh variety the spice of life—of *married life! En Verite* there has a change come o're the spirit of your letters, my brother. Dinna talk to me any more of connubial felicity. No—give me liberty; no husband to control me." Henry, on the other hand, though he wrote her about his political anxieties and doubts, left no question about the position he expected her to fill in his life. "My wife is not competent to advise the Statesman or the politician—her knowledge, her advice, her ministry is in a kindlier sphere. . . . She can hear my griefs, know of my troubles, understand the cause of my perplexities, be the confidant of my secret feelings and sympathize with me in them all. Blessed is she to me in that alone. I have poured out my heart to *her,* and now I feel better. I knew I would and therefore took up my pen to write to her."[24]

In segregating Ann into the private, domestic sphere of his life, Henry offered a typical though by no means universal male perspective. But his dependence on her for emotional support and comfort is mirrored in private correspondence as well as the divorce petitions throughout this period. In letters to male friends men frequently expressed their need to find "their long lost rib" to make their own lives complete and described the happiness they anticipated or enjoyed in married life. As the antebellum era drew to a close, one lovesick Romeo demonstrated the extent to which the prevailing perspectives on marriage had sunk in. Writing to his fiancée, Burrell Cook insisted that marriage was essential to a man's happiness. Only a wife provided "comfort in distress advice in difficulties attention in sickness and . . . consolation in an hour of death." While "her tenderness and Love" promised to "sweeten his toil and scatter sunshine in the pathway of his existence," he offered her his "protection and support." Both would share equally in whatever happened to them in their married life. He added in conclusion, "The surest foundation of connubial happiness is Religion."[25]

Independent of their class, men uniformly expected that marriage would bring them domestic comfort and emotional satisfaction. William Bayliss formally defined the purpose of marriage as "the promotion of happiness and a virtuous and lawful intercourse or connection. . . . It inculcates domestic peace, and a firm and abiding confidence between the parties contracting." Within the setting of home and family, the good marriage produced "domestic endearment and social affections." He expected "confidence" and "affection" and "respect." Charles Jones wanted "a companion with whom all Joys and Sorrows are shared." William Simpson hoped "to be happy or as much so as any person in my humble situation could be."[26]

Men frankly admitted their need for a wife and appear much more anxious to remarry than did women. John Peyton felt "that the natural propensities and inclinations of all men give them an attractive impulse toward the other sex the possession of whom greatly contributes to their happiness and comfort in life." He wanted another chance at "happiness to be engaged in the nuptial state." Jacob Freeze's wife had deserted him, committed adultery, and borne two children by another man; yet he confidently asserted his belief "that the married life tends more to the happiness of mankind than a single one." He wanted "the privilege of marrying some other woman, so that his happiness, heretofore marred by the prospect of perpetual celibacy, may be restored." Some men literally begged for a divorce. After describing his wife's multiple infidelities, a wretched William Simpson entreated the assembly to consider "the unhappy situation of a Man in the prime of Life compelled to drag out his days in connection with such a Woman." His prime was doubtless gone when sixteen years later he was finally granted a divorce without permission to remarry.[27]

It is not surprising that male petitioners typically present the adultery of their wives as a repudiation of an idyllic union. Like John Pryor, they described the early wedded years as a time of pure connubial bliss for both themselves and their wives. As far as Robert Campbell "knew or believed," his wife "enjoyed uninterrupted happiness, and content." James Thompson noted that for the first dozen years of his marriage to Nancy Bear, "all was peace, all was love and affection." In large part men attributed this happiness to their own successful efforts as husbands, fathers, and providers. For example, Michael Keaffer had brought his wife and two daughters with him when he immigrated to the United States from Germany. His family lived in Portsmouth. As a ship's officer Michael was forced to be away from home a great deal, but he claimed that he provided for his family and "always" left enough money to keep them supplied with food and necessities while he was gone. Moreover, "when at home all his consolation and happiness was being in the bosom of his family" and with the wife "he onice [sic] most affectionately loved."[28]

Virtually every male acknowledged in some fashion society's expectation that a responsible husband would provide physical protection and economic security for his wife and children. Self-presentation could be crucial to the success or failure of a petition. James Martin first asked for a divorce in 1840 on the grounds that, unknown to himself, his wife had been pregnant by another man when he married her. While passing herself off as "chaste and virtuous," the reality was otherwise. She had since abandoned him, and her "licentiousness" had become notorious.

Martin's divorce bill, however, got blocked in the Senate by one vote because of a "defect in the record." He had omitted any reference to his own "character" and motives for marriage. He drafted a new petition and had a second jury trial to validate his reputation. With that addition to his file, the divorce sped through the assembly. Favorite male self-descriptives include such republican virtues as honesty, fidelity, sobriety, and industriousness. Husbands accepted accountability for their wives' contentment and happiness. Felix Ferte claimed in typical fashion that he had done everything possible to make his spouse "contented and happy, and could not be charged with a single violation of the duties of a faithful husband." In contrast to John Pryor, some men also wrote, as Ferte and Keaffer did, of loving their wives, showing them tenderness and affection, and caring for their emotional needs. Nathaniel Needles claimed that with his wife "he has shared Cares and Troubles, bestowing on her every assistance and every fond attention that his situation in life would admit of. Altho he was poor, he was Kind and affectionate honest and industrious." James Settle simply stated that he had "loved his wife dearly."[29]

When men elaborated on their desiderata for marriage, their favorite adjective for a wife was "virtuous," which encompassed a series of expectations that she would be not only chaste or pure but also modest in her behavior, prudent in her conduct, and careful in fulfilling her domestic responsibilities toward children, servants, and home. In making his case for divorce, it was important for a man to prove that his wife had originally possessed those qualities, and especially that at the time of the wedding she had been "pure and unspotted," a woman of "unblemished Character." For Washington Cooper, marriage to Polly brought an added bonus, because she was not only a woman of virtue but also youthful and comely.[30] When female virtue became soiled, however, scorned husbands characterized their wives in the most degrading and condemnatory terms, calling them, for example, "lewd and profligate" or, most commonly, a "prostitute." That appellation held broader meaning in the nineteenth century than it does today. An irate husband could freely bestow it on any wife suspected of sex outside marriage, not just someone who plied her trade on the streets or in a bawdy house. Too late Samuel Irvine found he had chained himself to "a monster in female form." Nathaniel Hart described Eliza as "Determined to Wallow in the Filth of her Abominations." It grieved Valentine Powers enormously when he considered his wife's "filthy actions where with she hath Defiled herself, hath Conceived and Brought forth two Children to another

Man." In a dozen cases men discovered shortly after the wedding that their wives were already pregnant with another man's child. More commonly, however, the fall from grace was gradual. James Trotter's wife, in his words, "became by degrees, lewd, bold and profligate, till at last she became perfectly abandoned." Some husbands discussed the adultery of their wives as if it originated in a psychological predisposition. For example, Charles Bosher described the "temper of incontinency" of his wife, Susan; Charles Mahan attributed his wife's infidelity to "an infamous disposition."[31]

In numerous other situations, particularly when husbands and wives appear to have been reasonably well matched for many years, the petitions present what today might be termed a midlife crisis, as a result of which one spouse chose to leave a long-standing marital commitment. For example, the affidavits that accompanied the petition of William Croxton describe a marriage in which he and his wife lived happily for fourteen years. Mary Croxton had borne seven children when, in June 1808, she eloped with a married man, a neighbor, who left his wife with five children to take Mary to Kentucky and marry her there. Perhaps both adulterers simply wanted to escape from all their offspring. In a similar situation Pendleton County gossips must have enjoyed a field day at the end of the second decade of the nineteenth century. First, Suzanne Paulsen petitioned twice without success for a divorce from her husband, Henry Paulsen, on grounds of battery, bigamy, and desertion. Then Henry Stone asked for a divorce from his wife, Mary, accusing her of adultery and naming Suzanne's husband as one of her paramours. The Stones had been married for more than thirty years and had twenty children.[32]

Neither the presence of children nor the duration of a marriage inhibited some people from committing adultery or seeking a divorce. Benjamin and Mary Sewell of Russell County in southwest Virginia had been married for eighteen years. "Like the rest of mankind," Benjamin explained, he had trusted that marriage would promote his "happiness." Owning land and slaves and being well regarded in their community, the Sewells belonged to the middling class of small planters and had eight children. According to her husband, however, Mary was "possessed of an exceedingly Irritable temper, whimsical and unsteady." But he stayed with her in the hope that as she grew older, "her evil passions would subside and . . . she would become a prudent and affectionate wife." Instead she became an adulteress. For the benefit of the male legislators, the humiliated planter bitterly itemized the results: "every prospect of happiness blasted, his wife disgraced, himself dishonoured, and his poor children ruined. . . . She bartered away any affection she had for her husband; for her children; the respect she had for her Sex and for herself, for the foul embraces of a vile *Seducer*." He further informed the legislature that "his honor forbids" taking her back.[33]

REMEMBERING FORMER AFFECTION

Earlier, however, Benjamin Sewell had tried to reclaim his wife. What most differentiated John Pryor from many other cuckolds was his immediate repudiation of Anne as soon as he learned of her relationship with Charles. Whether or not the old soldier threatened physical violence, as Anne claimed, John certainly never intimated any desire for or possibility of forgiveness and reconciliation with his wife. Some of the other men behaved in a similar fashion, even acknowledging that they had driven their spouses from the house and would never live with them again under any circumstances.[34] But the majority of male petitioners alleged, as did Sewell, that they had made at least initial efforts to reclaim their spouses, and some had gone to extreme lengths. Frequently the adulterous affair had proceeded in stages and the husband had covered it up. Peter Stone had been mortified by his wife's liaisons during the last ten years of their marriage, but he feared becoming "the Public Panderer of his own shame" by making the local community "partakers in his disgrace." He was also so deeply concerned for the "reputation" of his numerous progeny that even after his wife and her lover had gone to Indiana, Peter had entreated her "repeatedly" but unsuccessfully to come home. Divorce for him was a last straw, not the first resort.[35]

But more than personal shame and concern for their children's good name made some husbands tolerate what others found impossible to stomach. The evidence is overwhelming that many men, like Peter Stone, were willing to overlook a wife's dalliance for a more or less extended period of time. Phoebe Caverley Arell's "adulterous and infamous practices" forced her husband to leave her on frequent occasions until "she became so base a prostitute that he found it absolutely impossible to live with her any longer." It is significant, however, that he repeatedly left her instead of forcing her out of the house. Phoebe held the fort. Other women successfully begged forgiveness of their husbands only to relapse into adultery.[36] The difficulty of obtaining a divorce undoubtedly kept some men from seeking one. More serious, practical considerations intervened as well. Apart from satisfying male emotional and sexual needs, a wife filled essential roles in caring for the home and raising the next generation. How would a man manage a household full of children by himself? Divorce posed severe consequences for both genders.

If a divorced woman confronted a situation of economic inequality from dower and alimony, divorced men, particularly middle- and lower-class nonslaveholders, faced domestic disaster. So deserted husbands sometimes tried to force their wives to come home. Providence Mountz pursued his wife to her hiding place across the Mississippi River and brought her back to Virginia, only to have her leave again and refuse to live with him. For all the vaunted legal rights enjoyed by the male party, his domestic control might actually be quite limited, as John Campbell's failed attempts to get his wife back demonstrate. He described himself to the assembly as "a young man just entering the theater of life with an anxious desire to be useful and respectable in society." He started poorly. At age twenty-three he married sixteen-year-old Ann Mariah Oliver. Within three months she left him and went home to her mother. John tried repeatedly to persuade her to return to him. Then a lawyer advised that he was within his rights in carrying Ann back home by force, so long as he did not commit a "breach of the peace." Taking several friends along for support, John made a valiant effort. But she threw rocks at him and told the men that she preferred "a part in hell" to life with her husband. Eventually they gave up, and Ann took John to court in a peace action. When John appeared before the judge, he saw his wife "sitting in a young man's lap." Despite his renewed entreaties, she still refused to come home with him. Her mother's house had become a brothel, and Ann had produced a bastard child by the time John petitioned for divorce.[37]

A husband possessed few resources against a wife determined to leave him. Archibald Rowsey and Betsy Noel had been married for almost twenty years and had ten children when, according to her uncle's testimony, Betsy developed "a fondness" for Bartlett Childress. Soon after Archey, as he was familiarly known, discovered his wife's affair, Betsy skipped out with Bartlett. Three weeks later she reappeared on the doorstep to check on her youngest child, who was just a year old. After a quick visit Betsy disappeared again, only to return four weeks later. According to her brother, William Noel, on this occasion Archey inquired whether "she had come to stay and hoped she had stayed off enough," but she told him that their marriage had ended. Rejecting Archey's entreaties to remain and his promise to "treat her as her wife" and "never" bring up "her conduct," Betsy left for a third time. In one last desperate attempt, remembering "his former affection" and concerned for his children, Archey sought his brother-in-law's assistance, and the two men went looking for Betsy. Eventually they discovered her with Bartlett in Rockbridge County across the Blue Ridge Mountains from Archey's home in Amherst. While Archey fruitlessly begged his wife to return with him and vowed to "forgive her" if she would come home, William Noel worked on Bartlett, asking how he could separate "a wife and mother from her young children." Betsy chimed in that it had been her idea to leave and she had "prevailed" upon Bartlett to take her away. Archey finally gave up hope of a reconciliation after Betsy bore Bartlett's child. By her adultery she had brought "disgrace and infamy . . . upon her Children and himself," Archey Rowsey wrote in his divorce petition.[38]

Archey's concern for his offspring typified many cuckolds. Neighbors and relatives of Betsy Rowsey admired the way Archey cared for his ten children after his wife moved out. In such situations men commonly kept the children, though occasionally they might divide them with the estranged spouse, along with their financial assets. The petitions frequently mention children as principal victims of the adultery and separation, and the adulterous wife as failing in the "duties of a mother."[39] In this respect it is interesting to speculate that John Pryor might have behaved differently toward Anne if she had borne a child. Washington Cooper was willing to take back his wife "on account of the Children" and expressed a willingness to forgive and forget his wife's adultery if "she returned home to him and behaved her self." When a paramour made his wife pregnant, however, Cooper withdrew the invitation. A few wives asked their husbands to take them back, but more commonly the women who appear in these proceedings acknowledge the truth of their spouses' accusations and, like Anne Pryor, signal to the legislature their desire for a divorce. Some women also chose to resume their unmarried name.[40]

Husbands such as Peter Stone, John Campbell, and Archibald Rowsey, anxious to get their wives home, frequently used intermediaries, such as family members, neighbors, or friends. Because John Tharp's wife was a "professor of religion," he tried to appeal to her through other members of her church community. Thompson Adams sought help from his father-in-law. His travail exemplifies the efforts that some men made to have their wives return, the involvement of family and neighborhood, and the freedom that women, like men in similar circumstances, enjoyed to leave marriage, family, and community. The verbal exchange reported in the divorce records represents the mentality of husband, father, and especially the woman fallen from grace.[41]

Thompson had married Martha Ann Burrus in 1839, and they had several children before she began a series of illicit affairs in their town of Gordonsville in Orange County. A carriage maker by trade, Thompson would frequently work at night in his shop while Martha Ann entertained young men at their nearby home. Peeking through the windows, George Parrott had seen one of them "setting in her lap, playing with her." During the daytime various individuals observed that she spent time "in the bushes" outside the village with assorted males who later bragged about making "connection" with her. When Martha Ann's reputation for sexual promiscuity eventually became notorious in 1844, she left her husband and children and moved into a brothel in Richmond, "a finishing blow to whatever of virtue remained to her."

Though Thompson later denied that he ever considered a reunion with his wife after she left their home, witnesses suggest that a reconciliation remained possible. He certainly tried to bring her back to Orange County. Accompanied by Martha Ann's elderly father, Joseph Burrus, Thompson went to Richmond and inquired of the police if they would "take her in charge." The police captain, Burrell Jenkins, denied having the authority to do so but offered to accompany Thompson and Joseph if they wished to take her. That evening the threesome appeared at the back door of Martha Stevens's brothel, where, responding to their knock, Martha Ann appeared on the stairs. Father and daughter embraced weeping. "My Daughter," Joseph exclaimed, "how could you have treated your mother and Mr. Adams in this way. If it dont Kill your Mother I think it will be the death of me!!" Martha Ann answered, "I Know that I have done wrong, but it is done now and Cant be helped."

Jenkins helped the men collect Martha Ann's trunks, and off they went to find a place to sleep, though the police captain warned that no hotel would give them rooms once the manager learned of Martha Anne's prostitution, a condition he would feel duty bound to report. Eventually he brought them to the jail to spend the night. Later that evening, while Thompson had gone to collect their children in the city, Joseph and Martha Ann had a conversation, reported later by Jenkins, that captures the intense father-daughter relationship, the social situation of a fallen woman, and the lure of the big city.

Initiating the exchange, Martha Ann asked her father, "Why did he come after her"? Joseph answered, "My dear child for the purpose of carrying you home with us, in hopes to reclaim you. Your Mother is willing to forgive you and so is Mr. Adams, and I will take you as a child again if you will do as you ought to do from this time." After staring at the floor for a bit, Martha Ann looked intently at her father and replied, "It is useless; you may carry me home now, but I will come back, for I wont stay there or in that neighbourhood." When her father asked the reason, she said that "she would not then be respected as other females were, and how Could she go to some church or meeting-House . . . and See other females looked upon differently to what I should be. And I will come back to Richmond where I can enjoy myself more in one week, than I can in the old neighbourhood for a whole year." Joseph replied, "Martha you are a member of the Church, and your character I am afraid is gone; now I want you to tell me, if you have ever been guilty of such bad conduct before you visited Richmond." She responded, "It is done, and over." Though the exchange is carried out gently, both sides reflect the mindset that Martha Ann's scorned husband expressed in describing his wife's adultery to the assembly: "She is forever lost to her husband, to her children, to her friends, to society, and to herself."

Joseph began crying again, so Jenkins joined the conversation. When Martha Ann insisted that she would return to Richmond, the policeman warned her that he would pick her up immediately. She replied that she would then go elsewhere, but that she would never remain with her husband. The next morning a train carried the family to Gordonsville, and Martha Ann was as good as her word. In 1845 Thompson Adams received an *a mesa* divorce from the Orange County Circuit Superior Court and then petitioned the assembly for an absolute divorce in order to avoid "a separation from all the enjoyments of domestic life."[42] True to male form, he wanted to marry again.

BATTERING AND BRAZEN WIVES

The legal subordination of women in the Old South did not necessarily express itself in predictable exchanges. Lip service to a husband's prerogative obscured the reality that spouses might find themselves in reverse power positions. Martha Ann Adams's defiance of her husband was not exceptional. Some marriages produced stormy relationships in which the wife maintained quite literally an upper hand, and her fist was clenched. Often enough she was intractable in the choice she had made, and sometimes liquor and drugs influenced her conduct, as they did for many men. At least a few wives were also capable of physically battering their husbands. Anthony Robiou claimed that the violent temper of his "ill-mannered" wife, Emily, frightened him, and she resisted all his efforts "to reform" her. Although Harden Fulcher described his early years with his wife, Louisa, as relatively peaceful, their marriage grew steadily more tempestuous. After she formed various adulterous relationships, her behavior grew "naughty refractory and unkind" until she became extremely "cruel and offensive" to Harden. Eventually Louisa tried to force her husband to move out of the house, but ultimately she herself left after she bore a child by a wealthy and powerful man in the neighborhood. Bertram Wyatt-Brown suggests that the assembly would sympathize with a poor man whose wife had been seduced by a rich one, but Fulcher did not gain a divorce in his 1849 suit, perhaps because he had repeatedly forgiven Louisa's adultery and continued to live with her. Condonation weakened the good order of a society that expected men to maintain proper discipline in their homes.[43]

Some husbands asserted that their wives had attempted to murder them. Poison was a favorite means. James Trotter's wife concocted a "potion" that practically destroyed his "health and constitution"; Sally Thomas fed her husband doses of arsenic. A court of inquiry into the facts alleged by John Copin against his wife found that Rebecca Copin displayed "a haughty, intractable, and violent temper." From practically the beginning of their wedded life, the couple had quarreled violently. The all-male jury sided with John in blaming Rebecca for the domestic conflict and for leaving her husband and their six children for extended periods "without reasonable causes" or John's approval. They also agreed that Rebecca had "threatened to shoot" her husband and once "prepared the means to do so," and that she had also tried to kill him by putting "arsenic in his coffee." Luckily he had found it. But the jury failed to substantiate John's claim that Rebecca had "scalded" him by pouring "boiling water" over "his leg, producing a painful wound and rendering him unfit for labor." Nor was there sufficient evidence that while he was slowly recovering from that injury and suffering from a high fever, Rebecca had "refused to nurse" him and had even beaten him "cruelly" using "one of his own crutches." As in the case of battering males, some of this violent behavior may have been related to alcohol. According to Ichabod Thomas, his wife, Sally, regularly got so drunk that she neglected her domestic responsibilities and disgraced "her family and her sex."[44]

Drug dependency probably induced the extraordinary attempt of Mildred Tate Williams to kill her bridegroom on their wedding night. A respected and prosperous slaveholding farmer in southwest Virginia, William B. Williams had fallen in love with Mildred while boarding in her parents' home. When she rejected his proposals of marriage, William dropped his suit. But then Mildred reversed herself and set a date for their wedding in January 1833. The celebration in the village of Rocky Mount continued for two days. After the last guests had finally left, the couple retired to their room in a boardinghouse. Because the bridegroom had "a slight cold," Mildred fixed "a potion" to drink that she told him was "burnt Baitmans Drops." Later he discovered that it was laudanum, an opium derivative. When the newlyweds retired to bed, Mildred, claiming extreme fatigue, said she wanted to sleep and urged William to do the same. But despite the drug, he could not fall asleep, as he later explained, due to "the novelty of his situation."

After lying quietly for a long period, Mildred suddenly got up and told her husband that she had dreamed of a remedy that would restore his graying hair to black. When she asked if she could make an experiment, William agreed. Though he thought the whole business "an idle fancy," he wanted "to indulge" his bride. Insisting that he lay on his side facing away from her, Mildred gave him a glass funnel to hold in his ear. After going to the fireplace, she returned to the bed and poured "a quantity of molten lead" into her husband's ear. As William jerked and rolled over with the fierce pain, Mildred bolted from the bedroom, and her screams roused the household.[45]

A doctor was quickly called who treated the suffering but well-drugged bridegroom while other witnesses collected the evidence of lead and laudanum and questioned Mildred. Within a week William began divorce proceedings, and multiple affidavits from Mildred's relatives, the attending physician, people sleeping in the house that night, and wedding guests confirmed his account. William later proposed that Mildred had deliberately planned his death because she loved someone else. Others had noticed her "attachment" to "a young gentleman." Mildred's friends and family testified to her strange behavior, which they generally attributed to an excessive use of laudanum. A storekeeper, Burwell Keath, reported that he had regularly sold Mildred the drug "for the tooth or head ache," but he had also noticed her wild mood swings in recent months. She had frequently complained of headaches. Shortly before the wedding Michael Holland, who worked for Keath, was alarmed by Mildred's odd behavior and "maniac stare." Other observers commented on her "mental alienation," that she appeared "not in her right mind," and that she was "completely deranged." Afterward Mildred told her brother and two women friends that she could not recollect the wedding at all and was amazed to discover that she had been married. Her brother, James Tate, was particularly active in soliciting support for the divorce. With the help of powerful friends in the House, William's bill sailed through the assembly despite the absence of a local court verdict of facts.[46]

Apart from the divorce petitions, evidence from the press, church records, and private correspondence indicates that a wide variety of abuse cases ranging from run-of-the-mill to bizarre never reached the legislative halls. For example, in 1838 William Austin, a sixty-year-old widower and farm laborer in Hanover County, married a widow perhaps twenty-five years younger. A few days after the wedding she began publicly complaining that Austin was "not a *man*," while he retorted "that he has all that nature gave him." Divorce seemed possible, particularly if an "examination" confirmed her assertions. Neighbors who found the exchange intriguing began digging into the past. One of them wrote to his brother, a Methodist minister, that "pretty good authority" recalled that Austin's first marriage had experienced its traumatic moments. During one fight with his first wife, probably over her adulterous relationship with a man "she liked as well as her husband," her paramour forcibly restrained Austin "while she with her teeth maimed him." According to several eyewitnesses at the trial, "for this outrageous offence" the magistrates ordered Austin's wife "put in the Pillary and stoned for one hour with rotten eggs."[47] But apparently no divorce had occurred.

It is sometimes difficult to know with certitude which spouse had rejected or left the other, and whether or not the wife separated voluntarily. According to her husband's petition, Susan Stratton had abandoned their home after he confronted her with proof of her adultery "strong as evidence of holy writ" and she "confessed her guilt." It was clear, however, that George Stratton had forced her to leave and would never take her back. Yet numerous other women of all ages and backgrounds obviously deserted their husbands and families. Young Larinda Stratham had married an equally youthful Jesse Wallin and had gone to live with his parents, a common arrangement for newlyweds who frequently could not afford their own home. That situation lasted three months before Larinda "became Fretful and abusive and vulgar in her language." Finally she told her husband there were "other young men" in her life, went back to her father's home, and refused Jesse's entreaties to return. After a few months of Larinda's "keeping vile company," her father drove her out, and she left for Kentucky with a boyfriend. Much older and married more than twenty years, Deborah Carty told the neighbors that she preferred "to die in the woods" before she would return to her husband and children.[48]

Like Deborah Carty, some women openly defied their husbands and society's expectations. When Rosewell Carter, an artisan at the Richmond armory, confronted his wife, Alice, with evidence of her adultery, she "frankly" admitted "her guilt" and told Rosewell that she preferred her paramour to him. Then Alice and her lover ran off together. Jacob and Eleanor Bagent had been married for five years when they rented a house owned by Jacob Waters. The latter's wife was ill, and Eleanor took care of her. Within a short time Eleanor left her husband, moved into Waters's home with two of her four children—presumably his wife had died—and had three children by him. When someone asked her why she had left her husband, she replied that "he was jealous of her." Jacob retorted "that he had good cause to be jealous."[49]

Jesse and Jemima Horton's stormy relationship illustrates the prolonged conflicts that afflicted numerous marriages as well as the rough verbal blows that wives could inflict. The fallout from the Hortons' problems spread legislative papers across the assembly's chambers through the second decade of the nineteenth century. Jesse's first attempt at divorce came in 1811. The couple had been married five years earlier. Despite a promising beginning, Jesse claimed that Jemima eventually exchanged his "Company" for "habits of Adultery with others at will." Neighbors first sensed the problematic situation in the Horton household when Jemima began boasting publicly that her second child was not Jesse's. Seeking to salvage his marriage, he proposed that the family relocate to another farm in the area. The feisty Jemima refused to go but suggested that Jesse could take his child when he went. When Jesse responded that "both [children] passed for his," Jemima retorted, "with nobody but a D——d fool like you this belongs to a Gentleman." Jesse, who owned five horses but no land, could not compete with James Fullin, his wife's paramour. When Jemima openly stated that she would rather be Fullin's "Whore" than Horton's "wife," Jesse finally left her and petitioned for a divorce, which the legislature swiftly rejected.[50]

Jemima received a rude awakening, however. When she wanted to move in with her wealthy lover, Fullin rejected her. Abandoned and destitute, she had second thoughts; "professing the utmost penitence for her crime," Jemima begged Jesse to take her back. The couple reconciled on condition that she amend her life. In later justifying the decision, Jesse pleaded that his primary concern had been for their motherless son. During their reunion Jemima bore another child, but Jesse soon discovered that she was incapable of reform. A wife who was "lost to all Sense of propriety Virtue and principle" had tricked him, he complained. According to their neighbors, while the husband and wife were living together, Jemima engaged in "Whoredom" with various young males. Marital relations boiled over with acrimony.

Despite Jesse's "tender" treatment, Jemima "proved very disagreeable and frequently and repeatedly abused" her husband. Witnesses testified that she accused him unjustly of adultery and even threatened "to poison" him. Disgusted with her "baseness" and fearful for his personal safety, Jesse separated from her a second time in 1815 and repetitioned the assembly. This time the lawmakers proved more favorable, perhaps because the talk among the neighbors was that Jemima had become "a common prostitute," and Jesse swore that he could never live with her again. The House approved a divorce bill, only to have the Senate reject it.[51]

As the law worked its way through the assembly in the winter of 1815–16, Jemima headed west to Tennessee and on to Indiana. Before she left Virginia, however, she signed a statement acknowledging "with shame" the pain she had inflicted on her husband, the justice of his separation and divorce petition, and her own "misconduct." She left her children behind—two with Jesse and one with Fullin. A neighbor encountered Jemima on the road with a male companion who verified her story that they would be married shortly. Jesse included this new information in his third divorce petition in 1816 along with a bevy of fresh affidavits. Among them was one from Isaac Lowe, who claimed that Jemima "frequently" said that "she beded [sic] with another Man as regular and constant as she ever did with her said husband and that she so intended to do so long as she had the opportunity." But once again the Senate rejected Jesse Horton's divorce bill after the House had passed it. Jesse made a fourth and final unsuccessful attempt in 1819. Generally speaking, at this time *a mensa* divorces might have been available for women for cases of extreme battery, but men were out of luck on any grounds apart from fraud or interracial adultery.[52]

Some women, like Jemima Horton, married again without benefit of a prior divorce; others chose to live so openly in adultery that they and their lovers were eventually presented in court for violation of the moral laws.[53] But few adulterous wives proved as brazen as Fanny Walling Bishop. Her husband, William Bishop, had been a widower of almost fifty with a few children by his first wife when in 1826 he married Frances Walling, a widow with five children. She and William added three more children to their collected progeny before their marriage fell apart. In William's words, an "ungrateful" and "discontented" Fanny finally notified him "that there were other men" in her life, and "she liked their little fingar better than [his] whole body." She proved it when she deserted William and their children and bore a child by Benjamin Porter and then another by John Neely. William must have thought she was gone for good when she left Virginia for several years. Then suddenly, much to his dismay, Fanny reappeared practically on his doorstep. Claiming her dower rights, she ensconced herself in a "cabin" on William's property and quite close to his home. There to the "great annoyance" of her husband and the neighbors, Fanny opened "a bodey house."[54]

The elderly cuckold—he was over seventy when he submitted his divorce petition to the 1850 session of the legislature—complained that his wife and "her cumrades" were "destroying the youth of the Country and demoralizing the Country." Moreover, "inicent families" were hurt by the activities at "Fanny Bishops house of Ill fame," where she and the other "inmates causes the inicent women of the Country to be beaten and abused by their husbands . . . and little children brought to begary and dry bred[,] and respectable young ladies" who walked past the house were "disgraced and slandered . . . by their slanderous tongs." Business must have been brisk at Fanny's establishment. It also appeared to be a family enterprise. Almost two years before William petitioned the assembly for a divorce, the county court had indicted Ruth Walling, probably one of Fanny's daughters by her first husband, "for keeping a house of ill fame, resorted to, for the purpose of prostitution and lewdness to the great Corruption of the Morals of the youth and other Citizens of the Country." By the time Ruth's case was scheduled for trial in the fall of 1850, she was married and living with her husband not far from her old haunt.[55]

Marriage was one way of quashing a criminal indictment for sexual misconduct. The same April grand jury that indicted Ruth Walling also presented twenty-two couples for "lewd and lascivious cohabitation." A state law passed the preceding year provided a fine of fifty dollars for this offense, but when trials began in September 1849, those couples who had gotten married only paid court costs.[56] Marriage had removed Ruth from prostitution, and Fanny was managing the operation when her husband sent his complaints to the legislature in the early weeks of 1851. Although he knew that the local circuit court could grant a divorce, that action would take until September. During the interval, he argued, Fanny's business could create "great distress in the neighbourhood." Sixty neighbors signed his petition in agreement. William Bishop's real objective was to evict Fanny from his property, but he could not do so as long as dower rights gave her an economic hold over him as her husband. After the legislature rejected William's request for a divorce, the estranged couple sold their real estate, valued at $2,000 in the 1850 census, to the children for cash and William's "maintenance during my natural life." Fanny probably took the cash.[57]

PROPERTY AND DOWER RIGHTS

Property issues and the legal obligations of husbands toward their wives are a not so subtle undercurrent in many of the divorce cases involving cuckolds. After Anne Pryor left Richmond with Charles Fremon, financial concerns certainly motivated John Pryor's swift action. He designed his newspaper announcement, the language of his divorce petition, and the questions he asked witnesses to quash any claims she might make on his estate. According to Anne's letter to her family, John had demanded that she draw up a written waiver of all financial rights she might have over him. The old Revolutionary warhorse was clearly accustomed to command and not above pressuring his wife to forfeit her economic prerogatives. Other men acted similarly. Before she left with her lover, Charles Bosher's wife, Susan, signed a statement in which she "voluntarily" confessed "that I have disgraced myself and injured my husband in the indulgence of a criminal intercourse" and gave up her claims on Charles and his property. Her paramour, Richard Grant, acknowledged "the truth" of her statement; but since three other men, two of whom were Bosher's kin, attested to this document, one can only wonder how much duress was applied.[58]

Sometimes, as we have seen, when both parties wished to be free of each other, spouses worked out a settlement notarized in a court or by a county justice dividing the land, home, or whatever resources they owned. Far more often, however, a wounded husband would complain, as John Pryor did, that his wife had absconded with property that rightfully belonged to him.[59] Other outraged males accused their wives of squandering their possessions, creating huge debts, and even spending their hard-earned money on their lovers. Again like John Pryor, deserted husbands commonly placed a notice in the press that they refused to be held responsible for any financial obligations their wives might incur. Some used the occasion to blow off steam. One deserted husband expressed his indignation in doggerel:

> Ill thrives the hapless family that shows,
> A Cock that's silent, and a hen that crows,
> I know not who live more unnatural lives,
> Than obeying husbands, and commanding wives.[60]

Other males, however, found that going public was too embarrassing. After Henry Carty's wife of twenty-eight years left him and their five children, she continued to run up large bills with merchants that he was forced to pay in order to keep his marital failure a secret. James and Mary Barnett may have been the longest-married couple to seek a divorce in Virginia. Wed in the last years of the eighteenth century, they lived together for almost fifty years and had thirteen children before "Mary became dissatisfied." A puzzled James watched her leave in 1843 "for causes unknown," and she refused his multiple entreaties to return. Discord between father and children followed, and James became practically destitute while Mary began "selling and sacrafising his property."[61] At least by consenting to a divorce, Mary Barnett offered her husband a way to limit his financial problems.

Not all wives were so cooperative. The law forbade a husband from selling property in land or slaves unless his wife consented, and her approval had to be given without her husband being present. Virginians debated the efficacy and reality of this arrangement in the 1840s when the assembly considered a married woman's property act. Some questioned whether a wife could be truly free to refuse a husband's wishes. They thought the separate examination was a sham. Significantly, however, when a wife and husband lived apart but were not divorced or had not formalized their situation through a separation agreement, the wife still maintained a legal hold on whatever property her husband owned. A strong-minded woman determined to maintain her rights could make life hell for a man who wanted to manage his estate independently of her wishes.

The case of Mariam and Benjamin Wright exemplifies this situation while it also demonstrates the legal action a cuckolded husband might take against his wife's paramour. When Jackson County was established in 1831, Ben Wright had been named clerk of the county court. His father, who owned and operated a prosperous mill, had been among the first settlers of that region on the Ohio River. In accepting Ben's proposal, Mariam Flowers had married well, at least from an economic perspective. Two children came soon. But marital problems surfaced. While Ben's important position kept him busy at the courthouse, Mariam began entertaining a lodger, John Greer, who clerked in a nearby store. Ben finally quit the house in 1834 or 1835, seven years after their marriage. Later he claimed that he had wanted to migrate to a place "where the evidence of his shame would not meet him in every object animate or inanimate that he saw." But he could not sell his property because of Mariam's dower claims, "which she has always loudly asserted whenever it suited her purposes so to do." Greer had helped Mariam acquire a lawyer.

Ben began the divorce process in July 1836 by filing papers in the Circuit Superior Court. He accused Mariam and John of adultery in his own home and in his "very bed." He also asserted that when John was away, his wife had sexual encounters with other men. More than a year passed before the divorce trial of facts opened on 15 September 1837. Mariam immediately requested a postponement, which the court granted. Concerned perhaps that John might skip town, Ben found a magistrate and swore out a writ of *capias ad respondendum,* an order to the sheriff to ensure that John would appear in court in October. Ben planned to institute a suit in the Circuit Superior Court for "criminal conversation," charging that John's adultery with Mariam had violated his right to the "comfort fellowship aid and assistance" of his wife. He wanted damages of $5,000. In England a parliamentary divorce first required a conviction of criminal conversation. Ben hoped that his suit would satisfy a Virginia legislature of the veracity of the facts he alleged. But John failed to appear in court for the next three months. In December the judge provisionally accepted Ben's version of events and ordered a trial. John finally showed up on 12 April 1838 claiming innocence, and his lawyer invoked the statute of limitations. Over the objections of Ben's attorney, the judge postponed John's trial until the next court term.[62]

That same day the court impaneled a jury and held a trial of facts for Ben's divorce petition. It proved disastrous for his cause. The jurors agreed that Mariam and John had committed adultery repeatedly and blatantly. But they also found that Ben had cohabited with his wife after he had left her and that he had continued to support her and their two children. Moreover, the jurors questioned whether Mariam had bestowed sexual favors on other men and noted that she had recently given birth to a child who could only have been conceived while John Greer was out of the county. Thus Ben appeared to have fathered the child at a time when he claimed he was living apart from his wife. Such clear-cut evidence of condonation would torpedo his petition.

His case against Greer for the seduction of Mariam now became crucial. That summer he arranged for depositions of witnesses living in Ohio in the suit of *Wright v Greer*. The Superior Court clerk handled this complicated process by sending a commission to two justices in Meigs County, Ohio, to depose Mariam's sister and brother-in-law, Sarah and Hugh Sinclair. Hugh's testimony to the adultery was firsthand. While Ben was away from home, Hugh had slept in one bed while Mariam and John occupied another a few feet away. Sarah swore to John's passion for her sister as well as his paternal love and concern for Mariam's new baby, Mary Jane. Other witnesses in Ohio and Illinois described how Mariam and John displayed great affection for each other "at *Frollicks and gatherings*" and when Mariam came to buy items at the store where John worked. Another witness observed "the whole transaction" between the two lovers both at Ben's home and later when John "layed her down by or near a log . . . in broad day light . . . in the act of adultery." The witnesses agreed that Ben had treated his wife well. In fact Sarah declared that she "would have given anything if she could have had a husband that would treat her so well and provide so well for her as said Wright did for his wife." One can only wonder if a sister's jealousy enhanced the deposition and what Hugh thought if he heard his wife's statement to the justice of the peace.[63]

That winter Ben submitted his divorce petition to the legislature. He took pains to explain that what the jurors had actually determined was that *perhaps* he had cohabited with his wife, but they were only guessing. He had really returned home to visit his children, hoping that this might conciliate Mariam into a real estate transfer. The jury presupposed that if he was at home, he and Mariam were having sexual relations. Their surmise was both unfortunate and mistaken. To bolster his case he included statements by ten of the twelve jurors that their verdict did not mean that Ben had had sexual relations with Mariam when he visited his former home, only that it was possible. Ben's petition said nothing, however, about the birth or paternity of Mary Jane, an issue the jury had raised. The assembly quickly rejected Ben's petition.[64]

When *Wright v Greer* came to trial in April 1839, the judge took John's plea of the statute of limitations under advisement and postponed the case again. In September he decided against John's plea but, at John's request, again put off the trial. More testimonies were taken that fall as Ben prepared a new petition. Back went the local justice to the Sinclair household, where young Nancy testified that she had seen "Aunt Mariam" and John Greer "in bead together very frequently." Jackson County's two deputy sheriffs discussed the "common rumor of the country" that John and Mariam were taking off for the West. The community knew Mariam's character and agreed that if Ben took up with her again, "he ought to be hooted out of Society." These affidavits, a new petition, and a copy of the proceedings thus far in Ben's "suit against the seducer" arrived in the capital on 13 January 1840. Ben informed the legislators that Mariam was again pregnant, courtesy of John Greer. His inability to transfer property irritated him most, though a lawyer advised that his wife's dower claims were questionable at best. By this time Mariam had evidently moved out, leaving Ben's house and their children, so she had deserted him. Ben no longer supported her. He begged release from a purely legal relationship "unsustained by . . . Justice or morality; and in direct conflict with the Laws of the Most High which expressly says that 'for adultery a Man may put away his wife.'" Was he not entitled to "pursue the path . . . to happiness, unburthened and unobstructed by the other"? The assembly thought not.[65]

Two and a half years after Ben filed his suit against Greer, the case finally came to trial in April 1840. Because the sheriff was Ben's brother-in-law and the county coroner was absent, the judge appointed a third party to seat the jurors. They found Greer guilty and ordered him to pay a fine of $700 in damages to Ben Wright plus the latter's court costs of $55.68. Greer's attorney asked for a new trial, but after a night's rest, the judge denied the motion. The court ordered the sheriff to bring Greer in until he paid his fine and costs, but he proved to be an insolvent debtor whose total property amounted to a note for $1.37½. At least Ben now had a court verdict for criminal conversation to present with his third divorce petition that December. It received somewhat more consideration before the House once again refused the divorce.[66]

After three rejections in three years, Ben Wright had temporarily run out of options. Mariam meanwhile had moved into a cabin by herself and was pregnant again. John became a regular houseguest. Eventually the lovers and their children settled down "in good family Style" near Hugh and Sarah Sinclair. But Mariam's own relations, if their testimony in 1844 is credible, had written her off. Her cousin's wife described Mariam as "a swearing scoling and mischief making dont care woman and further she saith not." She had said enough, however. In their 1844–45 session the assembly finally divorced Benjamin and Mariam Wright over the strenuous objections of one legislator, who was probably screaming condonation. As we have seen, that year marked a new acceptance by the assembly of adultery as grounds for absolute divorce. In a few years the law would catch up with legislative practice. Benjamin Wright was only forty when he received his divorce, yet he did not marry again, at least during the next six years. Although like virtually every other divorced male he probably wanted a wife, nightmares about dower rights may have kept him from the altar. Mariam's adultery had been a searing experience, but control of his estate had driven the proceedings. As his brother-in-law testified, Ben owned "considerable property." In 1850 he was living with his three teenaged children, his eighty-two-year-old mother, and a twenty-four-year-old woman named Roxanne Jones, who may have been a servant or perhaps something more.[67]

Ben Wright's situation was not unique. Like any man, a woman could also marry for money, and some husbands, like Matthew Watson, wanted a divorce in order to limit their losses. In more than twenty years of marriage to Lucy Bowe, he had only lived a few months with his wife. She left him once, returned briefly in response to his pleas, and finally departed for a life of adultery. As he grew older, Matthew's chief concern was to keep Lucy from his estate in case he should die first, because he did not want "the fruits of her adultery" to share the inheritance of "his own child." Even more revolting was the thought that Lucy "will revel in debauchery with [her] paramours upon the fruits of his honest and laborious earnings." Similar concerns preoccupied John Bane and William Horton. A disconsolate widower, Bane had foolishly married again only to increase "the bitterness of his sorrow." His new wife, Jane, would not live with him or carry out her wifely obligations, had run off with another man, and now only communicated with her husband to threaten him about "what proportion of [his] property . . . she intends to have." William Horton's wife, Nancy Ann, had committed adultery and even married another man in Alabama, yet she pursued William to Kanawha County and badgered him for alimony. Although he had offered to provide her with a home and support, according to one witness Nancy Ann expected Horton to give her "half of his estate."[68] The desire for ownership and control of property and wealth knew no gender.

Desires for property did not motivate Anne Whiting Pryor, however. For a few years she and Charles Fremon remained in Savannah, where he taught French and she took boarders into their home to help make ends meet. Their first child, John Charles, was born there in January 1813. A short time later they moved, first to Nashville and then back to Norfolk in 1817. Two more children were born before Charles Fremon died in 1818. Anne, who never remarried, soon left Virginia and raised her children in Charleston. The *t* was added to the end of their surname in the 1820s, before John Charles Frémont left school to find a profession and explore the West. His relationship with his mother remained especially close. As he wrote years later, "We were only two, my mother and I. We had lost my sister. My brother was away, making his own career, and I had to concern myself for mine. I was unwilling to leave my mother. Circumstances had more than usually endeared us to each other and I knew that her life would be solitary without me. . . . But my mother had an experience of sacrifice which with her true womanly nature it had been hard to learn."[69]

In her letters to her family, Anne regretted the unhappiness she had caused her husband. John Pryor was left to assuage the public shame that his wife and her lover had brought upon him and reclaim some semblance of personal honor. His press notice against Anne had been the first step in that process. His application for divorce had been the second. In the conclusion of his petition he pleaded with his male peers for that "relief" that would save him from "a series of sorrows and wretchedness" in his declining years. Although the legislators had not granted him a divorce, they had accepted in print his version of events and denied Anne's, thus substantially reducing any possibility she might have of obtaining a separate maintenance or alimony. Furthermore, this verdict also justified the next measure he would take. For third, and most important, he needed to demonstrate his manhood and capacity as a husband by acquiring a new wife.

In March 1815 the Richmond press announced John Pryor's marriage to "the amiable Miss Elizabeth Graves." A Presbyterian minister, Drury Lacy, performed the ceremony. Despite Pryor's failure to obtain a legal divorce, neither the state nor the church objected. He had, after all, proven his wife's adultery and desertion in the legislative forum. That was enough for his family, the local community, and the Westminster Confession of Faith, which permitted divorce in cases of adultery. In his will, probated after his death in 1823, Pryor claimed that he had re-married "under a well founded impression and confident belief that my late wife Ann Pryor had departed this life." But he also slipped in a clause that acknowledged Elizabeth "as my wife, none other having any fixed claim upon me or my estate, in that Character."[70]

Twenty-three years earlier, in what had been from his perspective an idyllic time in his first marriage, Pryor had drafted a will. The contrast between that document and the one probated after his death demonstrates the trauma he had experienced as a cuckold. The first text makes repeated references to Anne, his "dear well beloved wife." Had they remained together, on his death she would have received the great bulk of his property, including his Richmond home, $1,500, and whatever he eventually inherited from her father's estate. In the 1823 will Pryor's sparse references to Elizabeth, his second wife, are terse and perfunctory. She was to be paid $1,000 in lieu of her dower and inherit his furniture, except his organ and secretary. The bulk of the estate, however, went to various nieces and nephews. Another person is also mentioned in both documents. In his first will Pryor left 5,000 acres of Kentucky land to Edward Hazlewood, "late a soldier in Captain Blackburn's Company of Artilery." Apart from the executors, Hazlewood is the only nonfamily member named; the legacy might be understood as a reward from an officer to a soldier for some special service rendered during the Revolution. In 1823 the bequest was clarified when Pryor bequeathed $500 "to my natural son Edwin Hazlewood if he be living." Clearly no closeness existed between the two. Pryor was unsure of the man's first name and whether he was even still alive. But no matter what Anne or anyone else might have thought or speculated over the years, John Pryor wanted the world to know that he had not been impotent. He had fathered a son.[71]

III Consequences

CHAPTER 7

This Prejudice of Divorce

THE SOCIAL STIGMA

Sally McDowell Thomas's divorce became inevitable the day her father attacked her husband at a stagecoach stop. In itself the incident was unremarkable. Antebellum southern males were prone to violent reactions when provoked, and Frank Thomas had behaved despicably toward his wife, from whom he was separated. But the assault generated widespread gossip and even newspaper reports because Frank Thomas was the governor of Maryland and James McDowell, his father-in-law, was the governor of Virginia. James and Susanna McDowell were about to board the coach in Staunton on the last leg of their journey to Colalto, their plantation home on the outskirts of Lexington, Virginia. Suddenly their cordially detested son-in-law materialized on the sidewalk behind them.

Later that evening a shaken Susanna Preston McDowell described the scene in a letter to her daughter Mary. Her furious husband had wheeled about and demanded, "Where are you going?" "Fincastle," Thomas replied, indicating a destination farther down the Valley of Virginia that would take him through Lexington. James McDowell had lashed out with his umbrella, and the two governors grappled until bystanders intervened to end the fight. Quitting the public conveyance for a carriage provided by friends, the McDowells raced after the stage that carried Thomas south toward his estranged wife at Colalto. Before his coach arrived in Lexington, however, the Maryland governor disembarked at a tavern stop. Vowing revenge on the McDowells, he went to stay with a cousin in Glasgow, about eight miles from Colalto. Several years later in his account of the incident Thomas blamed his father-in-law for his wrecked marriage: "The divorce has been decreed by him in a street brawl."[1]

The McDowells had never wanted Thomas to marry their daughter.

In 1840 when the then-congressman had visited their home, Susanna McDowell wrote her husband, "The sound of his voice . . . rings through my ears as a death bell to all my fondly cherished hopes." She had avoided the unwelcome houseguest, but the dreaded interview was inevitable. I prefer to encounter "a rattlesnake," she opined. His personality and manners, not his politics, elicited her antagonism. Like James McDowell, Frank Thomas was a Democrat. His career, first in the state legislature and now for almost ten years in the House of Representatives, had been extremely successful.[2] Sally had met her future husband in Washington, D.C., in January 1836 when her parents sent the young girl not quite fifteen to be educated there. For more than a year she had lived with her aunt and uncle, Elizabeth and Thomas Hart Benton, the powerful Democratic senator from Missouri. The Bentons proudly exposed their impressionable young niece to Washington's glittering society. At White House receptions she met President Andrew Jackson. Vice-President Martin Van Buren squired her about the East Room. Letters to her parents detailed gorgeous parties and elegant dinners, theater performances, trips to Philadelphia and New York, politics, ladies' fashions, dancing and guitar lessons, and even a circus parade.

Like most congressional families, the Bentons shared a Capitol Hill rooming house with compatible Democrats. Their regular dining companions included Missouri's other senator, Lewis Fields Linn, who showered Sally with attention; his fat wife, Elizabeth, who ate quarts of ice cream; and the thirty-seven-year-old bachelor congressman from Maryland, Frank Thomas. When Sally moved from the Benton household to the Georgetown Female Seminary in March 1837, Frank gave her an elaborate "book of engravings" as a "momento," which she accepted with her aunt's approval. "I am glad," she wrote her mother, "that there are some persons in this world who, besides my own relations, desire to 'have a place in my memory.'"[3] Little did she imagine the nightmarish place Thomas would later occupy in her life.

Although the events surrounding her later marriage, separation, and divorce became notorious at the time and involved important personages, they have remained unknown to historians.[4] A case study of her experience makes an appropriate conclusion to this examination of divorce in its social context of kinship and community in the Old South. It serves, first, to summarize the legal procedures involved in legislative divorce, the conflicting emotions it aroused as a discursive process, and its growing acceptance by the time Sally McDowell petitioned the legislature in 1845.

Throughout Sally's ordeal her extended family provided emotional encouragement, and at critical junctures friends, neighbors, and the larger community in Lexington offered their support. Those same individuals and groups, however, also held expectations for a woman in Sally's position and sat in judgment on her conduct after as well as before the divorce. Thus her story reveals the enormous pressures suffered by people caught in marital traumas and the ambiguous social situation in which divorce placed them. Although gender, class, circumstances, and temperament rendered each person's experience distinctive, the narrative of her marital strife and its aftermath captures the upheaval divorce created in the antebellum era and the attendant problems divorced people faced in reconstructing their lives.

Society could be cruel and unyielding, even after the legal niceties had been settled. For both men and women, stable identities based at least partially on marriage had been destroyed. Broad familial, political, and cultural forces constructed new ones for divorced people that constricted their lives. Sally McDowell struggled to keep what she termed "the great catastrophe of my life" from destroying her life. First, she successfully maintained her "position" through the grim period of separation and divorce when multiple legal battles thrust her repeatedly into public view. Then, in the mid-1850s, she fought to overcome the extraordinary social prejudice against remarriage. In addition to personal letters and documents from the period of her marriage and divorce in the 1840s, she and John Miller, her second husband, left an extraordinary courtship correspondence of almost 500 letters. Even more than the divorce petitions, this rich source reveals the inner traumas of a failed marriage and public divorce as well as the social stigma divorced people bore afterward.[5]

During the years Sally McDowell spent completing her education at Miss English's academy in Georgetown, Frank Thomas became her "old friend."[6] The young Virginia woman was flattered, even overwhelmed, by Thomas's attention, and her obvious "fancy" for the rising politician prompted Washington gossips to predict that the couple would be married in the early months of 1840. She had left school in 1838 but returned to Washington for a visit at that time. In fact Sally was planning a wedding for the summer of 1839 until her parents discovered the betrothal and vigorously opposed it. The difference in their ages was not the principal problem. As Sally herself later explained, the McDowells thought Frank possessed "a jealous, irritable and bad temper which foreboded an unhappy union."[7] She broke off the engagement and returned to Colalto, but the Maryland congressman would not be put off and repeatedly visited Sally. He wrote a close friend that though rumors of an impending marriage were untrue, he would play the suitor until he discovered "whether I have power to win the affections of a fine woman." Despite her family's best efforts, he was ultimately persuasive. The marriage was, as her mother said, "her decision," and by December 1840 Sally was anticipating "a release from gloomy retirement" in the country. The day when parents determined the spouses for their children was long gone, if indeed it had ever existed since the colonial period.[8]

As Sally McDowell prepared for her wedding day, she must have anticipated for her future something like the relationship her own parents enjoyed. The marriage of Susanna Preston to James McDowell, Susanna's first cousin, exemplified the complementarity and reciprocity in marriage and domestic life that preachers and writers praised. A planter as well as a politician, James was frequently called away from home to administer family properties in other states as well as to attend to official duties in Richmond or Washington. Susanna managed home, family, and money as best she could, and her husband deferred to her. Their letters mainly revolved around their children and financial concerns, and James McDowell closed one exchange with a typical remark: "Think the whole matter out for yourself and I am very sure that your judgment and decision will be better than mine." But husband and wife also knew what their respective roles in marriage should be. At Christmas 1840 an exhausted Susanna McDowell wrote her husband, "I do long for your return. Our family is too large and I too frail to be without an efficient head." He replied from Mississippi, "I pray *you* be patient until I can come to your relief and take, as I ought, the *larger half* of your troubles." A few weeks later he reflected to Susanna on his domestic situation and his longing for home and family: "Thank God that I have a home to think of and go to, where my heart can feel no emotion but that of Kindness and confidence . . . that family fireside which Providence has given me— Would that I were at it with the wee one and Canty and Tom upon my Knee and all the rest around to greet me and make me happy. This I trust will soon be."[9] Sally may well have hoped for and expected a marital relationship like the one her parents enjoyed. The reality would prove a bitter disappointment.

Relatives and friends filled Colalto for the wedding on 8 June 1841. Although Sally's parents at last accepted the marriage as inevitable, they had repeatedly expressed their reservations and concerns to the bride. They knew their daughter possessed a lively, playful disposition that contrasted sharply with Frank Thomas's suspicious nature and morose seriousness. The humorless politician was ill at ease with the light banter that was part of Sally's casual manner among her young intimates. But overly impressed by his "uprightness, integrity and high gentlemanly qualities," she was oblivious to Frank's defective personality and the enormous risks it posed for her future happiness. Had she known her prospective husband's capacity for self-deception and his violent fantasies on the eve of the wedding, she might have drawn back at the last moment. Aware of the McDowell family's opposition to the marriage, Frank convinced himself and even told a few male friends that he would be physically assaulted at the ceremony and another groom substituted in his place. In preparation for this anticipated outrage, he brought two pistols to repel the attack that never came. Sally knew none of this at the time, but her rejection of parental advice later rendered her, in her own mind, all the more dependent on her husband "for happiness and protection." Should marital problems arise, she could hardly turn to her family for assistance. Thus Sally gave herself completely and irrevocably into Frank Thomas's hands.[10]

Three weeks after the wedding the couple traveled north to the groom's home outside Frederick, Maryland. Their honeymoon passed happily enough until Sally's cousin, Robert Taylor, whom Frank had invited to join his law practice the preceding winter, arrived in Frederick in July. Frank's first jealous explosion soon followed. Earlier he had confided to Sally that Robert was "profligate" and had acted indecently toward women—a charge she considered incredible because the two cousins had been raised together in Lexington and she regarded Robert like "a brother." Now as they visited and laughed together, Frank glowered in the background. In a lighthearted, joking mood, Sally once teased Frank, "As you know, you're not a man of truth or a gentlemen." Instantly she regretted it, for he became terribly angry. On another occasion Robert made a comical remark about Frank's clothes, and the older man took immediate, stormy offense. Later alone with Sally, Frank became enraged and accused his wife of behaving improperly. Then his mood suddenly shifted, and all was forgotten. He became tender and

loving, and Sally experienced "a feeling of quiet happiness, and of undis-
turbed confidence and repose in his affection."

The jealous suspicions returned with renewed intensity, however, and
his outbursts became more frequent. Toward the end of July he told Sally
that he had observed a secret meeting between the two cousins one evening in the garden. She denied it, but on Frank's orders Sally wrote a letter
to her parents asking them to meet her in Washington to take her home.
Frank, filled with remorse, begged her to stay and give their marriage
another chance. She destroyed the letter. This pattern was repeated from
day to day and week to week. The slightest incident provoked black looks,
even in public, to be succeeded, when husband and wife were alone, by
renewed accusations of impropriety and infidelity. Violent rages ended
in gloomy silence. He cajoled her repeatedly to confess to the evening
tryst with Robert, promising that if only she admitted the meeting, all
would be forgiven and the past entirely forgotten. As Frank played upon
her emotions and controlled her by his moody outbursts, Sally's anxiety
mounted. In the account she drew up a few years later, she described
this period: "My life was one of continual excitement—either fighting off
avowed suspicions—or in constant apprehension of them.—yet always
hoping, and with the credulity of strong affection, always believing that
every spell, would be the last."

At each stormy session he promised that if she just admitted the
truth of his accusations, sweet harmony would be restored. Eventually
Sally, knowing that she was not at fault, persuaded herself that perhaps
her cousin had in fact entertained "improper designs," as her husband
charged, and agreed to write him a dismissive letter, which Frank dictated. A few days later, when Robert wrote Frank asking for an explanation of the accusations, the latter demanded that Sally personally support
his version of every incident lest he be considered a "jealous husband."
Helpless to resist, she agreed, though in fact both husband and wife knew
that the charges were all lies. Robert left Frederick and returned to Virginia.[11]

"These admissions," she later wrote, "drawn from my weakness, and
from the powerful but perverted force of the strongest feelings of a
woman's nature," were then thrown back in her face when Frank admitted to her that he had never seen the meeting about which he had ex-
torted her confession. Afterward she found it strange that this behavior
had not shaken "her confidence" in her husband. The "lie" that she had
told against her cousin weighed on her conscience. Nor did Robert Tay-

Francis Thomas, ca. 1841 (Courtesy of The Library of Virginia)

lor's removal from the scene end her problems. Frank, fully engrossed in his campaign for governor, left his wife in the care of his father and sisters. From the time she arrived in Maryland, they had treated her with respect and kindness. Shortly before her husband went off electioneering, Sally suspected that she was pregnant but said nothing. Frank had previously announced to her that, against the opinions of two doctors, he was personally convinced that he was impotent. One night after Frank was gone, while sharing a room at her father-in-law's home with her sister-in-law Eliza Thomas, Sally became ill and in the morning discovered she had suffered a miscarriage. The family doctor was summoned and estimated that the fetus was two months old. Sally recovered quickly but delayed telling Frank what had taken place until he returned victorious from the election.

The tirade that followed dwarfed all previous scenes as the frenzied husband wildly accused his wife of aborting Robert Taylor's child with a potion furnished by her paramour. A frantic Sally declared her innocence, but Frank, demanding confession and promising forgiveness, "with a masterly hand" played "upon all the instincts and affections of my nature." The governor-elect threatened to disclose everything publicly and destroy her reputation, the honor of both their families, and even his own career. If she admitted "The Truth," however, he promised that his "affection" for her was so "intense" that "he would again take [her] trustingly to his bosom" and the matter would remain strictly between them. An emotional wreck, Sally ultimately said enough to produce a triumphant cry from her husband. According to her version of events, she instantaneously recovered her bearing and repudiated this confession. Sally had already falsely implicated Robert once, and she would not do so a second time. But her steadfast denials only further enraged her husband.

Other incidents followed as trivial encounters and casual conversations with Frank's family or friends occasioned fresh outbursts of jealousy and charges of infidelity. The last suspect, incredibly, was Dr. William Tyler, an older man with a wife and adult children and a relative of Frank's. When he came in early November to treat a toothache and infected gum that had swollen Sally's face, her ever watchful husband heard them laughing together and became convinced that she had formed yet another illicit liaison. Later that month at a dinner party the Thomases hosted for his friends, the Macgills from Hagerstown, Frank spied Tyler leave his chair, take one next to Sally, and engage her in quiet conversation. Her husband's face turned black with angry suspicions that worsened during the meal until his malevolent glares led Sally to exclaim, "Good God Mr. Thomas, remember where you are." Later the report went out that he "shook his fist in her face" and commanded her to leave the dining room. Such a scene of emotional conflict between husband and wife seriously violated social convention, which strictly segregated private spousal relations from public scrutiny. Frank Thomas was losing his self-control.[12] The miserable pattern continued through the fall, as Sally recalled, "ever suspicious—then relenting—violent—then unaffectedly affectionate—. . . declaring he would not live with me—then exclaiming 'how can I live without you'." Repeatedly he threatened to expose her by sending for her parents to take her away, only to reverse course after she had packed her bags. Twice in December he composed affidavits accusing his wife of conducting an "improper interview" and engaging in "unlawful intercourse," though she denied both charges in writing.[13]

Their married life together ended shortly after Frank was sworn in as governor at Annapolis on 3 January 1842. Nearby in Baltimore lived Sally's older brother, James McDowell Jr., a medical student at Johns Hopkins, and her mother's sister, Ann Sophonisba Breckinridge, the wife of Robert Jefferson Breckinridge, a well-known Presbyterian minister. But Frank did not contact them. Instead, in a furious moment he summoned Sally's aunt Elizabeth McDowell Benton to come from Washington to hear his charges against his wife. When Elizabeth Benton returned home, she informed her husband as well as another of Sally's powerful uncles, Senator William Campbell Preston of South Carolina. The family patriarchs mobilized to support their niece. Both wrote James McDowell to come at once to take his daughter home. Preston explained Frank's "derangement" as a "*mono*mania of the most distressing character." What the crisis demanded, he urged his brother-in-law, was someone with "the right and authority to command under most difficult and delicate circumstances and to assume responsibilities of the most decisive character."[14] Within the rigidly hierarchical South, such an extraordinary intervention challenged a husband's authority over his wife. The most appropriate person to make it would be the closest male relative, in this case the father.

True to form, Frank again reversed himself and ordered Sally to instruct her aunt not to inform her parents. But Sally's letter missed the mail. By mid-January James and Susanna McDowell had arrived in Baltimore and sent for their daughter. Though her husband followed her to the city and implored Sally to return to Annapolis, she left for Virginia with her parents. Years later while he was courting Sally, John Miller, soon to become her second husband, analyzed Frank Thomas's behavior: "He tortured you as a cat does a mouse, fondling you between the acts of his ordering you out of the house . . . and turning upon you so soon after your reconciliations as to make your living with him impossible." Sally agreed:

> My life was one of torture—all the more dreadful that it was mixed up with moods of tenderness. . . . I sat watching a cat, the other day, torturing a forlorn little mouse—I was just that poor suffering thing; without, however, the perfect certainty of death. I think I was in danger often of that fatal end, tho' I was unaware of it: and yet I dont know; he has all the cowardice of an opossin, and whilst he w[oul]d have killed me if he c[oul]d have concealed the deed, never w[oul]d, unless he had been in one of his storming passions, when there was a prospect of discovery.[15]

Years of separation passed before Sally could begin to comprehend the destructive forces that controlled her husband. Though confronted by numerous instances of his jealousy, she had found the idea incredible. In rejecting the counsel of her parents and friends, she had left all to give herself entirely into his care and was completely devoted to him. Once, in a rare moment of candor, Frank confessed that he had never really believed his accusations, and she thought he spoke truthfully. While she never understood the motives behind the pain he inflicted on her or himself, in the narrative she composed for the divorce trial, she suggested perceptively that perhaps something in childhood might have "left a sting that sometimes goaded him." His inner agonies drove him beyond "passion" or "anger" and created within the tortured man only "the deepest, bitterest misery." Sometimes at night he would awaken Sally, imploring her "to talk to him." The subject was not important, but the sound of her voice in the quiet would calm his desperate fears and soothe him to sleep.

Although she eventually came to pity Frank, Sally realized the psychological damage he had inflicted on her. Unreservedly she had given him her "whole heart with its most sacred feelings," only to find that "the object was unworthy." He had bullied and tormented her, yet almost up to the time of their separation she retained "the most abiding faith in his honour" and thought him "incapable of doing a wrong act." She operated, she later acknowledged, under "a most extraordinary delusion." Although Chesapeake society ultimately regarded Frank Thomas as demented, she saw him only as "a Mother does . . . a spoiled child in its anguish."[16] She would witness much more of that behavior in the months and years that followed first their separation and then their divorce.

His last-minute efforts to prevent Sally's departure having failed, Frank wrote repeatedly in early February 1842 pleading for a reconciliation. His first letter reminded her that sacred obligations still bound them together. With breathless understatement he acknowledged that he had not "fully performed" his "solemn delicate duties" as a husband "to comfort, nourish, cherish and protect you," but he blamed his conduct on a "painful delusion of your unworthiness," which he now recognized as entirely false. Desolate in her absence, seeking only her "happiness," he inquired plaintively, "Have I erred beyond forgiveness?" Senator Benton's letters had finally convinced him of her "entire innocence," and "with horror" he now reflected "upon the mental agony you must have experienced in the consciousness that all my sufferings and all your own, had their origin in a mere mistake." Frank pleaded for "an opportunity to make reparation" for all that she had suffered and assured Sally that his mental state was now "sound, sane and clear."[17]

The Maryland governor had a further concern, however. For the aspiring politician, Sally's departure had proven to be a public relations disaster of the first magnitude. Enemies were misrepresenting his "character and conduct," he wrote his wife, and capitalizing on the rumors that his tyrannical behavior had ruined their marriage and forced her to send for her parents. Reaching out for intercessors, he persuaded Reverdy Johnson, a distinguished Baltimore lawyer, to serve as his emissary and press Sally to return to Annapolis. Initially convinced of Frank's sincerity, Johnson bent his energies to the awkward task and in lengthy letters to Sally and her father detailed the emotional suffering and hearty repentance of Maryland's chief executive.[18] To Frank Thomas's growing consternation, Maryland society set its face against him. Already the press there and in Virginia had commented on his marital troubles and were representing Sally as the abused party. In any propaganda war Frank was doomed. As Norma Basch has pointed out in her study of divorce, nineteenth-century newspapers fed on juicy marital breakups and usually portrayed the accused women sympathetically as victims. From Baltimore in June, Aunt Sophonisba Breckinridge reported that public opinion regarded the governor with "perfect detestation and abhorrence," and except when essential government business demanded contact, people ostracized him.[19]

Frank desperately wanted her back, but a reconciliation posed serious problems for Sally. Her brother James wrote that "universal sentiment" in Baltimore regarded her as "an injured woman, and that it would affect her reputation *most* materially to return." Impartial observers agreed that under no circumstances should she reunite with Frank. Such action would only play into his hands and make him appear the innocent party. Virginians concurred with Maryland sentiment. While Frank writhed in Annapolis, the McDowells and their kinfolk circled the wagons around Sally in Lexington. Her grandmother Preston wrote, "the late distressing circumstance . . . must tend to make us all love each other more." As family members rallied to her cause, Sally became, in one aunt's terms, "our dear persecuted child." In parlors and across dining room tables throughout the Chesapeake region and beyond, tales were told of Frank's cruelty and his wife's "unmerited, barbarous" sufferings. She had "loved too fondly for her own peace," and her husband had used "her innocence and purity" to destroy her. Her parents' actions in bringing her home received general approbation from the "enlightened and virtuous." All agreed that the separation must be final and definitive. Reunion would prove a "fatal step . . . *fatal* to her happiness and character."[20]

Meanwhile, an increasingly distraught Governor Thomas reached out to old friends for support in his "domestic affliction" and suggested publicly in December 1842 that Sally would return to Annapolis in the spring. Her brother reported that tidbit along with his fixed judgment that any such action would jeopardize Sally's "honor . . . and that of her family." From the outset the essential cause was honor for Sally and her kin. The entire family's reputation was inexorably tied to her good name. But should the separation be rendered permanent and irrevocable by law? Aunt Sophonisba had suggested that her niece eliminate "all further embarrassment by getting a *divorce*." Sally's brother James concurred. "Why should *we* fear a thourough [*sic*] investigation of this subject before the tribunal of our State?" he wrote to his mother. For the time being, however, a permanent separation seemed the most viable option to Virginia's new governor. The fall elections had placed Sally's father in that office. Winter found him alone in Richmond while his wife and most of the children remained at Colalto. In mid-February of 1843 James McDowell wrote his oldest daughter warmly of his "anxiety and affection" and expressed admiration for the resolve she showed in rejecting a marital reunion. It was the only course pointed out by "safety or virtue or hope."[21]

The months passed sadly for Sally. While relatives and friends commiserated over her misfortune, she had another immediate concern:

the injustice she had done to her cousin, Robert Taylor. Writing to him shortly after her return to Colalto, she directly and frankly acknowledged that "*all accusations of dishonorable and base conduct on your part to me are utterly unfounded and false.*" Taylor may not have responded, because a few weeks later, carefully coached by her father, she wrote another apologetic letter, explaining that she had acted in "weakness, in anguish, in the fear and under the fear of horrors." But now she wanted to proclaim his entire "innocence, of the gross charges" made against him.[22]

She also confronted the attitude of southern society toward a woman who had separated from her husband. Even though the public did not hold her responsible for the collapse of the marriage, society now regarded Sally Thomas as damaged goods, a marked woman. Writing to his wife in February from Richmond, an assemblyman reported the capital gossip about Frank Thomas's outrageous behavior toward Sally, but then he added, "How deplorable her condition. So young and with such prospects to have such a destiny."[23] The past foreclosed her future. Even divorce would not alter that condition. Since her return to Colalto she had remained there as if in mourning, with the single exception of a visit to some nearby cousins. Her mother served as chief confidante and adviser. She spoke to no one about her situation, except very occasionally to her father. She did not lack invitations. An uncle suggested she spend time with her Preston kin in South Carolina, and her father thought she would enjoy a month or two in Richmond or perhaps a stay with cousins in the Piedmont outside the capital. But even the thought of social contact proved excruciatingly painful to the devastated young woman, so she remained at home while her mother traveled to Richmond. As she recalled much later, "the spring of life" was "broken." All her hopes and dreams had been ruined, and she existed in a kind of graveyard "'among the tombs' of every thing that made [life] a blessing."[24]

Toward the end of February 1843 yet another letter arrived from Frank expressing "bitter regret . . . at the failure of every attempt to learn [her] inclinations." Sally had been returning his mail without comment, but he refused to stop believing that one day she would be "adorning and enjoying that station I was ambitious to attain only for your sake. In that hope I live. When that hope is blasted this life has lost all attractions for me." Although he had received "no mercy" from Sally's father, he sympathized with the "pains and privations" of James McDowell's situation and begged his "very dear" wife to tell him what he must do "to reunite your Father's family" and to restore her "happiness and peace." In March he wrote again, hoping that Sally and her parents did not want a "final separation." He was unsure of their intentions, he claimed, because they had cut off all contact. But the fact that she had not returned his last letter gave him hope of reconciliation.[25]

The Virginia governor and his wife were in Richmond when Sally received this letter, and she postponed her response in expectation of their imminent arrival at Colalto. When they were delayed, she confided in an old family friend, Lexington physician Dr. Archibald Graham. She needed advice immediately because Frank had proposed that if a reunion was impossible, she should return his letter. Not to do so might indicate that she was wavering; swift action was imperative. The previous year her brother had suggested that Frank might visit Lexington after the legislature concluded its work in Annapolis.[26] He was prescient. Both the Maryland and Virginia assemblies had ended their respective sessions, freeing their chief executives to leave their offices. Thus they met in Staunton on 20 April 1843.

The violent encounter between the two governors created a sensation in southern social and political circles. From Columbia, South Carolina, William Preston congratulated his brother-in-law on "the blow you gave the reptile" and noted that "all men in this quarter" agreed that Frank Thomas deserved it "at your hands" even "if you had been ten times the governor." The Marylander had behaved in a "blackguard and ruffianly" fashion. Meanwhile Frank responded in the pages of the *Baltimore Republican*. He characterized James McDowell as a "cowardly assailant" and promised to vindicate himself before the public by exposing all the sordid details of his wretched marriage.[27] But the governor had misjudged his audience. Although it published his announcement, the newspaper severely criticized its author. From Baltimore a distraught Sophonisba Breckinridge wrote James McDowell that the popular uproar had reached a new pitch. Though "public sympathy . . . is decidedly with *us*," she advised him not to respond to Frank in the press or do anything that would expose the family to "public chit *chat*." She had urged his "fearfully excited" son James not to walk about with pistols but only a stout club to use as needed. A friendly lawyer had informed her that Frank had hired legal counsel; she suggested that the Virginia governor beat him to the punch by applying for a divorce in the Old Dominion. Up to this point Sally's parents had done everything possible to keep the public controversy from their daughter, but her aunt now thought that the time had come for her niece to "know all" and perform "firmly her duty to herself and to her large connection." Frank's "polluted tounge" [*sic*] was dragging her name through the mud.[28]

As evidence of Sally's infidelity, the Maryland governor produced a letter written to her in 1837 by the unhappy wife of Senator Linn of Missouri. In it she accused Sally of attempting to alienate her husband's affections when they were living in the Capitol Hill boardinghouse and insisted that she return his picture and lock of hair. At the time the bewildered young girl had turned the letter over to her aunt Elizabeth Benton, who wrote Elizabeth Linn denying the charges and demanding proof. After a further exchange, Linn retreated from her accusations. But three years later, when Frank became engaged to her niece, Elizabeth Benton had shown him the correspondence in an unsuccessful effort to dissuade a man she knew was suspicious by nature from a marriage that none of Sally's relatives favored. Unfortunately her ploy did not work, but Frank remembered the letters, insisted that Sally obtain them from her aunt after their marriage, and kept them when she returned to Colalto. Now he trotted them out and showed them about the Baltimore streets, her brother James reported, "to excite the ribald laughter of his dirty and vulgar associates."[29]

Throughout the rest of May and into June 1843 letters flew back and forth between Maryland and Virginia as Sally's family searched for ways to counter Frank's attacks on his wife's character. Following the overwhelming advice of family members and friends, Governor McDowell had not responded in the press to his son-in-law's defamation campaign, but clearly something had to be done. In a long letter to his wife he poured out his concerns: "[Frank Thomas] is bent upon the utter destruction of her character and peace, and that of us all, . . . It was dreadful enough for our dear child to find that she had placed all her hopes of happiness and protection upon an unworthy man; but how much more dreadful to find that he is not only unworthy but that he is pursuing her with the fiery spirit of the very devil himself that he may dishonor and destroy her." James McDowell was determined to move heaven and earth to protect his daughter against this "wretch" who had left her no choice but to treat him as "the worst of enemies." In his view Sally must use "every means of resistance necessary to vindicate and uphold herself."

With the greatest reluctance the governor concluded that a divorce was essential. Only divorce would legally free Sally from her husband.

But even more important, the judicial process followed by legislative action would publicly and definitely disprove Frank's accusations. Frank himself had provided the irrefutable evidence by the letters he had written Sally after their separation in which he apologized for his conduct, admitted her innocence and his delusions, and begged her to return. James McDowell now dispatched carefully attested copies to his son in Baltimore. Reverdy Johnson, previously Frank Thomas's personal advocate and legal counsel, had switched sides to support Sally. He gave permission to use his earlier letters describing Frank's remorse. Other Baltimore lawyers also enlisted in the cause. Meanwhile members of the Richmond bar bolstered the Virginia governor's conviction that no procedure short of divorce would offer the needed vindication.[30]

Sally, however, recoiled in horror at the sensational publicity a divorce would generate. Given the political and social positions of the principals, the press would have a field day exposing her marital trials. So writing to his wife, who remained with Sally at Colalto, her father marshaled his arguments. Frank, he reasoned, would not seek a divorce because the Maryland legislature would not grant him one, and he well knew that the proceedings would draw out "*all* the facts" which were in his interest to hide. But vengeful desires made men do strange things, even against their own interests, and so Frank might indeed destroy himself. Whatever his son-in-law did, James McDowell thought it critical for Sally's future that the sordid marriage be examined in judicial daylight. Matters had developed to the point where if Frank were to die now and the controversy be buried in oblivion, people would always wonder whether he had taken "secrets" against Sally to the grave. From this perspective, to remain in her private sphere beyond the glare of public scrutiny might prove the more dangerous choice and permanently compromise her reputation. In fact, if Frank suddenly withdrew all charges against her, some would think that he had acted out of "forbearance and charity" or an unwillingness to expose "the private affairs" of Maryland's chief executive.

Like so many other antebellum southerners confronting the spectacle of a public divorce, first in a courtroom and then in the legislative chambers, Susanna McDowell and Sally Thomas were not persuaded. James McDowell wrote again to urge the logic of his case. What choices do you have? he asked his wife and daughter rhetorically. Only two alternatives remained: "Go into the court for a divorce or go into the newspapers." Only a judicial tribunal guaranteed a full accounting with cross-examination. "Divorce," he insisted, "is the only efficient, direct customary and proper mode for the case and there is nothing to oppose to it except some morbidness of feeling, and a feeling too which regard more the *name* than any thing else." From her father's perspective, Sally was caught between the responsibility she owed Frank as his wife and the "natural and inalienable duty" she bore "to herself of protecting . . . her life, or her character." The only way she could fulfill the second obligation was by abandoning the first.

In speech and in deed Frank had "disowned her[,] . . . publickly declared that she was infamous," and "effectually destroyed" both "the moral bond of the marriage obligation" and any realistic hope of a genuine reconciliation. Therefore he had destroyed the marriage and liberated Sally from "the moral obligations of a wife." What was more important in a marriage, James McDowell asked his wife, the "legal obligations" or the moral ones? The legalities were "secondary and conventional." The state's sanction and control over marriage existed for the sake of a higher, moral responsibility. For the governor, morality rested on religion, and marriage followed God's law before all else. The acceptance of divorce, therefore, meant viewing the conditions surrounding that reality within the context of God's plan. Reaching out to his distraught wife and daughter, he summarized his position and blended the moral, legal, and personal realities behind divorce that would ultimately persuade so many southerners, however reluctantly, to accept divorce: "Mr. Thomas has taken from the marriage tie all that was sacred or binding in it; now let the law take off the rest. Especially let this be done once it is known to afford the only means of preserving uninjured the honor and pure name of my Child."[31] At stake was Sally's reputation, and inevitably it involved the honor of her entire extended family. Only a divorce would vindicate it.

National attention was already focused on the affair, and the public's sympathies overwhelmingly favored Sally's cause. Throughout Richmond, James McDowell informed his wife, he found widespread support for their daughter. From Missouri, Senator Benton wrote of the "universal and spontaneous feeling" of everyone toward "Our dear Sally." Returning from a trip to Philadelphia, William Swan Plumer, the most distinguished Presbyterian minister in Virginia, called upon the governor to assure him of his "warmest regard" for Sally and reported that everywhere he had been, the sentiment was the same. Later that summer Plumer wrote to Governor McDowell in Lexington of his support for the divorce. It was, in his considered judgment, justified according to the "law of God," supported by "public opinion," and likely of success in the legislature. Granting McDowell permission to make his letter public, the minister assured him, "I will do any thing in my power to serve you."[32] As we have seen, Plumer was not unique among southern clergymen in the 1840s. A generational shift had occurred, and numerous ministers now accepted divorce in cases of proven adultery and desertion. They found warrant in scripture, and their support, in turn, made divorce more generally acceptable in society, at least in certain cases. Could not a woman's honor, enfolded in that of her extended family, be one of them?

While Governor McDowell enlisted allies in a possible newspaper campaign against the "*lies*" that Frank Thomas was busily propagating, the Maryland governor momentarily retreated from the press attack and turned his guns against an old target. In August 1843 he wrote Robert Taylor an "outrageous and insulting letter," charging him with cowardice by hiding in Virginia after being "driven" from Maryland. Taylor recognized the gambit. Two years had passed since Frank had accused Robert of seducing his wife, and the latter had rejected the charge "in person and by letter as *false*." Now Frank had trumped up a new accusation. Did male honor require a duel? Like Sally, Robert turned to Archibald Graham for advice. After consulting with several other men, the sagacious doctor replied that the decision to accept or reject the challenge was entirely up to Robert. "No man can take the responsibility to decide for you," he wrote. But all his confidants agreed that the young man had sized up the situation correctly. Frank was trying to provoke a fight. Because the Marylander was more proficient with the pistol, Graham suggested Robert choose a different weapon and expressed a personal concern: "I cannot bear the idea of your risking your life for such a wretch."[33]

However Robert Taylor responded, no duel took place. Instead Frank again changed course and trained his sights on another previous victim of his jealous suspicions, his relative Dr. William Tyler. Charging the respected Frederick physician with drugging him, Frank threatened to "kill him" on sight. By this time the governor's credibility had evaporated. In any matter involving his estranged wife, Marylanders increasingly considered their chief executive to be insane. Nor was his failed marriage the sum of Frank Thomas's troubles. At age forty-four he found his political career in shambles and his business affairs in such collapse that his elderly father was forced to honor his financial obligations.[34]

In the fall of 1843, prompted by her father's need for an account of her marriage in whatever divorce suit might arise, Sally began writing a narrative of her relationship with Francis Thomas. Dredging up all the memories proved an excruciating experience, and it continued in fits and starts with much scratching out and rewriting for the next year and a half. Meanwhile, perhaps the universal discredit in which Frank was held persuaded the McDowells that they could avoid what Sally most dreaded: the embarrassment of a public trial in the court and legislature. But that hope proved illusory the following May when, in yet another printed circular, Frank described himself as the "victim of a cruel matrimonial fraud." According to his scenario, Thomas Hart Benton, a "filthy scoundrel" and "unscrupulous demon," instead of avenging Sally after she had been seduced while in his home in Washington, had conspired with his wife to trick "an unsuspecting and confiding man" into marrying her. Frank also announced that Benton and James McDowell had rejected his challenge of a "judicial enquiry." Because of this circular the Missouri senator later sued Frank for libel.[35]

Earlier in December 1843 Frank Thomas had sent James McDowell a printed broadside daring him to initiate divorce proceedings in Maryland. Virginia's governor had not responded. Though general sentiment in Baltimore held that James McDowell should ignore such missives, Frank's barrage continued. "His course is silently to undermine the character of his wife," James McDowell Jr. reported from that city in May. "This he is pursuing daily and assiduously . . . among the lower order of persons and dirty politicians." Writing in midsummer to the Annapolis *Democratic Herald*, Maryland's governor castigated the Whig press for publicizing his "private misfortunes" and repeated his previous charge: "Gov. McDowell has been invited, Col. Benton has been defied, to meet me before a Court of Justice." By this point shrewd observers such as Reverdy Johnson had become convinced that Frank Thomas was truly "*mad*" and could only be properly handled in court.[36] Out of respect for his daughter's feelings, McDowell demurred. In September Sally traveled north to visit relatives, and her mother went to Baltimore to spend several months with her sister, Sophonisba. The latter wrote her brother-in-law in Richmond to send his young daughters to visit also. Susanna McDowell questioned the propriety of Sally's siblings coming to that city with Frank nearby, but their Aunt Sophy opined, "It would be a pretty story if the movements of your family would be hampered by that most misirable [*sic*] creature." Both Susanna McDowell and her sister were ill that December, and Sophonisba Breckinridge died shortly before Christmas.[37]

ANNAPOLIS, *December* 21, 1843.

DEAR SIR: As Governor McDowell has declined to receive my letter, I have no alternative but to send to him in another form a copy of my letter to him, and of your letter to me.

This course is not taken to provoke a public discussion on this painful subject. That I am most anxious to avoid, if it can be done by any reasonable sacrifices on my part. In publishing these papers I am influenced by the hope that Governor McDowell, when he has seen and reflected upon the reasonableness of my request, will promptly take measures that will afford me a suitable opportunity, to repel the charges he and others have circulated to my prejudice. He can, I know, take a different course. He may continue to exhibit my strictly confidential letters to his daughter, without affording me an opportunity to shew, the means by which his friends managed to have those letters written, or the change in my opinions which further and very recent information has wrought. He may, write letters, besides those I have already heard of, without communicating to me copies, that I may at least know with what I am charged. He may, by refusing to go into a judicial investigation, deprive me of an opportunity to compel unwilling witnesses to disclose facts explanatory of my conduct. But when he remembers, the delicacy and forbearance with which I conducted this most irritating affair, in sending for him to take charge of his daughter, without communicating to any one but her nearest relations my reasons for desiring, if explanations could not be given, a seperation: and when he remembers, that I have been forced to speak on this subject, by conduct of others, whom I could not control: since, too, he claims to be considered a Virginia Gentleman, and knows, also, that his character in that respect is deeply implicated, I will not anticipate, that an unfair shrinking course, unjust alike to me and to all concerned, will be, if hastily adopted, pertinaciously pursued.

If Governor McDowell will not furnish to me copies of the letters he has written, and afford a decent opportunity for the vindication of my character, I may reasonably hope that he will cease circulating scandalous rumors to my prejudice.

Most sincerely your friend, FRANCIS THOMAS.

To ——— ——— Esq.

RICHMOND, *December* 15th, 1843.

His Excellency Governor THOMAS, *Annapolis:*

DEAR SIR: Your letter of the 6th inst., enclosing one for Gov. McDowell, was duly received. I called on him to deliver the letter, and in my interview stated the subject of it. He replied, in respectful terms, that he had come to the determination to decline all correspondence with you on that subject; and in accordance therewith would decline receiving the letter.

I informed him that I would advise you of what had occurred, that you might take such course as you might think proper, in the case.

I remain, with great respect, your friend and obedient servant, ——— ———

ANNAPOLIS, *December* 5, 1843.

His Excellency, JAMES McDOWELL, *Richmond:*

SIR: It is painful to me after all that has passed, to address to you this letter.

I understand that in Richmond, as well as elsewhere, letters written by you have been circulated in order to make known the circumstances, which you state led to the seperation of my wife from myself, and which were of course calculated to make me appear the party offending. Although I have not been able to inform myself what were the contents of those letters, yet I must take it for granted that the matters which you have thought proper to mention in them, justified, in your opinion, the seperation; and if so, they must justify, if not imperiously require, that measures should be taken to obtain a judicial investigation thereon.

I write to inform you that in Maryland either the High Court of Chancery, or the County Courts as Courts of Equity, have power to grant divorces, and to express my anxious desire that in behalf of your daughter you will take steps to have a judicial investigation of the subject.

It is not for me to say to you, how innocent I deem myself to have been of any act which authorised the seperation to be brought about. All that I will allow myself here to say in regard thereto is, that I shall not shrink from any investigation of my conduct and character: will throw no difficulties, technical or otherwise, in the way of a full and fair investigation, or in any way delay a decision.

Without such an investigation suspicions, injurious it may well be supposed to both parties, will exist, and therefore the innocent party must most cruelly suffer.

I earnestly request you to give an answer to this letter, so soon as you can, and let me know whether you will institute any such proceeding, or what course you would suggest, in order that all who have a right to feel an interest in the subject may be able to know the truth and the whole truth.

The Act of Assembly of Maryland, giving jurisdiction in such cases, will be found in the Laws of December session 1841, chapter 262, which were forwarded to your Department.

Your obedient servant, FRANCIS THOMAS.

Governor Francis Thomas's broadside, December 1843, challenging Governor James McDowell (Courtesy of The Library of Virginia)

In January 1845 Frank Thomas completed his gubernatorial term and retired to his law practice in Frederick. Senator Benton thought the opportunity was ripe for legal action. He began preparations for a libel suit against the ex-governor, and in concert with Reverdy Johnson he urged his brother-in-law to come to Washington and proceed with the divorce. To fail to respond, the senator argued, was tantamount to a confession that Frank's accusations were true and would bring upon Sally "all the guilt and infamy which he charges." She remained unwilling until early March, when her father mailed to her from Washington an extraordinary publication, a fifty-two-page pamphlet titled *Statement of Francis Thomas*. A copy had been placed on the desk of every member of Congress. In copious detail Frank unveiled his case against his wife, with himself in the role of victim and cuckold. The most electrifying charges asserted that she had committed adultery with Robert Taylor and had taken drugs to induce an abortion, charges he promised to prove if Governor McDowell ever allowed a court trial of the facts. Moreover, he claimed that during their short time together his wife had been intimate with several other men. Frank also maintained that the Bentons and the McDowells had urged the marriage until they had finally overcome his "extreme diffidence," and that Sally had initiated his actions against her cousin Robert Taylor. Only her pathetic pleas and his foolish love had kept him on numerous occasions from sending her back to Virginia.[38]

But Frank needed to confront the most damaging evidence the McDowells had gathered against him: the letters he had written after the separation in which he repeatedly acknowledged her "innocence" and his "delusions." He explained that Sally herself had created his suspicions by her "confessions." In his version of events he had been entirely passive while she concocted "strange errors" that roused anxieties in his mind and made both their lives miserable. Her departure for Virginia from Baltimore after he invited her return to Annapolis only raised fresh questions, for if indeed she was blameless, then she should have come home to him when he promised to receive her lovingly. Moreover, Frank repeatedly protested that throughout their unhappy marriage he had sought to keep their troubles private and shield his wife and himself from public notice. In her heavily annotated copy of the pamphlet, Sally wrote next to one of these assertions of husbandly reserve, "Every *stage coach* and tavern from Lex Va to Baltimore knows to the contrary." At the point in the story where he quoted her joking remark, "You are neither a gentleman nor a man of truth," she scrawled, "I didn't know how true it was!"[39]

Her insistence on remaining silent now ended. A complex mix of half-truths and outright lies, Frank's *Statement* shocked Sally into action. Her husband had answered her discreet reserve by publicly and deliberately attempting to destroy her reputation. She had no choice but to respond. "Be strong in your innocence," James McDowell urged his daughter, and with complete and absolute trust "pray to God that he would aid you in vindicating and maintaining it." Outraged by Frank's assault on her character, Sally immediately wrote her father a detailed account of the events surrounding her miscarriage and a rebuttal of other charges in the pamphlet. The next day she began afresh to compose for the trial a "connected narrative" of her married life from its inception.[40] This affair of honor would be fought in the court and legislature rather than in the press or on the dueling ground.

Venue was crucial as well for the sensibilities of the estranged woman. Baltimore lawyers advised caution, at least concerning a divorce suit in Maryland. One attorney, William Marshall, wrote James McDowell that he had not read the *Statement* and was afraid to bring it home lest it fall into the hands of his adolescent son. Apart from the case's "merits," he thought the issue of evidence was crucial; the necessity of introducing detailed documentation could bring Sally enormous personal embarrassment. Given that Maryland's ex-governor was already widely regarded as "a madman" and the object of "loathing and disgrace," was exposing his lies in court worth the potential damage it might cause to Sally's "delicate and susceptible mind?" Better that she take refuge among her family and "numerous friends who love and admire her," and if a divorce was to be attempted, then let it take place in Virginia. Marshall regretted Benton's law suit against Frank Thomas. A summons had already gone out for witnesses, and the Maryland lawyer's opinion was widely shared.[41] In mid-March the Missouri senator went before the grand jury in Washington to provide evidence for the indictment. A defense of insanity was broached, but Benton fended it off, arguing that it was up to the defense lawyers to raise that issue should they choose to do so. The grand jury not only indicted Frank Thomas on the libel charge but also independently "presented" his *Statement* as a "nuisance."[42]

As James McDowell hired lawyers to prepare the divorce case for the 1845 legislative session, the Virginia press and, even more significantly, Sally's friends and neighbors sprang to her support. At the end of March an extraordinary public meeting in Lexington expressed complete confidence in her "moral character" and that of Robert Taylor, who had also been attacked in Frank's pamphlet. The town assemblage appointed a committee of leading citizens to draft resolutions defending Sally against her husband's allegations. Southern men spoke eloquently. They had known this excellent woman from her "childhood." Since Frank Thomas's allegations were now public, they wished "to shield female character against an attack wicked and unmanly, if not insane" and to affirm that Taylor possessed "the character of a gentleman and a man of honor." After attesting to Sally's virtuous behavior among them before her marriage and after her separation—"as one of the liveliest of our women, and as one of the fairest ornaments of our society"—the resolutions suggested that Frank's accusations must be attributed to "insane jealousy" rather than any misdeeds by his wife. Moreover, the committee resolved that by publishing his marital troubles, "whether real or imaginary," Frank had acted in a manner "offensive to good taste, demoralizing in its tendency, and injurious to the peace and harmony of society."[43]

Neither the adverse press reaction nor his grand jury indictment seemed to faze Maryland's ex-governor. In May 1845 an old friend and political ally, Dr. Charles Macgill, encouraged Frank to run for his former seat in Congress, but he demurred on the grounds that he preferred to vindicate his reputation in court. There he would prove "that I have never knowingly done wrong to a human being." From Baltimore James McDowell Jr. reported to his mother the gossip that all over town Frank Thomas "sits down with the utmost composure, . . . and begins with a minute recital of his wrong and defames the character of his wife and her immediate friends with infinite delight." In August, however, James Lyons, one of Richmond's most distinguished attorneys, encountered Frank at the Astor House in New York City and thought the man dramatically changed: "He has fattened, stoops, is very grey, seems to be incessantly walking, not even sitting out the whole dinner, and I have never seen him speak to a single person, or one to him since I have been here." Because Frank stared savagely at the Virginian, Lyons thought that he must have received the legal notification of the divorce proceedings and knew Lyons was representing Sally.[44]

Frank Thomas's *Statement* had finally forced the issue. Sally's extensive clan now rallied for its resolution. From South Carolina Uncle William Preston wrote detailed letters of advice and enumerated the witnesses that should be called and the questions and issues to be raised in court. The fall passed in elaborate preparation for two trials, Benton's libel suit in Washington in November and the divorce case in Richmond in December. Meanwhile Frank instituted a divorce suit in Frederick County, Maryland, summoned an ever increasing list of witnesses for the libel trial, and ignored the legal action in Virginia.[45] Drawn by the drama of a contest involving such prominent families and politicians from Virginia, Maryland, and Missouri as well as the expectation of "wonderful disclosures," spectators packed the gallery when *United States v Francis Thomas* opened on 10 November 1845 in Washington Federal Circuit Court. Since all the participants were Democrats, this was, the *Richmond Whig* noted with delicious glee, a "family quarrel." But because two witnesses, including Elizabeth Linn, had not responded to the subpoenas, the judge granted Frank's request for postponement. Lyons was unsurprised by Frank's delaying action, because he never expected the trial to take place.[46]

A few days before Christmas, *Thomas v Thomas* opened before Judge Nicholas in Henrico County's Circuit Superior Court to assess the facts for a legislative divorce. After the judge overruled Frank's objection to the court's jurisdiction, the prosecution called as its first witness Reverdy Johnson, now a U.S. senator from Maryland. Johnson read aloud Frank's letters to his wife that confessed "that he had wronged her." He then testified that Frank had personally said the same thing to him. The "opportunity to give testimony in behalf of injured innocence," he told Benton afterward, gave him "the greatest satisfaction." It was really all the court needed to hear, but five more witnesses appeared, including Dr. Tyler and Robert Taylor, who both denied Frank's accusations of adultery. Without leaving the room to deliberate, the jury decided that Sally Thomas's statement of facts against her husband was true. In sum, Frank had treated Sally cruelly and by false and malicious charges had publicly attempted to destroy her honor and, by extension, that of her entire family.[47] Expressions of support for Sally included a letter from her old teacher Miss English, who evinced "confidence" in her final victory, and from William Preston addressed to "Miss Sally Campbell McDowell." Writing to Sally's father, Preston proposed, "Let her fling away his name which has been associated with nothing but shame and suffering and be again altogether identified with us—an honored and beloved member of our family."[48]

As Governor McDowell left office on 1 January 1846, the legislature prepared to consider his daughter's divorce bill, which also restored her surname to McDowell. In an extraordinary move the House suspended the rules and read the bill three times in succession. Though fully convinced that marriage was a "holy" relationship that should not be touched "lightly," one member spoke for all when he pledged his wholehearted support in this particular case "to sustain and protect female virtue and innocence." The delegates approved the divorce unanimously. The senators, however, did not move so expeditiously, and Lyons, a member of the House, sniffed out the opposition and urged James McDowell to use his influence. As Henry St. George Tucker had told his students twenty years earlier, the Senate regarded itself as the last redoubt in upholding the Old Dominion's traditional values, including opposition to divorce. The senators finally passed the bill in mid-January by a vote of 20 to 4. The next month the Maryland legislature swiftly and quietly enacted the divorce bill requested by Frank Thomas without affixing blame on either party.[49]

A decade later Sally McDowell, believing that Frank had been a notorious adulterer while they were still married, attempted to discover whether the legislative committee had considered adultery when drawing up her bill of divorce. Friends in Frederick substantiated her suspicion of Frank's sexual infidelity. But Willis Bocock, who had chaired the committee of the courts of justice and reported the divorce bill to the floor of the House, explained that the legislators had acted only on the facts that James Lyons had presented in the courtroom and the jury had found to be true. After searching the offices of both the clerk of the House of Delegates and the clerk of the circuit court, Bocock verified that Sally had charged Frank with "cruelty and defamation, in unkind treatment to her and in charging her with adultery with diverse persons." But neither her legislative petition nor the facts found by the jury mentioned Frank's adultery. To the best of Willis Bocock's recollection, the House committee had discussed nothing beyond the jury's findings. But his brother, John Bocock, a Presbyterian pastor and one of Sally's good friends, recalled that Frank' adultery had been common knowledge at the time, even though Sally had not included it among the allegations. "Could a *lady ever* allege such a cause," the minister wrote her, "if there were other grounds of allegation sufficient without it?"[50] In 1846 the assembly could approve a divorce for whatever reasons it chose, and such bills had become far more frequent in recent legislative sessions. Upholding a woman's honor provided ample cause, particularly when she was the daughter of a popular public figure such as Virginia's recent governor. Five years later, however, after the new state constitution ended legislative divorce, the best result Sally might have obtained in a courtroom, without proving adultery, would have been a legal separation on grounds of cruelty.

Sally McDowell returned her wedding ring to her former husband with a brief note. Since "the marriage . . . had been dissolved *at her request*," it would be improper to keep the ring that "was the pledge of feelings no longer existing."[51] Congratulations poured in to the McDowell household. An aunt wrote Sally of her "pride and heart full joy" in her niece's "signal victory." The divorce now presented Sally "before the world in the splendeur of innocence." The editor of the *Richmond Enquirer*, Thomas Ritchie, opened his letter to the "Late Gov of Virginia" with warm good wishes: "Permit me to congratulate you and your daughter, on the passage of the Act, which sets her free, and restores her to her proper rank in the enlightened Society which she is destined to adorn. — May her future path be stript of every thorn, and covered only with roses."[52]

MRS. MCDOWELL

At least one bramble thicket remained, however: Thomas Hart Benton's upcoming libel trial. By a special election for a seat in the House of Representatives, James McDowell replaced William Taylor, his brother-in-law who had recently died. Soon he was locating rooms at Gadsby's in Washington, where he busied himself in preparation for the trial.[53] By adding Sally McDowell to his list of witnesses, Frank Thomas threatened her with enormous public attention. From South Carolina William Preston correctly sized up his niece's situation. The divorce had been trauma enough. It had settled her legal problems and whatever lingering doubts might have existed in the public mind about her character. But Benton and Thomas, locked in male combat, had forgotten Sally and were now "trampling her in their fight." Benton's suit made her life a continuing "torture" because the extensive number of witnesses guaranteed a courtroom circus that would air her marital distress and further destroy her privacy.[54]

Frank Thomas first delayed the trial, however, on the plea that he was presenting Tyler on criminal charges before a Frederick grand jury and could not be present in Washington until late April at the earliest. In early May the court postponed the trial again because of Elizabeth Linn's absence. Her penchant for troublemaking had not been limited to Washington and the McDowells, and apparently she was fixated on the subject of sexual infidelity. In St. Louis she had recently stirred up a terrible ruckus by accusing a respectable Methodist minister of seducing a young woman. Without inquiring into the truth of the charges, the woman's outraged brother publicly flogged the poor clergyman. Too late he discovered Linn had been lying and had to beg forgiveness from the minister, who instituted a suit to clear his name.[55] Despite her questionable value as a witness, Linn was Thomas's only remaining support. Benton agreed that her testimony might be taken in St. Louis, so Thomas set out for that city while James McDowell sent James Jr., who was now practicing medicine there, elaborate instructions and questions for her cross-examination. The senior McDowell was now convinced that this "base and infamous creature" was responsible for the sufferings of "poor Sally and the whole family." He averred to his son, "Were she a man, shooting would be the proper punishment." Since that, however, was not an option, she would have to be exposed as a "*liar*" and a "slanderer." Throughout the whole affair, she had been Thomas's "malignant accomplice." Benton spoke truly when he called her a "hell-cat."[56]

Sally's brother used the same description when he reported in June that Elizabeth Linn's testimony would not be taken in St. Louis after all because she had reversed course and decided to go to Washington. That later proved to be a ruse, but she feared the prosecution's harsh treatment as well as popular opinion in Missouri.[57] Meanwhile, one summer evening in Washington, Congressman McDowell received startling information. A baker of reputable character had called on Benton after seeing Linn's name linked with Sally's in press reports of the trial. The man remembered that some years earlier, when another Sally McDowell, a "very handsome" prostitute in the capital, had died, her effects included a picture of Senator Linn. A local judge had drawn up the inventory of her possessions for a sale, and he also recalled that he had hushed up the finding in order to protect the Missouri senator's reputation. The baker suggested to Benton that either Elizabeth Linn or her Washington informant had confused one Sally McDowell with the other. This explained her accusation, which she insisted was true, that Sally had "stolen" her husband's picture.[58]

As Thomas's defense against the libel suit evaporated, he twice wrote Sally asking to meet with her. "I am still prepared," he insisted in July 1846, "to take any course that will releive you from odium if by the same means I can be sheilded from unmerited dishonor." Two weeks later he protested that his motives in seeking the meeting were only "the most generous, the kindest and most magnanimous towards yourself." He wanted to "spare" Sally further pain "without degrading myself." After having the letters copied, she sent them to her father and her Washington lawyer, Philip Fendall. Although she realized that he was trying to save his own skin, Sally felt sorry for her ex-husband: "From the bottom of my heart, I do pity him," she confided to her father. She wanted only "vindication" not "vengeance" and thought the whole business could end swiftly, if only Thomas made a "full recantation of all his accusations." That would be satisfaction enough for her, but he would have to discover that path by himself. She would neither write to nor meet with him. Fendall agreed with her analysis and informed Thomas that there would be no interview, but the attorney also warned Sally that her ex-husband was desperate and dangerous. Her father agreed. After Thomas had done everything possible to destroy her reputation, it was "a stretch of insolence as unpardonable as it is audacious" that he should seek a "confidential interview." The congressman urged his daughter to stay close to the house and to warn their friend Archibald Graham to be on the lookout in Lexington in case Thomas arrived uninvited. James McDowell averred that if he saw Thomas attempt a meeting with his daughter, he would shoot him.[59]

In November Sally returned to Frederick with her parents for the trial of William Tyler. Thomas had accused the doctor, who had been in practice for forty years, of "maiming him" in the spring of 1841 and then trying to poison him the following December. Tyler regarded the allegations as preposterous and "the motives of so depraved a wretch" beyond understanding. He invited the entire McDowell family to stay at his home during the trial, and Sally arrived to a warm welcome from friends.[60] After Tyler was acquitted, his accuser wrote a friend a letter filled with self-pity and self-justification. The case was not "fully and fairly tried by Attorneys," Thomas complained. His "conclusive testimony" had been refused "because it involved a woman." Earlier Tyler had assured Sally that the judge would treat her fairly and prevent offensive questioning. But Frank charged that he had been "sacrificed to save the feelings of those who had no sensibility."[61]

That same fall he again ducked the libel trial. The judge was sick, but so was the elusive Elizabeth Linn, whose doctor diagnosed a liver ailment and prescribed bed rest. The case was continued until March. By February, however, Thomas had been forced to waive Linn's testimony and was running out of excuses for delay. Clutching at straws, he asked his friend Charles Macgill for any information Macgill's wife, Mary, possessed that could be useful in the trial. Recently Charles had recalled a comment that Mary had made after a dinner party at the Thomas home in November 1841. She remarked then that Charles was wrong in thinking the newlyweds were happily married. This casual reference to an incident five years earlier revived Frank's long-standing suspicion of a romantic relationship between Sally and William Tyler. Perhaps Mary Macgill had witnessed "something pass" between the two. He desired her "facts" to free himself from "unmerited odium" and solace his aging father's last years. Again the ex-governor played the familiar dual roles of hero and victim. He wanted only to protect "an unfortunate woman" from further scandal. He had not sought "controversy," but Benton and McDowell and the "filthy scoundrels" supporting them refused to quit.[62]

A few days later, presumably after Macgill failed to respond, Thomas electrified Maryland by calling for the impeachment of John Carroll LeGrand, a former friend and protégé whom he had appointed as chief justice of the state's supreme court. The Maryland House of Delegates agreed to hear the charges, and the two men confronted each other in Annapolis. Thomas accused LeGrand of stealing papers that were needed for his defense at the pending libel trial, of cooperating in the theft of "two vials" that had contained the poison Tyler used against him, and of informing James McDowell where Thomas might be found in Staunton in April 1843 and thus providing the Virginia governor with an opportunity to kill him. The baffled judge replied that the charges were the product of Thomas's "diseased brain and malicious heart" and proposed that "on the ground of his insanity, he may be placed in a Lunatic Hospital." LeGrand harbored no hostility, he later wrote Thomas's brother-in-law, because he thought the poor man suffered from "an unfortunate hallucination in regard to subjects, however incongruous, which his highly excited imagination connects with his matrimonial relations." The Baltimore press agreed that Thomas's charges were groundless and suggested that personal problems had overwhelmed a "noble mind."[63]

Still, LeGrand welcomed the opportunity to confront his accuser under oath. The Maryland assembly scheduled proceedings for 1 March, the day the libel trial was set to begin in Washington. Once again, as

James McDowell pointed out to his wife, Thomas was trying to postpone Benton's suit and gain a public forum to assail Sally and their family "without cost and with impunity."[64] The deeply embarrassed legislators closed the LeGrand trial to the public, excluded the testimony from the House journal, and forbade any newspaper publicity until after the event concluded. First, however, the governor, state senators, and judges of the Court of Appeals were admitted, and then the outcry against a closed trial became so great that the next day the House opened its doors to all who could fit inside. Ignoring the press gag, the Baltimore *Republican and Argus* reported that the hall was packed as James McDowell stood to defend "the honor and virtue of his daughter" and then verbally lacerated his former son-in-law. The last of several witnesses to be examined was the "Honorable Francis Thomas."[65]

It proved a pathetic, humiliating moment for Maryland's former governor in the same arena that had once marked his triumphs. The House exonerated LeGrand and concluded that the charges against Sally McDowell were "utterly groundless," the product of "an unhappy delusion of the mind of their author." The legislators further affirmed "that they regard her real character and conduct, both as maid and wife, to render her deserving of all the felicity and fair fame that can fall to the lot of woman." Finally, they ordered all testimony in the case destroyed. Even then many members thought a maligned Sally McDowell insufficiently vindicated and wanted to demonstrate further their indignation at Thomas's "reckless assault" on her reputation and their revulsion at his "systematic malice and his towering audacity." Having done everything he could to ruin his former wife's reputation, Frank had destroyed only himself.[66]

That same day James Lyons sent Sally his regrets that he would be unable to attend the libel trial but questioned its necessity, given "the farce at Annapolis." Certainly, he opined, she did not need to be "the martyr of another trial now." All the world knew that Thomas was "deranged, from vice and malignancy," while she had been completely exonerated. Thomas's lawyers concurred. Two days after the Maryland resolution, his three attorneys resigned out of "honor and conscience." Their client, they wrote, operated under "the overmastering power of morbid delusion" in attacking "a lady deeply injured in her prospects and happiness" and blameless in her character. Benton also withdrew his suit. From the outset his only desire had been to vindicate his niece from the allegations in Thomas's *Statement*. This the Maryland legislature had accomplished. The district attorney in Washington closed the case. "A very extensive community," wrote a Richmond newspaper, rejoiced to see Sally McDowell's drawn-out ordeal concluded.[67] Her friends and family savored the victory as a collective achievement. From St. Louis James wrote of his delight that a trial, which would have required testimony "deeply mortifying to us," had been avoided. Finally, after six nerve-wracking years, Sally and her clan were free from "anxiety and suspense." So at least her brother believed, and Sally herself must have hoped.[68]

Wishing Frank Thomas away, however, would not cause him to disappear. Controlling his ex-wife had become an obsession. In a long, rambling letter to James McDowell in September 1847, he proposed "to alleviate the very heavy misfortunes of your daughter," whose "mangled character" and "cruel fate" rendered her existence so wretched that she must "call upon the earth to cover her and hide her from the shame." He offered his assistance, available only by "personal interview." Over the next two years he wrote repeatedly to Sally's father. In one letter he defended himself as "an indulgent, a generous, doting and affectionate husband." In another missive he confessed that "extraneous and powerful influences" had driven him "to tease and torment" her.[69] James McDowell did not respond to this extraordinary one-way correspondence.

The divorce and attendant anxieties profoundly affected Sally. Even as the legislature's action brought freedom, vindication, and a measure of privacy, she experienced a severe depression, "a sorrow too deep for the reach of human aid." In the midst of an intense, solitary sadness, however, a religious conversion brought relief and a new awareness that life was not over. In her own words, she heard "the tones of One who commended himself to me as being 'acquainted with grief,'" and a peaceful calm followed. An awareness of new possibilities, of "*duties*" and "a sense of my responsibility" reinvigorated her. Sally's conversion experience probably followed her mother's death in the fall of 1847, when she assumed charge of Colalto and the care of her underage sisters and brother. After her father died in 1851, Sally bought the plantation from her siblings, occupied herself with its management and plans for a biography of her father, and traveled to the Northeast and Montreal. Religious sentiment and church affairs figured prominently in her family letters. In all this she found a new purpose and meaning for her state as a single woman.[70] Outwardly all seemed peaceful, yet she carried through these years the burden of the divorce. People were kind to her but tended to treat her like an invalid. As she traveled from place to place, she was aware of people's comments; her very "name . . . told its own sad story." An anomaly in her family and social set, she was properly titled Mrs. McDowell, though some were unsure at first how to address her.[71]

Frank Thomas remained a distant, sometimes threatening presence. After James McDowell's death, he wrote boldly to "dearest Sally" regretting the failure to achieve a "reconciliation and reunion" and urging a meeting before they also died "without exchanging sincere assurances of a perfect forgiveness for acts in which we were both entirely free from malice." Her uncle John Floyd, the new governor of Virginia, urged her simply to return the letters without reply.[72] But she had already written Thomas to cease correspondence, and when more unwelcome mail arrived proposing a reconciliation, she responded with a forthright denunciation of his "apocryphal expressions of tenderness" and "insincerity." Anger and anguish spilled over as she blistered her ex-husband:

> After all that, by repeated and voluminous publications you have endeavored to prove me to the world to be; after having for years maligned, defamed and attempted to degrade me . . . how can you harbor for one moment the thought of a re-union!
>
> And I, I who have seen you ruthlessly, ceaselessly, cruelly break the promises to love, honor and protect me which you once so solemnly made; I, I who have been dragged by you from the retirement in which my misfortunes sought both refuge and relief and held up to the gaze and derision and scoff of the world as an unfaithful wife—a dishonored woman; I, I who have seen you make merchandise of my character and gloat over . . . blackening and ruining it,—*I* after all this am appealed to by you the author of all to re-assume the relation and bring back to you again the trust and the respect and the affection of a wife! You know not what you propose,—you cannot know to whom your proposal is made.

Whether he operated from "remorse" and "repentance" or "malice and passion and revenge," she rejected with "loathing" his proposals. He had destroyed her love and the regard she had once had for him. Nothing was left, neither "respect" nor "affection." He could expect no further correspondence or contact.[73] Thought externally life appeared tranquil, her letter betrayed the intense hurt she carried. A proposal of marriage would resurrect it.

While vacationing at the Virginia springs in the summer of 1854, John Miller, a Presbyterian minister from Philadelphia, found himself in Lexington and visited Colalto. He and Sally had met before when Miller had been pastor in Frederick and she had come there for Dr. Tyler's trial. A thirty-five-year-old widower with two children, he was two years older than Sally. Completely enamored with the mistress of Colalto, he impulsively proposed a courtship. She was aghast and refused to see him again. Without mentioning her divorce, Sally wrote John of "the peculiarity of my condition in life" and its "*equivocal* nature." His declarations of love had assailed her "sense of womanly dignity and delicacy." All her natural "instinct" and "views of religious truth and duty" made a "new marriage" impossible. Within the context of southern society and a tight-knit and supportive family, she had constructed a new identity based on models of Christian duty and responsibility as Mrs. McDowell. She would never marry again. But Miller would not be deterred. From Philadelphia he initiated an extraordinary correspondence that lasted for twenty-six months with only brief, infrequent visits. In early September John proclaimed, "I love you wildly" and insisted that the Presbyterian confession of faith permitted her to remarry. The flustered divorcée found the whole topic "most embarrassing" and discussed it with no one, she wrote John, not even her "most trusted and familiar friends."[74]

Through the privacy of the mails, however, Sally bared her soul. In several long letters she revealed the traumatic effects of her marriage, separation, and divorce. Reasons of "safety and honor" had finally made her consent to "a divorce," and she added parenthetically, "Can you concieve how excessively painful that word is to me?" But though civil law permitted her to remarry, divine law only allowed it on grounds of the first spouse's adultery. That did not apply in her case, she thought; but even if it did and she was free, "the instinct of my nature . . . would forbid any new connection during the life of the other party." What she meant and only gradually revealed was a deep-seated anxiety that she could never have the absolute "confidence" of another husband while Frank Thomas was alive. John argued, however, that she was indeed free because of Frank's notoriously public sexual license in Frederick. Drawing on her own sources for information about her ex-husband, Sally soon accepted that view of what they termed the "moral issue." Still she drew back. "No woman in my circumstances" no matter how free she might be to remarry, could do so without "losing *caste* in society," she wrote.[75]

Preserving social status, however, was only one among several inter-related concerns. She also feared that as a divorcée she would damage his ministerial career and hurt the future of his children. Though Presbyterian clergy generally favored the match, some laity, particularly members of Sally's family and Miller's congregation, were not supportive. Sally shrank from the inevitable controversy. "I do so dread the gaze and sneer and remark of society," she wrote. Her closest friend, "Cousin John" Preston, warned that Miller might well suffer church penalties, and the "ladies" if not the "gentlemen" would surely censure her. At the end of April 1855, though, she finally consented. "Dear John," she wrote, "*At last I come to tell you that I am yours.*"[76]

The moral issue surfaced again. An informant had told Miller that in recommending the divorce the legislative committee had acted on its private knowledge of Thomas's sexual liaisons in Frederick, but this became difficult to substantiate. John urged a May wedding, but Sally wanted it delayed until the "facts" of Thomas's sexual license and the reasons for the legislature's action on the divorce bill became certain. Her older brother and assorted aunts, uncles, and cousins involved themselves as well. Among other worries, her brother James feared that her marriage would resurrect "the old scandal."[77] Meanwhile Frank Thomas, whom Miller aptly styled "crazy," again wrote to Sally. Earlier he had proposed remarriage. Now she returned his letter unopened, but she feared her former husband and the embarrassment he might cause them. Nevertheless these concerns were brushed aside as John journeyed to Lexington in mid-November 1855 for their wedding. When he arrived, however, he found that Sally's brother James had sent a strongly disapproving letter. After the couple talked about their concerns and considered the worries of "Cousin John" and reports from Philadelphia, they decided to postpone marriage indefinitely.[78]

On the eve of their pastor's planned wedding in Virginia, Miller's church trustees formally censured his marriage to a divorced woman whose husband was still alive. Although their debate over the biblical legitimacy of a new marriage was inconclusive, a majority voted that it would hurt "our prosperity as a Congregation . . . and injure and interfere with our Success as a Church and our Pastor's influence among us." Miller returned to Philadelphia, voluntarily resigned his pastorate, and retired to his mother's home in Princeton to write theology. Other clergymen there and in the South offered strong support, but his family and friends were much more reserved. Now the potential damage to

Sally's social status if they married became John's principal anxiety. "If you love that lady dont marry her," an older woman warned him. As John saw it, they had become the victims of "this prejudice of divorce."[79] Some time before he had contrasted Virginia's divorce procedures with those in the North. Northern legislatures rarely considered such business, while Virginians regarded divorce in "a totally different way" from people in New Jersey or Pennsylvania. The minister had thought that the prevalent feeling in the South, once the "moral question" was settled, might be "oppressive and wrong." But now he discovered that, at least in elite circles, the prejudgment against divorce was national, not regional or local. From Miller's perspective they would probably have to delay marriage until Frank Thomas's death. Equally dismayed by the turn of events, Sally saw no other alternative. Her "unfortunate marriage," she wrote John, had brought down "a sort of drop-curtain" over her life, "shutting out all that was prospective in it."[80]

The next spring she suffered a severe depression that only a strong religious faith made bearable. Sally dismissed Miller's fears for her social standing; her anxieties plunged much deeper and found root in the disastrous events of her former marriage. Her passion for Miller unnerved her. She had once lavished a similar love on Thomas until it "triumphed over his worthlessness and wickedness" and blinded her to his malice. How could she ever again give herself unreservedly to another person? In their correspondence she hung back from returning the expressions of love and commitment that Miller offered constantly. Haunted by fear of betrayal, she wrote of her apprehension "that, after all you may not love me." She wondered whether, if they married, he might become disappointed in her. Though repeatedly he protested his undying love, she worried that he would "change." In July 1856 she confessed her anxiety: "I suffer so much under the torture of a growing distrust of every human being. I am afraid of everybody; and yearn with inexpressible yearning just to lay my head in your lap and be assured I need have no fear there and that you were so far unlike other people that you *couldn't* change."[81]

Miller thought she was not free to marry because of her position in society. Sally disagreed and said so. Increasingly she resented the "social prejudice," particularly from her relatives, that blocked her happiness. As Miller in his letters protested unswerving affection, she tried to reciprocate his expressions of love. "If ever a woman opened her treasures of love and faith and poured them out lavishly, I think I have done it. . . . Whatever I have, I have given you," she claimed a bit defensively. When

Sally McDowell, ca. 1855, when she and John Miller were considering marriage (Courtesy of Raleigh C. Minor)

she hesitated to reveal herself fully, he implored her to trust him. "Are we not all one creature?" he asked in early September, and two days later he begged her to throw *"all doubts of my constancy . . . to the winds."* The logic of his argument unfolded: "I don't doubt *your* love. Why should you be doubting mine[?] I dont say you will prove faithless. Why should you suppose I will[?]"[82]

Finally Sally exposed her last reservations. She had feared that John's anxieties, which had prevented their marriage the preceding November, sprang from causes other than regard for her social status. Granted that their public engagement had damaged her "position." Whatever social and familial rejection she experienced became the "marriage-portion" she brought her husband. In return she expected that his "love was to recompense me for every loss—was to be to me home and friends and station." Though John had represented her loss of social stature as the major reason for canceling the wedding, she was terrified that the heat of "public disapproval" would wither his love. The "censure and neglect of the world" did not bother her, Sally wrote, but she "could not consent to run the risk of having *you* turn against me in our own home." Once before she had given herself completely to a man and been betrayed. She could not endure the thought that this might happen again, that after their marriage John might reject her love as Frank Thomas had done. These fears tortured her, though she had never before expressed them so directly.

Now she evaluated not only their relationship but the entire male domination of courtship. She had never enjoyed parity in the discussions of their future. "A woman's rights," Sally wrote, "are always ignored by others and she fails to urge them herself out of the horror she feels at even seeming to assume the attitude of the wooer; and out of the shame she could not brook of appearing to thrust herself upon an unwilling lover." In the decision to abort the marriage the preceding November they had agreed, but they had reached that judgment by very different routes.[83]

At last John began to comprehend the nature of their relationship. It was, he wrote, "a love baptized by sorrow," and he added, "I think we already love each other more than most married people." He called for her to drop all reserve, and she did, exclaiming to him that delaying their marriage had been "*a great mistake.*" It had not made either of them happier or enhanced Sally's social status.[84] That letter transformed Miller's perspective. Clergy he consulted supported their marriage, and a week of prayer confirmed that judgment in his mind. Meanwhile Sally mused over her own history and how divine favor had supported her:

Many an innocent wife, no doubt, has suffered and fallen nearly under her husband's attack—but, for me, God willed it otherwise. There was everything *against* me, but He ruled *for* me. And since then, I have led a vagrant life, living in different communities, among different kinds of people, in circumstances of much exposure. I was young and handsome and unusually attractive, (now I don't say this out of vanity, but as marking out the case truly and strongly), and yet, under all and thro all, no voice has been raised against me;—and more than that, *I myself* have stood firmly, not only receiving respect, but respecting myself. Now, why is this? and how is it? Truly very simply and naturally—it has been, out and out, God's work—not mine in any part.[85]

For the next few weeks letters flew back and forth as they revisited all the issues involved in their marriage: the "moral issue" and scriptural warrant for her divorce and remarriage, the effect on Miller's ministry and children as well as any children they might have, Sally's guardianship of her youngest sister, the reactions of relatives and friends, and the financial arrangements for her property. The decision was fixed and the date was set. In the end, as she made clear, John's love freed Sally from the tragic identity that society had assigned her. His "affection" had given her "a great feeling of independence as to that of other people." John Miller agreed. Their "passion" for each other more than outweighed whatever "prejudice" they might experience.[86]

Sally's Presbyterian pastor married the couple at Colalto on 3 November 1856. John Miller moved to Lexington, managed Sally's farm, and supplied nearby Presbyterian churches. During the Civil War he served in Stonewall Jackson's army and then as a pastor in Petersburg during Ulysses S. Grant's siege. The Millers raised their children there after the war until 1871, when John retired to Princeton to write theology. Sally was away for some weeks that summer visiting relatives in the South when John scribbled a letter to her from their new home. Reflecting on the deprivations of their courtship, when visits were rare and brief and their relationship depended almost entirely on letters, he ruminated that those "years of trial" had made their love for each other even more passionate than that of "most people." It would further grow and deepen for another quarter-century until they died a week apart in 1895.[87]

In contrast to her divorce from Frank Thomas, Sally McDowell's marriage to John Miller represented a triumph over the social prejudice that confronted divorced persons to a greater or lesser degree in the antebellum era. After Frank Thomas publicly attacked his wife, divorce became acceptable and even necessary for her vindication. Sally's closest male and female family members and friends urged her to relinquish the private sphere for the sake of her own reputation and the honor of her family. First in Virginia and then in Maryland the discursive process of a legislative divorce and subsequent trials in Frederick and Annapolis established her in the public mind as an icon of virtue and moral rectitude. While membership in the elite class as the daughter of a popular governor had certainly facilitated the divorce, her social status severely constrained her future. The remarriage of a divorced person while the other party still lived, even though permitted by law, was frowned upon not so much by men, even evangelical clergymen, as by "ladies," who were the guardians of antebellum propriety. They molded popular opinion and upheld the social conservatism embedded in the foundations of southern culture.[88]

Sally McDowell's major critics were women, particularly members of her own family. By her remarriage she repudiated the identity they had constructed for her and fashioned her own self, a person capable of decision and action while still keenly conscious of her social identity and responsibility. John Miller made that possible, even as he lost his pulpit because of intolerance in his Philadelphia congregation. John's insistent love enabled Sally to overcome both the social stigma that surrounded divorced persons and the fear of personal rejection that had burdened her since Frank Thomas had repudiated her love. Her story exemplifies the prejudice faced by other women and men before the Civil War who were caught up in marital tragedies and forced in some fashion to reconstruct their identities. Sally McDowell Miller's triumph came only after an enormous personal struggle.

Petitioners

On a warm day in early June I arrived at Colalto on the outskirts of Lexington. The stately plantation home of the McDowell family loomed, big and empty, at the end of a gravel drive. The front door was unlocked. The staff at the town's visitors' center had told me I could go inside. Though Washington and Lee University owned the property, a sale was in process, and the house had been stripped of its furnishings. The previous evening I had flown into Dulles Airport and driven straight up the Shenandoah Valley. Another summer of research was beginning, but before ensconcing myself in Richmond, I felt compelled to visit Sally McDowell's home.

Her divorce petition had been missing from the Library of Virginia's collection, so the name did not register in my mind when I first came across it in the card file at the Alderman Library. Sally's papers provided the one piece my research still lacked: the personal reflections of someone who had endured a divorce. What were the people behind the petitions experiencing? No document written for public consumption could adequately disclose that inner person. But in her intensely private letters and the narrative of her relationship with Frank Thomas, Sally fully and eloquently revealed the horror of her first marriage, the shame she felt in its failure, and her unequivocal repugnance for divorce. Now I walked through the house where she had married Frank Thomas and lived for years in seclusion after their separation and divorce. Sally had so often described her feelings at Colalto that strolling through its rooms and about the grounds I sensed her presence. She remains there as, for example, Monticello holds Thomas Jefferson. Place helps to fix people.

In some cases place also proved indispensable in uncovering people's lives after divorce. That knowledge in turn revealed how divorce affected them and the kind of people they were or became. For some of the women and men in this book, closure became important. Over fifty pages in typescript, Evelina Gregory Roane's petition traced a year and a half of

The approach to Colalto, the McDowell plantation home just outside Lexington

the hell she experienced with her first husband before divorce broke the conjugal chains in 1825. How had she fared afterward? She waited almost a decade before she married again. When her second husband died after a few years, Evelina inherited his ample estate. She soon married again and bore two children with a third husband, William Brookes. By 1860, however, he had died, and Evelina was living alone at age fifty-six. Then she disappeared from the records.

One Sunday afternoon I left Richmond in search of Evelina. Before the Civil War she had owned a farm and ferry service on the Mattaponi River across from West Point. An illustrated book of King and Queen County included a picture of her home.[1] Finding the building deserted, I asked a neighbor if he had ever heard of Evelina Brookes. He pointed to a house across the field where some of her descendants live. They graciously hauled out a box of her papers, which revealed yet another marriage. Later I stopped at Elsing Green, the former Gregory plantation in rural King William County. Evelina contracted her disastrous first marriage to Newman Roane in its parlor and is buried nearby in the Gregory family cemetery. She outlived four husbands and died at age eighty-one, bequeathing a substantial estate to her son. Her portrait as a mature woman confirms what the paper trail indicated: Evelina had been a strong, capable woman who knew her own mind and lived life on her own terms. That strength of character enabled her to surmount her first marriage and divorce and renew her life.

Many of the petitioners, like Evelina, appear to have been survivors. The storm that broke over Sarah Turnbull showed the stuff of which she was made. After taking Robert to court for a financial settlement, she retired to Baltimore and lived in style for almost two more decades. When she died in 1811, Sarah's remarkable will displayed her shrewd business sense, a keen knowledge of women's legal disabilities, and a basic goodness of heart. She left extensive bequests to a wide circle of relatives, friends, and charities. A devout Methodist, she freed her slaves who were over twenty-one and all the rest when they reached that age, except two women who were freed immediately. To three older women slaves she bequeathed their own children and grandchildren until their maturity, as well as homes, furniture, and sufficient funds from a stock sale to assure their financial independence.[2] Like many other women and men, Sarah showed in later life that it was possible to overcome personal tragedy, that the future need not be foreclosed.

The future might even provide redemption. Though some petitioners were more sympathetic figures than others, the divorce process displayed the flaws and limitations in virtually everyone it touched. Sometimes, however, their later lives disclosed more promising aspects. Joseph Mettauer offers a case in point. In three attempts to divorce Jemima, he cast her in the worst possible light. Ultimately, however, most legislators had not bought the half-truths lacing his petitions and resisted the pressures brought to bear from his friends and neighbors. Now what would he do? He did not leave Virginia. Nor did Joseph defy the law and marry again or take a common-law wife. Several young men whom he prepared for medical school boarded in his home. Had the living situation been notorious, they probably would have gone elsewhere.[3] But more important, Joseph had the reputation and future of his two sons to consider. To supply them with the best possible education, he sent them to Hampden-Sydney College and then to the University of Pennsylvania's medical school. When Joseph died in 1812 at age fifty-six, both men were practicing physicians. Although Jemima had renounced her dower rights years earlier, they obviously felt an obligation to care for their mother, and in 1813 they deeded property to her. Later the two men helped found Randolph-Macon Medical School, and one of them, John Peter Mettauer, became an outstanding surgeon and a pioneer in gynecology. Their father had not done so badly.[4]

The petition collection yielded a cross-section of ordinary southerners. Certain aspects of their stories resonate strongly in our own times. Like so many people in divorce courts today, they may have chosen the wrong partner or been psychologically unfit for the obligations that marriage entails. Frequently they appear to have wed in haste, pressured by passion, relatives, or economic circumstances. Sometimes serious problems such as a partner's infidelity, cruel temper, or alcohol abuse surfaced after the wedding. Despite differences in background and situation, these men and women discovered for themselves that not all weddings end happily, that a particular marriage may be unsustainable, and that divorce may be an absolute necessity. Personally they found it a difficult, even traumatic experience.

But there the similarities with our age end. Antebellum southerners faced a world far different from our own. The Old South privileged permanent, companionate marriages locked in by strong kinship and communal ties. If unhappy spouses sought to escape marital disaster, they generally encountered an unsympathetic culture. The social and political elites in particular tended to regard divorce as an unmitigated evil, a threat to values they considered essential to their society. Only the brave dared attempt it. And if a miserable wedded life and social disapproval had not already toughened those who ventured to seek divorce, a draconian legal system must have done so. The cumbersome process of drafting petitions, collecting affidavits, and after 1827, facing a court trial comprised the smaller portion of the challenge. The assembly supplied the bulk. Legislators made up divorce law as they went along, case by case, often without regard to precedent. The absence of statutes specifying grounds and regulating procedures created a kind of Alice in Wonderland world. Petitioners essentially operated at the mercy of politicians who, regardless of their intentions, frequently appear by turns obtuse, inflexible, and arbitrary. Finally, even after a legal divorce, a family or community could be socially restrictive and harshly judgmental toward those whose marriages had failed. No wonder so few unhappy spouses even attempted a legislative divorce. Thus from whatever aspect—personal, social, or legal—one may consider the situations of these women and men, they often displayed a personal courage that deserves both sympathy and respect. Out of the wreckage of marital catastrophe, they sought to reclaim their lives.

APPENDIX

Table A.1 Total Petitions and Petitioners

Total petitions	583			
From men	286 (49%)			
From women	292 (50%)			
From couples	5 (0.8%)			

Total petitioners	460			
Men	218 (47%)			
Women	242 (53%)			

Repeat petitioners	2nd	3rd	4th	5th
Men	48 (22%)	15 (6%)	5 (2%)	—
Women	38 (16%)	9 (4%)	2 (0.8%)	1 (0.4%)

Table A.2 Divorce Petitions/Divorces Granted

	1786–90	1791–95	1796–1800	1801–5	1806–10	1811–15	1816–20	1821–25	1826–30	1831–35	1836–40	1841–45	1846–50
Men	2/1	7/1	9/0	9/4	28/5	19/3	19/1	28/3	17/4	24/3	30/5	31/14	63/28
Women	2/1	2/0	4/0	1/0	24/4	17/2	40/8	38/7	17/5	18/5	40/8	29/5	60/36
Couples			1/0	1/0	1/0						1/0		1/0
Total	4/2	9/1	14/0	11/4	53/9	36/5	59/9	66/10	34/9	42/8	71/13	60/19	124/64
Percent granted	50	11	0	36	17	14	15	15	26	19	18	32	52

Note: Includes absolute divorces, conditional divorces, and legal separations.

Table A.3 Petitioners' Alleged Grounds for Divorce

	Women	Men
Adultery	61 (30%)	138 (81%)
Battery	86 (42%)	3 (2%)
Bigamy	33 (13%)	13 (8%)
Cruelty	14 (7%)	—
Deceit/fraud	8 (4%)	19 (11%)
Desertion	139 (68%)	102 (60%)
Impotence	2 (1%)	2 (1%)
Imprisonment	25 (12%)	1 (0.5%)
Incest	1 (0.5%)	1 (0.5%)
Insanity	2 (1%)	3 (2%)
Miscegenation	19 (9%)	23 (13%)
Neglect	31 (15%)	3 (2%)
Property	11 (5%)	2 (1%)

Note: Petitioners' reasons for requesting divorce have been located in 82 percent of the divorce cases considered by the Virginia General Assembly between 1786 and 1850. They came from 171 men, 204 women, and 4 couples.

Table A.4 Legislative Divorces Granted

Total legislative divorces	153 (33% of all petitioners)
Divorces granted men	72 (33% of male petitioners)
Absolute divorces	69 (96%; 2 men forbidden remarriage)
Conditional divorces	3 (4%)
Divorces granted women	81 (33% of women petitioners)
Absolute divorces	62 (72%)
Legal separations	15 (19%)
Conditional divorces	4 (5%)

NOTES

ABBREVIATIONS

AA	*Acts of the General Assembly of Virginia*
Aff(s).	Affidavit(s)
BC	Brock Collection, Henry E. Huntington Library, San Marino, California
CCD	Correspondence Concerning Divorce
CMP	Charles Macgill Papers
Co.	County
DAB	Allen Johnson et al., eds. *Dictionary of American Biography*. 22 vols. New York: Scribner, 1928–58.
DB	Deed Book
DP	Papers Related to Divorce
DU	Rare Book, Manuscript, and Special Collections Library, Duke University, Durham, North Carolina
DVB	John Kneebone et al., eds. *Dictionary of Virginia Biography*. 2 vols. to date. Richmond: Library of Virginia, 1998–2001.
GFP	Graham Family Papers
IWCC	Isle of Wight County Courthouse, Virginia
JHDM	*Journal of the House of Delegates of Maryland*
JHDV	*Journal of the House of Delegates of Virginia*
JMP	James McDowell Papers
JTMP	John Thompson Mason Jr. Papers, Maryland Historical Society, Baltimore
LC	Library of Congress, Washington, D.C.
LP	Legislative Petitions, Records Group 78, Library of Virginia, Richmond
LT	Land Tax Records
LVA	Library of Virginia, Richmond, Va.
MFP	McDowell Family Papers, Albert H. Small Special Collections Library, University of Virginia, Charlottesville
OB	Order Book
Pet(s).	Petition(s)
PPT	Personal Property Tax Records
RHB	Rough House Bills, Resolutions, etc., Virginia General Assembly
SHC	Southern Historical Collection, University of North Carolina, Chapel Hill

SLM   *Southern Literary Messenger*
UTS   Union Theological Seminary Library, Richmond, Virginia
UVA   Albert H. Small Special Collections Library, University of Virginia,
          Charlottesville
VBHS   Virginia Baptist Historical Society, University of Richmond, Richmond
VHS   Virginia Historical Society, Richmond
VTS   Bishop Payne Library, Virginia Theological Seminary, Alexandria
WB   Will Book
WMC   Earl Gregg Swem Library, College of William and Mary, Williamsburg,
          Virginia
WS   *Watchman of the South*

INTRODUCTION

1. Pet. of Wersley, LP.

2. See Bailey, *Popular Influence upon Public Policy,* and Bogin, "Petitioning and the New Moral Economy."

3. For a statistical summary, see the Appendix. The *JHDV* reports these petitions and assembly action. Most are available by county and date in LP. Bills passed are in Hening, *Statutes;* Shepherd, *Statutes;* and after 1806, *AA.*

4. Cott, "Eighteenth Century Family and Social Life" and "Divorce and the Changing Status of Women"; Wyatt-Brown, *Southern Honor,* 283–89, 300–306, 315–16; Lebsock, *Free Women of Petersburg;* Stevenson, *Life in Black and White,* 3–5, 140–56; Kierner, *Southern Women,* 191–229.

5. Clinton, *Plantation Mistress,* 79–85; Bardaglio, *Reconstructing the Household,* 32–34; Bynum, *Unruly Women,* 63–64, 68–77; McCurry, *Masters of Small Worlds,* 86–91. For brief mention, see Fox-Genovese, *Within the Plantation Household,* 203; McMillen, *Southern Women,* 20, 36–37, 40–47; and Wolfe, *Daughters of Canaan,* 20, 38, 92–93.

6. Chused, *Private Acts;* Censer, "'Smiling through Her Tears.'" Glenda Riley relied primarily on published laws for "Legislative Divorce in Virginia." Other studies of divorce in the pre–Civil War South include Johnson, *Ante-Bellum North Carolina,* 217–23, and Goodheart, Hanks, and Johnson, "Act for the Relief of Females."

7. James Hugo Johnston, *Race Relations in Virginia;* Robert McColley, review, *Journal of Southern History* 36 (1970): 594. For a recent discussion in a related context, see Popkin, "Historians on the Autobiographical Frontier."

8. Censer, "'Smiling through Her Tears,'" 35–37.

9. Howard, *Matrimonial Institutions,* 3:31; he elaborated on his objections in 2:360. For an earlier, nonjudgmental study of legislative divorce, see Bishop, *Commentaries on the Law of Marriage,* 1:545–75. General treatments of divorce include Blake, *Road to Reno;* Phillips, *Putting Asunder;* and Riley, *Divorce.* More recent treatments include Basch, *Framing American Divorce,* and Grossberg, *Judgment for Solomon.*

10. For this understanding of discourse, see Baker, "Ideological Origins." Also helpful is Pocock, *Virtue, Commerce, and History*, 1–33.

11. In a similar way William O'Neill used divorce to illustrate the contending moral values of the Progressive era in *Divorce in the Progressive Era*.

12. For a fine recent study, see Shade, *Democratizing the Old Dominion*.

13. For a similar conclusion for twentieth-century divorce, see DiFonzo, *Culture of Divorce*.

CHAPTER ONE

1. Aff. of William Cole, in Pet. of Turnbull, LP; Turnbull Family Bible Records, VHS; F[rederick] Johnston, *Old Virginia Clerks*, 105. In addition to his import business in Petersburg, he possessed numerous slaves and an extensive plantation; see Prince George Co. PPT and LT, 1789–90, LVA. For male dependence and concerns, see Filene, "Secrets of Men's History," 107–10, and Frank, *Life with Father*, 15–22.

2. For Sarah's family, see Lee, *Lee of Virginia*, 156–57. For Archibald Buchanan, see the obituary in *Maryland Journal*, 19 Aug. 1785; Archibald Buchanan, Last Will and Testament, box 20, folder 31; Inventory, 1786, box 30, folder 7; Account of Sale, 12 Dec. 1785, box 1, folder 33; and Accounts, 1787, box 24, folder 72, Hall of Records, Annapolis, Md.

3. Affs. of William Cole and David Robertson, in Pet. of Turnbull, LP; *Baltimore American*, 19 Mar. 1790; Boyd et al., *Papers of Jefferson*, 16:300. For Sarah's age, see *Baltimore American*, 13 Nov. 1811.

4. Affs. of William Cole and David Robertson, in Pet. of Turnbull, LP.

5. Smith, *Inside the Great House*, 22, 126–38, 286; Lewis, *Pursuit of Happiness*, chap. 5.

6. St. George Tucker, *Blackstone's Commentaries*, 2:441–45; Hartog, *Man and Wife*, 115–35, 168–69. For companionate marriage, see Stone, *Family, Sex, and Marriage*, 325–36, 361–74, and Degler, *At Odds*, chap. 1. See also Kulikoff, *Tobacco and Slaves*, chap. 5; Lerner, *Creation of Patriarchy*, 231–43; and esp. Bardaglio, *Reconstructing the Household*, 24–26, 241–42.

7. Affs. of William Cole and David Robertson, in Pet. of Turnbull, LP.

8. Stone, *Road to Divorce* and *Broken Lives*. For Virginia's adaptation of English marriage law, see St. George Tucker, *Blackstone's Commentaries*, 2:433–45. See also Moore and Briden, *English Canon Law*, 86–93, 130–53.

9. Dewey, *Jefferson*, 57–72.

10. Boyd et al., *Papers of Jefferson*, 2:556–58; the text of the approved bill is in Shepherd, *Statutes*, 1:130–36. Virginia's colonial law gave the General Court the authority to pronounce incestuous marriages (those in violation of the Levitical law on consanguinity and affinity) null and void. In 1788 the assembly, in a law later ruled unconstitutional, transferred this jurisdiction to the High Court of Chancery. See St. George Tucker, *Blackstone's Commentaries*, 2:433.

11. Pet. of Dantignac, LP.

12. For the initial draft, see "A Bill to Dissolve the Marriage of Ann Dantignac," RHB, 1789, box 12, LVA; the act is in Hening, *Statutes*, 13:97–98. The General Court had original as well as appellate jurisdiction in both civil and criminal matters. An excellent summary of the court system in Virginia at this time is in the introduction to Hobson, *Papers of Marshall*, xxviii–xxxiii.

13. Hening, *Statutes*, 13:227. The Virginia law states his name as Roberts. See Owsley, "Marriages of Rachel Donelson."

14. Aff. of William Cole, in Pet. of Turnbull, LP. For such paternal obligations, see Smith, *Inside the Great House*, 22, 25–54, 61–64, 82–125.

15. John Dawson to James Madison, 7 Nov. 1791; William Overton Callis to James Madison, 18 Nov. 1791; Francis Corbin to James Madison, 22 Nov. 1791, all in Hutchinson and Rachal, *Papers of Madison*, 16:97, 109, 124; *JHDV*, 22 Nov., 3, 5, 9 Dec. 1791, 73, 101, 102, 113.

16. Aff. of William Cole, in Pet. of Turnbull, LP.

17. Kaplan, Freedman, and Sadock, *Comprehensive Textbook of Psychiatry*, 567; Ricci, *Genealogy of Gynaecology*, 532. In the eighteenth century William Rowley covered convulsions at length and explained their symptoms and treatments, but he did not deal with or describe vaginismus; see Rowley, *Treatise on Diseases*, 344–77. Other contemporary medical writers did not mention this condition.

18. Hening, *Statutes*, 13:301; Bryson, "English Common Law in Virginia"; St. George Tucker, *Blackstone's Commentaries*, 2:433. Blackstone's judgment finds modern support in Helmholz, *Canon Law and English Common Law*.

19. Hening, *Statutes*, 13:302; Marshall to Rush, 6 Aug. 1792, in Johnson, Cullen, and Harris, *Papers of Marshall*, 2:123. The editorial note erroneously states that the assembly passed the Turnbull bill in the October 1792 session instead of 1791. Thus the editors mistakenly surmise from this letter that Turnbull first appealed to the chancery court before going to the legislature. For Marshall's fee, see Johnson, Cullen, and Harris, *Papers of Marshall*, 2:438.

20. Arthur Lee to Turnbull, VHS. This was a peculiar letter, but then so was its writer. For Arthur Lee's exasperating personality and poor judgment, see Nagel, *Lees of Virginia*, 93–94, 107, 133–35. Lee died within two weeks of writing this letter; see Potts, *Arthur Lee*, 280.

21. Because the case was never decided, it does not appear in Wythe, *Decisions of Cases*. For evidence of Robert Turnbull's remarriage, see Spotsylvania Co. DB, 27 Jan. 1796, and Brunswick Co. PPT and LT, 1800–1805, LVA; Turnbull, "Turnbull Family," VHS. For Hannah Turnbull's previous marriage, see Vogt and Kethley, *Brunswick County Marriages*, 91. Robert Turnbull died in 1804; see Prince George Co. and Brunswick Co. PPT and LT, 1804–5, LVA.

22. Arthur Lee to Turnbull, VHS; John Marshall to Charles Lee, 28 Dec. 1793, in Johnson, Cullen, and Harris, *Papers of Marshall*, 2:250. For a husband's obligations, see Hartog, *Man and Wife*, 155–66. For separate estates, see Hartog, *Man and Wife*, 169–76; Salmon, *Women and the Law of Property*, 81–119; and Lebsock, *Free Women of Petersburg*, 23–24, 58–67. Marshall's last entry for this case in his account book is for July 1793; see Johnson, Cullen, and Harris, *Papers of Marshall*, 2:462.

23. *JHDV*, 21 Nov. 1791, 71, and 26 Nov., 12 Dec. 1796, 43, 72. Established in 1787, the district court system did not handle matters of equity or fairness. In 1802 the legislature created Superior Courts of Chancery, which were equity courts; see Roeber, *Faithful Magistrates*, 222–25. Recording the vote count and names in the *Journal* indicates the intense concern divorce aroused. Only seven roll calls were taken in this session. For this theme of social stability, see Selby, *Revolution in Virginia*.

24. For the varied interactions involved in the discursive process, see Perinbanayagam, *Discursive Acts*. The significance of localism is emphasized in Shain, *Myth of American Individualism*, 84–95, and Bardaglio, *Reconstructing the Household*, 7–12. For the rituals of court days in the colonial and early national periods, see Isaac, *Transformation of Virginia*, and Roeber, *Faithful Magistrates*. For the Jacksonian era, see [Carter], "March Court," and "Court Day."

25. Pet. of Ritchie, LP; Emory L. Hamilton, "Samuel Ritchie."

26. Pet. of Bonnell, LP. For the prevalence of "self-divorce," see Cott, *Public Vows*, 37–38.

27. See, for example, *Virginia Journal and Alexandria Advertiser*, 4 Dec. 1788; *Virginia Gazette and Weekly Advertiser*, 20 May 1790; *Virginia Gazette and General Advertiser*, 21 Dec. 1796, 23 Mar. 1803, 12 Oct. 1805, 10 Sept. 1806, 22 Apr. 1807, 25 Aug. 1809; *Columbian Mirror and Alexandria Gazette*, 21 July 1795, 2 June, 16 Aug. 1796, 2 Mar. 1797; and *Virginia Argus*, 18 Jan., 28 June 1808, 9 May, 4 Aug. 1809.

28. See, for example, the notice of Ann McHenry in *Virginia Journal and Alexandria Advertiser*, 17 June 1790.

29. Pet. of Netherland, LP; Spoden, *Richard Netherland*, 23–26.

30. Lebsock, *Free Women of Petersburg*, 69; Separation Agreement, in Pet. of Margaret Cox, LP; Pet. of Daws, LP. See also Articles of Separation, in Pet. of Wills, LP. For a typical press announcement, see *Virginia Gazette and General Advertiser* 25 Apr. 1804. For their use in the South, see Salmon, *Women and the Law of Property*, 62–80, and Chused, *Private Acts*, 6, 19–21. An example from the colonial era is in Prince William Co. DB Q, 3 Nov. 1766, 404, LVA.

31. Indenture, 5 May 1808, in Pet. of Whitfield, LP.

32. Aff. of Mildred Hood, in Pet. of Cocke, LP; Pet. of Sally Carter, LP. For an evaluation, see Henry St. George Tucker, *Commentaries on the Laws*, 1:106–8. See also Bishop, *Commentaries on the Law of Marriage*, 1:527–41, and Hartog, *Man and Wife*, 29–39.

33. *Richmond Enquirer*, 18 Jan. 1805; R. B. Tunstall, "Littleton Tazewell," *DAB*, 18:357. For the church-state legislation, see Shepherd, *Statutes*, 2:149, 314–16.

34. Kight, "In Rural Virginia"; Eggleston, "Francis Joseph and John Peter Mettauer"; Adolph Michaelis to Mrs. W. Mettauer Crute, 21 July 1977, Sheppard Papers, Tompkins-McCaw Library, Medical College of Virginia, Richmond.

35. Pet. of Mettauer, 1796, LP; Mettauer Family Genealogical Notes, Eggleston Family Papers, sec. 31, VHS.

36. Pet. of Mettauer, 1796, LP.

37. *JHDV*, 30 Oct., 4, 10 Dec. 1793, 26, 112–13, 124. No file exists for 1793. His

single petition from the 1790s is undated and filed under Prince Edward Co., 14 Nov. 1796, LP.

38. Affs. of Mary Barrett, Betty Gaulding, Samuel W. Venable, Philip Holcombe, and Johnston, subscribers to Edmund Randolph, undated, in Pet. of Mettauer, 1796, LP; *JHDV*, 14 Nov., 21 Dec. 1796, 14, 91; Reardon, *Edmund Randolph*, 348–60.

39. Bradshaw, *Prince Edward County*, 302, 354–55; for his economic prosperity, see Prince Edward Co. PPT and LT, 1788–1810, LVA.

40. Pet. of Mettauer, 1804, and Aff. of John Woodson, in ibid., LP; *JHDV*, 16 Jan. 1805, 86.

41. *Richmond Enquirer*, 18 Jan. 1805; *JHDV*, 16 Jan. 1805, 85.

42. In the earliest affidavit, dated 12 Nov. 1792, Betsy Gaulding stated that Jemima had told her she had not wanted "to yield" to "the young Doctor . . . John Peter Mettauer" (Aff. of Betsy Gaulding, in Pet. of Mettauer, 1796, LP).

43. Pet. of Mettauer, 1796, LP.

44. *Richmond Enquirer*, 18 Jan. 1805. The London consistory court and the Court of Arches, the appeals court for all consistory courts in the Anglican province of Canterbury, heard cases at Doctors' Commons. Lawrence Stone corrects Tazewell's common error in Stone, *Road to Divorce*, 304–8.

45. Pets. of Wilson, Grantham, and William and Martha Chapman, LP.

46. Articles of Separation, in Pet. of Wills, LP; see also "Marriage and Divorce" and Lewis, *Pursuit of Happiness*, 203–5.

47. Gordon S. Wood, *Creation of the American Republic*, 53–54; Roeber, *Faithful Magistrates*, 240–44; Weaver, "Two Types of American Individualism," 82.

48. *Richmond Enquirer*, 15 Feb. 1823. For similar sentiments in the Carolinas, see Bynum, *Unruly Women*, 68–72, and McCurry, *Masters of Small Worlds*, 86–91.

49. McCurry, *Masters of Small Worlds*, 21, 86–89; Cashin, *Family Venture*, 32–39. See also Konig, "Jurisprudence and Social Policy."

50. *JHDV*, 18, 25 Jan., 1 Feb. 1808, 79, 86, 97; ["A Bill Concerning Divorces"], RHB, 1807, box 22, LVA.

51. Pet. of Brough, LP; *AA* (1808), chap. 42, 43; chap. 43, 44; chap. 49, 50; chap. 60, 57.

52. *JHDV*, 8, 30 Dec. 1809, 12, 13 Jan. 1810, 15, 47, 62; "References to authorities upon various subjects discussed in the Virginia Assembly, session of 1809–1810," box 7, Cabell Papers, UVA; "A Bill Concerning Divorces" and "Resolutions," RHB, 1809, box 23, LVA.

53. Henry St. George Tucker to St. George Tucker, 3 Mar. 1808, 14 Jan. 1809, 1 Mar. 1810, box 28, Tucker-Coleman Papers, WMC. For the growing conservatism, see Bruce, *Rhetoric of Conservatism;* Jordan, *Political Leadership in Jefferson's Virginia;* Phillip Forrest Hamilton, "Tucker Family"; and Owen, "Legal Profession."

54. B. Estill to David Campbell, 17 Jan. 1821, and David Campbell to Arthur Campbell, 15 Jan. 1822, Campbell Family Papers, DU.

55. *JHDV*, 29 Dec. 1815, 82; 20 Feb. 1821, 206; 14 Feb. 1823, 196; *Richmond Enquirer*, 22 Feb. 1821, 15 Feb. 1823.

56. *AA* (1821), chap. 108, 82. For male reaction in such cases, see Wyatt-Brown, *Southern Honor*, 289–91. For a bigamy case, see Pet. of Jourdan, LP, and *AA* (1814), chap. 99, 146.

57. *JHDV*, 7 Dec 1816, 72; 10 Jan. 1818, 110; 4 Dec. 1821, 70; 6 Dec. 1822, 20; 14 Dec. 1823, 48; *AA* (1823), chap. 94, 99.

58. "Amendments proposed . . . to the Bill divorcing Mary Brady," RHB, 1819, box 35, LVA; *AA* (1819), chap. 132, 100.

59. *Richmond Enquirer*, 22 Jan. 1820.

60. Walter R. Daniel to William Brent Jr., 8 Dec. 1824, box 17, Cabell Papers, UVA; Robert E. Cummings to David Campbell, 15 January 1826, and David Campbell to James Campbell, 16 Jan. 1826, Campbell Family Papers, DU.

61. *JHDV*, 8, 17, 20, 26 Dec. 1825, 15, 35, 44, 59; *Richmond Enquirer*, 10, 17 Dec. 1825; "A Bill Regulating . . . applications for Divorce," RHB, 1825, box 42, LVA; Robert E. Cummings to David Campbell, 15 January 1826, Campbell Family Papers, DU. For Blackburn, see Brent Tarter, "Samuel Blackburn," *DVB*, 1:518–19.

62. "J" to "M," 22 Jan. 1826, *Virginian*, 16 Feb. 1826; *Richmond Enquirer*, 7 Jan. 1826; "Bill Divorces," RHB, 1825, box 42, LVA.

63. Henry St. George Tucker, *Notes on Blackstone's Commentaries*, bk. 1, 440 (unpaginated; numbers refer to sections in St. George Tucker, *Blackstone's Commentaries*); W. Hamilton Bryson and E. W. Marshall Tucker, "Henry St. George Tucker," in Bryson, *Legal Education*, 600–613.

64. *JHDV*, 10, 11, 14 Feb., 9 Mar. 1826, 161, 162, 164, 207; *Richmond Enquirer*, 7 Jan. 1826; "Mr. Bryce's Substitute to Bill Divorces," RHB, 1825, box 42, and "Amendments Proposed by the Senate," RHB, 1825, oversize box, LVA.

65. Tucker advised his student that because the civil law now "invested" specific courts "with the ecclesiastical jurisdiction in cases of divorce," they would follow "the rules of the ecclesiastical courts . . . except so far as they are in conflict with the general principles of our laws, or particular statutory provisions" (Henry St. George Tucker, *Commentaries on the Laws*, 1:24).

66. *AA* (1826–27), chap. 23, 21–22. It is curious that the 1827 law ignored interracial sexual liaisons. Presumably the legislators preferred to deal with such divorces themselves. The Superior Courts of Law were established in 1808 as successors to the District Courts. In 1831 the Circuit Superior Courts of Law and Chancery replaced the Superior Courts of Chancery and the Superior Courts of Law. For helpful surveys of Virginia's complicated judicial history, see Brent Tarter, "An Introduction to the Courts of Virginia" (unpublished guide, 1994), and Thomas Jefferson Headlee Jr., "The Virginia State Court System" (unpublished guide, 1969), LVA. For an appeal, which Judge Francis Brooke denied, see *Graves v Graves*.

67. No system was foolproof, however. See Court Transcript and Isaiah Cherry Jr. to [J. W.] Murdaugh, 2 Dec. 1829, in Pet. of Evans, LP.

68. Robinson, *Practice in the Courts*, 153; Pet. of Cloud, LP; *AA* (1838–39), chap. 262, 199; Pet. of Warwick, LP.

69. Robert Young Conrad to Elizabeth Powell Conrad, Richmond, 7 Feb. (first quote), 17, 24 Jan. 1841, Conrad Papers, VHS; *JHDV*, 13, 15, 17, 22 Mar. 1841, 199,

203, 214, 237; "A Bill Concerning Divorces," RHB, 1840, box 66, LVA; *AA* (1840–41), chap. 71, 78–79. Two years later a brief law explained that a legal separation had the same effects as an absolute divorce on "personal rights and legal capacities" and reiterated the prohibition against remarriage after separations; see *AA* (1842–43), chap. 80, 55–56. For the need for this law, see *Richmond Whig*, 10 Feb. 1843.

70. *Richmond Whig*, 16 Mar., 21 Dec. 1841. The invocation of Fanny Wright blended sexual license and religious infidelity in antebellum America. See Ginzberg, "Fanny Wright."

71. James McDowell Jr. to Susan S. McDowell, 22 Dec. 1842, and S[ophonisba] Breckinridge to Susan S. McDowell, 25 June 1842, CCD, MFP.

72. Pets. of Benjamin Wright, 1839, 1840, LP; *Richmond Enquirer*, 6 Feb. 1845; *AA* (1844–45), chap. 165, 135.

73. To sample legislative activity, see *Richmond Enquirer*, 6 Feb. 1845, 13 Jan. 1846, and *Richmond Whig*, 7 Feb. 1845, 22 Feb. 1847.

74. *JHDV*, 10, 16, 22 Dec. 1846, 26, 36, 52, and 23 Dec. 1847, 24 Feb., 18 Mar. 1848, 86, 279, 370; *Richmond Enquirer*, 11 Feb. 1848; *AA* (1847–48), chap. 122, 165–66.

75. Henry St. George Tucker, *Commentaries on the Laws*, 1:105; *AA* (1847–48), chap. 122, 165–67; Pet. of French, LP; *JHDV*, 2 Jan. 1850, 113.

76. See, for example, Pet. of Callaway, Pet. of Stevens, and Sidney Gribb to Henry L. Thomas, 26 Jan. 1848, in Pet. of Yonson, 1848, LP.

77. Aff. of Walter Powell, in Pet. of Martha A. Allison, LP; *AA* (1847–48), chap. 361, 348–49.

78. Pet. of Zinn, Monongalia Co., 1839, LP; *JHDV*, 1 Apr. 1839, 249; Aff. of John M. Gault, 14 Dec. 1849, in Pet. of Zinn, Marion Co., 1849, LP; *Richmond Whig*, 22 Mar. 1850; *JHDV*, 11, 18, 29 Dec. 1849, 2, 11 Feb. 1850, 62, 82, 108, 213, 245. The assembly in 1835–36 rejected another petition for divorce on insanity grounds; see Pet. of Hope, LP. Successful petitioners who alleged insanity included a second ground for divorce. See, for example, Pets. of Williams and Huston, LP, and *AA* (1832–33), chap. 239, 197, and (1836–37), chap. 338, 283.

79. *Richmond Whig*, 22 Mar. 1850; Virginia Constitution of 1851, Article 4, *AA* (1852–53), 332. The legislators still set the grounds for granting divorces. They expanded them in 1853; see *AA* (1853–54), chap. 28, 47–48.

80. For a narrowly averted injustice, see Pet. of Moore, LP, and *JHDV*, 31 Jan. 1849, 217.

81. See, for example, *JHDV*, 2 Jan. 1843, 52; 10, 16, 22 Dec. 1846, 26, 36, 52; 23 Dec. 1847, 86; and 25 Jan. 1849, 191.

82. Virginia General Assembly, *Code of Virginia*, 1849, 2:472; Shepard, "Lawyers Look at Themselves."

CHAPTER TWO

1. Pet. of Bartlam, LP.
2. Pets. of Bailey and John J. Campbell, LP. Bartlam was divorced by the 1844–

45 session; see *AA* (1844–45), chap. 161, 134. Bailey and Campbell were divorced the following year; see *AA* (1845–46), chap. 213, 159, and chap. 215, 160. For similar appeals, see Pets. of Benjamin Wright, 1839, and Harper, LP.

3. Howison, *History of Virginia*, 2:478; W. Hamilton Bryson, "Robert Reid Howison," in Bryson, *Virginia Law Reporters*, 112–17. See also Boles, "Evangelical Protestantism."

4. Howard, *Matrimonial Institutions;* Geertz, *Interpretation of Cultures*, 89–90. For Geertz's analysis, see Pals, *Seven Theories of Religion*, 233–67.

5. Fischer, *Albion's Seed*, 7, 8, 795. For criticisms of Fischer's analysis and his rejoinder, see "Albion's Seed."

6. Howard, *Matrimonial Institutions*, 2:228–63, 353–76; Fischer, *Albion's Seed*, 232–36, 281–86, 332–39. For the vitality of Virginia Anglicanism, see Gunderson, *Anglican Ministry*, and Bond, *Damned Souls*.

7. Doe, *Legal Framework*, 368; Witte, *From Sacrament to Contract*, 8–10, 165–76 (quote on 175). Not all the divines agreed; see Winnett, *Divorce and Remarriage*, 60–108.

8. Phillips, *Putting Asunder*, 191–226; Dewey, "Jefferson's Notes on Divorce."

9. "On Celibacy; or, The Condition of Old Maids and Bachelors," *Richmond Enquirer*, 17 Nov. 1804; Pet. of Fletcher, LP.

10. St. George Tucker, *Blackstone's Commentaries*, 2:433–40; Charles T. Cullen, "St. George Tucker," in Bryson, *Legal Education*, 657–86.

11. Chused, *Private Acts*, 43, 120–24, 184–86; Johnson, *Ante-Bellum North Carolina* 217–23; Boatwright, *Status of Women*, 61; Hudson, "From Constitution to Constitution."

12. Basch, *Framing American Divorce*, 37.

13. Thompson, *Presbyterians in the South*, 1:127–30, 252–59, 275–83.

14. Lower Banister Baptist Church, "Church Covenant," 2 Sept. 1798, 3, LVA. Recent studies of Baptist growth include Alley, *Baptists in Virginia*, and Wills, *Democratic Religion*.

15. Stith Mead to John Kobler, 15 May [1795], Mead Letterbook, VHS. Recent studies include Lyerly, *Methodism and the Southern Mind;* Wigger, *Taking Heaven by Storm;* and Andrews, *Methodists and Revolutionary America*.

16. For Moore's theology and ethics, see Moore to Edmund J. Lee, 23 Oct. 1817, and Moore to [William] Meade, 12 Mar. 1822, Moore Letterbook A, VTS; Lawrence L. Brown, "Richard Channing Moore"; and Johns, *Life of William Meade*.

17. *Virginia Argus*, 21 July 1809; Drury Lacy to Ashbel Green, 6 Oct. 1804, Gratz Collection, Pennsylvania Historical Society, Philadelphia.

18. *Richmond Enquirer*, 16 Oct. 1810; Mary Pocahontas Cabell to Susan Hubard, 21 Mar. 1815, ser. 1.4, folder 36, Hubard Family Papers, SHC; "Meeting of the General Committee, 1815," VBHS; *Virginian*, 26 May 1828.

19. *Virginia Religious Magazine*, Oct. 1804, vi, vii; *Christian Monitor*, 8 July 1815, 3. Rice published a "Prospectus" for his periodical in the *Virginia Argus*, 25 Feb. 1815.

20. "Sunday Schools," *Christian Monitor*, 10 May 1817, 276; Mathews, "Second Great Awakening"; "Meeting of the General Meeting, 1817," 8, VBHS.

21. Kennedy to Elizabeth Gray, 19 Aug. 1828, quoted in Bohner, "John Kennedy's Chronicle," 320; Nathaniel Beverley Tucker, "Sermon on the Death of Adams and Jefferson," box 2, Bryan Family Papers, UVA. For Tucker's religious beliefs at this stage in his life, see Brugger, *Beverley Tucker,* 67–72. For Randolph's *"conversion,"* see John Randolph to "My Good Friend," 25 Sept. 1818, in Randolph, "Mss. of John Randolph," 462–63. See also Davis, *Intellectual Life in Jefferson's Virginia,* 127–28, and Arthur Thomas, "Reasonable Revivalism." Even men who never joined a church regularly attended. Membership figures are deceptive because they include only full communicants, of whom a large majority were women.

22. Pets. of Settle, Waterfield, and Osbourne Parker, LP.

23. Bourne, *Marriage Indissoluble,* 12, 86, 67, 68.

24. Ibid., 51, 110. Blackstone pointed out the difference between impediments, such as an existing prior marriage, that rendered a marriage null from the beginning and those that could be grounds for a court annulment; see St. George Tucker, *Blackstone's Commentaries,* 2:435–40.

25. Bourne, *Marriage Indissoluble,* 12, 86; Shain, *Myth of American Individualism,* 38–41. For the significance of marriage to republicanism, see Lewis, "Republican Wife."

26. Bourne, *Marriage Indissoluble,* 24, 86, 113. For expectations that young women should marry, see Farnham, *Education of the Southern Belle,* 171.

27. Rice, *Duties of a Minister,* 27; Hanover Presbytery, Minutes, 11 Apr. 1807, 218–20, UTS; Bayley, *Marriage As It Is;* Bourne, *Marriage Indissoluble,* 23. For family religion and the sacralization of the home, see Mathews, *Religion in the Old South,* 98–101, 111–20.

28. Hite, Commonplace Book, VHS; for Hite, see Robertson, "Biographical Sketches," 27–28.

29. Betsy Watts to Sarah C. Watts, 29 May 1807, Watts Papers, WMC. See also Johnson, *Ante-Bellum North Carolina,* 209–17.

30. E. E. Wiley, "The Word of God: The Only Safeguard amid the Perils of Youth," in Smithson, *Methodist Pulpit South,* 353. For one town's efforts to regulate them better, see Albemarle Co. Pet., 8 Dec. 1815, LP.

31. Synod of Virginia, "Address to the Churches," 27 Oct. 1814, in "Minutes," vol. 4, UTS; see also Dover Baptist Association Records, 1817, 9–10, VBHS.

32. Weems, *God's Revenge against Adultery.*

33. "Mark 9:43–49. 'If thy hand offend thee,'" 4 Mar. 1830, Jared Rice Sermons, 1829–92, Protestant Episcopal Church in the U.S.A., VHS.

34. See, for example, Antioch Baptist Church, Minutes, 8 Aug. 1829, 13 Nov. 1831, 9 Mar. 1839, 1:59, 63, 2:23; Brock's Gap Baptist Church, Records, 17 Sept., 8 Oct. 1814, 79; Goose Creek Baptist Church, Minutes, 6 Aug. 1836, 74; and Lower Banister Baptist Church, Minutes, 17 Mar. 1804, 16 Feb. 1805, 20 Sept. 1806, 40, 51, 59, LVA; Buck Marsh Baptist Church, Minutes, 2 June 1797, 62, and Colosse Church, Minutes, 23 Oct. 1831, 24 June 1832, VBHS.

35. Richard Channing Moore to Col. H[ugh] Mercer, 4, 16 Nov. 1831, and

to William Meade, 12 Nov. 1831, Moore Letterbook M, VTS; Watkins Leigh to William Henry Lyons, 4 Apr. 1848, box 32, Lyons Family Papers, BC.

36. Bayley, *Marriage As It Is*, 48, 49; Garnett, *Lectures on Female Education*, xxiii, 203, 228.

37. *JHDV*, 11, 15, 19, 21 Dec. 1810, 18, 25, 32, 35; *Richmond Enquirer*, 20 Dec. 1810; *Virginia Argus*, 21 Dec. 1810, 1 Jan. 1811.

38. Shepherd, *Statutes*, 1:133–34; Virginia General Assembly, *Revised Code*, 1:400. For example, Jacob Warner of Winchester was convicted of bigamy in 1817 and was sentenced to serve one year; see *Richmond Enquirer*, 17 Oct., 6 Dec. 1817. See also the trial report, *Wm. Moore alias Jas. A. Robertson v Commonwealth*, in *Richmond Enquirer*, 21 June 1839.

39. Frying Pan Spring Baptist Church, Records, 17 July 1793, VHS.

40. La Rouchefoucauld-Liancort, *Travels*, 2:117; Jared Rice, untitled sermon, Sermons, Protestant Episcopal Church in the U.S.A., VHS; Goose Creek Baptist Church, Minutes, Sept. 1809, 32, LVA.

41. Broad Run Baptist Church, Minutes, 14 June 1785, LVA. It is worth noting that Drury's wife was not a church member.

42. Buckingham Baptist Church, Minutes, 30 Aug. 1833, 118, LVA; Strawberry Baptist Association Records, ? Mar., 26 June 1824, VBHS.

43. Goose Creek Baptist Church, Minutes, June 1788, 3, LVA. See also Saylor Creek Baptist Church, Minutes, 11 Oct. 1808, 34, LVA, and Dover Baptist Association Records, 1810, 6, VBHS.

44. Garnett, *Lectures on Female Education*, 228; Bayley, *Marriage As It Is*, 54; Bourne, *Marriage Indissoluble*, 86.

45. Garnett, *Lectures on Female Education*, xxi, xxiii, 223, 226.

46. Betsy Watts, Bedford, to Sarah C. Watts, 4 Apr., 29 May 1807, Watts Papers, WMC.

47. Buckley, "Duties of a Wife," 104; Bayley, *Marriage As It Is*, 61. See also "Marriage," *WS*, 30 Nov. 1843. For examples of women who married for wealth, see Pease and Pease, *Family of Women*, 48–57.

48. Garnett, *Lectures on Female Education*, 222; Pet. of Rowsey, LP. See also Lystra, *Searching the Heart*, 197–98.

49. [Methodist Episcopal Church], *Doctrines and Discipline*, 243; Coe, *John Wesley and Marriage*, 55–57; *Semi-Weekly Enquirer*, 30 Aug. 1805.

50. General Association Records, Oct. 1788, and Virginia Portsmouth Association Records, 26, 27 May 1793, 4, 5, VBHS; Schwarz, *Twice Condemned*, 12. For slave marriages, see Walsh, *From Calabar to Carter's Grove*, 83–85, and Philip D. Morgan, *Slave Counterpoint*, 499–501, 530–40.

51. Christopher Collins to Robert Carter, 11 Jan. 1788, Carter Family Papers, VHS. For Collins, see Hammond Family Papers, VHS. For concern over separating families, see Gutman, *Black Family*, 284–92.

52. Woolman, *Journal*, 59; Moreau, *American Journey*, 306.

53. Shepherd, *Statutes*, 1:134; Virginia Portsmouth Association Records, 27 May 1793, 4, VBHS. For a firsthand account of a slave wedding performed by a

black minister, see Adams, *Sketch Book*, 36–37. See also Nathaniel Beverly Tucker, "Essay on the Relation between Master and Slave."

54. Hanover Presbytery, Minutes, 2 Apr., 1 Aug. 1791, 37, 44, UTS.

55. Semple, *Baptists in Virginia*, 93–94; Dover Baptist Association Records, 14 Oct. 1793, 4; Virginia Portsmouth Association Records, 26, 28 May 1792, 27 May 1793, 26 May 1794, 2, 3, 4, 5; Baptist General Committee, Minutes, 13 May 1793, 7; and Strawberry Baptist Association Records, 26 May 1793, 58, VBHS.

56. Buck Marsh Baptist Church, Minutes, 1 Oct., 4 Nov. 1791, 31 Mar. 1792, 4 May, 2 Aug. 1794, 21, 22, 26, 39, and Ketocton Association Records, 17 Aug. 1809, 4–5, VBHS. See also Betty Wood, "African Americans and Church Discipline"; McCurry, *Masters of Small Worlds*, 138–48; and Sobel, *World They Made Together*, 190–97.

57. Pet. of Subscribers, in Pet. of Nancy H. Knight, 1811, LP; Roanoke Baptist Association Records, 10 May 1813, 3, VBHS. For Johns, see Taylor, *Virginia Baptist Ministers*, 11–12.

58. Dover Baptist Association Records, 11 Oct. 1819, 5, 14, VBHS; Pet. of Subscribers, in Pet. of Sewell, LP.

59. St. George's Parish, Vestry Book, 13 July, 26 Sept. 1808, 29 Apr., 6 May (quotation), 10 June 1809, LVA.

60. Low to Trustees of the Episcopal Church in the Town of Fredericksburg, 10 June 1809, and W[illiam] Taylor and Hugh Mercer to Samuel Low, 15 June 1809, St. George's Parish, Vestry Book, 10, 15 June 1809, 9 Apr. 1811, LVA.

61. Meade, *Old Churches*, 1:30, 71; St. George's Parish, Vestry Book, 9 Apr. 1811. See Slaughter, *History of St. George's Parish*, 34–36, and Brydon, "List of Clergy," 410, 411. For Maryland Episcopalians, see Chused, *Private Acts*, 43–44.

62. Hite, Commonplace Book, VHS. See Phillips, *Putting Asunder*, 90–94.

63. Bourne, *Marriage Indissoluble*, 86; Hite, Commonplace Book, VHS; Bayley, *Marriage As It Is*, 38.

64. Henry St. George Tucker, *Commentaries on the Laws*, 607. See "William Scott, Lord Stowell," and "Joseph Chitty the elder," in Stephen and Lee, *Dictionary of National Biography*, 17:1046–50, 4:266–67. For the difference between divorce law in New York and Virginia, see Robinson, *Practice in the Courts*, 153. For the importance of New York's judicial decisions, see Hartog, *Man and Wife*, 15–16.

65. *WS*, 6 Feb. 1840. For Plumer, see White, *Southern Presbyterian Leaders*, 286–92.

66. Robert Young Conrad to Elizabeth Powell Conrad, Richmond, 6 Dec. 1840, 17, 24 (quote) Jan. 1841, 14 Jan., 2, 11 Dec. 1843, Conrad Papers, VHS. For hardline opposition to divorce, see *WS*, 2 Mar. 1843, and Reid, Diary and Copybook, 111–15, Reid Papers, DU.

67. [Lynch], "Influence of Morals," 148; Pet. of Harper, LP; *JHDV*, 2 Jan. 1843, 52.

68. Robert M. Balls to Edmund J. Lee, 17 Nov., 10 Dec. 1847; Edmund J. Lee to Robert M. Balls, 23 Nov., 19 Dec. 1847 (copies); Edmund J. Lee to [Caroline Octavia Hudgson] Balls, 23 Dec. 1847 (copy), Lee Papers, DU.

69. Edmund J. Lee to R[obert] M. Balls, 17 Aug. 1849, Lee Papers, DU; Pet. of Balls, LP; *AA* (1850–51), chap. 297, 197.

70. *AA* (1847–48), chap. 122, 165–67; "John Mercer Patton," *DAB*, 14:316–17; Richard A. Claybrook Jr., "Conway Robinson," in Bryson, *Virginia Law Reporters*, 57–64.

71. [Patton and Robinson], *Report*, chap. 109, 561–64.

72. Ibid., 561. This is handwritten in the margin of the copy at VHS; see also Virginia General Assembly, *Code of Virginia*, 2:471–74.

73. *Richmond Whig*, 13 Jan. 1846; *Richmond Enquirer*, 13, 20 Jan. 1846.

74. *Richmond Whig*, 22 Mar. 1850.

75. Pets. of Stevens, Ferdinand S. Heiskell, Huldah Heiskell, and Rucker, LP; *AA* (1849–50), chap. 336, 230; chap. 327, 228; chap. 334, 230.

76. *Richmond Enquirer*, 22 Feb. 1848; Conway Robinson to Jaquelen Taylor, 13 Nov. 1852, Taylor Papers, VHS. In 1853 the assembly amended the divorce laws to permit absolute divorce in cases of desertion or abandonment for a five-year period; see *AA* (1852–53), chap. 28, 47.

77. John B. Minor, *Institutes*, 1:254–265 (quotes on 254, 259, 264, and 265); Holly B. Fitzsimmons, "John Barbee Minor," in Bryson, *Legal Education*, 417–30.

CHAPTER THREE

1. Aff. of Martha Walton, in Pet. of Nancy H. Knight, 1809, LP. See Kulikoff, *Tobacco and Slaves*, chap. 6; Censer, *North Carolina Planters*, 25–28; Kenzer, *Kinship and Neighborhood;* and Friedman, *Enclosed Garden*, 8–11.

2. Smith, *Inside the Great House*, 26–27; "George Walton Family Bible," 89–90; Will of George Walton, 2 Sept. 1796, Walton Family Papers, and sec. 168, Grigsby Papers, VHS; Bradshaw, *Prince Edward County*, 76–77. In 1782 his sixty-four slaves made George Walton the second largest slaveholder in the county; see Bradshaw, *Prince Edward County*, 271.

3. Aff. of John Billups, in Pet. of Walton Knight, LP; Bell, *Old Free State*, 1:268, 269; Knorr, *Marriages of Prince Edward County*, 45; Lunenburg Co. PPT and LT, 1805, LVA.

4. Bell, *Old Free State*, 1:334; Knorr, *Marriages of Prince Edward County*, 88; Lunenburg Co. PPT and LT, 1805, LVA.

5. Joseph Yarbrough to Walton Knight, 27 Feb., 20 Sept., 20 Dec. 1804, 6 Jan., 9 Apr. 1805, and undated, in Pet. of Nancy H. Knight, 1811, LP.

6. Aff. of John Billups, in Pet. of Walton Knight, LP; Knorr, *Marriages of Prince Edward County*, 45; H[enry] S[t.] G[eorge] Tucker to [Ann] Evelina [(Hunter)] Tucker, 6 Nov. 1831, box 8, Randolph-Tucker Papers, BC; Beeman, *Evolution of the Southern Backcountry*, 202–3. For marriages between cousins, see Bardaglio, *Reconstructing the Household*, 41–44; Wyatt-Brown, *Southern Honor*, 217–23; Censer, *North Carolina Planters*, 84–88; and Cashin, "Antebellum Planter Families."

7. *Walton v Knight*, packet Dec. 1809/Jan.–Feb. 1810, box 13, Circuit Court Papers, Prince Edward Co., LVA.

8. Aff. of Martha Walton, in Pet. of Nancy H. Knight, 1809, LP. See also Aff.

of Desha W. Morton, in ibid. For a wife's duties, see Clinton, *Plantation Mistress*, 22–25, and Lystra, *Searching the Heart*, 137–38.

9. Aff. of Martha Walton, in Pet. of Nancy H. Knight, 1809, LP.

10. Compare Fox-Genovese, *Within the Plantation Household*, 30, 192–241, with Clinton, *Plantation Mistress*, 3–15, 164–79.

11. Affs. of John Billups and Elizabeth Smith Walton, in Pet. of Nancy H. Knight, 1811, LP.

12. Affs. of Sarah L. Morton and Desha W. Morton, in ibid.

13. Affs. of Elizabeth Atkins, Pettus Shelburne, and John Billups, in ibid.

14. Prince Edward Co. OB no. 16 (1807–11), Nov. Court, 1807, 29, 30, 34, 40, 49, 86, 87, 479–81; Mar. Court, 1808, 116, 118; May Court, 1808, 142–43; and Aug. Court, 1808, 189, LVA.

15. Aff. of Martha Walton, in Pet. of Nancy H. Knight, 1809, and Walton Knight to Nancy H. Knight, 4 June 1808, in Pet. of Nancy H. Knight, 1811, LP.

16. Walton Knight to Nancy H. Knight, 5 July 1808, in Pet. of Nancy H. Knight, 1811, LP.

17. Ibid., 16 July 1808.

18. Ibid., 2, 4 Aug. 1808.

19. Ibid., 9, 18 Aug., [?] Sept. 1808.

20. Ibid., 18 Mar. 1809.

21. Nancy Hughes [sic] to Walton Knight, 3 July 1809; Walton Knight to Nancy H. Knight, 30 Aug. 1809; Notice of Nancy H. Knight; and Joseph Yarbrough to Walton Knight, 7 Sept. 1809, all in Pet. of Nancy H. Knight, 1811, LP. Her "property" is listed in the Aff. of Elizabeth Walton, ibid.

22. Aff. of Anderson Bagley, in Pet. of Walton Knight, LP.

23. Pet. of Nancy H. Knight, 1809, LP; *JHDV*, 5 Jan. 1810, 53.

24. Affs. of Elizabeth Hightower (quote), Thomas Farmer, John Jordan, and Boswell B. DeGraffenreid, in Pet. of Nancy H. Knight, 1811, LP.

25. Pet. of Nancy H. Knight, 1811, LP; Memorial of subscribers, Lunenburg Co., 17 Dec. 1811, LP; *JHDV*, 20 Dec. 1811, 3 Jan., 10, 18, Feb. 1812, 43, 61–62, 129, 142.

26. Pet. of Nancy H. Knight, 1812, LP; *JHDV*, 1 Jan. 1813, 93; *AA* (1812–13), chap. 103, 119.

27. Pet. of Nancy H. Knight, 1813, LP; *JHDV*, 8, 15, 23 Dec. 1813, 38, 59, 80.

28. Warren, *Virginia District Courts*, 56–57; *Knight v Yarbrough*, Walton Family Papers, VHS; Asa Dupuy's answer in *Neal v Walton's administrator*, and Court Order, 19 Mar. 1823, Grigsby Papers, VHS; Yarbrough, Will, VHS.

29. Robert S. Brooke to Margaret L. Brooke, 16 Jan. 1843, Brooke Papers, UVA; Aff. of Francis T. Brooke, in Pet. of Hamilton, LP; Brent Tarter, "Francis Taliaferro Brooke," *DVB*, 2:259–61.

30. Affs. of Francis T. Brooke, M[ary] C. Brooke, and Dr. Martin Burton, in Pet. of Hamilton, LP.

31. Helen B. Hamilton to Captain [George] Hamilton, 12 May 1844, and [unsigned] to Helen Hamilton, 13 May 1844, in ibid.

32. Robert Hamilton to George Hamilton, 18 Oct. 1844, 10 May 1845, in ibid.

33. Rob[er]t Hamilton to Helen Brooke, 15 Jan. 1843; R[obert] Hamilton to Mrs. C[harlotte] Thornton, 28 Apr. 1845; Robert Hamilton to [George Hamilton], 19 May 1845; and Robert Hamilton to Helen Hamilton, 29 May 1845, in ibid.

34. Aff. of Francis T. Brooke, in ibid.; *AA* (1846–47), chap. 275, 231. For her father's mention of the divorce, see Brooke, *Narrative of My Life*, 77. Helen later married Thomas M. Forman from Georgia; see *Richmond Enquirer*, 9 Oct. 1849.

35. Pet. of Cauffman, 1824, LP; Simon Cauffman to [Rachel Cauffman], 15 May 1819, in Pet. of Cauffman, 1825, LP. Simon's age and occupation are given in "Mayors Court," Philadelphia, 9 Sept. 1819, in Pet. of Cauffman, 1825, LP. See also Berman, *Richmond's Jewry*, 80.

36. Sentence of Simon Kauffman [*sic*], "Mayors Court," Philadelphia, 9 Sept. 1819, and Simon Cauffman to [Rachel Cauffman], 19 Sept. 1819, in Pet. of Cauffman, 1825, LP.

37. Simon Cauffman to [Rachel Cauffman], 22 Dec. 1820, in ibid. For Jewish divorce law, see Breitowitz, *Between Civil and Religious Law*, 5–19, and Freid, *Jews and Divorce*.

38. Simon Cauffman to [Rachel Cauffman], 29 May 1821, in Pet. of Cauffman, 1825, LP.

39. *State of Maryland v Simon Kauffman* [*sic*], Baltimore City Court, June term, 1821, and Simon Cauffman to [Rachel Cauffman], 6 Aug. 1821, in ibid.; Pet. of Cauffman, 1824, LP.

40. Court Record, Pet. of Olympia Blood, LP; Pet. of Fleming and Friendless Blood, LP; *AA* (1848–49), chap. 325, 248.

41. See, for example, Pets. of Saunders, 1825, 1826, LP.

42. David Dryden to Christopher Clise, 30 Sept. 1809, and Aff. of Samuel Lewis, in Pet. of Dryden, LP.

43. Pets. of Hillary and Robertson, LP. For an example of parental intervention, see Pet. of Corbin, LP.

44. Pets. of Harris, 1838, 1839, 1840, LP.

45. Pets. of Stanbery and Crawford, LP; John Tyler to James Lyons, 16 Dec. 1840, box 33, Lyons Family Papers, BC; Atkinson, *Bench and Bar*, 23–24, 54–55.

46. Aff. of Elizabeth Carter, in Pet. of Toomes, LP; Pets. of Kimberlin, Corbin, Lane, and Burke, LP.

47. Pet. of Lyon, LP; Aff. of Polly Smith, in ibid. See also Pets. of Rousseau and Carothers, LP.

48. Hening, *New Virginia Justice*, 745–46; Pets. of Dantignac and Dowdall, LP. See also Burke, *Property Rights of Married Women in Virginia;* Salmon, *Women and the Law of Property*, 81–119; Lebsock, *Free Women of Petersburg*, 54–86; and Chused, "Married Women's Property Law."

49. Buckley, "Evelina Gregory Roane"; Pet. of Walke, LP.

50. Pet. of Saunders, 1826, LP.

51. Pets. of Falkler and Peyton, 1845, LP; Aff. of Catherine Cooper, in Pet. of Cooper, LP.

52. Response of Ferdinand Heiskell, *Heiskell v Heiskell*, in Pet. of Ferdinand S. Heiskell, LP.

53. Affs. of William R. Richardson and John Pate, in Pet. of Cocke, LP; Cocke, *Hanover County Wills and Notes,* 39, 137–38; Hanover Co. PPT and LT, 1817, 1818, LVA; Pets. of Fanny Pollock and James T. Pollock, LP.

54. Pets. of Cloud, Davis, Carty, Fogg, Bourn, Leatherman, and Moran, LP. For a charge of brother-sister incest, see Pet. of Warwick, LP.

55. Aff. of Martha Walton, in Pet. of Nancy H. Knight, 1809, LP.

56. Aff. of Meriweather Hunt, in Pet. of Nancy Hughes Knight, 1812, LP; Affs. of John Jordan and Elizabeth Hightower, in Pet. of Nancy H. Knight, 1811, LP.

57. Aff. of Rolly Kern, in Pet. of Saunders, 1825, LP. See also Pets. of Mace, Joyner, and McGinty, LP.

58. Aff. of Robert Gonoe, in Pet. of Noseman, LP; Aff. of Daniel K. Hewett, in Pet. of Yonson, 1847, LP.

59. Bender, *Community and Social Change,* 7.

60. Aff. of subscribers, in Pet. of William Dinwiddie, LP.

61. Pet. of Nancy Dinwiddie, LP.

62. Pet. of Cole, LP; Affs. of Robert Harris, Wilkins Hall, Isham Cheatham, Robert Wilkinson, and Elam Cheatham, in ibid.

63. Affs. of James R. Gates, Elam Cheatham, Edward Bass, and Robert Baugh, in Pet. of Cole, LP.

64. Court Record, Chesterfield Clerk's Office, and Affs. of Robert Harris, Wilkins Hall, and Robert Baugh, in ibid.

65. Affs. of Philip Turpin and James Gates, in ibid.; Chesterfield Co. PPT and LT, 1824, LVA; *AA* (1824–25), chap. 107, 103.

66. Pet. of Dixon, LP.

67. Pet. of subscribers, in Pet. of Irvine, LP.

68. Pet. of Bell, LP; Pet. of subscribers, in ibid. For similar subscribed petitions, see Pet. of Thomas Alexander; Pet. of subscribers, in Pet. of Sewell; and Pet. of subscribers, in Pet. of Falkler, LP.

69. Affs. of Dr. Francis G. Taylor and Wyatt L. Lowry, in Pet. of Anna Woolfolk, LP.

70. Answer of Bentley B. Woolfolk, in ibid.

71. Affs. of Robert B. Smith, Charles M. Smith, Wyatt Lowry, Edmund Winston, William D. Taylor, William W. Mallory, and Robert A. Dosewell, in ibid.; Pet. of Bentley B. Woolfolk, LP.

72. Pets. of Anna Woolfolk and Bentley B. Woolfolk, and Aff. of William W. Dickinson, in Pet. of Anna Woolfolk, LP; *AA* (1850–51), chap. 310, 200. For another perspective on this case, see Wyatt-Brown, *Southern Honor,* 288–89.

73. Shepherd, *Statutes,* 1:133. See Bardaglio, "'Outrage upon Nature'" and *Reconstructing the Household,* 41–42.

74. Strawberry Baptist Association, Minutes, Oct. 1792, 51, and "Circular Letter," Dover Baptist Association Minutes, 1808, VBHS; *Minutes of the Dover Baptist Association . . . 1813,* 15. For Broaddus's life, see Taylor, *Virginia Baptist Ministers,* 238–77, and E. Brooks Holifield, "Andrew Broaddus," *DVB,* 2:239–40.

75. See, for example, John Matthews to William Hill, 25 Dec. 1810, box 3, Hill Papers, UTS.

76. *American Beacon*, 8 Nov. 1816. This statement by Elizabeth and William Dwyer was notarized 22 Nov. 1815.

77. *Virginia Herald*, 13 Mar. 1816; *Minutes of the Dover Baptist Association . . . 1817*, 13; [John D. Blair] to S[amuel Stanhope?] Smith, [ca. 1818], box 45, Blair Papers, BC; Maurice Duke, "John Durburrow Blair," *DVB*, 1:546–47.

78. *Richmond Enquirer*, 18 Apr. 1817, 19 Feb. 1818; *Attorney General v Broaddus and Wife*, 116–18. Andrew Broaddus won the case, but the marriage collapsed in 1822 when, according to his clerical biographer, Jane "proved entirely unworthy of his affections" and "he repudiated her" (Broaddus, *Sermons and Other Writings*, 40).

79. *Attorney General v Broaddus and Wife*, v, vi. For Roane, see Huebner, *Southern Judicial Tradition*, chap. 1.

80. The bill sped through the House in just four days. See *JHDV*, 18, 19, 20, 21 Feb. 1818, 209, 213, 214, 215, and Virginia General Assembly, *Revised Code*, 1:399–400.

81. Pets. of John Moore and Jesse Parker, LP. See also Pet. of Gill, LP.

82. *JHDV*, 7, 11 Jan. 1819, 94, 99, 100; *AA* (1818–19), chap. 29, 41–42; "To the Editor of the Enquirer," *Richmond Enquirer*, 3 Feb. 1820.

83. Pet. of subscribers, Northampton Co., LP. See also Pet. of Roper, LP; Pet. of subscribers, Preston Co., LP; and Pet. of Slade, LP.

84. *Richmond Enquirer*, 16 Dec. 1824. For these House actions, see *JHDV*, 13, 23, 24, 31 Jan. 1823, 115, 143, 150; 1 Jan., 17 Feb. 1824, 99, 172; 3, 6, 7, 11, 13, 14, 15 Dec. 1824, 14, 19–20, 22, 32–33, 34, 39, 41. The texts of these defeated proposals are in RHB, 1822, 1823, and 1824, box 39 and oversize box, LVA.

85. Henry Lee to Lewis, VHS. For this scandal, see Templeman, "Black Horse Harry Lee," and Nagel, *Lees of Virginia*, 204–30. Nagel questions whether Elizabeth ever became pregnant and had a stillborn child.

86. In elaborating on his argument to Lewis in 1833, Lee credits Uphsur's reasoning in the legislative debate; see Henry Lee to Lewis, VHS. For a firsthand report of the debate, see "J" to "M," 22 Jan. 1826, *Virginian*, 16 Feb. 1826.

87. Blackburn, *Speech on a Bill*, 3, 5; *JHDV*, 20 Jan. 1826, 121; John Campbell to David Campbell, 19 Jan. 1826, Campbell Family Papers, DU; Henry Lee to Lewis, VHS.

88. *JHDV*, 8, 23, 28 Feb. 1826, 157, 181, 186, and 16 Feb. 1827, 166; Virginia General Assembly, Senate, *Journal*, 2 Mar. 1826, 124; RHB, 1825, box 42, LVA; *AA* (1826–27), chap. 24, 22. "Incestuous Marriages," *Virginian*, 2 Mar. 1826, reported the House debate and vote.

89. *JHDV*, 12 Dec. 1822, 41, 72, 78, 82, and 13 Dec. 1824, 34, 40, 48, 50, 76, 93, 95; *Commonwealth v Leftwich*.

90. *Commonwealth v Edmund Perryman and Kiturah Perryman*. See also Pet. of Luck, LP.

91. *JHDV*, 19 Jan., 8 Mar. 1847, 93, 182; Virginia General Assembly, *Code of Virginia*, 1:470–71. Some legal authorities continued to object to the relaxation of these laws. See John B. Minor, *Institutes*, 1:261.

92. Pet. of subscribers, in Pet. of Tilson, LP; Buckingham Baptist Church, Minutes, 20 Nov. 1841, LVA.

1. Pet. of Fouch, LP; Aff. of Jane Campbell, in ibid. See also Stevenson, *Life in Black and White*, 145–46, 156.

2. Shepherd, *Statutes*, 1:134–35; Virginia General Assembly, *Code of Virginia*, 1:401. For southern law and attitudes, see Bardaglio, *Reconstructing the Household*, 48–64, and Sommerville, "Rape Myth."

3. General Association, Minutes, Oct. 1788, and Dover Baptist Association Records, 14 Oct. 1805, 6, VBHS.

4. Timothy Pickering to John Marshall, 17 Jan. 1826, Marshall Papers, LC. See Higginbotham and Kopytoff, "Racial Purity and Interracial Sex"; Williamson, *New People;* and Philip D. Morgan, *Slave Counterpoint*, 398–412.

5. See Hodes, *Sex across the Color Line* and *Sex, Love, Race*, and Rothman, "Freed from Thate Curs."

6. McCurry, *Masters of Small Worlds*, 48; PPT for Accomac Co. (1805); Amherst Co. (1807, 1834); Bedford Co. (1807, 1817); Culpeper Co. (1806, 1842); Fairfax Co. (1832); Fauquier Co. (1815); Fluvana Co. (1802); Frederick Co. (1840); Henry Co. (1848); James City Co. (1833); King William Co. (1824, 1836, 1837); Monroe Co. (1828); Norfolk Co. (1802, 1803, 1835, 1837); Northampton Co. (1813, 1814); Powhatan Co. (1815); and Prince William Co. (1806, 1807); LT for Accomac Co. (1805); Amherst Co. (1807, 1834); Culpeper Co. (1806, 1842); Fairfax Co. (1832); Fauquier Co. (1815); Frederick Co. (1840); James City Co. (1833); King William Co. (1824, 1836, 1837); Nansemond Co. (1826, 1840); Norfolk Co. (1835, 1737); Northampton Co. (1813, 1814); and Powhatan Co. (1815); Will of Elizabeth Owen, 17 Jan. 1802, Patrick Co. WB 1, 41, LVA.

7. Edmund Morgan, *American Slavery, American Freedom*, 338, 344–45, 364–69, 380–81. Historians divide over whether class differences produced conflicting ideas about white female purity. Hodes, *Sex across the Color Line*, 4–5, argues that this perspective belonged to the planter elite. But for the congruence between planter and yeoman classes in outlook, see Bynum, *Unruly Women*, 8–10, though Bynum places poor whites, whom she defines as those without land or slaves, in a class by themselves. See also Hagler, "Ideal Woman."

8. Kathleen Brown M., *Good Wives, Nasty Wenches*, 126, 131–33, 194–211, 237–40, 355–56.

9. William Brockenbrough to Joseph C. Cabell, 14 May 1802, box 2, Cabell Papers, UVA; Hening, *Statutes*, 11:39; Shepherd, *Statutes*, 1:122, 239; Egerton, *Gabriel's Rebellion*.

10. Affs. of James McNeilege, Ann McNeilege, and Jane Campbell, in Pet. of Fouch, LP; Hening, *Statutes*, 12:184; Shepherd, *Statutes*, 2:458–59, 3:26, 231, 321; *JHDV*, 28 Jan. 1809, 91; *AA* (1808–9), chap. 41, 84–85. For Maryland, see Chused, *Private Acts*, 22–23.

11. Pets. of Fouch and Dabney Pettus, LP; Affs. of James Thompson and James Daniel, in Pet. of Bayliss, 1833, LP; Pets. of Butt, Rose, and Hall, LP.

12. Pet. of subscribers, in Pet. of Rose, LP; Pets. of Dabney Pettus, Tatham, Gresham, and Mosby, LP.

13. Aff. of Jane Rose, in Pet. of Rose, LP; Aff. of Elizabeth G. Merryman, in Pet. of Fouch, LP; Pet. of Mosby, LP.

14. Pets. of Tatham, Cook, David Parker, and Richard Jones, LP.

15. Pets. of Bayliss, 1833, and Butt, LP; Pet. of subscribers, in Pet. of Rose, LP; Pet. of Owens, LP.

16. Pets. of Fouch and Richard Jones, LP.

17. Aff. of Thomas Whitlock, in Pet. of Owens, LP; Court Transcript, in Pet. of Rawls, LP; Pets. of Howard, 1807, 1809, LP. For the committee reports, see *JHDV,* 28 Dec. 1807, 42; 11 Dec. 1809, 17; 15 Jan. 1812, 82.

18. Aff. of Elizabeth Merryman, in Pet. of Dabney Pettus, LP; Aff. of Anna Masden, in Pet. of Butt, LP; Pet. of David Parker, LP; Aff. of Rachel Purkell, in Pet. of Fouch, LP.

19. Statement of Elizabeth Pettus, in Pet. of Dabney Pettus, LP; Statement of Benjamin Butt Jr. and Lydia Butt, in Pet. of Butt, LP; Articles of Agreement, in Pet. of Tatham, LP; Accomac Co. DB 10, 22 Mar. 1804, 499–500, and DB 11, 24 June 1805, 247–48, LVA.

20. Aff. of Th[omas] Miller, in Pet. of Mosby, LP; Aff. of John Daniel, in Pet. of Bayliss, 1833, LP; Pet. of Hall, LP.

21. Aff. of Jane Campbell, in Pet. of Fouch, LP.

22. Court Transcript, in Pet. of Gresham, LP. The jurors' residences are determined by Williamsburg City and James City Co. PPT and LT, 1832–33, LVA.

23. Court Transcript, in Pet. of Culpeper, LP.

24. Horner, *Blair, Banister, and Braxton Families,* 160; Henry St. George Tucker to St. George Tucker, 7, 18 May, 16 Aug. 1803, box 23; 21 Aug. 1810, box 30; 26 June 1818, box 36 (first quote); 27 Mar. 1820, box 38 (second quote), Tucker-Coleman Papers, WMC. For the challenges facing young lawyers, see "Memoir of the Ambitious Lawyer."

25. Virginia General Assembly, *Revised Code,* 1:270–71; [Benjamin Blake Minor], "Legal Profession."

26. Pet. of Bourne, 1824, and Affs. of Peter Wade, Thomas W. Pulliam, Daniel A. Molloy, and Richard Woodson, in Pet. of Bourne, 1825, LP. See also Hodes, *Sex across the Color Line,* chap. 4.

27. Affs. of John Richardson, Thomas Anderson, Anderson Bowles, Lewis Bourne, and William Bourne, in Pet. of Bourne, 1825, LP.

28. Pet. of Bourne, 1824, and Affs. of William Bourne and Pleasants Proffit, in Pet. of Bourne, 1825, LP; *JHDV,* 3, 5 Dec. 1823, 35, 40, 46, 47.

29. Statement of Doratha Bourne and Aff. of Delphy Hooker, in Pet. of Bourne, 1825, LP.

30. Affs. of Keziah Mosely and Shandy Perkins, in Pet. of Bourne, 1825, LP; *JHDV,* 5 Feb. 1825, 151.

31. Salmon, *Women and the Law of Property,* 15–19, 31–32, 39, 144, 151–56; *AA* (1847–48), chap. 122, 166.

32. *Watkins and Wife v Carlton,* 593, 594, 595, 596, 602, 603; Philip M. Grabill Jr., "Benjamin Watkins Leigh," in Bryson, *Virginia Law Reporters,* 49–56.

33. Pet. of Bayliss, 1831, LP; Court Transcript, in Pet. of Bayliss, 1833, LP; Pet. of Hall, LP.

34. Keith Thomas, "Double Standard."

35. *Virginian*, 1 Jan. 1827; *Richmond Whig*, 4 Jan. 1842; E. Lee Shepard, "Briscoe Gerald Baldwin," in *DVB*, 1:296–97. For Baldwin's divorce case, see Pet. of Rankin, LP.

36. La Rouchefoucauld-Liancort, *Travels*, 2:82; Bayard, *Travels*, 20. But see Wyatt-Brown, *Southern Honor*, 307–24. For Jefferson, see Gordon-Reed, *Thomas Jefferson and Sally Hemmings*.

37. Sally C. P. McDowell to Susan S. McDowell, [Feb. 1836], MFP; Thomas Brown, "Miscegenation of Richard Mentor Johnson."

38. Aff. of Thomas Jenkins, in Pet. of Ball, LP.

39. Pets. of Hunter, Rowland, Dunlap, and Harwell, LP.

40. Pet. of Brewer, LP. For this time in antidivorce feminism, see Basch, *Framing American Divorce*, 74–77.

41. Aff. of Stephen Terry, in Pet. of Dobyns, LP; *AA* (1817–18), chap. 222, 220–21.

42. Pet. of Barbara W. Pettus, LP. Barbara got a separate maintenance from the Louisa County court; see Aff. of Charles Thompson, in ibid.

43. Pet. of Roane, LP; Buckley, "Evelina Gregory Roane." But see also Susan Miller, *Assuming the Positions*, 257–62.

44. Pet. of Roane, LP; Aff. of Thomas S. W. Gregory, in ibid.; *AA* (1824–25), chap. 106, 102.

45. Pets. of Alvis and Watts, LP; Court Transcript, in Pet. of Eubank, LP; Court Transcript, in Pet. of Pannill, LP; *AA* (1828–29), chap. 173, 154; (1834–35), chap. 212, 238; (1836–37), chap. 337, 283; (1838), chap. 303, 220.

46. Court Transcript, in Pet. of Pannill, LP.

47. Robert Hamilton to Helen Brooke, 15 Jan. 1843, and Aff. of Francis T. Brooke, in Pet. of Hamilton, LP.

48. Pet. of Norman, LP; Extracts from Depositions, in ibid.; *AA* (1848–49), chap. 322, 247; *Richmond Whig*, 2 Feb. 1849.

49. Aff. of Elizabeth G. Merryman, in Pet. of Dabney Pettus, LP; Aff. of Benjamin Butt Sr., in Pet. of Butt, LP; Aff. of Mary Gregory, in Pet. of Roane, LP; Court Transcript, in Pet. of Pannill, LP. On slaves' use of poison and whites' fears, see Schwarz, *Twice Condemned*, 92–113, 200–205, 295–97.

50. Pet. of Brewer, LP. For the situation faced by female slaves, see Bardaglio, *Reconstructing the Household*, 66–69.

51. Aff. of Thomas Jenkins, in Petition of Ball, LP; *Milly, "a free negro woman," v Egbert Harris*, Powhatan Co. OB, 16 Feb. 1814, 3, and *Anna Cooper, "a free negro woman," v Samuel Williams*, Powhatan Co. OB, 21 Oct. 1816, 487, LVA. See also Jacqueline Jones, *Labor of Love, Labor of Sorrow*, 11–43; Sterling, *We Are Your Sisters*, 1–84; and McLaurin, *Cecilia*.

52. Buckingham Baptist Church, Minutes, 16 May 1827, 44–45, LVA.

53. Accomac Co. OB, 28 May 1804, 1, and Isle of Wight Co. Court Judgments,

1 May 1815, LVA. For the development of an "oppositional" identity, see Sidbury, *Ploughshares into Swords*.

54. Pet. of Robert Wright, LP; Will of Thomas Wright, Campbell Co. WB 2, 1800–1810, 226, and Campbell Co. PPT and LT, 1806–18, LVA.

55. Pet. of subscribers, in Pet. of Robert Wright, LP; *JHDV*, 16 Nov. 1816, 26. For the family's legal tangles, see Buckley, "Unfixing Race." After the Civil War, Virginia law made an interracial marriage void from the outset; see John B. Minor, *Institutes*, 1:261, 262.

CHAPTER FIVE

1. Affs. of R. H. Bradford and Ja[me]s Johnson, in Pet. of Ann P. Cowper, LP; Crocker, "Parkers of Macclesfield," 421.

2. The literature is abundant. See, for example, Breines and Gordon, "New Scholarship on Family Violence"; Giles-Sims, *Wife Battering;* Walker, *Battered Woman* and *Battered Woman Syndrome;* Kurz, "Perspectives on Wife Abuse"; and Gelles and Loseke, *Current Controversies.*

3. Peterson del Mar, *What Trouble I Have Seen;* Pleck, *Domestic Tyranny;* Nadelhaft, "Wife Torture"; Griswold, "Law, Sex, Cruelty, and Divorce."

4. Hening, *New Virginia Justice*, 675–85; Lebsock, *Free Women of Petersburg*, 34–35; Samuel M. Walker Jr., "William Waller Hening," in Bryson, *Virginia Law Reporters*, 19–24. Marshall is quoted in Conrad, *Old County Court System*, 17.

5. *Almond v Almond*, 667–68. An earlier alimony case upheld the Court of Chancery's jurisdiction to hear such cases. See *Purcell v Purcell*.

6. Henry St. George Tucker, *Commentaries on the Laws*, 101.

7. Pet. of Ann P. Cowper, LP; Crocker, "Parkers of Macclesfield," 421; *Norfolk Herald*, 8 May 1802.

8. Pet. of Ann P. Cowper, LP; *Waterfield v Cowper*, 7 Oct. 1806, 29 July 1807, Isle of Wight Co. Court Judgments, LVA.

9. Will of Josiah Parker, in Pet. of William Cowper, 1811, LP. Joseph Baker was the son of Ann's stepsister. For these family connections, see Crocker, "Parkers of Macclesfield," 421, and Boddie, *Southside Virginia Families*, 8, 9. Josiah Parker's estate was considerable. In addition to houses and lots in several towns, the estate paid taxes on twenty slaves, six horses, a carriage, and more than 2,000 acres of land in Isle of Wight; see Isle of Wight Co. PPT, 1811, and LT, 1821, LVA.

10. Affs. of R. H. Bradford, J[ames] B. Southall, and Sally Copeland, in Pet. of Ann P. Cowper, LP.

11. *Cabell v Cowper*, Isle of Wight Co. OB, 1810–13, 1 July 1811, 147, IWCC.

12. Pets. of Ann P. Cowper; William Cowper, 1811; and Ann Pierce Parker Cowper, LP; *JHDV*, 19 Dec. 1811, 42.

13. Pet. of Ann P. Cowper, LP. The agreement, notarized by Thomas Pierce and dated 5 Dec. 1811, is in Pet. of Ann Pierce Parker Cowper, LP.

14. Affs. of Sally Copeland and James Johnson, in Pet. of Ann P. Cowper, LP.

15. *Commonwealth v Cowper*, peace warrant and recognizance, 26, 27 Feb. 1812, Isle of Wight Co. Court Judgments, LVA.

16. Sup. Ct. of Law, 9 May 1812, 64–65, Isle of Wight Co. OB, 1809–28, IWCC. The chancery records were destroyed, but Ann Cowper included a certified copy of her court statement and Judge Nelson's decree in Pet. of Ann P. Cowper, LP. For this trial and Tazewell's role, see Ann P. P. Cowper to Joseph C. Cabell, 26 Dec. 1816, in Pet. of Ann P. Cowper, LP. For Tucker's friendship with Cowper, see Philip Barraud to St. George Tucker, 13 July 1810, box 8, Randolph-Tucker Papers, BC. See also Joseph C. Cabell to [Philip] Barraud, 4 July 1803, box 23, Tucker-Coleman Papers, WMC.

17. Pet. of Thomas Hancock, Aug.–Sept. 1812, Isle of Wight Co. Court Judgments, LVA.

18. *Baker adm. v Pitts and Whitfield*, Apr. 1815, Isle of Wight Co. Court Judgments, LVA; "Baker against Cowper: In Trespass," Isle of Wight Co. OB, 1809–28, Sup. Ct. of Law, 9 May 1814, 9 May 1816, 94, 141, IWCC.

19. Guardian Records, Isle of Wight Co., 9 Nov. 1815, 237, LVA; Aff. of Thomas Hancock, in Pet. of Ann P. Cowper, LP; Isle of Wight Co. OB, 1809–28, Sup. Ct. of Law, 9 May 1812, 63, IWCC; William Cowper to Littleton W. Tazewell, 6 May 1814, box 7, Tazewell Family Papers, LVA; Pets. of William Cowper, 1811, 1812, 1815, 1816, LP; *Jones and Riddick v Cowper*, Petition for Counter Security, Aug. 1815, Isle of Wight Co. Court Judgments, LVA. For Cowper's debts, see Cowper to Lightfoot, Deed of Trust, 1 June 1815; *Davis v Cowper*, Aug. 1816; and *Barbers admin v Cowper*, Mar. 1817, Isle of Wight Co. Court Judgments, LVA. For the estate's loss of value, see Isle of Wight Co. PPT, 1810–18, LVA.

20. Pet. of Ann P. Cowper, LP; Ann P. Cowper to Joseph C. Cabell, 26 Dec. 1816, in ibid.; *AA* (1816–17), chap. 119, 175–76.

21. Rotundo, "Learning about Manhood," 35–37. Rotundo's research is based on northern middle-class men, but his conclusions apply to William Cowper, whose Norfolk base connected him to the coastal and West Indies trade. See also Rotundo, *American Manhood*, and Ditz, "Shipwrecked."

22. Ann Cowper to the Chancery Court, 1812, in Pet. of Ann P. Cowper, LP. See Stevenson, *Life in Black and White*, 92, and Gordon, "Ideal Husband," 145–57.

23. Pet. of Ann P. Cowper, LP; Aff. of Sally Copeland, in ibid.

24. Pet. of Ann P. Cowper, LP; Gelles and Loseke, *Current Controversies*, 37; Gelles, "Family Violence."

25. Gelles and Loseke, *Current Controversies*, 38. See also Gelles, "Exchange/Social Control Theory," and Aff. of Nathaniel Young, in Pet. of Ann P. Cowper, LP.

26. Walker, *Battered Woman*, 55–70.

27. Affs. of Thomas Pierce and Sally Copeland, and R. H. Bradford to Joseph C. Cabell, 26 Dec. 1816, in Pet. of Ann P. Cowper, LP.

28. Pet. of Ann P. Cowper, LP; Affs. of Andrew Woodley, Matt[hew] Jordan, John Dorlon, Nathaniel Young, Arthur Smith, and others (quote), in ibid.; McMillen, *Motherhood in the Old South*.

29. Will of John Kirk, Lancaster Co. WB 28, 312; Lancaster Co. PPT and LT, 1826–36; Indenture between John W. A. Edmonds, Addison Hall, and William H.

Kirk, 20 Feb. 1832; Indenture between John W. A. Edmonds, Robert T. Dunaway, and William T. Cowles, 24 Aug. 1834; and reports of public sales, 15 Dec. 1834, 19 Jan. 1835, in Lancaster Co. DB 34, 53–54, 248–49, 268–69, 269–71; Affs. of Judith George and Elizabeth Schofield, Court Record, 26 Aug. 1834, in Pet. of Edmonds, LP.

30. Pet. of Rankin, LP.

31. James B. Norman and Lucy W. Price, 14 Nov. 1842, Marriage Bonds, Henry Co., 186, LVA. John Price had married Lucy Pratt in 1825 and Lucy W. Harris on 13 July 1842; see ibid., 81, 131. Also, Will of John Price Sr., 3 Oct. 1842, Henry Co. WB 4, 446; Henry Co. PPT and LT, 1842–50; and U.S. Census Bureau, Seventh Census, 1850, and Eighth Census, 1860, Henry Co., Va., LVA; Pet. of Norman, LP; Indenture between James B. Norman and J. Tyler Hairston, 27 Mar. 1846, and Indenture between James B. and Lucy Norman and Patrick F. Hopper, 21 May 1846, in Henry Co. DB 13, 209–10, 234–35, LVA.

32. Aff. of Polly Wicker, in Pet. of Cocke, LP; Court Record, in Pet. of Eubank, LP; Pet. of Polly Stone, LP.

33. Admin. of estate of William Edrington, 22 Oct. 1821, Fauquier Co. WB 8, 111, LVA; Pet. of Combs, LP; Will of Seth Combs, 22 Aug. 1853, Fauquier Co. WB 21, 289–90, LVA.

34. Pets. of Godwin, Martha Barnett, and Boling, LP; Aff. of Stephen Terry, in Pet. of Dobyns, LP.

35. Pet. of Grantham, LP; *Richmond Enquirer*, 11 Jan. 1814. For the follow-up on the Robertson case, see *Richmond Enquirer*, 29 Jan. 1814; *AA* (1813–14), chap. 86, 143–44; and Pet. of Robertson, LP.

36. Pet. of Rollins, LP; Aff. of Juliana Baker, 31 Oct. 1806, in Pet. of Ball, LP; Pet. of Roberts and Court Order, in ibid.

37. Buckley, "Evelina Gregory Roane," 50; Eliza Thomson to Sally W. Griffith, n.d., transcript, Randolph Family Papers, VHS; Pet. of Amelia M. Alexander, LP. See also Nadelhaft, "Alcohol and Wife Abuse."

38. Statement of Huldah Heiskell, *Heiskell v Heiskell*, and Ferdinand Heiskell to Huldah Heiskell, 22 Sept. 1849, in Pet. of Ferdinand S. Heiskell, LP. The next year Huldah received a divorce; see *AA* (1849–50), chap. 327, 228.

39. Pets. of Waterfield, Crow, Cole, and Dobyns, LP; Affs. of Susan Witlow and Harrison W. Garrott, in Pet. of Wingo, LP.

40. Answer of Ferdinand S. Heiskell, *Heiskell v Heiskell*, in Pet. of Ferdinand S. Heiskell, LP; Pet. of Bayne, LP; *JHDV*, 15 Dec. 1808, 24.

41. Court Record, in Pet. of Hutchings, LP; Pet. of Boling, LP; Affs. of Juliana Baker and Elizabeth Evans, in Pet. of Ball, LP. For pregnancy as an illness, see Clinton, *Plantation Mistress*, 151–56, and Lewis and Lockridge, "'Sally Has Been Sick.'"

42. Pets. of Bayne and Boling, LP; Aff. of Travers Barnes, in Pet. of Ball, LP; Pets. of Roane, Ballinger, and Barbara W. Pettus, LP.

43. Pets. of Polly Stone and Dobyns, LP.

44. Pets. of Maxwell, Lowry, and Cole, LP.

45. Pets. of Wells and Cole, LP.

46. For example, Hoff, *Battered Women*, 32–78, and Stordeur and Stille, *Ending Men's Violence*, 37–54.

47. Jabour, *Marriage in the Early Republic;* Frank, *Life with Father*, 38. See also "Marriage and Divorce" and Cashin, *Our Common Affairs*, 1–12.

48. Buckley, "Duties of a Wife," 100, 101. For its republication and attribution to Madison, see "A Letter of Advice," *Richmond Enquirer*, 6 Mar. 1818; "Advice from a Father to his Only Daughter," *SLM* 1 (1834): 187–88; and "Advice of a Father to an Only Daughter," *WS*, 21 Nov. 1839.

49. *SLM* 1 (1834): 186; [DuPre], "Woman." See also [Dew], "On the Characteristic Differences."

50. Bayley, *Marriage As It Is*, 131; Garnett, *Lectures on Female Education*, 235. See also Lystra, *Searching the Heart*, 127–28, and Ann E. J. Wise to Henry Alexander Wise, 21 Dec. [1834–36], Wise Family Papers, VHS.

51. Garnett, *Lectures on Female Education*, 230, 232; Bayley, *Marriage As It Is*, 132–37; "The Wife at Home," *WS*, 9 Nov. 1843. See also Charles Colcock Jones, *Glory of Woman*, 21–23.

52. Pet. of Brown, LP; Abner Campbell to Scotty [Brown], 4 Oct. 1847, in ibid.

53. St. George Tucker, *Blackstone's Commentaries*, 1:432.

54. Aff. of Francis Sibert, in Pet of Ball, LP; "To the Honourable John Scott Judge," in Pet. of Combs, LP; Pet. of Bayne, LP. Nancy moved in with her parents, and the men worked out a property settlement.

55. Brent Tarter, "George Wilhelm Blaetterman," *DVB*, 1:533–34.

56. Pet. of Dobyns, LP. Jonah's penniless condition probably kept him from engaging a lawyer and going to court; see Bedford Co. PPT and LT, 1807–22, LVA.

57. Pet. of Eleanor A. Allison, LP; *AA* (1837–38), chap. 299, 219. See Dobash and Dobash, "Community Response to Violence."

58. Aff. of Andrew Woodley and Jam[e]s Johnson, in Pet. of Ann P. Cowper, LP; *Cabell v Cowper*, Isle of Wight Co. OB, 1810–13, 1 July 1811, 147, IWCC. William Cowper's proclivity for brawling seems to have placed him outside the circle of gentlemen. See Gorn, "'Gouge and Bite, Pull Hair and Scratch.'"

59. Isle of Wight Co. OB, 1816–18, 7 Apr., 31 May 1817, 5 Mar. 1818, 154–55, 173–74, 295–96, IWCC.

60. Virginia General Assembly, *Revised Code*, chap. 75, 266–67; Hening, *New Virginia Justice*, 405–17; F. Thorton Miller, *Juries and Judges*, 6–8, 19–21, 27–30. For glowing praise of Virginia's jury system by a self-described "state reformist," see Thomas [Crump] Mead to Frederick Casper, 32 May 1822, Miscellaneous Manuscript Collection, LC.

61. Isle of Wight Co. PPT and LT, 1816–17, LVA.

62. *Richmond Enquirer*, 11 Jan. 1817; *AA* (1816–17), chap. 119, 175. See also Grossberg, "Who Gets the Child?," and Bardaglio, *Reconstructing the Household*, 80–97.

63. Isle of Wight Co. OB, 1816–18, 5 May, 4 Aug. 1817, 168, 206, and Guardian bond of William Cowper for Josiah Parker, 4 Aug. 1817, Loose Papers, IWCC. Because the chancery papers were burned, this court's decision is unknown, but it most likely upheld the legislative act.

64. Pet. of William Cowper, 1817, LP; *JHDV*, 1817 sess., 34, 95, 111, 142; F. Thorton Miller, *Juries and Judges*, 5–6, 8–11, 18, 111–12.

65. Aff. of Nathaniel Gray, 24 Nov. 1818, and Edmund Godwin to Wm Exam Eley, 26 Nov. [1818], in Pet. of Godwin, LP. Edmund Godwin served on the jury that rejected Ann Cowper's legal right to Macclesfield; see Isle of Wight Co. OB, 1816–18, 31 May 1817, 174, IWCC. By mid-1819 Jane Godwin had become a widow; see Presentment of William Perkins, Aug. 1819, Isle of Wight Co. Court Judgments, LVA.

66. Resolution by Committee on Courts of Justice on E. Dowdall's Petition, 14 Dec. 1809, RHB, 1809, LVA; Pet. of Dowdall, LP. For a similar discussion, see *Richmond Enquirer*, 6 Jan. 1810, and *Richmond Whig*, 16 Mar. 1841.

67. Aff. of Eliza Hazelwood, 4 Jan. 1850, in Pet. of Harriet Z. H. Mallory, 1850, LP; Pets. of Garland A. Mallory and Harriet Z. H. Mallory, 1851, LP. For Macfarland, see Christian, *Reminiscences*, 6–7. For another contested divorce case in which the assembly sided with the husband, see Pet. of Elizabeth Watson, LP, and *Watson v Watson*, September 1832, box 62, Circuit Court Papers, Prince Edward Co., Jan. 1831–Apr. 1836, LVA.

68. *Richmond Enquirer*, 22 Jan. 1820. A criminal conviction, however, might ease the way for a divorce. See, for example, *AA* (1817–18), chap. 210, 220.

69. Pet. of Trueman, LP; Court Record, in ibid.

70. "Rights of Married Women," *Richmond Whig*, 16 July 1849; see also "The Bill to protect the property of Married Women," ibid., 27 Feb. 1949. Earlier legislative discussions are in *JHDV*, 26 Dec. 1843, 57; 14 Jan. 1847, 81; 31 Jan. 1848, 211–12; 8 Dec. 1848, 50.

71. "General Assembly of Virginia," *Richmond Whig*, 17 July 1849.

72. "Rights of Married Women," *Richmond Whig*, 21 Aug. 1849. The state also sanctioned institutional violence against women. When in 1843 the lower House passed a bill to eliminate whipping as a punishment for white women, the Senate rejected the measure; later in the session when the House passed an amended bill abolishing whipping for all whites, the Senate killed the proposal. See *JHDV*, 26, 29 Dec. 1843, 8, 12 Feb. 1844, 57, 64, 148, 172.

73. Walker, *Battered Woman Syndrome*, 10. For a sample of these cases, see *Cowper v Bullock*, Isle of Wight Co. OB, 1816–18, 3 Aug. 1818, 362; *Chapman exec. v Ann P. Parker*, Isle of Wight Co. OB, 1818–20, 2 Mar. 1819, 93; and *Drew v Ann P. Parker*, Isle of Wight Co. OB, 1818–20, 2 Mar. 1819, 98, IWCC. See also Higgins, *Resilient Adults*.

74. Pet. of Josiah Cowper, LP; *AA* (1823–24), chap. 103, 104; Indenture of Josiah C. Parker to Ann P. Cowper, 4 Mar. 1823, Isle of Wight Co. DB 26, 236, LVA.

75. Indenture of Ann P. Cowper to Bartholomew Lightfoot, 7 Jan. 1828, Isle of Wight Co. DB 27, 414; Indenture of Ann P. Cowper to Edwin Morrison, 1 Dec. 1841, Isle of Wight Co. DB 34, 232; and Account of sale, Ann P. Cowper by Edwin Morrison, Trustee, 9 June 1849, Isle of Wight Co. DB 37, 474, LVA; Crocker, "Parkers of Macclesfield," 421.

1. John Pryor to Thomas Massie, 13 Mar. 1799, Massie Family Papers, VHS. The Pryors had wed on 13 Oct. 1796; see *Virginia Gazette and General Advertiser,* 19 Oct. 1796.

2. John Pryor to Thomas Massie, 26 Dec. 1809, 29 Mar., 21 May 1803, Massie Family Papers, VHS.

3. Anne [Pryor] to John Lowry, 28 Aug. 1811, in Pet. of Pryor, LP (Pryor's property holdings are listed in his 1800 will in Pet. of Pryor); "Whiting Family," 260; "Notes to Virginia Council Journals," 131. Anne's daughter-in-law, Jessie Benton Frémont, visited the Whiting family in Virginia and took notes for a campaign biography by John Bigelow when John Charles Frémont ran for president on the Republican ticket in 1856. Her notes and Bigelow's first chapter are riddled with errors and inaccuracies, however. See Herr and Spence, *Letters of Frémont,* 115–18, and Bigelow, *Memoir of Frémont,* 11–21. Somewhat more reliable is Nevins, *Frémont,* 1:2–8.

4. Pet. of Pryor, LP; Anne [Pryor] to John Lowry, 28 Aug. 1811, in ibid.

5. Pet. of Pryor, LP; Aff. of Robert Quarles, in ibid.; Nevins, *Frémont,* 1:5–6. For the scandal involving Frémont and the threat it posed to Girardin's academy, see *Virginia Patriot,* 12, 23, 26, 30 July, 23 Aug. 1811.

6. Affs. of Robert Quarles and Archibald Blair, in Pet. of Pryor, LP.

7. Anne [Pryor] to John Lowry, 28 Aug. 1811, and Aff. of Robert Quarles, in Pet. of Pryor, LP. For Thomas Whiting's will, see Bigelow, *Memoir of Frémont,* 14–18.

8. Affs. of Archibald Blair and John Lataste, in Pet. of Pryor, LP.

9. *Virginia Argus,* 11 July 1811; *Virginia Patriot,* 12 July 1811; Henry St. George Tucker, *Commentaries on the Laws,* 2:442; *Purcell v Purcell.* See also *Richmond Enquirer,* 10 Oct. 1809; Lebsock, *Free Women of Petersburg,* 23–24, 68; and Salmon, *Women and the Law of Property,* 74, 76–78, 151–56.

10. Anne [Pryor] to John Lowry, 28 Aug. 1811, in Pet. of Pryor, LP. Bigelow reprinted the court records that list Lowry as Susanna's husband; see Bigelow, *Memoir of Frémont,* 17. Anne's version of events differs significantly from that given years later to Jessie Benton Frémont by her Whiting relatives. See Herr and Spence, *Letters of Frémont,* 116.

11. Anne [Pryor] to John Lowry, 28 Aug. 1811, in Pet. of Pryor, LP. In his 1800 will John left bequests to two living sisters, Elizabeth Hankins and Mary Quarles, and to the children of his deceased sister, Salley Taylor; see will of John Pryor, in Pet. of John Pryor, LP.

12. Anne [Pryor] to John Lowry, 28 Aug. 1811, in ibid.

13. Pet. of Pryor, LP; *JHDV,* 7, 11 Dec. 1811, 16, 29.

14. Pets. of Robert Campbell and Bosher, LP; Shepherd, *Statutes,* 3:163, 408.

15. Pets. of Mills, Ritchie, and Needles, LP; Wyatt-Brown, *Southern Honor,* 298–307.

16. Pets. of Ferte; Stratton; Thompson; Wright, 1839; and Smith, LP.

17. Pet. of Hobbs, LP.

18. Pets. of Kenney and Needles, LP.

19. Pets. of Hare, Turner, and Stratton, LP. See also Pets. of Daws and Yonson, 1848, LP, and Wyatt-Brown, *Southern Honor*, 306–7.

20. Pets. of Hart and Carty, LP.

21. Court Transcripts for Pets. of Martin, 1941; Ledington; and Hobbs, LP.

22. [St. George Tucker], "On Domestic Happiness," 20 Mar. 1809, folder 1, Barraud Family Papers, WMC; Bayley, *Marriage As It Is*, 127, 130. See also Bourne, *Marriage Indissoluble*, 38; "Whisper for Husbands," *WS*, 6 Mar. 1845; and Matthews, *"Just a Housewife,"* 3–34.

23. John H. Cocke to Louisa M. Holmes, 5 June, 9, 10 July 1821, and L[ouisa] Holmes to John H. Cocke, 3 July 1821, box 34, Cocke Papers, UVA. See also Smith, *Inside the Great House;* Lewis, *Pursuit of Happiness;* Buza, "'Pledges of Our Love'"; and Jabour, *Marriage in the Early Republic.*

24. Ann E. J. Wise to Henry Alexander Wise, 11 Jan., 15 Feb. 1836, and Henry Alexander Wise to Ann E. J. Wise, 23 Jan. 1837, Wise Family Papers, VHS. See also Torrence, "Letters of Mrs. Ann Wise."

25. J. J. Winn to Jeremiah S. B. Tinsley, 27 July 1842, box 17, Tinsley Family Papers, BC; Burrell H. Cook to Kate [?], 24 Mar. 1855, box 1, folder 2, Cook-Luttrell Papers, WMC. See also John Weylie to William Meade, 9 June 1807, box 1, folder 1, Meade Papers, WMC; Archibald Stuart to John B. Roy, 1 Oct. 1816, box 84, Garland Family Papers, BC; Benjamin W. Cabell to John B. Roy, 28 [Nov.?] 1816, box 48, Cabell Family Papers, BC; Beverley Kennon to James Lyons, 18 Dec. 1830, box 32, Lyons Family Papers, BC; Meade, *Recollections of Two Beloved Wives*, 36–37, 47.

26. Pets. of Bayliss, 1831; Charles Jones; and Simpson, LP. For similar sentiments in the North, see Frank, *Life with Father*, 85–92.

27. Pets. of Peyton, 1847; Freeze; and Simpson, LP; *AA* (1829–30), chap. 148, 133.

28. Pets. of Robert Campbell, Thompson, and Keaffer, LP.

29. Pets. of Martin, 1840, 1841; Needles; Ferte; and Settle, LP.

30. Pets. of Jesse Horton, 1815; Kinnamon; and Cooper, LP.

31. Pets. of Irvine, Hart, Powers, Trotter, Bosher, and Mahan, LP. See also Pets. of Kenney, Carty, Thomas, Sewell, John J. Campbell, George W. Foster, Nicholas, and Nutter, LP.

32. Pet. of Croxton, LP; *JHDV*, 8 Dec. 1819, 12, 67, 71, 78, 82, 151, and 19 Dec. 1820, 53; Pet. of Peter Stone, LP. See also Pet. of Marshall, LP.

33. Pet. of Sewell, LP; Russell Co. PPT and LT, 1825, LVA.

34. For typical examples, see Pets. of Arell and Turner, LP.

35. Pet. of Peter Stone, LP.

36. Pet. of Arell, LP. See also Pets. of Simpson, Mahan, Mills, and Blackburn, LP.

37. Pets. of Mountz and John J. Campbell, LP.

38. Affs. of Larkin Byers and William Noel, in Pet. of Rowsey, LP.

39. Affs. of John Hall, Larkin Byers, and William Noel, in Pet. of Rowsey, and Pet. of Netherland, LP. For other examples, see Pets. of Keaffer, Mills, Hobbs, and Marshall, LP.

40. Aff. of William Terry, in Pet. of Cooper, and Pets. of Keaffer, Mahan, Turner, and Pierce, LP.

41. Pets. of Tharp and Adams, LP.

42. Affs. of George Parrott and Burrell Jenkins, Court Transcript, in Pet. of Adams, LP. For a sample of failed reclamation efforts, see Pets. of Bonnell, Sewell, Mills, Settle, and John Foster, LP. For this kind of father-daughter relationship, see Clinton, *Plantation Mistress*, 44, and Stowe, *Intimacy and Power*, 171–79.

43. Pets. of Robiou and Fulcher, LP; Wyatt-Brown, *Southern Honor*, 303–4.

44. Pets. of Trotter and Thomas and Court Transcript, Pet. of Copin, LP.

45. Pet. of Williams, LP. Williams owned at least twenty slaves in 1830; see U.S. Census Bureau, Sixth Census, 1830, Franklin Co., Va, LVA.

46. Pet. of Williams; Affs. of John S. Hale, Burwell Keath, Michael Holland, Robert H. Calhoun, Elizabeth Calhoun, James C. Tate, and Harriet Hale, in Pet. of Williams; and James C. Tate to "Dear Sirs," 12 Feb. 1833, in Pet. of Williams, LP; *Lynchburg Virginian*, 25 Feb. 1833; *JHDV*, 19 Feb. 1833, 195, 232, 253, 255, 266. For the use of laudanum among southern women, see McMillen, *Southern Women*, 74–75, 108.

47. W. B. Sydnor to Thomas W. Sydnor, 2 Nov. 1838, box 1, Sydnor Papers, UVA.

48. Pets. of Stratton, Wallin, and Carty, LP. For a sample of wives who apparently chose to leave their husbands, see Pets. of Bonnell, Robert Campbell, Noseman, Cyrus, Thompson, Turnell, Mills, Settle, Joyner, Hobbs, Falkler, John Foster, and Marshall, LP. For the economic situation of newly married couples, see Stevenson, *Life in Black and White*, 67.

49. Pets. of Rosewell Carter and Bagent, 1841, 1844, and Aff. of John Bagent, in Pet. of Bagent, 1844, LP.

50. Pet. of Jesse Horton, 1811, and Affs. of George McConnell and John Osborne, in ibid., LP; Russell Co. PPT and LT, 1811, LVA; *JHDV*, 13 Dec. 1811, 29.

51. Pet. of Jesse Horton, 1815, and Affs. of John Hawl, John Blevins, Daniel Blevins, and George Jackson, in ibid., LP; *JHDV*, 9 Dec. 1815, 23, 30 Jan. 1816, 26, 136, 147.

52. Aff. of Jemima Horton, in Pet. of Jesse Horton, 1815; Pet. of Jesse Horton, 1816; Affs. of S[amuel] Ritchie Jr. and Isaac Lowe, in Pet. of Jesse Horton, 1816; and Pet. of Jesse Horton, 1819, LP; *JHDV*, 22 Nov. 1816, 2 Dec., 10, 31 Jan. 1817, 44, 59, 143, 179, and 24, 29 Dec. 1819, 70, 81.

53. For examples, see Pets. of Kinnamon, Powers, Ferte, Sewell, and Nottingham, LP.

54. Pet. of Bishop, LP; Fugate, *Scott County Marriages*, 12. William Bishop's first wife was Elizabeth Pogue, whom he married in 1808; see Fleet, *Washington County Marriage Register*, 13.

55. Pet. of Bishop, LP; Scott Co. OB 2, 11 Apr. 1849, and *Commonwealth v Ruth Walling*, Scott Co. Court, Causes Determined, Sept. 1850, LVA. Ruth Walling married Thomas A. Newman on 7 Oct. 1849 when they were both twenty-seven years old; see Fugate, *Scott County Marriages*, 104, and U.S. Census Bureau, Seventh Census, 1850, Scott Co., Va., LVA.

56. Scott Co. OB 2, 11 Apr., 10 Sept. 1849, 8, 10 Apr., 9 Sept. 1850, 265, 274, 289, 298, 314, LVA. For the pertinent "decency and morality" laws, see Virginia General Assembly, *Code of Virginia*, chap. 196, 740.

57. Indentures between William Bishop Sr. and William Bishop Jr. and between William Bishop Sr. and Sarah Wallin, formerly Sarah Bishop, George Bishop . . . , 19 Mar. 1851, Scott Co. DB 9, 371–72, LVA; U.S. Census Bureau, Seventh Census, 1850, Scott Co., Va., LVA.

58. Statements of Susan Bosher and Richard S. Grant, Richmond, 8 Apr. 1807, in Pet. of Bosher, LP.

59. Pets. of Sheppard, Tharp, John Cox, and Settle, LP.

60. Pets. of Sewell, Rosewell Carter, and Noseman, and Court Record, Pet. of Joyner, LP; notice by Charles Crenshaw, *Virginia Gazette and General Advertiser*, 12 Aug. 1807.

61. Pets. of Carty and James Barnett, LP.

62. Pleas held at the Court House, 12 Apr. 1838, and Court Transcript, in Pet. of Benjamin Wright, 1839, LP. For the use of the writ of *capias ad respondendum*, see Hobson, *Papers of Marshall*, 5:xxvi–xxvii.

63. Affs. of Hugh Sinclair, Sarah Sinclair, Elias Hughs, and James Smith, in Pet. of Benjamin Wright, 1839, LP.

64. Aff. of Jurors, Nov.–Dec. 1838, in Pet. of Benjamin Wright, 1839, LP. In each case the legislative action is written on the petition. The divorce file also contains an indenture dated 3 Mar. 1837 in which Ben, his wife, and his widowed mother sold 256 acres to Cyrus Perkins for $3,000.

65. Affs. of Nancy Sinclair, Edsen P. Harding, and William B. McMahan, in Pet. of Benjamin Wright, 1940, and Pet. of Benjamin Wright, 1840, LP.

66. *Wright v Greer*, 13, 14, 17 Apr. 1840, in Pet. of Benjamin Wright, 1839. For the pertinent laws governing this trial, see Henry St. George Tucker, *Commentaries on the Laws*, 2:72–73. Tucker notes, "In general the court will not grant a new trial to the defendant on account of excessive damages—in so henious a light is the offence viewed by the law. . . . Yet the damages are not to be looked on as a punishment, but merely in the light of compensation for injury" (2:73).

67. Affs. of Mary Hunt, Joseph Bennett, Hugh Sinclair, and Sarah Sinclair, in Pet. of Benjamin Wright, 1839; *AA* (1844–45), chap. 165, 135; *Richmond Enquirer*, 6 Feb. 1845; U.S. Census Bureau, Seventh Census, 1850, Jackson Co., Va., LVA.

68. Pets. of Matthew Watson and Bane and Aff. of Thomas Buster, in Pet. of William Horton, LP.

69. John Charles Frémont, *Memoirs*, 1:21–22 (quote), 56, 412–13; Nevins, *Frémont*, 1:8–18. John C. Freemon was living on Church Street in Norfolk in 1817. He owned two slaves; see Norfolk City PPT, 1817, LVA.

70. *Virginia Argus*, 1 Mar. 1815; *Richmond Enquirer*, 25 Mar. 1823; Will of John Pryor, Richmond City Hustings WB 3, 21 Mar. 1823, 302, LVA.

71. Will of John Pryor, 4 Feb. 1800, in Pet. of Pryor, LP; Will of John Pryor, Richmond City Hustings WB 3, 21 Mar. 1823, 303, LVA.

1. S. S. McDowell to Mary [McDowell], 20 Apr. [1843], undated file, Barrington-McDowell Family Papers, LC. For a typical press account, see *Daily National Intelligencer*, 9 May 1843, and [Francis Thomas], *Statement*, 51.

2. Susan S. McDowell to James McDowell, 2 Sept. 1840, MFP; Williams, *History of Frederick County*, 256–63; *DAB*.

3. Sally C. McDowell to Susan S. McDowell, 7 Mar. 1837, MFP.

4. The only detailed account is in Williams, *History of Frederick County*, 258–61. He argues that Frank Thomas's treatment of Sally "cost him the presidency" in 1844 (ibid., 261).

5. Buckley, *Courtship Letters*. For the value of such letters, see Lystra, *Searching the Heart*.

6. E. Benton to Sally C. McDowell, 2 Jan. 1839, MFP.

7. E. H. Benton to [Sally C. McDowell], 8 Dec. 1839, MFP; Sally McDowell, "Narrative," DP, MFP; Sally C. McDowell to James McDowell Jr., 12 May 1846, CCD, MFP.

8. Francis Thomas to Charles Macgill, [1841], box 1, CMP, DU; S[usan] S. McDowell to James McDowell, 8 Dec. 1840, JMP, DU. For this freedom in courtship and marriage choices, see Censer, *North Carolina Planters*, 65–83.

9. James McDowell to Susan S. McDowell, 9 Jan. 1838, MFP; S[usan] S. McDowell to James McDowell, 22 Dec. 1840, and James McDowell to Susan S. McDowell, 8, 20 Jan. 1841, ser. 1.3, folder 35, JMP, SHC; Lystra, *Searching the Heart*, 20–21, 129–31. Steven Stowe, *Intimacy and Power*, 248, argues that such separations typified marriage among the elite. See also Stevenson, *Life in Black and White*, 84–87.

10. Sally McDowell, "Narrative," DP, MFP; William C. Preston to Susan S. McDowell, 15 June 1845, CCD, MFP; *Richmond Enquirer*, 22 June 1841. For an account of the wedding by Sally's cousin, see Jesse Benton Frémont, *Souvenirs of My Time*, 45–47.

11. Sally McDowell, "Narrative," DP, MFP. For Thomas's version of events, see [Francis Thomas], *Statement*, 9–14.

12. Sally McDowell, "Narrative," DP, MFP; William Tyler to Sally C. McDowell, 13 Oct. 1846, CCD, MFP; Robert S. Brooke to Margaret L. Brooke, 16 Feb. 1842, Brooke Papers, UVA.

13. Sally McDowell, "Narrative," DP, MFP; [Francis Thomas], *Statement*, 22–23.

14. William C. Preston to [James McDowell], [? Jan. 1842], CCD, MFP.

15. Miller to McDowell, 17 Oct. 1856, and McDowell to Miller, 22 Oct. 1856, in Buckley, *Courtship Letters*, 852, 860–61.

16. Sally McDowell, "Narrative," DP, MFP.

17. Francis Thomas to [S. C. Thomas], 3, 9 Feb. 1842, copies in James McDowell to Archibald Graham, 25 May 1843, box 2, GFP, DU.

18. Francis Thomas to [S. C. Thomas], 9 Feb. 1842; Reverdy Johnson to James

McDowell, 18 Feb. 1842; and Reverdy Johnson to S. C. Thomas, 18 Feb. 1842, box 2, GFP, DU.

19. For reports of Frank Thomas, see James McDowell [Jr.] to Susanna S. McDowell, 28 Feb. 1842, MFP, and George H. Young to James McDowell, 6 Apr. 1842, box 1, JMP, DU. For Thomas's concern, see Francis Thomas to John Thompson Mason, 2 Mar. 1842, box 5, JTMP; Basch, *Framing American Divorce*, 147–68; and S[ophonisba] Breckinridge to Susan S. McDowell, 25 June 1842, CCD, MFP.

20. James McDowell [Jr.] to Susanna S. McDowell, 28 Feb. 1842, MFP; Sarah B. Preston to Susanna S. McDowell, 26 Feb. 1842; Edmonia M. Preston to Susanna S. McDowell, 1 Mar. 1842; and Eliza H. Carrington to Susan McDowell, 6 Mar. 1842, CCD, MFP.

21. Francis Thomas to Charles Macgill, 10, 31 Sept. 1842, box 1, CMP, DU; James McDowell Jr. to Susan S. McDowell, 22 Dec. 1842; S[ophonisba] Breckinridge to Susan S. McDowell, 25 June 1842; and James McDowell to Sally C. McDowell, 16 Feb. 1843, CCD, MFP.

22. S. C. Thomas to R. J. Taylor, 20 Feb., 12 Mar. 1842, CCD, MFP.

23. Robert S. Brooke to Margaret L. Brooke, 16 Feb. 1842, Brooke Papers, UVA.

24. James McDowell to Sally C. McDowell, 16 Feb. 1843, and to Susan S. McDowell, 5 Jan. 1843, CCD, MFP; S. C. Thomas to Archibald Graham, 11 Apr. 1843, box 2, GFP, DU; McDowell to Miller, 13 Oct. 1854, in Buckley, *Courtship Letters*, 15.

25. Francis Thomas to Sally C. Thomas, 20 Feb. 1843, CCD, MFP; Francis Thomas to Sally C. Thomas, 26 Mar. 1843 (copy), box 2, GFP, DU.

26. S. C. Thomas to Archibald Graham, 11 Apr. 1843, box 2, GFP, DU; Francis Thomas to Sally C. Thomas, 20 Feb. 1843, CCD, MFP; James McDowell [Jr.] to Susanna S. McDowell, 28 Feb. 1842, MFP.

27. Wm. C. Preston to James McDowell, May 1832, CCD, MFP. The press announcement was reprinted in the *Richmond Whig*, 12 May 1843.

28. A[nn] S. Breckinridge to James McDowell, 10 May 1843, box 1, JMP, DU.

29. Sally McDowell, "Narrative," DP, MFP; James McDowell to Susan S. McDowell, 20 May 1843, and James McDowell Jr., to Susan S. McDowell, 21 May 1843, CCD, MFP. Francis Thomas published some Linn letters in his *Statement*, 14–17.

30. James McDowell to Susan S. McDowell, 20 May 1843, DP, MFP. See also James McDowell to Susan S. McDowell, 27, 30 May, 4, 11 June, 1842, CCD, MFP.

31. James McDowell to Susan S. McDowell, 30 May, 4 June 1843, CCD, MFP.

32. Thomas H. Benton to James McDowell, 15 Aug. 1843, and William S. Plumer to James McDowell, 5 July 1843, box 1, JMP, DU; James McDowell to Susan S. McDowell, 30 May 1843, CCD, MFP.

33. *Richmond Whig*, 6 June 1843; Robert J. Taylor to Archibald Graham, 16 Aug. 1843, and Archibald Graham to Robert J. Taylor, 19 Aug. 1843, box 2, GFP, DU.

34. William Taylor to James McDowell, 26 Dec. 1843, CCD, MFP; James McDowell Jr. to Susan S. McDowell, 26 Dec. 1843, MFP.

35. Sally's narratives, dated 6 Sept. 1843 and 8 Mar. 1845, are in DP, MFP. The printed circular, dated 15 May 1844, is in box 1, CMP, DU.

36. James E. McDowell to William Campbell Preston, 28 May 1844, McDowell Family Papers, VHS; *Richmond Whig*, 6 Aug. 1844; James McDowell Jr. to James McDowell, 3 Aug. 1844, CCD, MFP. Frank's challenge to a divorce is in his Broadside, 1843, T45 box, LVA.

37. James McDowell Jr. to James McDowell, 18 Sept. 1844, MFP; A. S. Breckinridge to James McDowell, 23 Oct. 1844, and James McDowell Jr. to James McDowell, 5, 23 Dec. 1844, box 1, JMP, DU.

38. Thomas Hart Benton to James McDowell, 21 Feb. 1845, box 2, JMP, DU; [Francis Thomas], *Statement*, 8. The pamphlet is dated 19 Feb. 1845 from Montevue, Frank's father's home near Frederick. Portions are republished in Chused, *Private Acts*, 208–22, but the account is inaccurate; see Chused, *Private Acts*, 143–46.

39. [Francis Thomas], *Statement*, 29; [Francis Thomas], *Statement* (Sally McDowell's copy), 2, 10, DP, MFP.

40. James McDowell to Sally C. Thomas, 5 Mar. 1845, and Sally C. Thomas to James McDowell, 7 Mar. 1845, CCD, MFP; Sally McDowell, "Narrative," DP, MFP. For a very different example of a woman's journey from the private to the public sphere, see Cohen, "Respectability of Rebecca Reed."

41. Wm. L. Marshall to James McDowell, 20 Mar. 1845, CCD, MFP; Robert J. Taylor to Susan Taylor, 3 Mar. 1845, and Robert Breckinridge to James McDowell, 14 Mar. 1845, box 2, JMP, DU.

42. Thomas Hart Benton to James McDowell, 19 Mar. 1845, CCD, MFP; *Richmond Enquirer*, 9 Apr. 1845.

43. Resolutions of Lexington Meeting, CCD, MFP. The resolutions were widely republished. See, for example, *Richmond Whig*, 8 Apr. 1845; *Richmond Enquirer*, 9 Apr. 1845; and John Alexander to James McDowell, 2 Apr. 1845, box 2, JMP, DU.

44. Francis Thomas to Charles Macgill, 20 May 1845, box 1, CMP, DU; James McDowell Jr. to Susan S. McDowell, 24 May 1845, and James Lyons to James McDowell, 27 Aug. 1845, CCD, MFP. For Lyons, see Christian, *Reminiscences*, 7.

45. William C. Preston to Susan S. McDowell, 15 June 1845, and to [James] McDowell, 11 Aug. 1845, and Wm. Schley to James McDowell, 31 Oct. 1845, CCD, MFP; Thomas H. Benton to James McDowell, 3, 17, 23, 30 Oct. 1845, and James Hoban to James McDowell, 19 Sept., 22 Oct. 1845, box 2, JMP, DU; Frederick Co. Court, Equity Docket, 1842–51, MSA C783, 144–45, #2009, Hall of Records, Annapolis, Md.

46. *Richmond Whig*, 18 Nov. 1845; *Richmond Enquirer*, 14 Nov. 1845; James Lyons to James McDowell, 12 Nov. 1845, CCD, MFP.

47. *Richmond Whig*, 25 Dec. 1845; Thomas H. Benton to James McDowell, 30 Dec. 1845, box 2, JMP, DU. See also W[illis] P. Bocock to [John H. Bocock], 19 Jan. 1856, in Buckley, *Courtship Letters*, 514.

48. L. S. English to Sally C. Thomas, [25 Dec. 1845], and William C. Preston

to Sally Campbell McDowell and to James McDowell, 31 Dec. 1845, CCD, MFP.

49. *Richmond Enquirer*, 2, 16 Jan. 1846; James Lyons to James McDowell, 10 Jan. 1846, and W. H. Merrick to Sarah C. McDowell, 23 Feb. 1843, CCD, MFP; Henry St. George Tucker, *Notes on Blackstone's Commentaries*, 1:440; *AA* (1845–46), chap. 219, 160; Maryland Divorce Law, DP, MFP; *JHDM* 12, 13, 17 Feb. 1846, 249, 257, 274.

50. Miller to McDowell, 29 Dec. 1855, and John H. Bocock to McDowell, 4 Feb. 1856, in Buckley, *Courtship Letters*, 465–66, 513–14.

51. "Statement of James Lyons," in James Lyons to S. C. McDowell, 14 Aug. 1856, CCD, MFP.

52. Ann F. Preston to [S. C. McDowell], 12 Jan. [1846], MFP; Thomas Ritchie to James McDowell, 16 Jan. 1845 [*sic*], CCD, MFP.

53. Thomas H. Benton to James McDowell, 17 Jan. 1846, box 2, JMP, DU; James McDowell to Susan S. McDowell, 8 Feb. 1846, CCD, MFP; James McDowell to Philip R. Fendall, 9 Mar. 1846, Fendall Papers, LC.

54. P. R. Fendall to William C. Preston, 30 Mar. 1845, and William C. Preston to James McDowell, 2 Apr. 1846, CCD, MFP.

55. P. R. Fendall to William C. Preston, 30 Mar. 1846, and James McDowell to Sally C. McDowell, 11 Mar. 1846, CCD, MFP.

56. *Richmond Whig*, 8 May 1846; James McDowell to James McDowell Jr., 13, 26 May 1846, CCD, MFP.

57. James McDowell Jr. to James McDowell, 17 June 1846, and Judge Lawless to [Thomas H.] Benton, 18 May 1846, CCD, MFP.

58. James McDowell to Susan S. McDowell, 6 July 1846, CCD, MFP.

59. Francis Thomas to Sally C. P. McDowell, 16, 31 July 1846 (copies); Sally C. McDowell to James McDowell, 6 Aug. 1846; Philip R. Fendall to Sally C. McDowell, 3, 10 Aug. 1846; and James McDowell to Sally C. McDowell, 10 Aug. 1846, CCD, MFP.

60. William Tyler to James McDowell, 29 Sept. 1846; William Tyler to S. C. McDowell, 21 Sept., 13 Oct. 1846; and James McDowell Jr. to S. C. McDowell, 26 Nov. 1846, CCD, MFP.

61. Francis Thomas to John Thompson Mason, 12 Nov. 1846, JTMP; William Tyler to S. C. McDowell, 13 Oct. 1846, CCD, MFP.

62. Philip R. Fendall to Sally C. McDowell, 26 Oct., 16 Nov. 1846, and P. R. Fendall to S. C. McDowell, 8 Feb. 1847, CCD, MFP; Francis Thomas to Charles Macgill, 13 Feb. 1847, box 1, CMP, DU.

63. *JHDM*, 18, 19 Feb. 1847, 294–95, 301–2, 306–7, 312–14; *Republican and Argus*, 19, 20 Feb. 1847; John C. LeGrand to Richard S. Blackburn, 17 Mar. 1847, printed copy, in LeGrand to Charles Macgill, 18 Jan. 1861, box 1, CMP, DU.

64. *Richmond Whig*, 22 Feb. 1847; James McDowell to Susan S. McDowell, 22 Feb. 1847, CCD, MFP.

65. *JHDM*, 2, 3, 4 Mar. 1847, 413–14, 420, 421, 431; *Republican and Argus*, 4, 5, Mar. 1847.

66. *JHDM*, 6 Mar. 1847, 468; Charles F. Meyer to James McDowell, 6 Mar. 1847, CCD, MFP.

67. James Lyons to S. C. McDowell, 6 Mar. 1847, CCD, MFP; *United States v Francis Thomas*, DP, MFP; *Watchman and Observer*, 18 Mar. 1847.

68. James Lyons to S. C. McDowell, 10 Mar. 1847, and James McDowell Jr. to S. C. McDowell, 19 Mar. 1847, and to Susan S. McDowell, 17 Mar. 1847, CCD, MFP.

69. Francis Thomas to James McDowell, 20 Sept. 1847, 28 Sept. 1848, 12 Feb. 1849 (copies), CCD, MFP.

70. McDowell to Miller, 13 Oct. 1854, in Buckley, *Courtship Letters*, 15; S. C. McDowell to Susan Carrington, 23 Nov. 1848, McDowell Family Papers, VHS; S. C. McDowell to James McDowell, 21 Apr., 2 May, 23 Nov. 1853, box 2, JMP, DU; S. C. McDowell to Sophonisba McDowell, 25 Aug. 1853, MFP.

71. McDowell to Miller, 6 Dec. 1854, in Buckley, *Courtship Letters*, 24; James Lyons to S. C. McDowell, 17 Aug. 1846, CCD, MFP.

72. Francis Thomas to S. C. McDowell, 3 Sept. 1851 (copy), and John B. Floyd to S. C. McDowell, 6 Oct. 1851, CCD, MFP.

73. S. C. McDowell to Francis Thomas, 9 July 1852, CCD, MFP.

74. McDowell to Miller, 7 Aug., 12 Sept. 1854, and Miller to McDowell, 5 Sept. 1854, in Buckley, *Courtship Letters*, 1, 8, 2.

75. McDowell to Miller, 12 Sept., 13 Oct. 1854, and Miller to McDowell, 21 Sept. 1854, in ibid., 9, 14–15, 10, 11.

76. McDowell to Miller, 1 Jan., 22 Feb., 7 Mar., 30 Apr. 1855, in ibid., 39, 89, 113, 187.

77. Miller to McDowell, 27 Mar. 1855, and McDowell to Miller, 10, 14, 21 May 1855, in ibid., 140, 204, 211, 223.

78. Miller to McDowell, 20 Mar. 1855, 20 Oct. 1856, and McDowell to Miller, 30 Oct. 1855, in ibid., 126, 857, 416, 417.

79. Resolutions of Arch Street Presbyterian Church, 13 Nov. 1855, CCD, MFP; Philadelphia Presbytery, Minutes, 6 Dec. 1855, 390, Presbyterian Historical Society, Philadelphia, Pa.; *Central Presbyterian*, 2 Feb. 1856; Miller to McDowell 27 Nov., 1 Dec. 1855, in Buckley, *Courtship Letters*, 438, 448, 449.

80. Miller to McDowell, 13 Nov. 1854, 27 Nov. 1855, and McDowell to Miller, 29 Nov. 1855, in Buckley, *Courtship Letters*, 19, 437, 443.

81. McDowell to Miller, 18 Feb., 2 May, 2 July 1856, in ibid., 508, 569, 634.

82. McDowell to Miller, 15 July, 9, 26 Aug. 1856, and Miller to McDowell, 4, 6 Sept. 1856, in ibid., 648, 398, 741, 754, 757.

83. McDowell to Miller, 18 Sept. 1856, in ibid., 777, 778.

84. Miller to McDowell, 25 Sept., and McDowell to Miller, 27 Sept. 1856, in ibid., 787, 795.

85. McDowell to Miller, 8 Oct. 1856, in ibid., 825.

86. McDowell to Miller, 29 Oct. 1856, and Miller to McDowell, 30 Oct. 1856, in ibid., 870, 873.

87. John Miller to Sally Miller, 7 Aug. 1871, in ibid., 875; for their married life, see the introduction to ibid., xxii–xxvii.

88. See, for example, McDowell to Miller, 7 Mar. 1855, in ibid., 113; William L. White to S. C. McDowell, 3 Oct. 1856, MFP.

EPILOGUE

1. Cox and Weathers, *Old Houses*, 34–35.

2. Sarah Turnbull, Last Will and Testament, 1811, bk. 9, fol. 184, Hall of Records, Annapolis, Md.

3. The 1810 census lists Joseph Mettauer living with five males between sixteen and twenty-six, and twenty-two slaves. No white women lived there. See U.S. Census Bureau, Third Census, 1810, Prince Edward Co. Va., and Prince Edward Co. LT, 1788–1812, LVA.

4. Prince Edward Co. WB 4, 31 December 1811, 20 January 1812, 311; DB 15, 15 Feb. 1813, 51–53, 53–54, LVA; subscribers to Edmund Randolph, undated, in Pet. of Mettauer, 1796, LP; Kight, "In Rural Virginia"; Rucker, "Dr. John Peter Mettauer."

BIBLIOGRAPHY

MANUSCRIPT SOURCES

Alexandria, Virginia
    Bishop Payne Library, Virginia Theological Seminary
        Richard Channing Moore Letterbooks (xerox)
Annapolis, Maryland
    Hall of Records
        Archibald Buchanan, Last Will and Testament
        Sarah Buchanan Turnbull, Last Will and Testament
        Frederick County Court Records
Baltimore, Maryland
    Maryland Historical Society
        John Thompson Mason Jr. Papers
Chapel Hill, North Carolina
    Southern Historical Collection, University of North Carolina
        Hubard Family Papers, #360
        James McDowell Papers, #459
Charlottesville, Virginia
    Albert H. Small Special Collections Library, University of Virginia
        Robert S. Brooke Papers, 1831–63 (#38-137)
        Bryan Family Papers, 1770–1918 (#3400)
        Joseph C. Cabell Papers, 1796–1887 (#38-111)
        John Hartwell Cocke Papers, 1725–1931 (#640)
        McDowell Family Papers, 1892–95 (#2969)
            Correspondence Concerning Divorce
            Papers Related to Divorce
        McDowell, Miller, Warner Papers (#2969a)
        Thomas White Sydnor Papers, 1825–90 (#38-146)
Durham, North Carolina
    Rare Book, Manuscript, and Special Collections Library, Duke University
        Campbell Family Papers, 1797–1969
        Graham Family Papers, 1773–1885
        Edmund Jennings Lee II Papers, 1797–1877
        James McDowell Papers, 1767–1888
        Charles Macgill Papers, 1793–1906

Henry Reid Papers, 1839–46
Isle of Wight County, Virginia
County Courthouse
County Court Order Books, 1810–20
Loose Papers
Superior Court of Law Order Book, 1809–28
Philadelphia, Pennsylvania
Pennsylvania Historical Society
Gratz Collection
Presbyterian Historical Society
Philadelphia Presbytery, Minutes, vol. 5 (1850–55)
Richmond, Virginia
Library of Virginia
Antioch Baptist Church, Sussex County, Minute Books, 1772–1837
(xerox, #27920a); 1837–92 (xerox, #27920b)
Broad Run Baptist Church, Fauquier County, Minute Book, 1762–1873
(microfilm reel 472)
Brock's Gap Baptist Church, Rockingham and Shenandoah Counties,
Records, 1756–1844 (typescript, #19984)
Buckingham Baptist Church, Buckingham County, Minute Book, 1826–56
(photostat, #26757)
Circuit Court Papers, 1831–36, Prince Edward County
County Court Judgments, Isle of Wight County
County Deed Books (microfilm)
County Land Tax Records (microfilm)
County Order Books (microfilm)
County Personal Property Tax Records (microfilm)
County Will Books (microfilm)
Goose Creek Baptist Church, Bedford County, Minute Books, 1787–1821
(xerox, #26296); 1822–69 (xerox, #29865)
Guardian Records, Isle of Wight County
Legislative Petitions, Records Group 78
Thompson Adams, Orange County, 11 Dec. 1845
Amelia M. Alexander, Frederick County, 13 Dec. 1825
Thomas Alexander, Miscellaneous Collection, 22 Dec. 1803
Eleanor A. Allison, Hampshire County, 2 Feb. 1838
Martha A. Allison, Fairfax County, 15 Feb. 1848
Mary Alvis, Richmond City, 4 Dec. 1828
David Arell, Alexandria, 16 Nov. 1790
Jacob Bagent, Loudoun County, 10 Dec. 1841, 4 Dec. 1844
Leonard G. Bailey, Wythe County, 20 Jan. 1845
Charlotte Ball, Culpeper County, 9 Dec. 1806
Sally Ballinger, Bedford County, 2 Jan. 1838
Caroline Octavia Balls, Loudoun County, 14 Jan. 1851
John Bane, Brooke County, 28 Dec. 1818

James Barnett, Scott County, 5 Dec. 1850
Martha Barnett, Patrick County, 12 Dec. 1818
William Bartlam, Chesterfield County, 10 Dec. 1844
William P. Bayliss, Fairfax County, 8 Dec. 1831, 30 Dec. 1833
Nancy Bayne, Bedford County, 12 Dec. 1808
Susan W. Bell, Sussex County, 6 Dec. 1832
William Bishop Sr., Scott County, 11 Feb. 1851
William H. Blackburn, Henrico County, 18 Dec. 1847
Fleming and Friendless Blood, King William County, 13 Jan. 1849
Olympia Blood, King William County, 11 Jan. 1841
Susannah Boling, Harrison County, 6 Dec. 1824
John Bonnell, Harrison County, 10 Nov. 1796
Charles Bosher, Richmond City, 13 Dec. 1807
Elizabeth Bourn, Louisa County, 13 Dec. 1802
Lewis Bourne, Louisa County, 16 Dec. 1824, 20 Jan. 1825
Delilah Brewer, Fairfax County, 11 Dec. 1820
Margaret Brough, Halifax County, 9 Dec. 1808
Scotty Catherine Brown, Shenandoah County, 4 Jan. 1848
Mary Burke, Miscellaneous Collection, 20 Dec. 1817
Benjamin Butt, Norfolk County, 7 Dec. 1803
Cynthia Ann Callaway, Wayne County, 16 Dec. 1848
John J. Campbell, Nelson County, 17 Dec. 1844
Robert Campbell, Richmond City, 13 Dec. 1804
Kukama Carothers, Harrison County, 11 Jan. 1839
Rosewell Carter, Richmond City, 7 Dec. 1810
Sally Carter, Wythe County, 16 Nov. 1816
Henry Carty, Montgomery County, 3 Dec. 1823
Rachel Cauffman, Richmond City, 10 Dec. 1824, 15 Dec. 1825
William and Martha Chapman, Isle of Wight County, 24 Jan. 1840
Mary Cloud, Frederick County, 26 Jan. 1839
Judith Cocke, Hanover County, 5 Dec. 1821
Pamelia B. Cole, Chesterfield County, 14 Dec. 1824
Margaret A. Combs, Stafford County, 6 Dec. 1850
John Cook, Botetourt County, 2 Dec. 1812
Washington Cooper, Montgomery County, 14 Dec. 1815
John Copin, Kanawha County, 9 Dec., 1834
Elizabeth Corbin, Harrison County, 6 Mar. 1835
Ann P. Cowper, Isle of Wight County, 20 Nov. 1816
Ann Pierce Parker Cowper, Isle of Wight County, 19 Dec. 1811
Josiah Cowper, Isle of Wight County, 8 Dec. 1823
William Cowper, Isle of Wight County, 19 Dec. 1811, 16 Dec. 1812,
    6 Dec. 1815, 14 Nov. 1816, 12 Dec. 1817
John Cox, Miscellaneous Collection, 6 Dec. 1822
Margaret Cox, Greenbrier County, 6 Dec. 1821
Virginia Crawford, Ohio County, 4 Dec. 1840

Amanda Crow, Buckingham County, 21 Dec. 1844
William Croxton, Brooke County, 6 Dec. 1809
Thomas Culpeper, Norfolk County, 9 Dec. 1835
Solomon Cyrus, Campbell County, 21 Dec. 1820
Anne Dantignac, Prince William County, 12 Nov. 1789
Peter C. Davis, Buckingham County, 23 Dec. 1845
William Daws, Elizabeth City County, 13 Dec. 1802
Nancy Dinwiddie, Campbell County, 19 Dec. 1826
William Dinwiddie, Campbell County, 19 Dec. 1826
Catherine Dixon, Russell County, 2 Jan. 1838
Sopha Dobyns, Bedford County, 17 Dec. 1817
Elizabeth Dowdall, Hardy County, 8 Dec. 1809
Elizabeth Dryden, Rockbridge County, 5 Dec. 1809
Ellen Dunlap, Augusta County, 12 Oct. 1814
Ann Edmonds, Lancaster County, 2 Feb. 1836
Ann Eliza Eubank, King William County, 9 Dec. 1836
James W. Evans, Norfolk County, 12 Dec. 1829
Catlip Falkler, Nicholas County, 14 Dec. 1847
Felix Ferte, Norfolk County, 23 Dec. 1819
Drury Fletcher, Lee County, 7 Dec. 1809
John Fogg Jr., Essex County, 11 Dec. 1800
George W. Foster, Nicholas County, 14 Dec. 1847
John Foster, Portsmouth, 14 Dec. 1849
Isaac Fouch, Loudoun County, 24 Jan. 1809
Jacob Freeze, Page County, 26 Jan. 1841
S. Bassett French, Chesterfield County, 2 Jan. 1850
Harden Fulcher, Patrick County, 23 Jan. 1850
Thomas Gill, Nansemond County, 9 Dec. 1818
Jane D. Godwin, Isle of Wight County, 23 Dec. 1818
Sarah C. Grantham, Prince George County, 13 Dec. 1817
Joseph Gresham, James City County, 10 Dec. 1833
Richard B. Hall, Orange County, 28 Jan. 1838
Helen A. W. Hamilton, Richmond City, 14 Dec. 1846
Wyatt Hare, Nelson County, 27 Feb. 1852
Watkins Harper, Essex County, Dec. 2, 1842
John Harris, Bedford County, 20 Jan. 1838, 12 Jan. 1839, 2 Dec. 1840
Nathaniel Hart, Brooke County, 8 Dec. 1806
Elizabeth S. Harwell, Petersburg, 13 Dec. 1820
Ferdinand S. Heiskell, Augusta County, 17 Jan. 1849
Huldah Heiskell, Augusta County, 11 Dec. 1849
Catherine Hillary, Rappahannock County, 12 Dec. 1845
William Hobbs, Lee County, 30 Dec. 1841
John Hope, Washington County, 5 Jan. 1836
Jesse Horton, Russell County, 4 Dec. 1811; Scott County, 6 Dec. 1815,
    22 Nov. 1816, 20 Dec. 1819

William Horton, Kanawha County, 11 Dec. 1821
William Howard, Amherst County, 23 Dec. 1807, 6 Dec. 1809,
Janet Hunter, Petersburg, 15 Dec. 1823
Elizabeth C. Huston, Harrison County, 6 Mar. 1835
Elizabeth C. Hutchings, Rockbridge County, 31 Dec. 1841
Samuel Rose Irvine, Lynchburg, 23 Dec. 1835
Charles Jones, Brooke County, 18 Dec. 1811
Richard Jones, Northampton County, 2 Nov. 1814
Oney Jourdan, Bedford County, 21 Oct. 1814
Asabel Joyner, Southampton County, 4 Dec. 1839
Michael Keaffer, Portsmouth, 23 Dec. 1807
Matthias Kenney, Berkeley County, 15 Dec. 1815
Elizabeth Kimberlin, Wythe County, 8 Dec. 1808
Richard Kinnamon, Washington County, 21 Dec. 1815
Nancy H. Knight, Lunenburg County, 6 Dec. 1809, 17 Dec. 1811,
    15 Dec. 1812, 15 Dec. 1813
Walton Knight, Lunenburg County, 6 Dec. 1809
Nancy D. Lane, Surry County, 3 Dec. 1845
Abraham George Leatherman, Hampshire County, 9 Dec. 1846
Mary Ledington, Lee County, 30 Dec. 1841
Mary H. Lowry, Louisa County, 1 Dec. 1824
James C. Luck, Caroline County, 22 Dec. 1831
Judith Lyon, Amherst County, 7 Dec. 1809
Daniel McGinty, Marion County, 7 Dec. 1847
Henry Mace, Harrison County, 7 Dec. 1809
Charles Mahan, Norfolk Borough, 6 Dec. 1809
Garland A. Mallory, Richmond City, 31 Jan. 1850
Harriet Z. H. Mallory, Richmond City, 8 Feb. 1850, 4 Feb. 1851
Wilson Marshall, Rockingham County, 2 Jan. 1850
James M. Martin, Lee County, 19 Dec. 1840, 9 Dec. 1841
Elizabeth Maxwell, Cabell County, 7 Dec. 1809
Joseph Mettauer, Prince Edward County, 14 Nov. 1796; Cumberland
    County, 12 Dec. 1804
Alexander Mills, Lee County, 9 Dec. 1830
Susan Moore, Loudoun County, 31 Jan. 1849
John Moore, Southampton County, 9 Dec. 1818
Robert Moran, Marion County, 11 Dec. 1847
Hezekiah Mosby, Powhatan County, 6 Dec. 1815
Providence Mountz, Ohio County, 6 Jan. 1848
John Netherland, Powhatan County, 12 Nov. 1796
Nathaniel Needles, Monongalia County, 11 Dec. 1815
George Nicholas, Lewis County, 6 Jan. 1848
Lucy W. Norman, Henry County, 20 Dec. 1848
John Noseman, Monroe County, 10 Dec. 1818
Thomas G. Nutter, Harrison County, 4 Dec. 1850

Leonard Owens, Patrick County, 11 Dec. 1809

Elizabeth A. Pannill, King William County, 5 Mar. 1837

David Parker, Nansemond County, 8 Dec. 1826

Jesse Parker, Southampton County, 19 Dec. 1818

Osbourne Parker, Richmond City, 18 Dec. 1823

Barbara W. Pettus, Louisa County, 13 Dec. 1819

Dabney Pettus, Fluvanna County, 13 Dec. 1802

John Peyton, Cabell County, 27 Jan. 1845, 9 Dec. 1847

Fanny Pollock, Montgomery County, 8 Dec. 1813

James T. Pollock, Jefferson County, 13 Dec. 1813

Valentine Powers Jr., Hardy County, 16 Dec. 1813; Lewis County, 10 Dec. 1818

John Pryor, Richmond City, 7 Dec. 1811

Ann Rankin, Augusta County, 22 Dec. 1829

Bryant Rawls, Nansemond County, 14 Dec. 1840

Samuel Ritchie, Russell County, 5 Oct. 1792

Evelina Roane, King William County, 2 Dec. 1824

Mary A. E. Roberts, Norfolk Borough, ? Dec. 1850

John Robertson, Nottoway County, 17 Dec. 1818

Anthony J. Robiou, Chesterfield County, 31 Jan. 1851

Susan Rollins, Spotsylvania County, 14 Dec. 1849

John Roper, Campbell County, 6 Dec. 1823

Daniel Rose, Prince William County, 9 Dec. 1806

Nancy L. Rousseau, Patrick County, 19 Dec. 1826

Nancy Rowland, Henry County, 7 Dec. 1820

Archey Rowsey, Amherst County, 18 Dec. 1812

William Rucker, Allegany County, 5 Mar. 1849

Nancy Saunders, Prince Edward County, 7 Dec. 1825, 26 Dec. 1826

James Settle, Monongalia County, 16 Feb. 1837

Benjamin Sewell, Russell County, 7 Dec. 1826

Nathan Sheppard, Ohio County, 18 Nov. 1796

William Simpson, Montgomery County, 9 Dec. 1813

Miles Slade, Southampton County, 16 Dec. 1824

Barney Smith, Gilmer County, 31 Dec. 1850

Job Stanbery, Ohio County, 4 Dec. 1839

James M. Stevens, Marshall County, 14 Jan. 1850

Peter Stone, Pendleton County, 8 Dec. 1821

Polly Stone, Henry County, 9 Dec. 1806

George Stratton, Powhatan County, 13 Dec. 1825

subscribers, Northampton County, 3 Dec. 1824

subscribers, Preston County, 3 Dec. 1824

Ayres Tatham, Accomac County, 13 Dec. 1805

John Tharp, Halifax County, 7 Dec. 1810

Ichabod Thomas, Pittsylvania County, 7 Dec. 1825

James Thompson, Shenandoah County, 7 Dec. 1826

David Tilson, Smythe County and Washington County, 7 Dec. 1833

Polly Toomes, Essex County, 18 Dec. 1809

James G. Trotter, Petersburg, 11 Dec. 1809

Rebecca Trueman, Chesterfield County, 10 Dec. 1828

Robert Turnbull, Prince George County, 31 Oct. 1791

Richard Turnell, Accomac County, 23 Dec. 1828

Kirchen Turner, Nansemond County, 8 Jan. 1848

Edwin Walke, Norfolk Borough, 13 Jan. 1849

Jesse Wallin, Scott County, 11 Feb. 1851

Henry Warwick, Amherst County, 16 Dec. 1839

Elizabeth Waterfield, Northampton County, 18 Dec. 1817

Elizabeth Watson, Prince Edward County, 26 Jan. 1839

Matthew Watson, Albemarle County, 17 Dec. 1822

Lucy Watts, Amherst County, 8 Dec. 1834

Catherine M. Wells, Ohio County, 2 Dec. 1824

Susanah Wersley, Hanover County, 20 Nov. 1786

George Whitfield, Portsmouth City, 19 Dec. 1808

William B. Williams, Franklin County, 19 Feb. 1833

Nathaniel H. Wills, Washington County, 25 Jan. 1835

Polly Wilson, Miscellaneous File, 6 Dec. 1800

Mildred Ann Wingo, Buckingham County, 17 Jan. 1852

Anna Woolfolk, Hanover County, 9 Jan. 1851

Bentley B. Woolfolk, Hanover County, 3 Feb. 1851

Benjamin Wright, Jackson County, 10 Jan. 1839, 13 Jan. 1840

Robert Wright, Campbell County, 16 Nov. 1816

William Yonson, Loudoun County, 21 Jan. 1847, 31 Jan. 1848

Samuel Zinn, Monongalia County, 1 Mar. 1839; Marion County, 11 Dec. 1849

Lower Banister Baptist Church, Pittsylvania County, Minute Book, 1798–1845 (xerox, #27902)

Rough House Bills, Resolutions, etc., Virginia General Assembly

Saylor Creek Baptist Church, Prince Edward County, Minute Book, 1801–49 (xerox, #27523)

St. George's Parish, Spotsylvania County and Fredericksburg, Vestry Book, 1746–1842 (microfilm reel 363)

Tazewell Family Papers (#24194)

Francis Thomas Broadside, 1843

U.S. Census Bureau, Census of Virginia, 1810–60 (microfilm)

Tompkins-McCaw Library, Medical College of Virginia

L. Benjamin Sheppard Papers

Union Theological Seminary Library

Hanover Presbytery, Minutes

William Hill Papers

Synod of Virginia, Minutes

Virginia Baptist Historical Society, University of Richmond
    Baptist General Committee, Meetings, 1815, 1817
    Buck Marsh Baptist Church, Berryville, Clarke County, 1785–1841;
        Frederick County, Minute Book
    Colosse Church, Minute Book, 1814–34
    Dover Baptist Association Records
    General Association, Minutes
    Ketocton Association Records
    Roanoke Baptist Association Records
    Strawberry Baptist Association, Minute Book, 1787–1822 (photostat)
    Virginia Portsmouth Association Records
Virginia Historical Society
    Carter Family Papers, 1651–1861
    Holmes Conrad Papers, 1794–1859
    Eggleston Family Papers, 1788–1975
    Frying Pan Spring Baptist Church, Fairfax County, Records, 1791–1908
        (copy)
    Hugh Blair Grigsby Papers, 1745–1944
    Hammond Family Papers, 1796–1836
    Isaac Hite, Commonplace Book, 1785, 1819–99
    Arthur Lee to Sarah [Brooke (Lee) Buchanan] Turnbull, 1 Dec. 1792
    Henry Lee to [William Berkeley] Lewis (copy), 26 July 1833
    McDowell Family Papers, 1777–1963
    Massie Family Papers, 1698–1856
    Stith Mead Letterbook, 1792–95
    Protestant Episcopal Church in the U.S.A., Virginia (Diocese) Papers,
        1709–1972
    Randolph Family Papers, 1786–1970
    Alexander Fenelon Taylor Papers, 1837–71
    Benjamin Walton Turnbull, comp., "The Turnbull Family of Brunswick
        County, Virginia," 1986
    Turnbull Family, Bible Records
    Walton Family of Prince Edward County, Va., Papers, 1796–1830
    Wise Family Papers, Barton H. Wise Collection (old catalog, typescripts)
    Joseph Yarbrough, Will, 20 May 1827
San Marino, California
    Henry E. Huntington Library, Brock Collection
        John Durburrow Blair Papers
        Cabell Family Papers
        Garland Family Papers
        Lyons Family Papers
        Randolph-Tucker Papers
        Tinsley Family Papers
Washington, D.C.
    Library of Congress

Barrington-McDowell Family Papers, 1780–1897
Philip R. Fendall Papers
John Marshall Papers
Miscellaneous Manuscript Collection
Williamsburg, Virginia
Earl Gregg Swem Library, College of William and Mary
Barraud Family Papers
Cook-Luttrell Papers
William Meade Papers
Tucker-Coleman Papers
Sarah C. Watts Papers

VIRGINIA SUPREME COURT CASES

Almond v Almond, 25 Va. Reports [4 Randolph] 662 (1826).
Attorney General v Broaddus and Wife, 20 Va. Reports [6 Munford] iii, 116 (1818).
Commonwealth v Edmund Perryman and Kiturah Perryman, 29 Va. Reports
[2 Leigh] 779 (1830).
Commonwealth v Leftwich, 26 Va. Reports [5 Randolph] 657 (1827).
Graves v Graves, 28 Va. Reports [1 Leigh] 37 (1829).
Purcell v Purcell, 14 Va. Reports [4 Hening and Munford] 507 (1810).
Watkins and Wife v Carlton, 37 Va. Reports [10 Leigh] 586 (1840).

MAGAZINES AND NEWSPAPERS

American Beacon (Norfolk), 1816
Baltimore American, 1790–1811
Central Presbyterian (Richmond), 1856
Christian Monitor (Richmond), 1815–17
Columbian Mirror and Alexandria Gazette, 1795–97
Daily National Intelligencer (Washington, D.C.), 1843–47
Lynchburg Virginian, 1833
Maryland Journal (Baltimore), 1785
Norfolk Herald, 1802
Republican and Argus (Baltimore), 1847
Richmond Enquirer, 1804–50
Richmond Whig, 1841–49
Southern Literary Messenger, 1836–50
Virginia Argus (Richmond), 1808–15
Virginia Gazette and General Advertiser (Richmond) 1790–1809
Virginia Gazette and Weekly Advertiser (Richmond) 1790–95
Virginia Herald (Fredericksburg), 1816
Virginia Journal and Alexandria Advertiser, 1788–90

Virginia Patriot (Richmond), 1811
Virginia Religious Magazine (Richmond), 1803
Watchman and Observer (Richmond), 1845–50
Watchman of the South (Richmond), 1837–45

PUBLISHED PRIMARY SOURCES

Adams, Ephraim. *Sketch Book.* San Francisco: Sorg Printing, 1968.
Bayard, Ferdinand M. *Travels of a Frenchman in Maryland and Virginia with a Description of Philadelphia and Baltimore in 1781.* Translated and edited by Ben C. McCary. Ann Arbor: University of Michigan Press, 1950.
Bayley, John. *Marriage As It Is and As It Should Be.* New York: M. W. Dodd, 1857.
Blackburn, Samuel. *General Blackburn's Speech On a Bill, to alter and amend an Act . . . .* Richmond: T. H. White, [1826].
Bourne, George. *Marriage Indissoluble and Divorce Unscriptural.* Harrisonburg, Va.: Davidson and Bourne, 1813.
Boyd, Julian P., et al., eds. *The Papers of Thomas Jefferson.* 29 vols. Princeton: Princeton University Press, 1950– .
Broaddus, A[ndrew], ed. *The Sermons and Other Writings of the Rev. Andrew Broaddus with A Memoir of His Life, By J. B. Jeter, D.D.* New York: Sheldon, Lamport and Blakeman, 1855.
Brooke, Francis Taliaferro. *A Narrative of My Life; For My Family.* Richmond: Macfarlane and Fergusson, 1849.
Buckley, Thomas E., ed. "The Duties of a Wife: Bishop James Madison to His Daughter, 1811." *Virginia Magazine of History and Biography* 91 (1983): 98–104.
———. *"If You Love That Lady Don't Marry Her": The Courtship Letters of Sally McDowell and John Miller, 1854–1856.* Columbia: University of Missouri Press, 2000.
[Carter, St. Leger Landon]. "March Court." *Southern Literary Messenger* 2 (1836): 302–4.
Cashin, Joan E., ed. *Our Common Affairs: Texts from Women of the Old South.* Baltimore: Johns Hopkins University Press, 1996.
Cocke, William Ronald, III, comp. *Hanover County Chancery Wills and Notes.* Columbia, Va.: W. R. Cocke III, 1940.
"Court Day." *Southern Literary Messenger* 2 (1836): 433–34.
[Dew, Thomas Roderick]. "On the Characteristic Differences between the Sexes, and on the Position and Influence of Woman in Society." *Southern Literary Messenger* 1 (1834–35): 493–512, 621–32, 672–91.
[DuPre, Paulina]. "Woman." *Southern Literary Messenger* 2 (1835–36): 309–11.
Fleet, Beverly. *Washington County Marriage Register, 1782–1820.* Baltimore: Genealogical Publishing, 1961.
Frémont, Jessie Benton. *Souvenirs of My Time.* Boston: D. Lothrop, 1881.
Frémont, John Charles. *Memoirs of My Life.* Chicago: Belford, Clarke and Co., 1887.

Garnett, James M. *Seven Lectures on Female Education, Inscribed to Mrs. Garnett's Pupils, at Elm-Wood, Essex County.* 2nd ed. Richmond: T. W. White, 1824.

"The George Walton Family Bible." *Southsider* 8 (1989): 89–91.

Hening, William Waller. *The New Virginia Justice: Comprising the Office and Authority of a Justice of the Peace.* 3rd ed. Richmond: J. and G. Cochran, 1820.

———, ed. *The Statutes at Large: Being a Collection of All the Laws of Virginia, from the First Session of the Legislature, in the Year 1619 . . . .* 13 vols. Richmond: Samuel Pleasants Jr., 1809–23.

Herr, Pamela, and Mary Lee Spence, eds. *The Letters of Jessie Benton Frémont.* Urbana: University of Illinois Press, 1993.

Hobson, Charles F., ed. *The Papers of John Marshall.* Vol. 5, *Selected Law Cases, 1784–1800.* Chapel Hill: University of North Carolina Press, 1987.

Hutchinson, William T., and William M. E. Rachal, eds. *The Papers of James Madison.* 17 vols. Chicago: University of Chicago Press, 1962–91.

Johnson, Herbert A., Charles T. Cullen, and Nancy G. Harris, eds. *The Papers of John Marshall.* 10 vols. Chapel Hill: University of North Carolina Press, 1974– .

Jones, Charles Colcock. *The Glory of Woman Is the Fear of the Lord: A Sermon.* Philadelphia: Wm. S. Martien, 1847.

La Rouchefoucauld-Liancort, Francois Alexandre Frederic, duc de. *Travels Through the United States of North America . . . in the Years 1795, 1796, and 1797.* Translated by H. Newman. 2 vols. London: R. Phillips, 1799.

[Lynch, E. A.]. "The Influence of Morals on the Happiness of Man, and the Stability of Institutions." *Southern Literary Messenger* 4 (1838): 145–51, 273–80, 415–24.

Maryland General Assembly, House of Delegates. *Journal of the House of Delegates of Maryland.* Annapolis, 1846–47.

Meade, William. *Old Churches, Ministers, and Families of Virginia.* Philadelphia: J. B. Lippincott, 1891.

———. *Recollections of Two Beloved Wives. By Bishop Meade.* N.p., [1857].

"Memoir of the Ambitious Lawyer." *Southern Literary Messenger* 1 (1835): 645–46.

[Methodist Episcopal Church]. *The Doctrines and Discipline of the Methodist Episcopal Church in America, revised and approved at the General conference . . . in Nov., 1792.* Philadelphia: Parry Hall, 1792.

[Minor, Benjamin Blake]. "The Legal Profession: Lawyers and Lawyers' Fees in the 'Old Dominion.'" *Southern Literary Messenger* 13 (1847): 611–18.

Minor, John B. *Institutes of Common and Statute Law.* 4 vols. in 6. Vol. 1, *The Rights Which Relate to the Person.* 2nd ed. Richmond: the author, 1876.

Minutes of the Dover Baptist Association . . . 1813. Richmond, 1813.

Minutes of the Dover Baptist Association . . . 1817. Richmond, 1817.

Moreau de Saint-Méry, Médéric Louis Elie. *American Journey, 1793–1798.* Translated and edited by Kenneth Roberts and Anna M. Roberts. Garden City, N.J.: Doubleday, 1947.

Owen, Samuel. "The Legal Profession." *Southern Literary Messenger* 13 (1847): 356–59.

[Patton, John Mercer, and Conway Robinson]. *Report of the Revisors of the Civil Code of Virginia, Made to the General Assembly.* Richmond: S. Shepherd, 1847–49.

Randolph, John. "Mss. of John Randolph." *Southern Literary Messenger* 2 (1835–36): 461–64, 568–71.

Rice, John Holt. *A Sermon on the Duties of a Minister of the Gospel . . . 1809.* Philadelphia: William W. Woodward, 1810.

Robinson, Conway. *The Practice in the Courts of Law and Equity in Virginia.* Vol. 2, *Containing Practice in Suits of Equity.* Richmond: Samuel Shepherd, 1835.

Semple, Robert B. *A History of the Rise and Progress of the Baptists in Virginia.* Richmond: the author, 1810.

Shepherd, Samuel, ed. *The Statutes at Large of Virginia, . . . 1792, to . . . 1806: Being a Continuation of Hening.* 3 vols. Richmond: S. Shepherd, 1835–36.

Slaughter, Philip. *A History of St. George's Parish, in the County of Spotsylvania and Diocese of Virginia.* New York, J. R. M'Gown, 1847.

Smithson, William T., comp. *The Methodist Pulpit South.* 3rd ed. Washington, D.C.: William T. Smithson, 1859.

[Thomas, Francis]. *Statement of Francis Thomas.* N.p., 1845.

Tucker, Henry St. George. *Commentaries on the Laws of Virginia, Comprising the Substance of a Course of Lectures Delivered to the Winchester Law School.* 2 vols. Winchester, Va.: Winchester Virginian, 1831.

———. *Notes on Blackstone's Commentaries, for the Use of Students.* Winchester, Va.: S. H. Davis, 1826.

Tucker, Nathaniel Beverley. "An Essay on the Moral and Political Effect of the Relation between the Caucasian Master and the African Slave." *Southern Literary Messenger* 10 (1844): 329–39, 470–80.

Tucker, St. George. *Blackstone's Commentaries: With Notes of Reference, to the Constitution and Laws, of the Federal Government of the United States; and of the Commonwealth of Virginia.* 5 vols. Philadelphia: William Young Birch and Abraham Small, 1803.

Virginia General Assembly. *The Code of Virginia: With the Declaration of Independence and Constitution of the United States; and the . . . Constitution of Virginia.* Richmond: W. F. Ritchie, 1849.

———. *The Revised Code of the Laws of Virginia: Being a Collection of All Such Acts of the General Assembly . . . with a General Index.* 2 vols. Richmond: Thomas Ritchie, 1819.

Virginia General Assembly, House of Delegates. *Journal of the House of Delegates of the Commonwealth of Virginia.* Richmond, 1786–1851.

Virginia General Assembly, Senate. *Journal of the Senate of Virginia.* Richmond, 1786–1851.

Weems, Mason L. *God's Revenge against Adultery, Exemplified in the Following Cases of American Crim. Con.* Baltimore: Ralph W. Pomeroy and Co., 1815.

——. *God's Revenge against Murder: or The Drown'd Wife.* 11th ed.
Philadelphia: printed for the author, 1823.

Woolman, John. *The Journal of John Woolman and a Plea for the Poor.* New York:
Corinth Books, 1971.

Wythe, George. *Decisions of Cases in Virginia by the High Court of Chancery [1788-
1799], with Remarks upon Decrees, by the Court of Appeals, Reversing Some of
those Decisions.* 2nd. ed. Richmond: J. W. Randolph, 1852.

SECONDARY SOURCES

"Albion's Seed: Four British Folkways in America—A Symposium." *William and
Mary Quarterly,* 3rd ser., 48 (1991): 224–308.

Alley, Reuben Edward. *A History of Baptists in Virginia.* Richmond: Virginia
Baptist General Board, 1974.

Andrews, Dee E. *The Methodists and Revolutionary America, 1760-1800.*
Princeton: Princeton University Press, 2000.

Atkinson, George W., ed. *Bench and Bar of West Virginia.* Charleston, W.V.:
Virginia Law Book Co., 1919.

Bailey, Raymond C. *Popular Influence upon Public Policy: Petitioning in Eighteenth
Century Virginia.* Westport, Conn.: Greenwood Press, 1979.

Baker, Keith Michael. "On the Problem of the Ideological Origins of the
French Revolution." In *Modern European Intellectual History: Reappraisals and
New Perspectives,* edited by Dominick LaCapra and Steven L. Kaplan, 197–
19. Ithaca: Cornell University Press, 1982.

Bardaglio, Peter W. "'An Outrage upon Nature': Incest and the Law in the
Nineteenth-Century South." In *In Joy and in Sorrow: Women, Family, and
Marriage in the Victorian South, 1830-1900,* edited by Carol Bleser, 32–51. New
York: Oxford University Press, 1991.

——. *Reconstructing the Household: Families, Sex, and the Law in the Nineteenth-
Century South.* Chapel Hill: University of North Carolina Press,
1995.

Basch, Norma. *Framing American Divorce: From the Revolutionary Generation to
the Victorians.* Berkeley: University of California Press, 1999.

Beeman, Richard R. *The Evolution of the Southern Backcountry: A Case Study of
Lunenburg County, 1746-1832.* Philadelphia: University of Pennsylvania Press,
1984.

Bell, Landon C. *The Old Free State: A Contribution to the History of Lunenburg
County and Southside Virginia.* 2 vols. Richmond: William Byrd Press, 1927.

Bender, Thomas. *Community and Social Change in America.* New Brunswick, N.J.:
Rutgers University Press, 1978.

Berman, Myron. *Richmond's Jewry, 1769-1976: Sabbat in Shockoe.* Charlottesville:
University Press of Virginia, 1979.

Bigelow, John. *Memoir of the Life and Public Services of John Charles Frémont.* New
York: Derby and Jackson, 1856.

Bishop, Joel Prentiss. *Commentaries on the Law of Marriage and Divorce, of Separation Without Divorce, and of the Evidence of Marriage in All Issues.* 2 vols. 4th ed. Boston, 1864.

Blake, Nelson Manfred. *The Road to Reno: A History of Divorce in the United States.* Westport, Conn.: Greenwood Press, 1962.

Boatwright, Eleanor Miot. *Status of Women in Georgia, 1783-1860.* Brooklyn: Carlson, 1994.

Boddie, John Bennett. *Southside Virginia Families.* Vol. 1. Redwood City, Calif.: Pacific Coast Publishers, 1955.

Bogin, Ruth. "Petitioning and the New Moral Economy of Post-Revolutionary America." *William and Mary Quarterly,* 3rd ser., 45 (1988): 391–425.

Bohner, Charles H. "*Swallow Barn:* John Kennedy's Chronicle of Virginia Society." *Virginia Magazine of History and Biography* 68 (1960): 317-30.

Boles, John B. "Evangelical Protestantism in the Old South: From Religious Dissent to Cultural Dominance." In *Religion in the South,* edited by Charles Reagan Wilson, 13-34. Jackson: University Press of Mississippi, 1985.

Bond, Edward L. *Damned Souls in a Tobacco Colony: Religion in Seventeenth-Century Virginia.* Macon, Ga.: Mercer University Press, 2000.

Bradshaw, Herbert Clarence. *History of Prince Edward County, Virginia: From Its Earliest Settlements through Its Establishment in 1754 to Its Bicentennial Year.* Richmond: Dietz Press, 1955.

Breines, Wini, and Linda Gordon. "The New Scholarship on Family Violence." *Signs: Journal of Women in Culture* 8 (1983): 490-531.

Breitowitz, Irving. *Between Civil and Religious Law: The Plight of the "Agunah" in American Society.* Westport, Conn.: Greenwood Press, 1993.

Brown, Kathleen M. *Good Wives, Nasty Wenches, and Anxious Patriarchs: Gender, Race, and Power in Colonial Virginia.* Chapel Hill: University of North Carolina Press, 1996.

Brown, Lawrence L. "Richard Channing Moore and the Revival of the Southern Church." *Historical Magazine of the Protestant Episcopal Church* 35 (1966): 3-63.

Brown, Thomas. "The Miscegenation of Richard Mentor Johnson as an Issue in the National Election Campaign of 1835-1836." *Civil War History* 39 (1993): 5-30.

Bruce, Dickson D., Jr. *The Rhetoric of Conservatism: The Virginia Convention of 1829-30 and the Conservative Tradition in the South.* San Marino, Calif.: Huntington Library, 1982.

Brugger, Robert J. *Beverley Tucker: Heart over Head in the Old South.* Baltimore: Johns Hopkins University Press, 1978.

Brydon, G. MacLaren. "A List of Clergy of the Protestant Episcopal Church Ordained after the American Revolution . . . ." *William and Mary Quarterly,* 2nd ser., 19 (1939): 397-434.

Bryson, W. Hamilton, "English Common Law in Virginia." *Journal of Legal History* 6 (1985): 249-56.

————, ed. *Legal Education in Virginia, 1779-1979: A Biographical Approach.* Charlottesville: University Press of Virginia, 1982.

————. *The Virginia Law Reporters before 1880.* Charlottesville: University Press of Virginia, 1977.

Buckley, Thomas E., ed. "'Placed in the Power of Violence': The Divorce Petition of Evelina Gregory Roane, 1824." *Virginia Magazine of History and Biography* 100 (1992): 29–78.

————. "Unfixing Race: Class, Power, and Identity in an Interracial Family." *Virginia Magazine of History and Biography* 102 (1994): 349–80.

Burke, M[artin] P. *Notes on the Property Rights of Married Women in Virginia.* Lynchburg, Va.: J. P. Bell, 1894.

Buza, Melinda S. "'Pledges of Our Love': Friendship, Love, and Marriage among the Virginia Gentry, 1800–1825." In *The Edge of the South: Life in Nineteenth-Century Virginia,* edited by Edward L. Ayers and John C. Willis, 9–36. Charlottesville: University Press of Virginia, 1991.

Bynum, Victoria E. *Unruly Women: The Politics of Social and Sexual Control in the Old South.* Chapel Hill: University of North Carolina Press, 1992.

Cashin, Joan. *A Family Venture: Men and Women on the Southern Frontier.* New York: Oxford University Press, 1991.

————. "The Structure of Antebellum Planter Families: 'The Ties that Bound us Was Strong.'" *Journal of Southern History* 56 (1990): 55–70.

Censer, Jane Turner. *North Carolina Planters and Their Children, 1800–1860.* Baton Rouge: Louisiana State University Press, 1984.

————. "'Smiling through Her Tears': Ante-Bellum Southern Women and Divorce." *American Journal of Legal History* 25 (1981): 24–47.

Christian, George L. *Reminiscences of Some of the Dead of the Bench and Bar of Richmond.* [Richmond: Virginia Law Register, 1909].

Chused, Richard H. "Married Women's Property Law, 1800–1850." *Georgetown Law Journal* 71 (1983): 1357–1425.

————. *Private Acts in Public Places: A Social History of Divorce in the Formative Era of American Family Law.* Philadelphia: University of Pennsylvania Press, 1994.

Clinton, Catherine. *The Plantation Mistress: Woman's World in the Old South.* New York: Pantheon, 1982.

Coe, Bufford W. *John Wesley and Marriage.* Bethlehem, Pa.: Lehigh University Press, 1996.

Cohen, Daniel A. "The Respectability of Rebecca Reed: Genteel Womanhood and Sectarian Conflict in Antebellum America." *Journal of the Early Republic* 16 (1996): 419–61.

Conrad, Holmes. *The Old County Court System of Virginia: Its Place in History.* Paper read before the Virginia State Bar Association. Richmond: Richmond Press, 1908.

Cott, Nancy F. "Divorce and the Changing Status of Women in Eighteenth-Century Massachusetts." *William and Mary Quarterly,* 3rd ser., 33 (1976): 586–614.

————. "Eighteenth Century Family and Social Life Revealed in Massachusetts Divorce Records." *Journal of Social History* 10 (1976): 20–43.

————. *Public Vows: A History of Marriage and the Nation.* Cambridge: Harvard University Press, 2000.

Cox, Virginia D., and Willie T. Weathers. *Old Houses of King and Queen County Virginia.* Richmond: King and Queen County Historical Society, 1973.

Crocker, James F. "The Parkers of Macclesfield, Isle of Wight County, Va." *Virginia Magazine of History and Biography* 6 (1899): 420–24.

Davis, Richard Beale. *Intellectual Life in Jefferson's Virginia, 1790-1830.* Chapel Hill: University of North Carolina Press, 1964.

Degler, Carl N. *At Odds: Women and the Family in America from the Revolution to the Present.* New York: Oxford University Press, 1980.

Dewey, Frank L. *Thomas Jefferson: Lawyer.* Charlottesville: University Press of Virginia, 1986.

————. "Thomas Jefferson's Notes on Divorce." *William and Mary Quarterly,* 3rd ser., 39 (1982): 216–23.

DiFonzo, J. Herbie. *The Popular and Legal Culture of Divorce in Twentieth Century America.* Charlottesville: University Press of Virginia, 1997.

Ditz, Toby L. "Shipwrecked; or, Masculinity Imperiled: Mercantile Representations of Failure and the Gendered Self in Eighteenth-Century Philadelphia." *Journal of American History* 81 (1994): 51–80.

Dobash, Russell, and R. Emerson Dobash. "Community Response to Violence against Wives: Charivari, Abstract Justice, and Patriarchy." *Social Problems* 20 (1981): 563–81.

Doe, Norman. *The Legal Framework of the Church of England: A Critical Study in a Comparative Context.* New York: Oxford University Press, 1996.

Egerton, Douglas R. *Gabriel's Rebellion: The Virginia Slave Conspiracies of 1800 and 1802.* Chapel Hill: University of North Carolina Press, 1993.

Eggleston, J. D. "Francis Joseph and John Peter Mettauer." *William and Mary Quarterly,* 2nd ser., 8 (1928): 96–97.

Farnham, Christie Anne. *The Education of the Southern Belle: Higher Education and Student Socialization in the Antebellum South.* New York: New York University Press, 1994.

Filene, Peter. "The Secrets of Men's History." In *The Making of Masculinities: The New Men's Studies,* edited by Harry Brod, 103–19. Boston: Allen and Unwin, 1987.

Fischer, David Hackett. *Albion's Seed: Four British Folkways in America.* New York: Oxford University Press, 1989.

Frank, Stephen M. *Life with Father: Parenthood and Masculinity in the Nineteenth-Century American North.* Baltimore: Johns Hopkins University Press, 1998.

Freid, Jacob, ed. *Jews and Divorce.* New York: KTAV Press, 1968.

Friedman, Jean E. *The Enclosed Garden: Women and Community in the Evangelical South, 1830-1900.* Chapel Hill: University of North Carolina Press, 1985.

Fox-Genovese, Elizabeth. *Within the Plantation Household: Black and White*

Women of the Old South. Chapel Hill: University of North Carolina Press, 1988.

Fugate, Mary D. *Scott County Marriages, 1815-1853.* Athens, Ga.: Iberian Publishing, 1989.

Gelles, Richard J. "An Exchange/Social Control Theory." In *The Dark Side of Families: Current Family Violence Research,* edited by D. Finkelhor et al., 151-65. Beverly Hills, Calif.: Sage Publications, 1983.

———. "Family Violence, Abuse, and Neglect." In *Families and Change: Coping with Stressful Events,* edited by Patrick C. McKenry and Sharon J. Price, 262-80. Thousand Oaks, Calif.: Sage Publications, 1994.

Gelles, Richard J., and Donileen R. Loseke, eds. *Current Controversies on Family Violence.* Newbury Park, Calif.: Sage Publications, 1997.

Geertz, Clifford. *The Interpretation of Cultures.* New York: Basic Books, 1973.

Giles-Sims, Jean. *Wife Battering: A Systems Theory Approach.* New York: Gilford Press, 1983.

Ginzberg, Lori D. "'The Hearts of Your Readers Will Shudder': Fanny Wright, Infidelity, and American Freethought." *American Quarterly* 46 (1994): 195-226.

Goodheart, Lawrence B., Neil Hanks, and Elizabeth Johnson. "An Act for the Relief of Females. . . ? Divorce and the Changing Legal Status of Women in Tennessee, 1796-1860." *Tennessee Historical Quarterly* 44 (1985): 318-39, 402-16.

Gordon, Michael. "The Ideal Husband as Depicted in the Nineteenth-Century Marriage Manual." In *The American Man,* edited by Elizabeth H. Pleck and Joseph H. Pleck, 145-57. Englewood Cliffs, N.J.: Prentice-Hall, 1980.

Gordon-Reed, Annette. *Thomas Jefferson and Sally Hemmings: An American Controversy.* Charlottesville: University Press of Virginia, 1997.

Gorn, Elliott J. "'Gouge and Bite, Pull Hair and Scratch': The Social Significance of Fighting in the Southern Backcountry." *American Historical Review* 90 (1985): 18-34.

Griswold, Robert L. "Law, Sex, Cruelty, and Divorce in Victorian America, 1840-1900." *American Quarterly* 38 (1986): 721-45.

———. "Sexual Cruelty and the Case for Divorce in Victorian America." *Signs: Journal of Women in Culture and Society* 11 (1986): 529-41.

Grossberg, Michael. *A Judgment for Solomon: The D'Hauteville Case and Legal Experience in Antebellum America.* New York: Cambridge University Press, 1996.

———. "Who Gets the Child? Custody, Guardianship, and the Rise of Judicial Patriarchy in Nineteenth-Century America." *Feminist Studies* 9 (1983): 235-60.

Gunderson, Joan R. *The Anglican Ministry in Virginia, 1723-1766: A Study of a Social Class.* New York: Garland, 1989.

Gutman, Herbert G. *The Black Family in Slavery and Freedom, 1750-1925.* New York: Pantheon, 1976.

Hagler, D. Harland. "The Ideal Woman in the Antebellum South: Lady or Farmwife?" *Journal of Southern History* 46 (1980): 405–18.

Hamilton, Emory L. "Samuel Ritchie of Scott County Virginia." *Historical Sketches of Southwest Virginia* 12 (1978): 21–23.

Hamilton, Phillip Forrest. "The Tucker Family and the Dynamics of Generational Change in Jeffersonian Virginia, 1775–1830." Ph.D. diss., Washington University, 1995.

Hartog, Hendrik. *Man and Wife in America: A History.* Cambridge: Harvard University Press, 2000.

Helmholz, R. H. *Canon Law and English Common Law.* London: Selden Society, 1983.

Higginbotham, A. Leon, Jr., and Barbara K. Kopytoff. "Racial Purity and Interracial Sex in the Law of Colonial and Antebellum Virginia." *Georgetown Law Journal* 77 (1989): 1967–2029.

Higgins, Gina O'Connell. *Resilient Adults: Overcoming a Cruel Past.* San Francisco: Jossey-Bass, 1994.

Hodes, Martha. *Sex across the Color Line: White Women and Black Men in the Nineteenth-Century American South.* New Haven: Yale University Press, 1997.

———, ed. *Sex, Love, Race: Crossing Boundaries in North American History.* New York: New York University Press, 1999.

Hoff, Lee Ann. *Battered Women as Survivors.* London: Routledge, 1990.

Horner, Frederick. *The History of the Blair, Banister, and Braxton Families Before and After the Revolution, with a Brief Sketch of their Descendants.* Philadelphia: J. B. Lippincott, 1898.

Howard, George Elliott. *A History of Matrimonial Institutions, Chiefly in England and the United States.* 3 vols. Chicago: University of Chicago Press, 1904.

Howison, Robert R. *A History of Virginia, From its Discovery and Settlement by Europeans to the Present Time.* 2 vols. Philadelphia: Carey and Hart, 1846–48.

Hudson, Janet. "From Constitution to Constitution, 1868–1895: South Carolina's Unique Stance on Divorce." *South Carolina Historical Magazine* 98 (1997): 75–96.

Huebner, Timothy S. *The Southern Judicial Tradition: State Judges and Sectional Distinctiveness, 1790–1890.* Athens: University of Georgia Press, 1999.

Isaac, Rhys. *The Transformation of Virginia, 1740–1790.* Chapel Hill: University of North Carolina Press, 1982.

Jabour, Anya. *Marriage in the Early Republic: Elizabeth and William Wirt and the Companionate Ideal.* Baltimore: Johns Hopkins University Press, 1998.

Johns, J[ohn]. *A Memoir of the Life of the Rt. Rev. William Meade, D.D. Bishop of the Protestant Episcopal Church in the Diocese of Virginia.* Baltimore: Innes and Co., 1867.

Johnson, Guion Griffis. *Ante-Bellum North Carolina: A Social History.* Chapel Hill: University of North Carolina Press, 1937.

Johnston, F[rederick]. *Memorials of Old Virginia Clerks.* Lynchburg, Va.: J. P. Bell, 1888.

Johnston, James Hugo. *Race Relations in Virginia and Miscegenation in the South, 1776-1860.* Amherst: University of Massachusetts Press, 1970.

Jones, Jacqueline. *Labor of Love, Labor of Sorrow: Black Women, Work, and the Family from Slavery to the Present.* New York: Basic Books, 1985.

Jordan, Daniel P. *Political Leadership in Jefferson's Virginia.* Charlottesville: University Press of Virginia, 1983.

Kaplan, Harold I., Alfred M. Freedman, and Benjamin J. Sadock. *Modern Synopsis of Comprehensive Textbook of Psychiatry.* 3rd ed. Baltimore: Williams and Wilkins, 1981.

Kenzer, Robert C. *Kinship and Neighborhood in a Southern Community: Orange County, North Carolina, 1849-1881.* Knoxville: University of Tennessee Press, 1987.

Kierner, Cynthia A. *Southern Women in Revolution, 1776-1800: Personal and Political Narratives.* Columbia: University of South Carolina Press, 1998.

Kight, John R. "In Rural Virginia, World-Class Medicine: John Peter Mettauer, 1787-1878." *Virginia Medical Monthly* 116 (1989): 66-70.

Knorr, Catherine L. *Marriages of Prince Edward County Virginia, 1754-1810.* Privately printed, 1950.

Koehler, Lyle. *A Search for Power: The "Weaker Sex" in Seventeenth-Century New England.* Urbana: University of Illinois Press, 1980.

Konig, David Thomas. "Jurisprudence and Social Policy in the New Republic." In *Devising Liberty: Preserving and Creating Freedom in the New American Republic,* edited by Konig, 178-216. Stanford: Stanford University Press, 1995.

Kulikoff, Allan. *Tobacco and Slaves: The Development of Southern Cultures in the Chesapeake, 1680-1800.* Chapel Hill: University of North Carolina Press, 1986.

Kurz, Demie. "Social Science Perspectives on Wife Abuse: Current Debates and Future Directions." In *Violence against Women: The Bloody Footprints,* edited by Pauline B. Bart and Eileen Geil Moran, 252-69. Newbury Park, Calif.: Sage Publications, 1993.

Lebsock, Suzanne. *The Free Women of Petersburg: Status and Culture in a Southern Town, 1784-1860.* New York: Norton, 1984.

Lee, Edmund Jennings. *Lee of Virginia, 1642-1892.* Baltimore: Genealogical Publishing, 1974.

Lepore, Jill. "Historians Who Love Too Much: Reflections on Microhistory and Biography." *Journal of American History* 88 (2001): 129-44.

Lerner, Gerda. *The Creation of Patriarchy.* New York: Oxford University Press, 1986.

Lewis, Jan. *The Pursuit of Happiness: Family and Values in Jefferson's Virginia.* New York: Cambridge University Press, 1983.

———. "The Republican Wife: Virtue and Seduction in the Early Republic." *William and Mary Quarterly,* 3rd ser., 44 (1987): 689-721.

Lewis, Jan, and Kenneth A. Lockridge. "'Sally Has Been Sick': Pregnancy and

Family Limitation among Virginia Gentry Women, 1780–1830." *Journal of Social History* 22 (1988): 5–19.

Lyerly, Cynthia Lynn. *Methodism and the Southern Mind, 1770–1810*. New York: Oxford University Press, 1998.

Lystra, Karen. *Searching the Heart: Women, Men, and Romantic Love in Nineteenth-Century America*. New York: Oxford University Press, 1989.

McCurry, Stephanie. *Masters of Small Worlds: Yeoman Households, Gender Relations, and the Political Culture of the Antebellum South Carolina Low Country*. New York: Oxford University Press, 1995.

McLaurin, Melton A. *Cecilia: A Slave*. Athens: University of Georgia Press, 1991.

McMillen, Sally G. *Motherhood in the Old South: Pregnancy, Childbirth, and Infant Rearing*. Baton Rouge: Louisiana State University Press, 1990.

———. *Southern Women: Black and White in the Old South*. Arlington Heights, Ill.: Harland Davidson, 1992.

"Marriage and Divorce." *Southern Quarterly Review* 26 (1854): 351–53.

Mathews, Donald G. *Religion in the Old South*. Chicago: University of Chicago Press, 1977.

———. "The Second Great Awakening as an Organizing Process, 1780–1830: An Hypothesis." *American Quarterly* 21 (1969): 23–43.

Matthews, Glenna. *"Just A Housewife": The Rise and Fall of Domesticity in America*. New York: Oxford University Press, 1987.

Miller, F. Thorton. *Juries and Judges versus the Law: Virginia's Provincial Legal Perspective, 1783–1828*. Charlottesville: University Press of Virginia, 1994.

Miller, Susan. *Assuming the Positions: Cultural Pedagogy and the Politics of Commonplace Writing*. Pittsburgh: University of Pittsburgh Press, 1998.

Moore, E. Garth, and Timothy Briden. *Moore's Introduction to English Canon Law*. 2nd ed. London: Mowbray, 1985.

Morgan, Edmund. *American Slavery, American Freedom: The Ordeal of Colonial Virginia*. New York: Norton, 1975.

Morgan, Philip D. *Slave Counterpoint: Black Culture in the Eighteenth-Century Chesapeake and Lowcountry*. Chapel Hill: University of North Carolina Press, 1999.

Nadelhaft, Jerome. "Alcohol and Wife Abuse in Antebellum Male Temperance Literature." *Canadian Review of American Studies* 25 (1995): 15–43.

———. "Wife Torture: A Known Phenomenon in Nineteenth-Century America." *Journal of American Culture* 10 (1987): 39–59.

Nagel, Paul C. *The Lees of Virginia: Seven Generations of an American Family*. New York: Oxford University Press, 1990.

Nevins, Allan. *Frémont: Pathmaker of the West*. New York: D. Appleton-Century, 1939.

"Notes to Virginia Council Journals." *Virginia Magazine of History and Biography* 32 (1924): 127–43.

O'Neill, William L. *Divorce in the Progressive Era*. New Haven: Yale University Press, 1967.

Owsley, Harriet Chappell. "The Marriages of Rachel Donelson." *Tennessee Historical Quarterly* 36 (1977): 479–92.

Pals, Daniel L. *Seven Theories of Religion.* New York: Oxford University Press, 1996.

Pease, Jane H., and William H. Pease. *A Family of Women: The Carolina Petigrus in Peace and War.* Chapel Hill: University of North Carolina Press, 1999.

Perinbanayagam, R. S. *Discursive Acts.* New York: Aldine de Gruyter, 1991.

Peterson del Mar, David. *What Trouble I Have Seen: A History of Violence against Wives.* Cambridge: Harvard University Press, 1996.

Phillips, Roderick. *Putting Asunder: A History of Divorce in Western Society.* New York: Cambridge University Press, 1988.

Pleck, Elizabeth H. *Domestic Tyranny: The Making of Social Policy against Family Violence from Colonial Times to the Present.* New York: Oxford University Press, 1987.

Pocock, J. G. A. *Virtue, Commerce, and History: Essays on Political Thought and History, Chiefly in the Eighteenth Century.* New York: Cambridge University Press, 1985.

Popkin, Jeremy D. "Historians on the Autobiographical Frontier." *American Historical Review* 104 (1999): 727–48.

Potts, Louis W. *Arthur Lee: A Virtuous Revolutionary.* Baton Rouge: Louisiana State University Press, 1981.

Reardon, John J. *Edmund Randolph: A Biography.* New York: Macmillan, 1975.

Robertson, J. Dallas. "Biographical Sketches of Selected Revolutionary War Era Personalities from the Winchester Area." In *Men and Events of the Revolution in Winchester and Frederick County, Virginia,* 3–29. Winchester, Va.: Winchester-Frederick County Historical Society, 1975.

Roeber, A. G. *Faithful Magistrates and Republican Lawyers: Creators of Virginia Legal Culture, 1680–1810.* Chapel Hill: University of North Carolina Press, 1981.

Rothman, Joshua D. "'To Be Freed from Thate Curs and Let at Liberty': Interracial Adultery and Divorce in Antebellum Virginia." *Virginia Magazine of History and Biography* 106 (1998): 443–81.

Rotundo, E. Anthony. *American Manhood: Transformations in Masculinity from the Revolution to the Modern Era.* New York: Basic Books, 1993.

———. "Learning about Manhood: Gender Ideals and the Middle-Class Family in Nineteenth-Century America." In *Manliness and Morality: Middle-Class Masculinity in Britain and America, 1800–1940,* edited by J. A. Mangan and James Walvin, 35–51. New York: St. Martin's Press, 1987.

Ricci, James V. *The Genealogy of Gynaecology: History of the Development of Gynaecology throughout the Ages, 2000 B.C.–1800 A.D.* Philadelphia: Blakiston, 1943.

Riley, Glenda. *Divorce: An American Tradition.* New York: Oxford University Press, 1991.

———. "Legislative Divorce in Virginia, 1803–1850." *Journal of the Early Republic* 11 (1991): 51–67.

Rowley, William. *A Treatise on Female, Nervous, Hysterical, Hypochondriacal, Bilious, Convulsive Diseases; Apoplexy and Palsy; with Thoughts on Madness, Suicide, &c.* London: C. Norse, 1788.

Rucker, Pierce. "Dr. John Peter Mettauer: An Early Southern Gynecologist." *Annals of Medical History*, n.s., 10 (1938): 36–46.

Salmon, Marylynn. *Women and the Law of Property in Early America.* Chapel Hill: University of North Carolina Press, 1986.

Schwarz, Philip J. *Twice Condemned: Slaves and the Criminal Law of Virginia, 1705-1865.* Baton Rouge: Louisiana State University Press, 1988.

Selby, John E. *The Revolution in Virginia, 1775-1783.* Williamsburg, Va.: Colonial Williamsburg Foundation, 1988.

Shade, William G. *Democratizing the Old Dominion: Virginia and the Second American Party System, 1824-1861.* Charlottesville: University Press of Virginia, 1996.

Shain, Barry Alan. *The Myth of American Individualism: The Protestant Origins of American Political Thought.* Princeton: Princeton University Press, 1994.

Shepard, E. Lee. "Lawyers Look at Themselves: Professional Consciousness and the Virginia Bar." *American Journal of Legal History* 25 (1981): 1–23.

Sidbury, James. *Ploughshares into Swords: Race, Rebellion, and Identity in Gabriel's Virginia, 1730-1810.* New York: Cambridge University Press, 1997.

Smith, Daniel Blake. *Inside the Great House: Planter Family Life in Eighteenth-Century Chesapeake Society.* Ithaca: Cornell University Press, 1980.

Sobel, Mechal. *The World They Made Together: Black and White Values in Eighteenth-Century Virginia.* Princeton: Princeton University Press, 1987.

Sommerville, Diane Miller. "The Rape Myth in the Old South Reconsidered." *Journal of Southern History* 61 (1995): 481–518.

Spoden, Muriel M. C. *Ancestry and Descendants of Richard Netherland, Esquire, 1764-1832.* Privately printed, 1979.

Stephen, Leslie, and Sidney Lee, eds. *The Dictionary of National Biography: . . . from the Earliest Times to 1900.* 22 vols. London: Oxford University Press, 1921–22.

Sterling, Dorothy, ed. *We Are Your Sisters: Black Women in the Nineteenth Century.* New York: Norton, 1984.

Stevenson, Brenda E. *Life in Black and White: Family and Community in the Slave South.* New York: Oxford University Press, 1996.

Stone, Lawrence. *Broken Lives: Separation and Divorce in England, 1660-1857.* New York: Oxford University Press, 1993.

———. *The Family, Sex, and Marriage in England, 1500-1800.* New York: Harper and Row, 1977.

———. *Road to Divorce: England, 1530-1987.* New York: Oxford University Press, 1995.

Stordeur, Richard A., and Richard Stille. *Ending Men's Violence against Their Partners: One Road to Peace.* Newbury Park, Calif.: Sage Publications, 1989.

Stowe, Stephen M. *Intimacy and Power in the Old South: Ritual in the Lives of the Planters.* Baltimore: Johns Hopkins University Press, 1987.

Taylor, George Braxton. *Virginia Baptist Ministers.* 3rd ser. Lynchburg, Va.: J. P. Bell, 1912.

Templeman, Eleanor Lee. "Black Horse Harry Lee." *Northern Neck Historical Magazine* 38 (1988): 4344–47.

Thomas, Arthur Dicken, Jr. "Reasonable Revivalism: Presbyterian Evangelization of Educated Virginians, 1787–1837." *Journal of Presbyterian History* 61 (1983): 316–34.

Thomas, Keith. "The Double Standard." *Journal of the History of Ideas* 20 (1959): 195–216.

Thompson, Ernest Trice. *Presbyterians in the South.* 3 vols. Richmond: John Knox Press, 1963–73.

Torrence, Clayton, ed. "Letters of Mrs. Ann (Jennings) Wise to Her Husband, Henry A. Wise." *Virginia Magazine of History and Biography* 58 (1950): 492–515.

Vogt, John, and T. William Kethley Jr., eds. *Brunswick County Marriages, 1750–1853.* Athens: University of Georgia Press, 1988.

Walker, Leonore E. *The Battered Woman.* New York: Harper and Row, 1979.

———. *The Battered Woman Syndrome.* 2nd ed. New York: Springer, 2000.

Walsh, Lorena S. *From Calabar to Carter's Grove: The History of a Virginia Slave Community.* Charlottesville: University Press of Virginia, 1977.

Warren, Mary Bondurant, comp. *Virginia District Courts, 1789–1809, Records of the Prince Edward District.* Danielsville, Ga.: Heritage Papers, 1991.

Weaver, Richard M. "Two Types of American Individualism." In *The Southern Essays of Richard M. Weaver,* edited by George M. Curtis III and James J. Thompson Jr., 77–103. Indianapolis: Liberty Fund, 1987.

White, Henry Alexander. *Southern Presbyterian Leaders.* New York: Neale Publishing, 1911.

"Whiting Family." *Tyler's Quarterly Historical and Genealogical Magazine* 12 (1931): 259–62.

Wigger, John H. *Taking Heaven by Storm: Methodism and the Rise of Popular Christianity in America.* New York: Oxford University Press, 1998.

Williams, T. J. C. *History of Frederick County, Maryland.* Baltimore: Regional Publishing, 1967.

Williamson, Joel. *New People: Miscegenation and Mulattoes in the United States.* New York: Free Press, 1980.

Wills, Gregory A. *Democratic Religion: Freedom, Authority, and Church Discipline in the Baptist South, 1785–1900.* New York: Oxford University Press, 1997.

Winnett, Arthur Robert. *Divorce and Remarriage in Anglicanism.* London: Macmillan, 1958.

Witte, John, Jr. *From Sacrament to Contract: Marriage, Religion, and Law in the Western Tradition.* Louisville, Ky.: Westminster John Knox Press, 1997.

Wood, Betty. "'For Their Satisfaction or Redress': African Americans and Church Discipline in the Early South." In *The Devil's Lane: Sex and Race in the Early South,* edited by Catherine Clinton and Michele Gillespie, 109–23. New York: Oxford University Press, 1997.

Wood, Gordon S. *The Creation of the American Republic, 1776–1787*. Chapel Hill: University of North Carolina Press, 1969.

Wolfe, Margaret Ripley. *Daughters of Canaan: A Saga of Southern Women*. Lexington: University Press of Kentucky, 1995.

Wyatt-Brown, Bertram. *Southern Honor: Ethics and Behavior in the Old South*. New York: Oxford University Press, 1982.

INDEX